LESBIAN AND GAY LIBERATION IN CANADA:
A SELECTED ANNOTATED CHRONOLOGY, 1964–1975

LESBIAN AND GAY LIBERATION IN CANADA: A SELECTED ANNOTATED CHRONOLOGY, 1964–1975

Donald W. McLeod

Toronto: ECW PRESS/HOMEWOOD BOOKS, 1996

Third printing, 2022.

CANADIAN CATALOGUING IN PUBLICATION DATA

McLeod, Donald W. (Donald Wilfred), 1957–
Lesbian and gay liberation in Canada

Includes bibliographical references and index.
ISBN 1-55022-273-2

1. Gay liberation movement – Canada – Chronology.
1. Title.

HQ76.8.C3M35 1996   305.9'0664'0971   C95-933023-2

This book has been published with the assistance of an award
from the John Damien Educational Trust and a grant from
the Lesbian and Gay Community Appeal of Toronto.

The publisher gratefully acknowledges the financial assistance
of The Canada Council and the Ontario Arts Council.

Design and imaging by ECW Type & Art, Oakville, Ontario.
Printed by Imprimerie d'Éditions Marquis, Montmagny, Québec.

Distributed by General Distribution Services,
30 Lesmill Road, Don Mills, Ontario M3B 2T6.

Published by ECW PRESS/HOMEWOOD BOOKS,
2120 Queen Street East, Suite 200
Toronto, Ontario M4E 1E2.

CONTENTS

This book is for

James Fraser
(1946–1985)

and

Michael Lynch
(1944–1991)

PREFACE

For most of the past ten years I have worked part-time as a volunteer archivist at the Canadian Lesbian and Gay Archives. I have found that the researchers who come to use the Archives often have the most elementary notions about recent Canadian lesbian and gay history. Typically, they are bright university undergraduates or graduate students. Often they do not know that Canada had an organized homophile movement before Stonewall, or they have never heard of some of the major figures or events prominent during the early 1970s, when visible and vibrant lesbian and gay community groups began to form in cities across Canada.

An encounter with one such student frustrated me. It was during the autumn of 1989, and I was trying to help him with research for an undergraduate paper. I mentioned that he should examine copies of *The Body Politic* and was surprised to learn that he had never heard of it. Canada's gay newsmagazine of record for the period 1971 to 1987 had only ceased publication two years before and was now, I feared, forgotten.

This event left me uneasy. I felt that I had to do something to help to preserve the Canadian lesbian and gay past while at the same time easing access to it. And I came to question my own knowledge of Canadian lesbian and gay history. Sure, I knew a little about the late 1970s and had come to know somewhat more about Canadian lesbian and gay life in the 1980s through my work at the Archives. I had met many people who had actually been involved in making this history. But what did I *really* know? I was determined to find out. I started with the standard published sources, including Gary Kinsman's *The Regulation of Desire: Sexuality in Canada* (Black Rose, 1987), William Crawford's *Homosexuality in Canada: A Bibliography* (second edition, Canadian Gay Archives, 1984), and James Fraser and Alan V. Miller's *Lesbian and Gay Heritage of Toronto* (Canadian Gay Archives, 1982). I also started to poke about the collections of the Archives. The more I searched, the more I found. I soon realized that there was a great deal of published (and unpublished) material on the recent Canadian lesbian and gay past, some of it extremely obscure, scattered in many sources.

I became particularly fascinated by "Victories and Defeats: A Gay and Lesbian Chronology 1964–1982," compiled by James Fraser and published in Ed Jackson and Stan Persky's anthology *Flaunting It!: A Decade of Gay Journalism from* The Body Politic (New Star Books; Pink Triangle Press, 1982). We used it all the time at the Archives as a quick reference tool to solve simple questions about dates of Canadian lesbian or gay events. I was impressed by its straightforward utility but was sometimes dismayed that it gave no bibliographic sources with its information. Then I had an idea. I thought that if somehow a chronology of major events outlining Canadian lesbian and gay history for a particular period could be combined with a brief, selected bibliography of sources for each event, the result would be an authoritative reference guide to the origins and development of lesbian and gay liberation in Canada. And so, I set to work.

SCOPE OF THE WORK

I began this project in 1989 and worked on it in my spare time for six years. When I started I intended to expand the coverage of the "Victories and Defeats" chronology to the end of 1990, complete with bibliographic citations for each entry. The more I read, however, the more I realized this was impossible to do in a single volume. The 1980s saw an explosion of lesbian and gay activity in Canada, with dozens of new groups forming. And how would I deal with the AIDS crisis? An annotated chronology of Canadian lesbian and gay organizing around AIDS could easily fill a separate volume. I then decided to end the chronology at the end of 1981, the year in which AIDS first came to public attention, but even this proved untenable. A detailed, though selected, chronology of the period to the end of 1981 would still be several hundred pages long. A sharper focus yet was called for.

This *Chronology* covers the first twelve years of the homophile/gay liberation movement in Canada, from 1964 (when the Association for Social Knowledge [ASK], Canada's first large-scale homophile organization, was formed in Vancouver) through 1975 (the year of the founding of the National Gay Rights Coalition/Coalition nationale pour les droits des homosexuels [NGRC/CNDH], the first truly national coalition of Canadian lesbian and gay groups). Coverage is selective and focusses on self-declared lesbians and gay men and their activities in regard to the forging of lesbian and gay communities and liberation in Canada. Special attention has been given to important demonstrations, political action and lobbying, and legal reform. In addition to these areas, artistic and cultural contributions with significant lesbian or gay content are included, such as books, dramatic productions, films, etc. A number of heterosexuals (some friendly, some not) who somehow became embroiled in the struggle for lesbian and gay liberation in Canada are included. Several foreign events are listed in that they had a direct impact on the climate of liberation in this country: Stonewall is the prime example. Other foreign events are included if Canadian lesbians or gays were involved directly, such as the opening of Michel Tremblay's play *Hosanna* on Broadway or the attendance of Canadian academics at the Gay Academic Union conferences in New York.

There are twelve chapters, one for each year, and entries are chronological within each. Closely related entries are linked by internal references, and through an index. The early chapters are brief (less was happening then), while the chapters for 1974 and 1975 are more than fifty pages each. The full form of the name of an organization is used the first time it appears but the acronym is used thereafter (see pages xv–xvii for a full listing of abbreviations used).

The *Chronology's* three appendices provide useful supplementary information. The first is a checklist of lesbian and gay organizations in Canada active during 1964–75, arranged geographically and chronologically. The second appendix is a checklist of Canadian lesbian and gay periodicals published during the period, arranged alphabetically by title. Appendix three is a preliminary checklist of Canadian lesbian and gay bars and clubs active during 1964–75, arranged geographically.

A NOTE ABOUT SOURCES

I have cast a wide net to examine and list both published and unpublished sources that help to verify the contents of each entry. The holdings of three institutions were of key importance in this regard: the Canadian Lesbian and Gay Archives, Toronto; the Archives gaies du Québec, Montréal; and the Canadian Women's Movement Archives, Ottawa. I was also able to examine or verify materials held in numerous other institutions, from the archives of the University of British Columbia to the New York Public Library, either in person or by mail. Finally, I have corresponded with or spoken to more than fifty lesbians and gay men who were directly involved in some of the events chronicled in this book. They were helpful in providing leads to new sources and in correcting errors or misconceptions on my part. More than ten of them were asked to examine an earlier draft of the project and were able to offer cogent advice.

The Canadian Lesbian and Gay Archives was my base of operations. It is a remarkable institution and contains one of the finest collections of lesbian and gay material in the world. It began in 1973 as an offshoot of *The Body Politic*. It is this connection that accounts for its superb collection of lesbian and gay Canadiana from the 1970s. The Archives started as the back files of the newspaper, and grew from there. Almost every gay or lesbian liberation group formed in Canada during the 1970s was in some way connected to *The Body Politic* either through direct correspondence or through the exchange of newsletters or publications. This correspondence still exists, in *The Body Politic* papers in the Archives, as do all of the posters, pamphlets, flyers, buttons, newsletters, books, and other items that were sent to the paper. When some of these groups went out of business, they sent their organizational records to the Archives also. The Archives is fortunate to have the records of several key Canadian organizations from this period. Of course, Toronto-based groups predominate — from the University of Toronto Homophile Association (UTHA) to the Community Homophile Association of Toronto (CHAT) to the Coalition for Gay Rights in Ontario (CGRO) — but several key non-Ontarian groups are also represented. These include the papers of Gay Alliance toward Equality (GATE) (Vancouver), Gays for Equality (GFE) (Winnipeg), Gays of Ottawa/Gays d'Ottawa (GO), and Gay Alliance for Equality (GAE) (Halifax).

In the course of researching this project I conducted a systematic search through the following components of the Canadian Lesbian and Gay Archives:

- The James Fraser Library (includes literature, non-fiction, and reference works)
- Canadian Daily Press Clippings Collection (arranged chronologically)
- Canadian Vertical Files Collection (a quick-reference collection of files on individuals and organizations)
- Archival Accessions (includes the fonds and collections of papers of individuals and organizations)
- Monograph Collection (mostly pamphlets)
- Photographic Image Collection (includes the photo archive of *The Body Politic*)
- Poster Collection
- Non-Lesbian/Gay Periodicals Collection (mostly clippings on lesbian or gay subjects printed in mainstream publications)
- Lesbian and Gay Periodicals Collection (includes the most complete collection of Canadian lesbian and gay publications in existence)

The materials found here provided a strong foundation for the project, and were augmented by items located at other institutions, particularly the Archives gaies du Québec, Montréal, and the Canadian Women's Movement Archives, Ottawa.

HOW I HOPE YOU WILL USE THIS WORK

This book should *not* be viewed as a history of lesbian and gay liberation in Canada between 1964 and 1975. It is a chronology, with additional bibliographical support. I do believe that any serious history of Canadian lesbian and gay liberation for the period must take into consideration the material presented here. But there are other sources, too, that require study. Oral histories and the correspondence of organizations and individuals, for example, might be particularly fruitful areas to research. And, of course, history moves beyond the marshalling of simple facts and references when it uses these sources to present a thesis or to draw conclusions.

Many leads have been presented here. It is up to you to use them, and others you may find, to reach conclusions as to what it was like to be a lesbian or gay activist during the early years of lesbian and gay organizing in Canada. I hope that *Lesbian and Gay Liberation in Canada: A Selected Annotated Chronology, 1964–1975* will be seen as no more than a handy point of departure, a stepping-stone toward further, more advanced, research.

Don McLeod
Toronto
September 1995

NOTE: Several of the sources listed here are obscure and may be available at only one or two institutions in Canada. If you have trouble locating them, please contact me (or one of my colleagues) at the Canadian Lesbian and Gay Archives, P.O. Box 639, Station A, Toronto, Ontario M5W 1G2.

ACKNOWLEDGEMENTS

I would like to thank the following individuals for showing an interest in this project and for providing information or advice:

Barry Adam	Robert K. Martin
Harold Averill	Philip McLeod
Edna Barker	Robin Metcalfe
Rick Bébout	Alan V. Miller
Jay Cassel	Jearld Moldenhauer
David Churchill	Ken Popert
Gale Comin	Bob Radke
Charles Dobie	Neil Richards
John Forbes	Marie Robertson
Margaret Fulford	Becki Ross
Gerald Hannon	Bruce Russell
Bob Harris	Douglas Sanders
Gens (Doug) Hellquist	George Smith
Ross Higgins	Jim Thomas
Charlie Hill	Chris Vogel
George Hislop	Tom Warner
Ed Jackson	Tom Waugh
Sidney Katz	Cynthia Wright
Gary Kinsman	Ian Young
John Alan Lee	Peter Zorzi

The collections of several libraries and archives were consulted in researching this book. I would like to thank the staff at the following institutions in particular for their kind support in finding material and answering queries:

- Archives and Special Collections, University of British Columbia, Vancouver (George Brandak)
- Archives gaies du Québec, Montréal (Ross Higgins)
- Canadian Lesbian and Gay Archives, Toronto (especially Harold Averill and Alan V. Miller)

- Canadian Women's Movement Archives, Morisset Library, University of Ottawa, Ottawa (Christine Banfill)
- Cinematheque Ontario Library, Toronto
- IGIC Collection, Manuscripts Division, New York Public Library, New York, N.Y.
- McLennan Library, McGill University, Montréal
- Metropolitan Toronto Reference Library, Toronto
- National Library of Canada, Ottawa
- Robarts Library, University of Toronto, Toronto

Thanks to Edna Barker and Scott Mitchell for help with editing and proofreading, Paul Davies of ECW *Type & Art* for his design and typesetting skill, and to Jack David for his advice.

Finally, I must thank the John Damien Educational Trust and the Lesbian and Gay Community Appeal of Toronto for providing funds toward the publication of this work.

LIST OF ILLUSTRATIONS

NOTE: All images used in this book are courtesy of the Canadian Lesbian and Gay Archives, Toronto, unless noted otherwise

ABBREVIATIONS

ACT	Association for Canadian Transsexuals
AHM	Association homophile de Montréal [see also GMA]
ASK	Association for Social Knowledge
BBB	Brown Breast Brigade
CGAA	Canadian Gay Activists Alliance
CGRO	Coalition for Gay Rights in Ontario
CHAL	Centre humanitaire d'aide et de libération
CHAN	Community Homophile Association of Newfoundland
CHAT	Community Homophile Association of Toronto
CHUM	Centre homophile urbain de Montréal
CNDH	Coalition nationale pour les droits des homosexuels [see also NGRC]
ECHO	East Coast Homophile Organizations (U.S.)
ECM	L'Église communautaire de Montréal [see also MCC]
ELF	Edmonton Lesbian Feminists
FHQL	Front homosexuel québécois de libération
FLH	Front de libération homosexuelle
GAE	Gay Alliance for Equality
———	Gay Associations of Edmonton
GATE	Gay Alliance toward Equality
GAU	Gay Academic Union
GAY	Gay Alliance at York
———	in Montréal: the early name for Gay McGill
GCCS	Gay Community Centre of Saskatchewan
GFE	Gays for Equality
GHAP	Groupe homosexuel d'action politique
GIRC	Gay Information and Resources Calgary

GLF	Gay Liberation Front
GLM	Gay Liberation Movement
GMA	Gay Montreal Association [see also AHM]
GO	Gays of Ottawa/Gays d'Ottawa/Gais de l'Outaouais
GPA	Gay People's Alliance
GSA	Gay Students Alliance
Gay TRIC	Gay Transient Referral and Information Centre [see also TRIC]
HALO	Homophile Association of London, Ontario
HASP	Heather, Adrienne, Sue, Pat [the Brunswick Four]
HIM	Homophile Information Media
HMHA	Hamilton-McMaster Homophile Association
ISEA	International Sex Equality Anonymous
MCC	Metropolitan Community Church
——	Montreal Community Church [see also ECM]
MHA	McMaster Homophile Association
NACHO	North American Conference of Homophile Organizations
NDP	New Democratic Party
NGEC	National Gay Election Coalition
NGRC	National Gay Rights Coalition [see also CNDH]
PLC	People's Liberation Coalition
QUHA	Queen's University Homophile Association
SEARCH	Society for Education Action Research and Counselling on Homosexuality
SEHQ	Service d'entraide homophile de Québec
SIR	Society for Individual Rights (U.S.)
SOL	Slightly Older Lesbians
TAG	Toronto Area Gays
TGA	Toronto Gay Action
TRIC	Transient Referral and Information Centre [see also Gay TRIC]
UGHA	University of Guelph Homophile Association
USHA	University of Saskatchewan Homophile Association
UTHA	University of Toronto Homophile Association
UU	Unitarian Universalists

UWOHA   University of Western Ontario Homophile Association
Van-Gay Vancouver Gay Information Service
WGU   Windsor Gay Unity
YUHA   York University Homophile Association

1964

—— * Montréal * Paul Chamberland's book of poetry *L'afficheur hurle* was published by Éditions Parti pris.

[André Gaulin, "*L'afficheur hurle*," in *Dictionnaire des oeuvres littéraires du Québec*, ed. Maurice Lemire et al., vol. 4 (1960–69) (Montréal: Fides, 1984), pp. 4–7.]

—— * Montréal * Paul Chamberland's book of poetry *Terre Québec* was published by Librairie Déom.

[Maximilien Laroche, "*Terre Québec*," in *Dictionnaire des oeuvres littéraires du Québec*, ed. Maurice Lemire et al., vol. 4 (1960–69) (Montréal: Fides, 1984), pp. 868–70.]

—— * Montréal * Jean-Paul Pinsonneault's novel *Les terres sèches* was published by Éditions Beauchemin.

[Jacqueline Gourdeau, "*Les terres sèches*," in *Dictionnaire des oeuvres littéraires du Québec*, ed. Maurice Lemire et al., vol. 4 (1960–69) (Montréal: Fides, 1984), pp. 872–73.]

—— * Montréal * Paul Toupin's collection of essays *L'écrivain et son théâtre* was published by Le cercle du livre de France.

[Alonzo Le Blanc, "*L'écrivain et son théâtre*," in *Dictionnaire des oeuvres littéraires du Québec*, ed. Maurice Lemire et al., vol. 4 (1960–69) (Montréal: Fides, 1984), pp. 291–92.]

—— * Toronto * The weekly tabloid newspaper *Tab* (later a bi-weekly renamed *Tab International*) featured a regular, catty news and gossip column by Lady Bessborough entitled "The Gay Set." This became a prime source of information about happenings around Toronto's gay community, especially at the bars and clubs. Lady Bessborough was succeeded by Duke Gaylord, whose "Gay Set" column ran in *Tab International* as late as June 1985.

[*Tab* collection, Canadian Lesbian and Gay Archives, Toronto.]

—— * Toronto * By 1964 several Toronto physique photo studios, such as Frank Borck, Can-Art, Castillo, Jon Foto, C.K., and Harold Wells, provided photographs to the male physique and muscle-building magazines that were of some interest to gay men. These studios made contributions to Canadian examples of these periodicals, such as *Crew*, *Face and Physique*, and *Physique Illustrated*, published in Lachine, Québec, as well as to more obviously gay periodicals, such as *Gay International* and *Two*.

[William Crawford, comp., *Homosexuality in Canada*, second ed., Canadian Gay Archives Publication no. 9 (Toronto: CGA, 1984), pp. 267–68; M. Lasalle, "Littérature infame . . . ," *Zéro* 1 (? Autumn 1964): 7–8; *Lesbian and Gay Heritage of Toronto*, Canadian Gay Archives Publication no. 5 (Toronto: CGA, 1982), p. 11; Alan Miller, "Beefcake with No Labels Attached," *Body Politic*, no. 90 (1983), p. 33; Alan V. Miller, *Our Own Voices: A Directory of Lesbian and Gay Periodicals, 1890–1990, Including the Complete Holdings of the Canadian Gay Archives*, Canadian Gay Archives Publication no. 12 (Toronto: CGA, 1991), passim.; Alan Miller, "The Way We Were," *Action!: A Publication of the Right to Privacy Committee* 1 (1981): 4.]

—— * Washington, D.C. * The fifty-five page book *The Beginner's Guide to Cruising* was published by the Guild Press Ltd. It was written by George Marshall, of Toronto, who had worked as general manager of *Gay* magazine. In 1965 the Guild Book Service published a sequel, also written by Marshall, the seventy-seven page *Advanced Guide to Cruising*.

[Miles Johns, "In Review" (column; review of *The Beginner's Guide to Cruising*), *Two*, no. 11 (1966), p. 31; George Marshall, Interview, *Two*, no. 11 (1966), pp. 11–14; George Marshall, Letter, *Two*, no. 8 (1966), pp. 33–34.]

January 13 * Toronto * Nathan Cohen commented in his "Monday Miscellany" column in the *Toronto Daily Star* that local police feared that recently closed after-hours clubs had reopened as "hangouts for male and female homosexuals." On January 21, James Egan's letter of rebuttal, "Police Concern for Homosexual Clubs 'Illogical,' " was published in the *Star*. Egan was Canada's foremost gay activist during the period 1949–64. (See also August 5, 14, 1964.)

[Nathan Cohen, "Monday Miscellany" (column), *Toronto Daily Star*, night ed., 13 January 1964, p. 18; James Egan, "Police Concern for Homosexual Clubs 'Illogical' " (letter), *Toronto Daily Star*, night ed., 21 January 1964, p. 6 (reprinted in Robert Champagne, *Jim Egan: Canada's Pioneer Gay Activist*, Canadian Lesbian and Gay History Network Publication no. 1 [Toronto: CLGHN, 1987], p. 101).]

February * London, England; Toronto * Jane Rule's first novel, *The Desert of the Heart*, was published by Secker & Warburg in England and Macmillan of Canada. An American edition was released by World Publishing of New York later in 1964. A classic of lesbian literature concerning the relationship between a divorcée and a free-spirited woman in Reno, Nevada, during the 1950s, *The Desert of the Heart* has been reprinted many times, and was adapted by Donna Deitch into the film *Desert Hearts* in 1985.

["A Bibliography," *Canadian Fiction Magazine*, no. 23 (1976), pp. 133, 135–36; Martin Levin, "Reader's Report," *New York Times Book Review*, 1 August 1964, pp. 28–29; Jane Rule, "Jane Rule: The Woman behind *Lesbian Images*" (interview), *Body Politic*, no. 21 (1975), pp. 14–15, 17; V.T., "Under Covers: ASK Library Page," ASK *Newsletter* 2 (June 1965): 5; F.W. Watt, "Letters in Canada: 1964. Fiction," *University of Toronto Quarterly* 34 (July 1965): 380–81.]

February 22, March 7 * Toronto * *Maclean's* published a two-part series by Sidney Katz entitled "The Homosexual Next Door: A Sober Appraisal of a New Social Phenomenon." These are believed to be the first full-scale articles in a mainstream Canadian publication to take a generally positive view of homosexuality. Katz was influenced in his views through contact with James Egan, Canada's most prominent gay activist for the period 1949–64. The articles were later reprinted in a pamphlet of the same name by Pan-Graphic Press of San Francisco in its Mattachine Review Reprint Series.

[Robert Champagne (interviewing James Egan), "Canada's Pioneer Gay Activist: Jim Egan," *Rites* 3 (December 1986–January 1987): 14 (reprinted in Robert Champagne, *Jim Egan: Canada's Pioneer Gay Activist*, Canadian Lesbian and Gay History Network Publication no. 1 [Toronto: CLGHN, 1987], pp. 6–7); Sidney Katz, "The Homosexual Next Door: A Sober Appraisal of a New Social Phenomenon," *Maclean's*, 22 February 1964, pp. 10–11, 28–30; Sidney Katz, "The Harsh Facts of Life in the 'Gay' World," *Maclean's*, 7 March 1964, pp. 18, 34–38; Gary Kinsman, "Official Discourse as Sexual Regulation: The Social Organization of the Sexual Policing of Gay Men" (Ph.D. dissertation, University of Toronto, 1989), pp. 413–15; Gary Kinsman, *The Regulation of Desire: Sexuality in Canada* (Montréal: Black Rose Books, 1987), pp. 119–20, 160; "Treating the Homosexuals" (letters), *Maclean's*, 2 May 1964, pp. 7, 36.]

March 9 * Toronto * A joint meeting of the Catholic legal and medical guilds held at Osgoode Hall agreed unanimously that although homosexuality is a sin, it ought not to be a crime.

["Homosexuality Sin, Not Crime — Church Panel," *Toronto Daily Star*, night ed., 10 March 1964, p. 36.]

March 20 * Montréal * Pierre Patry's film *Trouble-fête*, in which Camille Ducharme played a predatory homosexual, opened at the Saint-Denis theatre.

[Robert Daudelin and Michel Patenaude, "La rentrée scolaire," *Objectif 64*, no. 28 (1964), pp. 36–37; Prat., "*Trouble-fête*," *Variety*, 20 May 1964, p. 6; D.J. Turner and Micheline Morisset, eds., *Canadian Feature Film Index, 1913–1985/Index des films canadiens de long métrage* (Ottawa: Public Archives, National Film, Television, and Sound Archives, 1987), entry 150; Thomas Waugh, "Nègres blancs, tapettes et 'butch': les lesbiennes et les gais dans le cinéma québécois," *Copie zéro*, no. 11 (1981), pp. 13, 15–16, 17.]

March 30 * Toronto * The first issue of the magazine *Gay* appeared. Published by the Gay Publishing Company, 122 Wellington Street W., it was

FOR THOSE WHO ARE HAPPY AND GAY

GAY INTERNATIONAL

50 Cents

LITHO'D IN CANADA   ADULTS ONLY

Acme

Vol. 2 No. 1   Feb.

Gay International, an early gay magazine published in Toronto.

one of the earliest periodicals to use the word "gay" in its title. *Gay* was a tabloid containing general articles on homosexuality (some reprinted from American homophile publications), fiction, photos, local gossip, jokes and cartoons, and personal ads. It was renamed *Gay International* with issue twelve (January 1965), and moved to 980 Queen Street E. It probably ceased publication after issue fifteen (about July 1965).

[Gary Kinsman, "Official Discourse as Sexual Regulation: The Social Organization of the Sexual Policing of Gay Men" (Ph.D. dissertation, University of Toronto, 1989), p. 399; Gary Kinsman, *The Regulation of Desire: Sexuality in Canada* (Montréal: Black Rose Books, 1987), pp. 158–59; Robert Maynard, "From the Editor's Desk" (column), *Gay International* 2 (February 1965): 4; Alan V. Miller, *Our Own Voices: A Directory of Lesbian and Gay Periodicals, 1890–1990, Including the Complete Holdings of the Canadian Gay Archives*, Canadian Gay Archives Publication no. 12 (Toronto: CGA, 1991), pp. 210, 231.]

Spring ✷ Toronto ✷ "Christian Attitudes toward Homosexuality," an article by Dr. Tibor Chikes, professor of pastoral care at the Wesley Theological Seminary, Washington, D.C., was reprinted (from *Concern*, 15 June 1963) in the 1964 annual report of the Board of Evangelism and Social Service of the United Church of Canada. Dr. Chikes argued that the self-organization of homosexuals and attempts to "glamorize" homosexuality are useless and that articles and books written by practicising homosexuals that try to further "the homosexual revolution . . . do homosexuals more harm than good."

[Tibor Chikes, "Christian Attitudes toward Homosexuality," in *Breaking the Barriers: 39th Annual Report, 1964 Board of Evangelism and Social Service, United Church of Canada* (Toronto: United Church House, 1964, pp. 142–47); Gary Kinsman, "Official Discourse as Sexual Regulation: The Social Organization of the Sexual Policing of Gay Men" (Ph.D. dissertation, University of Toronto, 1989), pp. 385–86.]

April ✷ Ottawa ✷ Member of Parliament Arnold Peters (NDP-Temiskaming) was preparing to introduce a private Member's bill calling for the modification of the Canadian Criminal Code to decriminalize homosexual acts between consenting adults in private. The bill never reached the floor of the House of Commons. Peters may have been influenced by the lobbying efforts of Garrfield D. Nichol (pseud. of Gary Nichols) of the Committee on Social Hygiene, Stittsville, Ontario. The Committee on Social Hygiene, pretty much a one-person operation, had been formed in 1963 to investigate the extent of homosexuality in eastern Canada and to quietly lobby for reforms to the Canadian Criminal Code. (See also May 26, 1965.)

["Committee on Social Hygiene" vertical file, Canadian Lesbian and Gay Archives, Toronto; Gary Kinsman, "Official Discourse as Sexual Regulation: The Social Organization of the Sexual Policing of Gay Men" (Ph.D. dissertation, University of Toronto, 1989), pp. 390–91; Gary Kinsman, *The Regulation of Desire: Sexuality in Canada* (Montréal: Black Rose Books, 1987), p. 155; Gary Kinsman (interviewing Bruce

ASK newsletter

association   for   social   knowledge

p   o   box 4277   vancouver 9 bc

"MAN'S ILLS ARE DUE TO HIS IGNORANCE OF NATURE."
— i'Helbach

JULY, 1964   VOL.1, No.4

EDITORIAL.....

This is a sad month for ASK. It is only our fifth month in existence, and we have had to sustain the news of the loss to the Association of both our Executive Advisor and our President.

Jaye has been a member of the Board of Directors since ASK's inception, and has been of invaluable help to us through her knowledge and work in the social field. She has been eloquent at business meetings and panel discussions, and also at the weekly executive coffeebar luncheons, where she has had a leading hand in the formulating of many of the Association's executive decisions. She leaves us to take up a post in the San Fransisco area, and we wish her well in her new venture. We are certainly going to miss her cheery "Committee Round-Up" news, but have the consolation of her promise to contribute a column from San Fransisco on activities of other organizations. We are pleased to announce that these will appear as often as we receive them. Good luck to you, Jaye, from all in ASK. We know we will be seeing you from time to time, so this is just au revoir.

Bruce has been our President from the beginning too, having been a leader in the early discussion groups that led to the formation of ASK. He guided the formative meetings through the initial stages, outlining to us all the need for ASK in Canada, the aims that the Association should have, the constitution and by-laws that the first members would have to hassle over, thrash out and weld into something meaningful and binding, the division of members into suggested committees and the work they would be expected to do for the betterment of the sexual variant in contemporary society. He was elected President of ASK by acclamation, and has worked tirelessly and selflessly to one end: to get ASK on its feet as a decent, effective organization working for the understanding and acknowledgment of homosexuals by themselves and the general public. Through press releases and reports of our activities we have established a small but sure footing on the contemporary scene, and there are many thousands of people throughout this world of ours who are aware of our existence and our purpose as a direct result of his efforts.

Being a president is not an enviable job. It involves levelheadedness when everything around you is chaotic and when everyone around you is hysterical;it involves farsightedness in making decisions which might appear to the less perceptive to be over-cautious or over-ambitious; it involves responsibility of person and of position, and the awareness of that responsibility at all times; it involves calmness of nature and temperament in the face of shortsighted pettiness; it involves firmness of conviction and principles in the face of setbacks and criticism; and, above all else, it involves dedication in the highest degree to the ideals and whole purpose of the corporation or organization which a president represents. Bruce has not been an unsuccessful president. He has displayed possession of all these qualities, and our best way to express appreciation to him for his work would be to aspire individually to these qualities in our continued efforts for ASK, and to emulate his sincere enthusiasm for all that ASK stands for.

Bruce leaves for Ottawa in August, and we wish him every success. It is with a heavy heart that we bid you adieu, Bruce; we will miss you.

/ * /

An issue of the ASK *Newsletter*, produced by the Association for Social Knowledge, Vancouver.

Somers), "Organizing in the Sixties: ASK: Canada's First Gay Rights Organization," *Rites* 3 (October 1986): 10; Wayne MacDonald, "New Democrats Push 'Hot' Bills," *Vancouver Sun*, four star ed., 11 April 1964, p. 8; G.N. (Gary Nichols), Letter, *Mattachine Review* 10 (October 1964): 29.]

April * Vancouver * The Association for Social Knowledge (ASK), the first homophile organization in Canada, was officially formed. It was inspired by the activities of the Mattachine Society in the United States, and was encouraged by Bruce Somers, a Vancouver interior decorator, who became ASK's first president. ASK was an independent organization established "to help society to understand and accept variations from the sexual norm." Its membership was almost equally divided between gay men and lesbians from the beginning. ASK supported law reform and sponsored public lectures and discussion groups, coffee parties (Gab 'N' Java), social events and outings, a lending library, and, eventually, a drop-in and community centre. The ASK *Newsletter* was filled with serious articles (some reprinted from other sources), news of local events, and Association news. ASK collapsed in the summer of 1965 but revived the next year; it disbanded early in 1969.

["Association for Social Knowledge (ASK)" vertical file, Canadian Lesbian and Gay Archives, Toronto; Bob Cummings, "The Lesbians: Part I," *Georgia Straight*, 13–19 September 1968, pp. 9–12; Gary Kinsman, "Official Discourse as Sexual Regulation: The Social Organization of the Sexual Policing of Gay Men" (Ph.D. dissertation, University of Toronto, 1989), pp. 376–84, 388–99; G.K. (Gary Kinsman), "Recovering History: ASK Reunion," *Rites* 3 (November 1986): 6; Gary Kinsman, *The Regulation of Desire: Sexuality in Canada* (Montréal: Black Rose Books, 1987), pp. 147–52, 154–58; Gary Kinsman (interviewing Bruce Somers and Douglas Sanders), "Organizing in the Sixties: ASK: Canada's First Gay Rights Organization," *Rites* 3 (October 1986): 10–11, 15; Gary Kinsman and Robert Champagne (interviewing Bruce Somers and Douglas Sanders), "ASK Reunion," *Angles* 3 (October 1986): 14–15; Neil Whaley, "His/Herstory: Gay Ground-breaker," *Vancouver Gay Community Centre News*, February 1983, pp. 39–41.]

April 11, 14, 15 * Toronto * A series of three articles on the "shadow world" of the homosexual entitled "Society and the Homosexual," by "a senior *Telegram* staff reporter" (Ron Poulton), was published in the *Toronto Telegram*. A vigorous rebuttal of the articles, written by "London Sociologist" (John Alan Lee), appeared in the *Toronto Telegram* on April 22, 1964. A more lengthy rebuttal, by James Egan, was published later in *Two*.

[James Egan, "*Two* Guest Editorial," *Two*, no. 2 (1964), pp. 13–19 (reprinted in Robert Champagne, *Jim Egan: Canada's Pioneer Gay Activist*, Canadian Lesbian and Gay History Network Publication no. 1 [Toronto: CLGHN, 1987], pp. 102–05); London Sociologist (John Alan Lee), "Gay Life Not a Shadow World" (letter), *Toronto Telegram*, final ed., 22 April 1964, p. 6 (reprinted in *Two*, no. 2 [1964], p. 20, and in Robert Champagne, *Jim Egan: Canada's Pioneer Gay Activist*, Canadian Lesbian and Gay History Network Publication no. 1 [Toronto: CLGHN, 1987], p. 106); Don Philip, "The

Biased I" (column), *Gay* 1 (15 May 1964): 7; (Ron Poulton), "Society and the Homosexual" (part 1), *Toronto Telegram*, final ed., 11 April 1964, p. 7; (Ron Poulton), "The Sick Life" (part 2), *Toronto Telegram*, final ed., 14 April 1964, p. 7; (Ron Poulton), "Church and Law" (part 3), *Toronto Telegram*, final ed., 15 April 1964, p. 7.]

April 13 * Toronto * The Roman Sauna Baths opened at 740 Bay Street. One of the largest and most modern bathhouses in Canada, the Roman Sauna Baths became a Toronto landmark. Renovated and expanded as the Romans II Health and Recreation Spa after a fire in 1977, the Romans survived the 1981 bath raids but eventually closed, on May 23, 1989.

[Jim Leahy, "Love amid the Ruins: Jim Leahy Spends a Last Night at the Roman's (sic) Health & Recreation Spa," *Xtra!*, no. 126 (1989), p. 13.]

April 29 * Vancouver * Rev. J.M. Taylor of East Burnaby United Church spoke on "The Church and Homosexuality" at the *Sun* Auditorium in the first public lecture sponsored by ASK. Twenty-five men and six women attended. Rev. Taylor called for the establishment of voluntary treatment centres for homosexuals, where a complete psychiatric and medical team could "assist the homosexual in his return to heterosexuality."

[Untitled article, ASK *Newsletter* 1 (May 1964): 2–3; "Hospital for Homosexuals Called for by Clergyman," *Vancouver Sun*, four star ed., 30 April 1964, p. 33; Gary Kinsman, "Official Discourse as Sexual Regulation: The Social Organization of the Policing of Gay Men" (Ph.D. dissertation, University of Toronto, 1989), pp. 384–85; Gary Kinsman, *The Regulation of Desire: Sexuality in Canada* (Montréal: Black Rose Books, 1987), pp. 151–52.]

May 15 * Montréal * Claude Jutra's film *À tout prendre/Take It All* opened at the Saint-Denis and Bijou theatres. A first-person, autobiographical narrative filmed between 1961 and 1963, *À tout prendre* was the first feature film made in Québec to explore a homosexual theme. It starred Jutra, Johanne Harrelle, and Victor Désy, and was shown at the Festival International du Film in Montréal in August 1963. English subtitles (written by Leonard Cohen) were added later.

[Denys Arcand, "Cinéma et sexualité," *Parti pris*, no. 9–11 (1964), pp. 94–97; Sy Oshinsky, "*Take It All*," *Motion Picture Herald*, 11 May 1966, pp. 519–20; Michel Patenaude, Review, *Objectif 63*, no. 23–24 (1963), pp. 41–43; Prat., "*À tout prendre (When All Is Said . . .)*," *Variety*, 28 August 1963, p. 18; D.J. Turner and Micheline Morisset, eds., *Canadian Feature Film Index, 1913–1985/Index des films canadiens de long métrage* (Ottawa: Public Archives, National Film, Television, and Sound Archives, 1987), entry 151; Thomas Waugh, "Nègres blancs, tapettes et 'butch': les lesbiennes et les gais dans le cinéma québécois," *Copie zéro*, no. 11 (1981), pp. 13, 22–24.]

May 20 * Vancouver * In an address to the John Howard Society of British Columbia, Minister of Justice Guy Favreau called for "a firm and comprehensive statement of the principles and policies that the Government of Canada proposes should be followed in the federal correctional field." This would include clarification of policies related to the treatment of convicted sex offenders, including homosexuals.

[D.E.S. (Douglas Sanders), "Straight Talk," ASK Newsletter 1 (July 1964): 3.]

June 3 * Vancouver * Mervin Davis, executive director of the John Howard Society of British Columbia, spoke to a public meeting sponsored by ASK and held at the Central YMCA. About twenty-five people attended. Davis said that homosexuals who don't infringe on the rights of "ordinary" citizens should not be punished.

["Our Society Needs ASK Says John Howard Executive Director," ASK Newsletter 1 (June 1964): 5.]

June 24 * Vancouver * The final spring meeting of ASK was held at the Vancouver Unitarian Church. A panel of three ASK members (David D., Lee L., and Bob T.) gave their views on the topic "ASK, Present and Future: What Should We Be Doing, and Where Should We Be Going?"

["The Roving Reporter . . . ," ASK Newsletter 1 (July 1964): 4.]

June 27 * Hamilton * Several hundred gay men from the Golden Horseshoe area attended a gala, open-air bottle party held at the home of Robert C. Hart, 63 Highcliffe Avenue. The party was raided by the police, who complained of noise, and the guests were forced to leave.

["Cops Queer Gala Fag 'Bottle Party': 800 Invitations Sent Out," Tab, 25 July 1964, p. 3.]

Summer * Montréal * The editors of the journal Parti pris caused a sensation when in their special summer issue, entitled "Portrait du colonisé québécois," they referred to "fédérastes" and "Confédérastie," a linking of Canadian federalists and pederasty.

[Robert Schwartzwald, "Fear of Federasty: Québec's Inverted Fictions," in Hortense J. Spillers, ed., Comparative American Identities: Race, Sex, and Nationality in the Modern Text (New York: Routledge, 1991), pp. 175–95; "Vulgarités," Parti pris, no. 9–11 (1964), p. 174.]

Summer * Toronto * Vice squad detectives Belcher and McGauty undertook a personal vendetta to harass and attempt to close the city's private gay clubs. Over several months the officers conducted a systematic campaign of harassment and threats against club managers and members, culminating in the laying of a charge of gross indecency against two men who were observed dancing together at the Melody Room, 457 Church Street. During the preliminary hearing, Belcher and McGauty produced conflicting testimony and the charges were dropped on September 24, 1964. The two detectives were not deterred, and they returned to the Melody Room in early 1965. At that time their disorderly conduct and verbal abuse led the manager to have them charged with trespassing after they refused to leave the club. (See also August 5, 14, 1964.)

[Alex Edmond, "A Case of Gross Indecency?" *Two*, no. 4 (1964), pp. 10–12, 21; "News: Toronto, Ontario: Disorderly Guests," *Gay International* 2 (February–April 1965): 12.]

Summer ∗ Vancouver ∗ ASK sponsored four discussion sessions open to the public: "Homosexual Marriages," "Lesbians," "Drag and Transvestism," and "Sadism, Masochism, and Fetishism."

[Announcement, ASK *Newsletter* 1 (August 1964): 8.]

July ∗ Toronto ∗ *Two* magazine was launched by Gayboy Publishing (later Kamp Publishing Company), with its editorial office listed as the Melody Room, 457 Church Street. Its name was inspired by the early American homophile magazine *One*. Beginning in April 1954, *One* had published a supplement entitled TWO (*Truth Will Out*); the Toronto publication was named after this. An occasional (later bi-monthly) collection of fiction, reviews, news, photos, and artwork, *Two*'s stated purpose was "to promote knowledge and understanding of the homosexual viewpoint among the general public and to educate homosexuals as to their responsibilities as variants from the current moral and social standards." *Two* ceased publication after issue eleven (July–August 1966).

[Gary Kinsman, "Official Discourse as Sexual Regulation: The Social Organization of the Sexual Policing of Gay Men" (Ph.D. dissertation, University of Toronto, 1989), pp. 399–402; Gary Kinsman, *The Regulation of Desire: Sexuality in Canada* (Montréal: Black Rose Books, 1987), pp. 158–59; "Second Time Around," *Gay* 1 (15 October 1964): 14.]

July ∗ Vancouver ∗ Jaye Haris, the first executive advisor of ASK, resigned her position to move to San Francisco, where she became involved with the Society for Individual Rights (SIR). At about the same time, Bruce Somers, the first president of ASK, resigned his position to move to Ottawa. Somers was succeeded by Douglas Sanders, who remained president of ASK until November 1967.

[Editorial, ASK *Newsletter* 1 (July 1964): 1.]

July 24 ∗ Toronto ∗ Journalist Sidney Katz announced plans for the formation in October of a Homophile Reform Society, to be based in either Toronto or Ottawa. A six-man committee had met to organize the society, whose first objective would be to press for the amendment of Section 149 of the Criminal Code, which concerned "gross indecency." Gary Nichols of the

Committee on Social Hygiene may have been a moving force behind the group, which appears to have never been very active.

[Sidney Katz, "Homosexuals Plan Own Organization," *Toronto Daily Star*, night ed., 25 July 1964, p. 2; Gary Kinsman, "Official Discourse as Sexual Regulation: The Social Organization of the Sexual Policing of Gay Men" (Ph.D. dissertation, University of Toronto, 1989), pp. 391–92; Gary Kinsman, *The Regulation of Desire: Sexuality in Canada* (Montréal: Black Rose Books, 1987), p. 155; "Seek to Form Society to Aid Sex Deviants," *Globe and Mail*, metro ed., 25 July 1964, p. 4; "Where Have All the . . . Gone?" *Two*, no. 5 (1965), p. 3.]

August 3 ✳ Hull, Qué. ✳ Member of Parliament Louis-Joseph Pigeon (PC-Joliette-L'Assomption-Montcalm), forty-two, was charged with indecently assaulting eighteen-year-old Raymond Emond on the main street of Hull, Québec. Emond claimed that Pigeon had led him into a laneway where he had made indecent propositions, upon which a struggle ensued. The charge was dropped when Judge Avila Labelle ruled that the Crown had not proved guilt beyond a reasonable doubt.

["'L'affaire' Pigeon s'instruit," *Le devoir*, 14 October 1964, p. 24; Malcolm Daigneault, " 'Statements to Police' Barred at M.P.'s Trial," *Toronto Telegram*, final ed., 14 October 1964, p. 44; "Indecent Assault Hearing Opens for Quebec M.P.," *Ottawa Citizen*, 13 October 1964, p. 28; "Judge Clears Pigeon of Indecent Assault: Reasonable Doubt Cited," *Globe and Mail*, metro ed., 24 October 1964, p. 3; "Louis-Joseph Pigeon est acquitté," *Le devoir*, 24 October 1964, p. 1; "M.P. Cleared of Assault Charge," *Ottawa Citizen*, 23 October 1964, p. 1; "M.P. Made Advances, Youth Tells Court," *Globe and Mail*, metro ed., 14 October 1964, p. 4; "Statement Ruled Out," *Ottawa Citizen*, 14 October 1964, p. 3.]

August 5, 14 ✳ Toronto; Vancouver ✳ In his August 5 column in the *Globe and Mail*, Michael Hanlon stated that Toronto police were worried about "the growing popularity of clubs for homosexuals in the city" — there were at least four at that time. The police were frustrated because ". . . behaviour in them is quite proper and no charges can be laid." Hanlon concluded that "What worries the police is not the activities in the clubs . . . but the fact that they are gathering places for homosexuals and as such offer a chance for homosexuality to spread by introduction." Less than two weeks later, Ormond Turner discussed the "problem" of clubs for homosexuals in Vancouver in his "Around Town" column in the Vancouver *Province*. An anonymous police officer was quoted as saying that the police had been " 'keeping track of them' " and that there had been more prosecutions involving gross indecency in the past six months than in the previous two years. Turner's conclusion was almost identical to Hanlon's: "What worries police is not the activities in the clubs . . . but the fact they are gathering places and, as such, offer a chance for homosexuality to spread by introduction."

[Michael Hanlon, "Homosexual Clubs Worry Metro Police" (column), *Globe and Mail*, metro edition, 5 August 1964, p. 8; Ormond Turner, "Around Town" (column), *Vancouver Province*, final home ed., 14 August, 1964, p. 21 (reprinted in the ASK *Newsletter* 1 [August 1964]: 3).]

September 14 * Vancouver * ASK sponsored a public discussion on "The Gay Bar in the Community."

[J.M., "Documenting 'Don Lucas Week,' " ASK *Newsletter* 1 (October 1964): 6.]

September 16 * Vancouver * ASK sponsored a lecture by Don Lucas, executive secretary of the Mattachine Society of San Francisco, on "The Homosexual Cause: The Aims and Activities of the Mattachine Society," held at Buchanan Penthouse, University of British Columbia.

[K.K., "Committee Round-Up Special: Programming," ASK *Newsletter* 1 (October 1964): 3; J.M., "Documenting 'Don Lucas Week,' " ASK *Newsletter* 1 (October 1964): 6.]

September 29 * Toronto * *The Gargoyle Magazine*, a student publication at University College, the University of Toronto, published Heather Dean's article on campus gay-bashing, entitled "The Varsity Sport Nobody Reports."

[*Gargoyle*, pp. 12–13 (reprinted in *Two*, no. 3 [1964], pp. 20–22).]

September 30 * Vancouver * Dr. Smith of the Vancouver Venereal Disease Clinic spoke on "Homosexuality and the Control of Venereal Disease" in a lecture sponsored by ASK, held at the Unitarian Hall.

[B.C., "ASK the Roving Reporter. . . ," ASK *Newsletter* 1 (October 1964): 11.]

October 12 * Montréal * John Watkins, Canada's ambassador to the Soviet Union from 1954 to 1956, died of a sudden heart attack during a month-long RCMP interrogation regarding his sexual activities and contacts while employed as a civil servant. This was but one incident (revealed only years later) relating to a massive hunt to identify male homosexuals in the Canadian civil service, and to eliminate them as security risks, conducted by the RCMP Security Service under Cabinet authority between 1959 and 1968.

[Dean Beeby, "Mounties Staged Massive Hunt for Gay Males in Civil Service: Police Kept Files on 8,200 during Diefenbaker-Pearson Era," *Globe and Mail*, metro ed., 24 April 1992, pp. A1, A2; Dean Beeby, "RCMP Was Ordered to Identify Gays: Only Carrying Out Cabinet Policy, Former Head of Mountie Security Says," *Globe and Mail*, metro ed., 25 April 1992, p. A5; Joe Clark, "Cold War Witch-Hunts Come to Light in Canada: Government Documents Expose a Wide-ranging Purge with Bizarre Twists," *Advocate* (Los Angeles), no. 604 (1992), pp. 44–45; Philip Girard, "From Subversion to Liberation: Homosexuals and the Immigration Act 1952–1977," *Canadian Journal of Law and Society* 2 (1987): 1–27; Philip Hannan, "McCarthyism Ottawa-Style: The Feds and the Fruit Machine," *Capital Xtra!*, no. 7 (1994), p. 11; "The

Homosexual Witch Hunt" and "The Fruit Machine" in John Sawatsky, *Men in the Shadows: The RCMP Security Service* (Toronto: Doubleday Canada, 1980), pp. 124–32, 133–37 ("The Homosexual Witch Hunt" reprinted in abridged form as "Security Paranoia & the Fruit Machine" in the *Body Politic*, no. 63 (1980), pp. 21–23); "John Watkins: Dead at 'Rockbottom,' " *Body Politic*, no. 81 (1982), p. 14; Gary Kinsman, " 'Character Weaknesses' and 'Fruit Machines': Towards an Analysis of the Anti-homosexual Security Campaign in the Canadian Civil Service," *Labour/Le travail*, no. 35 (1995), pp. 133–61; Gary Kinsman, "Pages from the Past: The Ottawa Purge Campaigns," *Centre/Fold: Newsletter of the Toronto Centre for Lesbian and Gay Studies*, no. 4 (1993): 12–13; Gary Kinsman, *The Regulation of Desire: Sexuality in Canada* (Montréal: Black Rose Books, 1987), pp. 120–23; B.L. (Bill Loos), "Cause of Death Due to 'Sudden': The Unexplained Demise of Diplomat John Watkins," *Body Politic*, no. 77 (1981), p. 9; Bill Loos, "Mounties Cleared in Watkins Inquest," *Body Politic*, no. 86 (1982), p. 12; Bill Loos, "Opening the Mounties' Closet: The McDonald Commission Pinpoints an RCMP Security Obsession: Homosexuals," *Body Politic*, no. 77 (1981), p. 9; "Operation Rock Bottom," in John Sawatsky, *For Services Rendered: Leslie James Bennett and the RCMP Security Service* (Toronto: Doubleday Canada, 1982), pp. 171–86; Daniel J. Robinson and David Kimmel, "The Queer Career of Homosexual Security Vetting in Cold War Canada," *Canadian Historical Review* 75 (September 1994): 319–45; John Sawatsky, "Homosexual Envoy Easy Prey for KGB: The Death of an Ambassador," *Toronto Star*, four star ed., 11 June 1981, pp. A1, A18; John Sawatsky, "Ottawa Discouraged RCMP's Spy Probe: The Death of an Ambassador," *Toronto Star*, four star ed., 12 June 1981, pp. A1, A16; John Watkins, *Moscow Dispatches*, ed. and introd. Dean Beeby and William Kaplan (Toronto: James Lorimer, 1987), pp. xiii-xxxii.]

October 14 * Vancouver * About sixty people attended a public panel discussion on "Religious Teaching and the Homosexual," sponsored by ASK and held at the Unitarian Hall. The panelists included Father James Roberts of Mount St. Joseph Hospital, Rev. A. Phillip Hewett, pastor of the Unitarian Church, and Prof. William Nicholls, an Anglican minister and head of the department of religious studies at the University of British Columbia. Nicholls stated that the criminal law should be changed to permit homosexual acts in private between consenting adults, and that the church should encourage stable unions between homosexuals.

["Change Law to Okay Homosexuals — Pastor," *Toronto Daily Star*, night ed., 16 October 1964, p. 51; K.K., "Homosexuality and Religion. Fall Lecture Series, Lecture # 3," ASK *Newsletter* 1 (November 1964): 9.]

October 28 * Vancouver * Douglas Sanders, president of ASK and also a lawyer, spoke on "Legal Reform and Homosexuality" at the Unitarian Hall in a lecture sponsored by ASK.

[Gary Kinsman, "Official Discourse as Sexual Regulation: The Social Organization of the Sexual Policing of Gay Men" (Ph.D. dissertation, University of Toronto, 1989), p. 389; "Legal Reform: Progress and Problems," ASK *Newsletter* 1 (November 1964): 2.]

November 18 ∗ Vancouver ∗ Dr. James Tyhurst, head of the department of psychiatry at the Vancouver General Hospital, delivered a lecture on "Psychiatry and Homosexuality," sponsored by ASK and held at the Unitarian Hall.

[B.C., "Programme Committee Annual Report," ASK *Newsletter* 2 (March 1965): 13.]

November 24 ∗ Canada ∗ CBC-TV telecast an hour-long discussion of legal, medical, and religious attitudes towards homosexuality on the program *Other Voices*. Several Canadian, British, and American "experts" were interviewed, but no open homosexuals. The program included a brief segment of a drag floor show filmed at the Music Room in Toronto.

["Drags at the CNE," *Two*, no. 3 (1964), p. 3; "*Other Voices*," CBC *Times*, 21–27 November 1964, p. 10; D.E.S. (Douglas Sanders), "Straight Talk," ASK *Newsletter* 1 (December 1964): 8.]

November 24 ∗ Toronto ∗ Rick Kerr, who was associated with the Music Room and the Melody Room clubs as well as *Two* magazine, spoke on "Hope for Homosexuals" before a group of University of Toronto students at a meeting of SCM. Kerr declared that homosexuality is a natural phenomenon and hoped that the public would come to accept it as just another minority position. This meeting resulted in informal talk of forming a homophile group in Toronto, but without result.

[Deanna Kamiel, "Pity the Pervert: No Fun and Nobody Wants Him. From Pink-panted Boys . . . to Respectable Citizens," *Varsity* (Univ. of Toronto), 25 November 1964, p. 1 (reprinted as "Hope for Homosexuals" in *Two*, no. 5 [1965], pp. 23–25).]

November 25 ∗ Toronto ∗ Sidney Katz of *Maclean's* spoke on "The Problem of Homosexuality" to the Humanist and Unitarian Society at University College, University of Toronto. Katz stated that homosexual acts between two consenting adults should not be criminal, but are instead a moral problem.

[Advertisement, *Varsity* (Univ. of Toronto), 25 November 1964, p. 5; "Over a Million Potential Criminals!" *Two*, no. 5 (1965), p. 3.]

November 30 ∗ Ottawa ∗ Member of Parliament Arnold Peters (NDP-Temiskaming) alleged that a former (unnamed) warden of St. Vincent de Paul penitentiary kept two homosexuals in the administration building at the prison and was a disgrace to the penitentiary service. The Ministry of Justice launched an investigation into the allegation.

["Probe Charge Pen Official Kept 2 Men," *Toronto Daily Star*, night ed., 1 December 1964, p. 4.]

December 11 ∗ Vancouver ∗ ASK's first theatrical venture, "ASKapades of 64," was held at the Unitarian Hall.

[R.M.C., "ASK at the Theatre: Reviewing a Revue," ASK *Newsletter* 2 (January 1965): 10; V.T., "ASKapades on Review," ASK *Newsletter* 1 (December 1964): 7.]

December 17 * Vancouver * Two members of ASK, a man and a woman, were interviewed by Jim Crossen on CJOR radio's hotline show *Crossfire*, followed by calls from the public. (See also December 18, 1964, and February 10, 1965.)

[J.M., "ASK Members under 'Crossfire,' " ASK *Newsletter* 2 (January 1965): 7.]

December 18 * Vancouver * Douglas Sanders, president of ASK, was interviewed by Jim Crossen on CJOR radio's hotline show *Crossfire*, followed by calls from the public.

[K.K., "ASK on the Spot: Our President on 'Crossfire,' " ASK *Newsletter* 2 (January 1965): 2.]

1965

—— * Englewood Cliffs, N.J. * Daniel Cappon's book *Toward an Understanding of Homosexuality* was published by Prentice-Hall. Cappon, a professor of psychiatry at the University of Toronto, claimed that homosexuality could be "cured" and that "There are no homosexuals — only people with homosexual problems." (See also October 9, 1968.)

["Kameny v. Cappon?" (editorial), YUHA *Newsletter*, January 1971, p. 2.]

—— * Longueuil, Qué. * Denis Vanier's *Je: poèmes* was published by Éditions le Crible. It was reprinted with additions in 1974 by Éditions l'Aurore.

[Roger Chamberland, "*Je* et *Pornographic Delicatessen*," in *Dictionnaire des oeuvres littéraires du Québec*, ed. Maurice Lemire et al., vol. 4 (1960–69) (Montréal: Fides, 1984), pp. 455–58.]

—— * Montréal * *Journal poétique, 1964–1965: élégie pour apprendre à vivre, suivie de pièces brèves*, by Jean Basile (pseud. of Jean-Basile Bezroudnoff), was published by Éditions du Jour.

[Michel Clément, "*Journal poétique 1964–1965*," in *Dictionnaire des oeuvres littéraires du Québec*, ed. Maurice Lemire et al., vol. 4 (1960–69) (Montréal: Fides, 1984), pp. 486–87.]

—— * Montréal * Marie-Claire Blais's novel *Une saison dans la vie d'Emmanuel* was published by Éditions du Jour. It garnered international acclaim and was awarded both the Prix Médicis and the Prix France-Canada. Translated into thirteen languages, the work was later adapted as a film.

[Annette Hayward, "*Une saison dans la vie d'Emmanuel*," in *Dictionnaire des oeuvres littéraires du Québec*, ed. Maurice Lemire et al., vol. 4 (1960–69) (Montréal: Fides, 1984), pp. 912–19; Mary Kandiuk, *French-Canadian Authors: A Bibliography of Their Works and of English-Language Criticism* (Metuchen, N.J.: Scarecrow Press, 1990), pp. 25, 36; Sinclair, "*Un saison dans la vie d'Emmanuel*," *Arcadie* (Paris), no. 156 (1966), pp. 582–83.]

—— * Toronto * The Gay Publishing Company, publishers of *Gay International*, printed the four-page pamphlet "How to Handle a Federal Interrogation/If You Are Arrested" for the East Coast Homophile Organizations (ECHO), the coalition of American homophile organizations formed in January 1963.

["East Coast Homophile Organizations (ECHO)" vertical file, Canadian Lesbian and Gay Archives, Toronto.]

—— * Toronto * Kamp Publishing Company, publishers of *Two*, *The Male Nude*, and *Gay Giggle*, moved from 457 Church Street to 292 Yonge Street. The operation soon opened K.K. Books, which stocked the largest selection of gay-oriented publications available in Canada at the time. In the early days, K.K. Books was run by Richard Kerr (of the Music Room and the Melody Room) and Kurt Lauer (of the Melody Room). The bookstore continued to operate into the early 1970s. (See also February 6, 1966.)

["Have You Heard?: Another First for Toronto," *Geo. Marshall's Queen City Gazette*, June 1965, p. 2; *Lesbian and Gay Heritage of Toronto*, Canadian Gay Archives Publication no. 5 (Toronto: CGA, 1982), p. 10.]

—— * Vancouver * Phyllis Webb's book of poetry *Naked Poems* was published by Periwinkle.

[Cecilia Frey, "Phyllis Webb: An Annotated Bibliography," in *The Annotated Bibliography of Canada's Major Authors*, ed. Robert Lecker and Jack David, Vol. 6 (Toronto: ECW Press, 1985), entries A4, D18–D23.]

February 6 * Montréal * An article by Norm Williams published in the *Montreal Star* discussed the increasing number of homosexuals being convicted in Montréal for soliciting, obscene displays, and "acting in a manner as to shock citizens." His research had been spurred by a comment made by Municipal Court Judge Pascal Lachapelle that homosexuality was on the rise in the city. Convictions for homosexual activities had increased from 25 in 1960 to 166 in 1964. Williams also interviewed members of Montréal's morality squad, who discussed gay night spots in town.

[Jean Côté, "L'homosexualité: les policiers de Montréal face á un probléme grandissant," *Le nouveau Samedi*, 20–26 March 1965, pp. 1, 14–17; Norm Williams, "Says Homosexuals on Increase Here: Judge's Observation," *Montreal Star*, final ed., 6 February 1965, p. 59.]

February 8 * Ottawa * Five gay men and four clergymen held an informal discussion with a view to forming "some type of organization to help homosexuals with their spiritual problems." Garrfield D. Nichol (pseud. of Gary Nichols) of the Committee on Social Hygiene was one of the organizers of the meeting. Further meetings were held on March 1 and March 29, 1965, and were a prelude to the formation of the Canadian Council on Religion and the Homosexual. (See also May 26, 1965.)

["Committee on Social Hygiene" vertical file, Canadian Lesbian and Gay Archives, Toronto.]

February 9 * Vancouver * Several members of ASK attended the annual general meeting of the John Howard Society of British Columbia to hear Dr. R.E. Turner, director of the Forensic Clinic attached to the Toronto Psychiatric Hospital, speak on the psychiatric treatment of the sexual offender. Dr. Turner was later interviewed by three members of ASK.

[Interview, ASK *Newsletter* 2 (April 1965): 3–8; J.M., "A Special Report: The John Howard Society and Forensic Psychiatry Facilities," ASK *Newsletter* 2 (February 1965): 5.]

February 10 * Vancouver * ASK held a discussion group to hear part of the CJOR radio program *Crossfire* taped on December 17, 1964, which featured two of ASK's members. Program host Jim Crossen attended the discussion.

[B.C., "ASK at the Discussion Groups," ASK *Newsletter* 2 (February 1965): 10.]

February 21 * Seattle, Wash. * ASK held its first meeting outside Vancouver, at the Friends' Center in Seattle, with guest speaker Dr. John Hampson of the department of psychiatry, University of Washington, discussing "Homosexuality and Psychiatry."

[B.C., "Programme Committee Annual Report," ASK *Newsletter* 2 (March 1965): 13; John Hampson, "Homosexuality and Psychiatry," ASK *Newsletter* 2 (March 1965): 5–7.]

March * Toronto * E.A. Lacey's *The Forms of Loss*, the first English-Canadian gay-identified book of poetry, was published by Muddy York Press. Poet Dennis Lee was one of the book's sponsors.

[Ronald Bates, "Books Reviewed: *The Forms of Loss*," *Canadian Forum*, February 1966, p. 259; Robert Fulford, "A Very Special Poet," *Toronto Daily Star*, night ed., 28 April 1965, p. 49; Dennis Lee, "Lacey Talented," *Varsity* (Univ. of Toronto), 19 March 1965, p. 14.]

March * Vancouver * Membership in ASK had risen to over sixty-five, and nearly one hundred people subscribed to the ASK *Newsletter*.

[K.K., "Membership Committee Annual Report," ASK *Newsletter* 2 (March 1965): 13.]

March * Vancouver * At the annual general meeting of ASK a committee was formed to enquire into the feasibility of starting a lesbian/gay social centre in Vancouver to be called The Circle. This would be a private social club that would cooperate with ASK but be separate from it. ASK disbanded temporarily in the summer of 1965 but reformed in 1966 and continued towards the goal of forming some sort of centre. The ASK Centre, the first community social centre in Canada run by a homophile organization, opened at the end of 1966. The idea for a social group called The Circle did not disappear, however. During the late 1960s and early 1970s, a non-profit homophile organization called The Circle was active in Vancouver under the direction of Mrs. D. Beck. It was devoted to education and personal counselling on homosexuality. (See also December 31, 1966.)

["The Circle," ASK *Newsletter* 2 (June 1965): 1; "The Circle" vertical file, Canadian Lesbian and Gay Archives, Toronto; Q.Q., "Page 69" (column), *Gay Canadian* 1 (7 September 1972): 6; Q.Q., "Page 69" (column), *Georgia Straight*, 2–9 September 1970, p. 20; Q.Q., "Page 69" (column), *Georgia Straight*, 22–29 June 1972, p. 17.]

May 26 * Ottawa * The Canadian Council on Religion and the Homosexual, a group of clergy and laypeople, was established to "aid in public education about homosexuality and the plight of the homosexual in society." The group's first executive included Rev. Philip Rowswell (Chairman), Garrfield D. Nichol (pseud. of Gary Nichols; Secretary), and Aurele J. Lebeau (Treasurer). Bruce Somers, first president of ASK, also helped to found the group, which sponsored discussion groups and was active until the autumn of 1966.

[Untitled article, ASK *Newsletter*, May 1967, p. 2; "Canadian Council on Religion and the Homosexual" vertical file, Canadian Lesbian and Gay Archives, Toronto; "Church Council Aims to Aid Homosexuals," *Globe and Mail*, metro ed., 2 June 1965, p. 9; Gary Kinsman, "Official Discourse as Sexual Regulation: The Social Organization of the Sexual Policing of Gay Men" (Ph.D. dissertation, University of Toronto, 1989), pp. 386–87; Gary Kinsman, *The Regulation of Desire: Sexuality in Canada* (Montréal: Black Rose Books, 1987), p. 153; "Tangents: Ottawa, Canada," *Tangents* 1 (October 1965): 16.]

May 26 * Stittsville, Ont. * The Committee on Social Hygiene, formed in 1963 by Garrfield D. Nichol (pseud. of Gary Nichols), was officially disbanded so that he could become active with the newly formed Canadian Council on Religion and the Homosexual.

[G.N. (Gary Nichols), Letter, *Mattachine Review* 10 (October 1964): 29; "Committee on Social Hygiene" vertical file, Canadian Lesbian and Gay Archives, Toronto.]

June 21 * Toronto * CBC-TV commentator Ed McGibbon chaired a panel discussion of sexuality with five lesbians during a fundraising event for Street Haven, a drop-in centre for women that had been founded at the Hotel Atalanta, 109–13 Carlton Street, in March 1965 by Peggy Ann Walpole. A number of Street Haven's clients were working-class lesbians. Three hundred and seventy-five people attended the event, held at the St. James Parish Hall.

[Marie Furtado, "Street Haven Site of Understanding," *Toronto Daily Star*, night ed., 13 March 1965, p. 57; Dorothy Howarth, "Lesbians Uphold 'Love,'" *Toronto Telegram*, final ed., 22 June 1965, p. 9; "Nurse Founds Haven from the Street for Prostitutes, Lesbians, Addicts," *Globe and Mail*, metro ed., 21 June 1965, p. 12; "We Think We Are Normal, Lesbian Panelist Says," *Globe and Mail*, metro ed., 22 June 1965, p. 9.]

July 6 ✱ Vancouver ✱ An article entitled "Homosexuality: Changing the Laws Could Raise Morality," by William Nicholls, an Anglican priest and head of the department of religious studies at the University of British Columbia, was published in the *Vancouver Sun*. Nicholls maintained that the present laws regarding homosexuality were "unjust and barbaric," and that homosexuality should be treated legally on the same basis as premarital intercourse between heterosexuals.

[William Nicholls, "Homosexuality: Changing the Laws Could Raise Morality," *Vancouver Sun*, four star ed., 6 July 1965, p. 6.]

August ✱ Northwest Territories ✱ Everett George Klippert, thirty-nine, a mechanic living in Pine Point, NWT, was questioned by the RCMP during an investigation of an arson. Klippert, who had not been involved in the fire, made a voluntary statement to the investigators that he had engaged in sexual acts with males on four occasions while living in the North. A native of Kindersley, Sask., Klippert had been convicted previously (in Calgary in 1960) of gross indecency and had been sentenced to four years in prison. Released in 1963 after serving three years, Klippert moved away and eventually settled in Pine Point. The RCMP charged Klippert with four counts of gross indecency involving non-violent acts with consenting adult males in private. He appeared before Magistrate P.B. Parker at Hay River, NWT, and pleaded guilty. On August 24, 1965, Klippert was sentenced to three years on each of the four counts, to be served concurrently. The Klippert case would become one of the most important criminal cases in Canadian history to deal with the matter of gay sexuality, and would prompt the introduction of amendments to the criminal code (Bill C-150) that came into effect in August 1969. (See also March 9, 1966, and November 7, 1967.)

[Gary Kinsman, "Official Discourse as Sexual Regulation: The Social Organization of the Sexual Policing of Gay Men" (Ph.D. dissertation, University of Toronto, 1989), pp. 161–65, 422–33, 438–40; "Everett Klippert" vertical file, Canadian Lesbian and Gay Archives, Toronto.]

September 27 ✱ Cardiff, Wales ✱ David Secter's film *Winter Kept Us Warm*, starring John Labow and Henry Tarvainen, premiered to critical acclaim at the Commonwealth Film Festival. This study of the "ambiguous" friendship between two male university students had been filmed at the University of Toronto by Secter, a twenty-two-year-old English major from Winnipeg. This was the first feature film with a homosexual theme made in English Canada.

[Adil., "*Winter Kept Us Warm*," *Variety*, 15 December 1965, p. 6; D.J. Turner and Micheline Morisset, eds., *Canadian Feature Film Index, 1913–1985/Index des films canadiens de long métrage* (Ottawa: Public Archives, National Film, Television, and

Sound Archives, 1987), entry 182; Tom Waugh, "Uncovering a Forgotten Canadian Gay Film — from 1965," *Body Politic*, no. 83 (1982), p. 36; "*Winter Kept Us Warm*," *Objectif 65*, no. 32 (1965), p. 19; "*Winter Kept Us Warm*," *Variety*, 7 February 1968, p. 22; "*Winter Kept Us Warm*" vertical file, Canadian Lesbian and Gay Archives, Toronto.]

November 15 * Toronto * In the November 15 issue of *The United Church Observer*, Rev. Mervyn Dickinson, pastoral counsellor at two United Churches in Toronto, declared that the church should welcome homosexuals warmly and openly into all phases of its life. Dickinson's statement that the church should give its blessing to some homosexual relationships alarmed some other members of Toronto's clergy.

["Cleric Asks Church Help Homosexuals," *Toronto Telegram*, final ed., 15 November 1965, p. 34; Mervyn Dickinson, "The Church and the Homosexual," *United Church Observer*, n.s. 27, no. 16 (15 November 1965): 22–23, 26, 40; "Homosexual Marriage Sick Idea, Priest Says," *Toronto Daily Star*, night ed., 20 November 1965, p. 13; "Minister Would 'Bless Some Homosexual Marriages,' " *Toronto Daily Star*, night ed., 6 November 1965, p. 36; "Tangents: Toronto," *Tangents* 1 (January 1966): 15–16.]

December 18 * Toronto * When four rowdy customers began to cause trouble at the Melody Room, manager Kurt Lauer called police for assistance. They arrived and arrested Lauer, who later sued Constable Russell Wilson for assault and false imprisonment.

["False Arrest, Assault Untrue, Officer Says," *Toronto Daily Star*, four star ed., 17 April 1968, p. 25.]

1966

—— * Montréal * *Joli tambour*, a play by Jean Basile (pseud. of Jean-Basile Bezroudnoff), was published by Éditions du jour. Based on historical events from New France in the 1750s, *Joli tambour* told the story of a drummer boy charged with rape who agreed to become the local executioner in order to escape a sentence of death. A gang of prisoners attempts to rape him, and the character LaRose is a bullying homosexual. *Joli tambour* was performed in English (as *The Drummer Boy*) in Toronto in January 1968. (See also January 17, 1968.)

[Paul Lefebvre, "*Joli tambour*," in *Dictionnaire des oeuvres littéraires du Québec*, ed. Maurice Lemire et al., vol. 4 (1960–69) (Montréal: Fides, 1984), pp. 475–76.]

—— * New York, N.Y.; Toronto * Leonard Cohen's novel *Beautiful Losers* was published by Viking in New York and McClelland and Stewart in Toronto. The central character is an aging scholar who ruminates about his past, including his homoerotic interest in a male friend named F.

[Robert K. Martin, "Two Days in Sodom; or, How Anglo-Canadian Writers Invent Their Own Quebecs," *Body Politic*, no. 35 (1977), pp. 28–30; Bruce Whiteman, "Leonard Cohen: An Annotated Bibliography," in *The Annotated Bibliography of Canada's Major Authors*, eds. Robert Lecker and Jack David, vol. 2 (Downsview, Ont.: ECW Press, 1980), entries A9, D50–D80.]

—— * Toronto * *Mazo de la Roche of Jalna*, Ronald Hambleton's biography of Canadian writer Mazo de la Roche, was published by General Publishing. De la Roche (1879–1961) had gained world-wide fame through her Jalna novels. For more than seventy years, she was involved in a very close relationship with her adopted sister Caroline Clement (who was actually a first cousin once removed). They were inseparable; according to Hambleton, Clement came to be seen as "almost Mazo's other self" (p. 16). Nowhere does he imply, hovever, that their relationship was in any way sexual. (See also 1972.)

[James Bannerman, "Bannerman on Books" (column), *Maclean's*, 19 November 1966, p. 62; Phyllis Grosskurth, "A Garrulous Account of Mazo of Whiteoaks," *Saturday Night*, December 1966, p. 46; George Hendrick, "Letters in Canada: 1966. Humanities," *University of Toronto Quarterly* 36 (July 1967): 410–11; Hilda Kirkwood, "*Mazo de la Roche of Jalna,*" *Canadian Forum,* February 1968, pp. 262–63; Dorothy Livesay, "Mazo Explored," *Canadian Literature,* no. 32 (1967), pp. 57–59.]

January * Toronto * An article by Daniel Dare (pseud.) in *The People's Magazine* advocated the execution of homosexuals. This magazine was the official organ of the People's Church, an independent evangelical church founded in 1930. Rev. J. Oswald Smith, the editor of the magazine, later claimed that the article had been published in error. (See also January 30, 1966.)

["Hang Homosexuals, Fundamentalist Says," *Globe and Mail,* metro ed., 7 January 1966, p. 5; "Sex Story an Error Says Cleric," *Toronto Telegram,* final ed., 7 January 1966, p. 3.]

January 29 * Toronto * Rev. Ian Rennie of Vancouver's Fairview Presbyterian Church was the guest speaker in the fourth program of a lecture series entitled "Man: Come of Age?," sponsored by Knox Presbyterian Church and held at New College, University of Toronto. During his talk before about 200 university students, Rev. Rennie declared that Toronto had become the Canadian centre for homosexuals. He viewed homosexuality as being a sinful choice rather than a "biological problem."

["Minister: Toronto Homosexual Centre," *Toronto Daily Star,* night ed., 31 January 1966, p. 23.]

January 30 * Toronto * Dr. Paul B. Smith of the People's Church, one of Toronto's leading fundamentalist Christian ministers, spoke to a congregation of 1,500 people on the topic "The Sin of Sodom." Dr. Smith stated that the law prohibiting homosexual acts between consenting adults should be abolished. He did view homosexuality as a sin, though, saying that it was as intolerable as other sins, such as adultery.

["Minister: Toronto Homosexual Centre," *Toronto Daily Star,* night ed., 31 January 1966, p. 23.]

February 6 * Toronto * Charges of possessing obscene literature for the purpose of distribution were laid against the Kamp Publishing Company, its secretary-treasurer Kurt Lauer, and Gary Somers, manager of the company's store (K.K. Books) at 292 Yonge Street. The store sold a large selection of titles of interest to gay men.

[Alan Miller, "The Way We Were," *Action!: A Publication of the Right to Privacy Committee* 1 (1981): 4; "Obscene Books Charge against Firm, 2 Men," *Toronto Daily Star,* night ed., 16 February 1966, p. 25.]

March 9 * Northwest Territories * Everett George Klippert was declared a dangerous sexual offender at the Territorial Court of the Northwest Territories, presided over by Justice J.H. Sissons. In August 1965, Klippert had been convicted on four counts of gross indecency involving non-violent acts with consenting adult males in private, and was sentenced to three years in prison on each count, to be served concurrently. Klippert had been convicted of gross indecency previously (in Calgary in 1960); his record of convictions had prompted Klippert's entry into the dangerous sexual offender sentencing procedure. In sentencing Klippert to an indefinite period of detention as a dangerous sexual offender, Justice Sissons said from the Bench, "I think the penitentiary term is going to do the accused considerable harm and will not help him and will not help the public." Klippert was transferred to the federal penitentiary at Prince Albert, Saskatchewan; his subsequent appeals were rejected. (See also November 7, 1967.)

[Cyril Greenland, "Dangerous Sexual Offenders in Canada," *Canadian Journal of Criminology and Corrections* 14 (1972): 47–48; Gary Kinsman, "Official Discourse as Sexual Regulation: The Social Organization of the Sexual Policing of Gay Men" (Ph.D. dissertation, University of Toronto, 1989), pp. 161–65, 422–33, 438–40.]

Spring ★ Garden City, N.Y. ★ Harold Horwood's novel *Tomorrow Will Be Sunday*, concerning a young man's (homo)sexual and moral coming-of-age in a Newfoundland outport, was published by Doubleday.

[James Bannerman, "Bannerman on Books: A Handy Guide to the Suburbs . . ." (column), *Maclean's*, 2 April 1966, p. 46; Arnold Edinborough, "New Canadian Fiction," *Saturday Night*, May 1966, pp. 45, 47–48; D. Kermode Parr, "Harold Horwood — 'Utterly Outspoken,' " *Atlantic Advocate* 56 (March 1966): 73.]

Spring ★ Montréal ★ A representative of the American homophile organization the Mattachine Society visited McGill University and delivered a talk on Mattachine and homosexuality. The event was sponsored by McGill's pre-med society.

[Unpublished interview with Charles Hill, ca. 1972, Charles Hill papers, 82–015/01, Canadian Lesbian and Gay Archives, Toronto.]

May 30 ★ Hamilton ★ During the second North American Conference on Church and Family Life, Dr. Gibson Winter, a professor of social ethics at the University of Chicago divinity school, maintained that homosexuality is natural for certain persons and could be considered moral. The conference was sponsored by the U.S. National Council of the Churches of Christ and the Canadian Council of Churches. (See also June 1, 1966.)

[Allen Spraggett, "Protestants Urged to Re-think Attitude on Homosexuals," *Toronto Daily Star*, night ed., 31 May 1966, p. 1.]

June 1 ★ Hamilton ★ Rev. George Johnston, professor of New Testament studies in the faculty of divinity at McGill University, declared that the

Christian Church could never approve or condone any type of homosexuality, and that it would always be impossible for a practising homosexual to be also a practising Christian. Rev. Johnston's remarks were made at the second North American Conference on Church and Family Life.

[Jack Cahill, "Pastor: Homosexual Cannot Be Christian," *Toronto Daily Star*, night ed., 2 June 1966, p. 14.]

June 16 ✳ Kelowna, B.C. ✳ A proposal by lawyers Sidney Simons and Douglas Sanders to relax laws concerning homosexual acts between consenting adults was defeated by the criminal justice committee at the annual convention of the British Columbia branch of the Canadian Bar Association. Simons and Sanders, sitting as a sub-committee, had proposed the resolution after studying the Wolfenden Report and conducting a two-year study of Section 49 of the Criminal Code, relating to acts of "gross indecency." The resolution called for the removal of criminal laws prohibiting homosexual acts in private between consenting parties over the age of eighteen. It also urged decriminalizing such acts between parties over the age of fourteen, providing the difference in their ages was not more than two years.

[Nate Cole, "Lawyers Support Homosexuality Ban: Bar Association Defeats Bid to Follow British Protocol," *Vancouver Sun*, four star ed., 16 June 1966, p. 24; Gary Kinsman, "Official Discourse as Sexual Regulation: The Social Organization of the Sexual Policing of Gay Men" (Ph.D. dissertation, University of Toronto, 1989), p. 392.]

August 25–27 ✳ San Francisco, Ca. ✳ Hazel M. and Douglas Sanders represented ASK at the second meeting of the National Planning Conference of Homophile Organizations.

[Bill Kelley, "Natl. Conference Progress Viewed (Part 2)," *Mattachine Midwest Newsletter*, October 1966, pp. 3, 9; "Roamings and Ramblings," ASK *Newsletter*, December 1966, p. 2.]

September 15, 17 ✳ Toronto ✳ The *Toronto Daily Star* published two columns in its "What Should I Do?" series that discussed solutions to questions about homosexuality submitted by readers. The columns were coordinated by the *Star's* social affairs expert Sidney Katz, and dealt mostly with medical and psychiatric opinions on treatments for the "homosexual problem."

[Sidney Katz, "What Should I Do?: Does Discussing Homosexuality Encourage It?" (column), *Toronto Daily Star*, night ed., 15 September 1966, p. 3; Sidney Katz, "What Should I Do?: How Can I Tell If My Son, 12, Is Homosexual?" (column), *Toronto Daily Star*, night ed., 17 September 1966, p. 3.]

October ✳ Ottawa ✳ Section 61 of a White Paper on immigration policy recommended that homosexuals "could safely be deleted from the specific list of prohibited persons" not allowed entry into Canada. Section 5 of the

Immigration Act stated that homosexuals, along with pimps, prostitutes, and drug addicts, were "undesirable" and therefore forbidden to enter Canada.

[Canada. Dept. of Manpower and Immigration, *White Paper on Immigration* (Ottawa: Queen's Printer, 1966), pp. 25–26; Philip Girard, "From Subversion to Liberation: Homosexuals and the Immigration Act 1952–1977," *Canadian Journal of Law and Society* 2 (1987): 1–27; Gary Kinsman, *The Regulation of Desire: Sexuality in Canada* (Montréal: Black Rose Books, 1987), pp. 123–24.]

October * Toronto * Renate Wilson's article "What Turns Women to Lesbianism?" was published in *Chatelaine*. She interviewed several lesbians in Vancouver and discussed the causes, frequency, and treatment of lesbianism with medical researchers such as Dr. R.E. Turner and Dr. J.W. Mohr of the Clarke Institute of Psychiatry in Toronto.

[Becki L. Ross, "The House That Jill Built: Reconstructing the Lesbian Organization of Toronto, 1976–1980," (Ph.D. dissertation, University of Toronto, 1992), p. 84; Renate Wilson, "What Turns Women to Lesbianism?" *Chatelaine*, October 1966, pp. 33, 130–32, 134.]

October 20 * Montréal * Marcel Dubé's play *Au retour des oies blanches* was performed at the Comédie-Canadienne. It was published by Leméac in 1969.

[Pierre Lavoie and Stéphane Lépine, "Théâtrographie," *Jeu: cahiers de théâtre*, no. 54 (1990), p. 127.]

December 31 * Vancouver * The ASK Community Centre opened at 1929 Kingsway with a Centennial New Year's Eve Ball. This was the first community social centre in Canada run by a homophile organization. The Centre provided space for business and executive meetings, a lending library, facilities for the production of the ASK *Newsletter*, some counselling and referral services, as well as a place for regular dances and speakers.

[Gary Kinsman, "Official Discourse as Sexual Regulation: The Social Organization of the Sexual Policing of Gay Men" (Ph.D. dissertation, University of Toronto, 1989), p. 382; Gary Kinsman, *The Regulation of Desire: Sexuality in Canada* (Montréal: Black Rose Books, 1987), p. 150; Gary Kinsman (interviewing Bruce Somers and Douglas Sanders), "Organizing in the Sixties: ASK: Canada's First Gay Rights Organization," *Rites* 3 (October 1986): 10–11, 15; "Roamings and Ramblings," ASK *Newsletter*, January 1967, p. 2; Neil Whaley, "His/Herstory: Gay Ground-breaker," *Vancouver Gay Community Centre News*, February 1983, pp. 39–41.]

1967

───── * Montréal * Marie-Claire Blais's novel *David Sterne* was published by Éditions du jour. An English translation of the same name was published in Toronto by McClelland and Stewart in 1973.

[Gabrielle Frémont, "*David Sterne,*" in *Dictionnaire des oeuvres littéraires du Québec,* ed. Maurice Lemire et al., vol. 4 (1960–69) (Montréal: Fides, 1984), pp. 247–48; Mary Kandiuk, *French-Canadian Authors: A Bibliography of Their Works and of English-Language Criticism* (Metuchen, N.J.: Scarecrow Press, 1990), pp. 25, 33.]

───── * Montréal * Jean-Paul Pinsonneault's play *Terre d'aube* was published by Fides.

[Lucie Robert, "*Terre d'aube,*" in *Dictionnaire des oeuvres littéraires du Québec,* ed. Maurice Lemire et al., vol. 4 (1960–69) (Montréal: Fides, 1984), pp. 866–67.]

January * Toronto * Scott Symons's "personal narrative" *Combat Journal for Place d'Armes,* in which a married, "respectable" Anglo-Canadian male spends three weeks in Montréal indulging in a variety of homosexual escapades, was published by McClelland and Stewart.

[J.G. (Jacques Godbout), "*Place d'Armes,*" *Liberté* (Montréal) 9 (March–April 1967): 89–90; W.D. Godfrey, "Andrea or Andre," *Canadian Forum,* May 1967, pp. 45–46; Robert K. Martin, "Cheap Tricks in Montreal: Scott Symons's *Place d'Armes,*" *Essays on Canadian Writing,* no. 54 (1994): 198–211; Robert K. Martin, "Two Days in Sodom; or, How Anglo-Canadian Writers Invent Their Own Quebecs," *Body Politic,* no. 35 (1977), pp. 28–30; "Scott Symons," in Charles Taylor, *Six Journeys: A Canadian Pattern* (Toronto: House of Anansi, 1977), pp. 191–243; Ronald Sutherland, "Brandy and Self-abasement," *Canadian Literature,* no. 33 (1967), pp. 84–85; Charles Taylor, "Scott Symons As Culture Hero: Son of Rosedale, Child of Our Disorder, Brother of Our Decline," *Toronto Life,* July 1977, pp. 50–53, 66–73; Charles Taylor, "The Spy Staying Out in the Cold to Fight Blandman and Methodism-on-the-Make," *Globe and Mail,* metro ed., 28 April 1973, p. 25.]

February 3 * Vancouver * Jean Lupien, vice-president of Central Mortgage and Housing Corporation and deputy commissioner-general of Expo '67, was arrested on a charge of attempted gross indecency when he was found at a local hotel in bed with a female impersonator. Lupien's defence was that he believed his companion was a woman. He was found guilty on June 27, 1967,

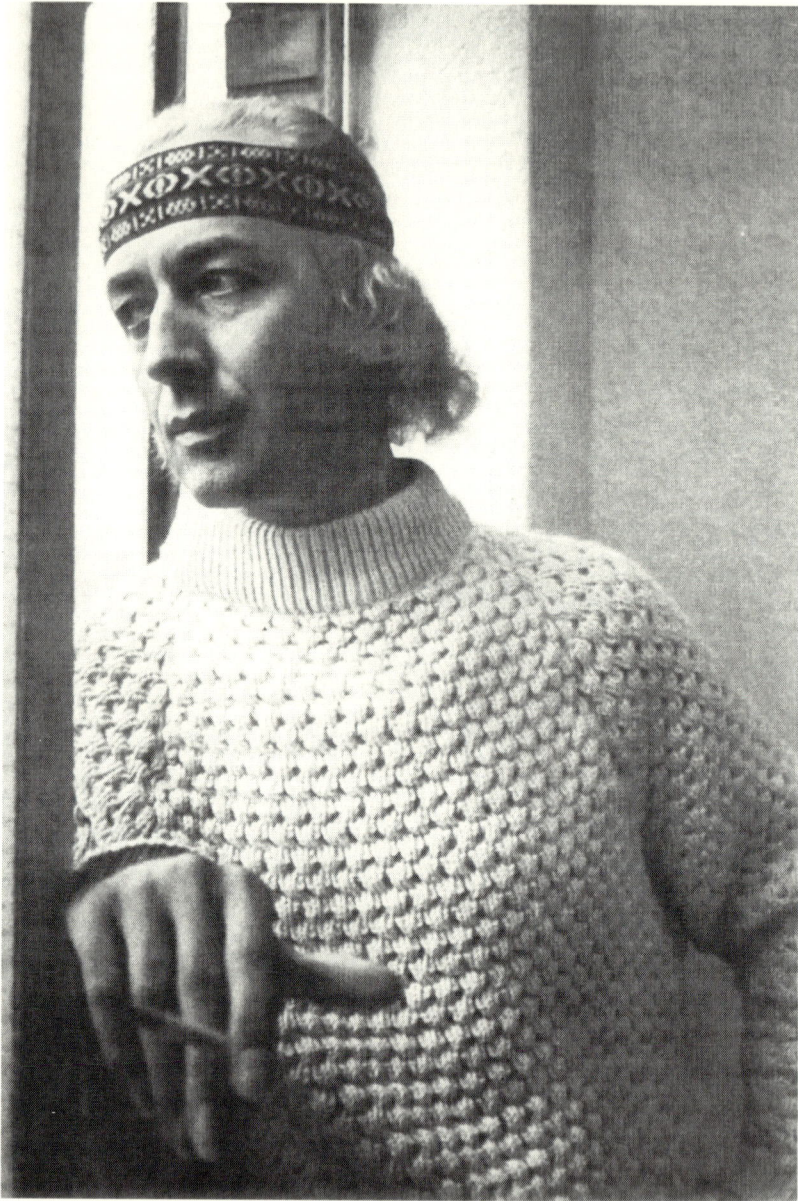

John Herbert, author of *Fortune and Men's Eyes.*

and fined \$750 (the other man, Serge Boisvert, was fined \$100), but the ruling was reversed by the British Columbia Court of Appeal. The case eventually went all the way to the Supreme Court of Canada, which reversed the ruling of the B.C. Court of Appeal and found Lupien guilty on November 17, 1969.

["High Court Upholds Indecency Conviction," *Toronto Daily Star*, all star ed., 18 November 1969, p. 55; Gary Kinsman, "Official Discourse as Sexual Regulation: The Social Organization of the Sexual Policing of Gay Men" (Ph.D. dissertation, University of Toronto, 1989), pp. 371–74; Douglas Sanders, "The Sentencing of Homosexual Offenders," *ASK Newsletter*, June 1967, p. 3 (reprinted in *Criminal Law Quarterly* 10 [November 1967]: 25–29); David N. Weisstub, ed., *Law and Psychiatry in the Canadian Context* (Toronto: Pergamon Press, 1980), pp. 300–303.]

February 14 ✳ New York, N.Y. ✳ *Fortune and Men's Eyes*, a play by Toronto writer John Herbert (born John Herbert Brundage), opened off-Broadway at the Broadway Actor's Playhouse. It concerns homosexuality and degradation in prison; Smitty, a straight student, is committed to jail for a minor drug offense and must share a cell with homosexuals. First staged in October 1965 in a Stratford (Ont.) Workshop production directed by Bruno Gerussi, *Fortune and Men's Eyes* opened in New York because the producers, David Rothenberg and Mitchell Nestor, had been unable to find a Canadian sponsor. Although it opened to mixed notices, *Fortune and Men's Eyes* became a very popular work. It was translated into six languages within three years and was staged internationally many times during the 1970s and 1980s. *Fortune and Men's Eyes* was filmed by Harvey Hart in 1971. (See also June 24, 1971.)

[Nathan Cohen, "Prison Drama Softened," *Toronto Daily Star*, four star ed., 17 April 1967, p. 22; Nathan Cohen, "Toronto Writer's Play: Too Good Not to Be Done," *Toronto Daily Star*, night ed., 15 October 1966, p. 31; Stan Fischler, "How Jack Brundage Found Fame — and Prison Inmates Found Fortune," *Toronto Daily Star*, three star ed., 9 November 1968, p. 33; "*Fortune and Men's Eyes*," *Guerilla* 2 (14 July 1971): 21; Robert Martin, "The Formidable Herbert Has Another Play," *Globe and Mail*, metro ed., 9 December 1972, p. 29; Frank Rasky, "Playwright John Herbert Insists He's No Has-been," *Toronto Star*, Saturday ed., 15 November 1975, p. F3; " 'That Man's Scope': John Herbert Now," *Body Politic*, no. 10 (1973), pp. 12–13, 25.]

February 19 ✳ Toronto ✳ Homosexuality, transvestism, and transsexuality were topics investigated in a program aired on CBC-TV's "Sunday" series. The program included a seven-minute film by Clifford Solway entitled *Gay Life*, filmed at a New York City gay bar in 1965.

[Ralph Thomas, "CBC's 'Sunday' Shows Men Cheek to Cheek," *Toronto Daily Star*, night ed., 18 February 1967, p. 39.]

February 24–26 ✳ Vancouver ✳ The official opening celebrations were held for the new ASK Centre. Activities included an open house, receptions, and a dance.

[Notice, *ASK Newsletter*, February 1967, p. 3.]

April 27 * Montréal * Expo '67 officially opened. In the months leading up to the event a number of gay bars and clubs were forced to close after the Québec Liquor Board refused to renew their licences. This was part of an attempt by authorities to clean up Montréal's image in preparation for Expo.

["Grapes from the Vine," *Two*, no. 1 (1964), p. 14; "Grapes from the Vine," *Two*, no. 9 (1966), p. 31; Bernard Morrier, "La Casbah donne du fil à retordre aux policiers," *La presse*, dernière ed., 15 April 1967, p. 6; John Yorston, "Club Charges Discrimination: Liquor Permit Hearing," *Montreal Star*, final ed., 22 April 1967, p. 21.]

May 22 * Washington, D.C. * The United States Supreme Court ruled, in a six-to-three decision, that homosexuals were ineligible for admission to the United States. Homosexuals were seen to fall within the definition of "afflicted with psychopathic personality" as used in the Immigration and Naturalization Act. The case had involved an order for deportation to Canada in March 1967 of Canadian citizen Clive Boutilier, who had admitted committing homosexual acts both before and after his entry to the United States in 1955. The U.S. Department of Justice did not relax its position on allowing gays and lesbians into the United States until September 1980, when it adopted a "don't ask, don't tell" policy.

[Chris Bearchell, "U.S. Loosens Ban on Homosexual Aliens," *Body Politic*, no. 68 (1980), p. 13; "Canadian Homosexual Deported from U.S.," *Toronto Daily Star*, four star night ed., 24 May 1967, p. 4; "Homosexual Alien Must Go, Supreme Court Rules in 6–3 Vote," *Pride Newsletter* 2 (July 1967): 6–7; "Homosexuals Ruled Ineligible to Enter U.S.," *Globe and Mail*, metro ed., 23 May 1967, p. 10.]

July * London, England * The Sexual Offences Bill, which partially decriminalized some homosexual activities in private between two consenting adults twenty-one years of age and older, passed third reading in the House of Commons on July 4 by a vote of 99 to 14. It passed third reading in the House of Lords on July 21, and was given Royal Assent July 27. The success of the Bill was due largely to the influence of the Wolfenden Report, published on September 4, 1957, and the lobbying efforts of the Homosexual Law Reform Society, formed in May 1958. This action on the part of the British Parliament in turn influenced the climate for legislative change in Canada, leading up to the passing of Omnibus Bill C-150 in May 1969.

["A Crucial Question" (editorial), *Vancouver Sun*, four star ed., 10 July 1967, p. 4; "Homosexual Bill Passes Commons," *ASK Newsletter*, August 1967, p. 2; "Homosexual Law Reform" (editorial), *Toronto Daily Star*, night ed., 29 May 1965, p. 6; "Homosexuality and the Law" (editorial), *Globe and Mail*, metro ed., 8 July 1967, p. 6; Stephen Jeffery-Poulter, *Peers, Queers, and Commons: The Struggle for Gay Law Reform from 1950 to the Present* (London: Routledge, 1991); Gary Kinsman, "Official Discourse as Sexual Regulation: The Social Organization of the Sexual Policing of Gay Men" (Ph.D. dissertation, University of Toronto, 1989), pp. 412–13; Anthony J. Lewis, "Homosexual

Reform Bill Passed by British M.P.s," *Globe and Mail*, metro ed., 5 July 1967, p. 4; "Metro Police Oppose U.K. Homosexual Law: Cases of Deviates Cited," *Globe and Mail*, metro ed., 7 July 1967, p. 5; Ron Poulton, "Homosexual Bill Passed in Britain after 9 Years," *Toronto Telegram*, final ed., 4 July 1967, p. 4.]

August ∗ Montréal ∗ International Sex Equality Anonymous (ISEA), an educational and social homophile organization, was founded by Paul Bédard. During 1967–68 Bédard was also involved with the Club Cherrier, 847, rue Cherrier, a discreet, semi-private mixed club for men. In September 1968, Bédard was acquitted of charges of gross indecency and contributing to juvenile delinquency after a member of the club was found to have used it to recruit customers for young male hustlers. By April 1969, Bédard and ISEA had opened the Gemini I club at 1285, boul. Maisonneuve O. ISEA was active until at least 1971. (See also April 19, 1969, and September 13, 1969.)

[Levy Beaulieu, "Une explosion de joie chez les 70,000 homosexuels du Québec," *Le semaine*, 17–23 June 1969, p. 6; "Ceux qui voulaient un jeune garçon n'auraient eu qu'a choisir parmi des photos cataloguées," *Le nouveau Samedi*, 31 August 1968, p. 3; Ross Higgins, "Lives, Oral Narratives, Writing the Past," revised version of a paper delivered at the Out of the Archives Conference, Department of History, York University, North York, Ont., 13–15 January 1994, pp. 14–20; ISEA file, University of Toronto Homophile Association (UTHA) papers, 82–006/01, Canadian Lesbian and Gay Archives, Toronto; Gary Kinsman, "Official Discourse as Sexual Regulation: The Social Organization of the Sexual Policing of Gay Men" (Ph.D. dissertation, University of Toronto, 1989), pp. 402–03; "Le président des homophiles acquitté!" *Montréal-matin*, 17 September 1968; "Le président du club des 'homophiles' est acquitté," *La presse*, métro ed., 17 September 1968, p. 33.]

August 17–19 ∗ Washington, D.C. ∗ Members of ASK attended the third National Planning Conference of Homophile Organizations (renamed the North American Conference of Homophile Organizations [NACHO]), which was sponsored by the Mattachine Society of Washington. ASK president Douglas Sanders became secretary of NACHO, a position he held until his resignation early in 1969.

[Bill Cae, "Third National Planning Conference," *Mattachine Midwest Newsletter* 2 (July 1967): 11; "Report of the Third Conference of Homophile Organizations," *ASK Newsletter*, September 1967, pp. 3–4; "Washington Conference," *Mattachine Midwest Newsletter* 2 (October 1967): 4.]

November ∗ Vancouver ∗ ASK's membership had grown to over one hundred fifty.

[Doug (Sanders), "President's Corner," *ASK Newsletter*, November 1967, p. 1.]

November 3 ∗ Toronto ∗ Lanny Salsberg's article "Witchcraft and Faggotry" was published in the *Varsity Review*. It examined the Yonge and King Street drag scenes during Halloween a few nights before, with particular emphasis on activities at Club 511 and Letros. The article was illustrated with photographs by John Swaigen.

[Lanny Salsberg, "Witchcraft and Faggotry," *Varsity Review* (Univ. of Toronto), 3 November 1967, pp. 8–9.]

November 4–5 * Seattle, Wash. * ASK sponsored the Western Regional Conference of Homophile Organizations, held in Seattle. Representatives from groups in Los Angeles, San Francisco, Seattle, and Vancouver attended.

["Report of the Third Conference of Homophile Organizations," *ASK Newsletter*, September 1967, p. 4.]

November 7 * Ottawa * In a three-to-two decision, the Supreme Court of Canada dismissed the appeal of Everett George Klippert, an admitted homosexual who had been sentenced to an indefinite period of detention in March 1966 as a dangerous sexual offender. Chief Justice John R. Cartwright, who had recommended quashing Klippert's preventive detention sentence, in a dissenting opinion suggested that the laws regarding homosexuality be clarified, and that it was not their intention to incarcerate harmless homosexuals for life. Intense media and political interest followed the dismissal of Klippert's appeal and influenced Justice Minister Pierre Trudeau in introducing amendments to the Criminal Code concerning homosexuality (Bill C-150). Although these amendments would eventually come into effect in August 1969, Klippert was not paroled until July 20, 1971. (See also November 8, and December 21, 1967.)

[Cyril Greenland, "Dangerous Sexual Offenders in Canada," *Canadian Journal of Criminology and Corrections* 14 (1972): 47–48; Sidney Katz, "Gentle George Klippert — Must He Serve Life?" *Toronto Daily Star*, four star ed., 18 November 1967, p. 10; Sidney Katz, "Homosexuals Shocked by Life Term Ruling: 'We're Society's Scapegoats,'" *Toronto Daily Star*, four star ed., 11 November 1967, p. 5; Gary Kinsman, "Official Discourse as Sexual Regulation: The Social Organization of the Sexual Policing of Gay Men" (Ph.D. dissertation, University of Toronto, 1989), pp. 161–65, 422–33, 438–40; Gary Kinsman, *The Regulation of Desire: Sexuality in Canada* (Montréal: Black Rose Books, 1987), pp. 161–64; Gerald McNeil, "In Canada: The Law Has Changed but Not for One Man," *Montreal Gazette*, final ed., 17 February 1971, p. 7; "Not Parliament's Intention," *Globe and Mail*, metro ed., 11 November 1967, p. 6; "Ottawa — November 7, 1967. — 'I Would Dismiss the Appeal...,'" *ASK Newsletter*, December 1967, p. 1; Gordon Pape,"Klippert's Case Helped Change the Law, but He Remains in 'Preventive Detention,'" *Montreal Gazette*, final ed., 26 December 1967, p. 7; Douglas Sanders (interviewing Everett Klippert), "An Exclusive Interview...," *ASK Newsletter* 5 (February 1968): 16–17; Douglas Sanders, "Homosexuality and the Law: The Mysterious Case of Everett Klippert,"*Georgia Straight*, 27 September–3 October 1968, pp. 10–11, 17; "Supreme Court Decision Means Homosexuals Can Face Imprisonment for Life," *Globe and Mail*, metro ed., 8 November 1967, p. 8; "Supreme

Court Ruling Makes Homosexual Liable to 'Life,' " *Toronto Daily Star*, all star ed., 7
November 1967, p. 1.]

November 7 * Ottawa * In the House of Commons, Bud Orange (L-North-
west Territories) asked Justice Minister Pierre Trudeau whether he would
consider amending the Criminal Code "so that Canadians will not be
subjected to preventive detention because they are victims of an unfortunate
social disease (homosexuality)." The question, arising from the Supreme Court's
verdict in the Klippert case, was ruled out of order, and Trudeau did not reply.
Outside the Commons, Trudeau told reporters that "there will be something
on preventive detention — whether it's too liberal or not liberal enough" in
his forthcoming omnibus bill to amend the Criminal Code (Bill C-150).

["Homosexual Detention Laws May Be Amended," *Toronto Telegram*, final ed., 8
November 1967, p. 36; "Law on Homosexuals Will Be Amended: No Life Sentences,"
Toronto Daily Star, three star ed., 8 November 1967, pp. 1–2.]

November 8 * Ottawa * Justice Minister Pierre Trudeau expressed approval
of liberalizing laws concerning homosexuality, and suggested that the law as
it concerned homosexuals be placed before the Ouimet committee on penal
reform. Trudeau's statement came in response to the dismissal of the appeal
of Everett Klippert by the Supreme Court of Canada the day before.

["Criminal Code to Be Revised — No Homosexual Life Sentences," *Toronto Daily
Star*, four star ed., 8 November 1967, p. 63; Tom Hazlitt, "Trudeau Backs New
Homosexuals' Law: He'll Ask Thorough Study," *Toronto Daily Star*, two star home ed.,
9 November 1967, p. 2; Lewis Seale, "Trudeau Says Ouimet Committee May Study
Homosexual Problem," *Globe and Mail*, metro ed., 9 November 1967, p. 8.]

November 29 * Vancouver * ASK elected a new executive. Norma K.
Mitchell, former treasurer of ASK, succeeded Douglas Sanders as president.

[Doug (Sanders), "President's Corner," ASK *Newsletter*, November 1967, p. 1.]

December * Ottawa * The article "Homosexuality among Women," by
Réjane Rancourt and Thérèse Limoges, was published in *Canadian Nurse*.
They described lesbianism as an "addiction," "deviation," and "retarded
psychosocial development."

[Réjane Rancourt and Thérèse Limoges, "Homosexuality among Women," *Canadian
Nurse* 63 (December 1967): 42–44; Becki L. Ross, "The House That Jill Built:
Reconstructing the Lesbian Organization of Toronto, 1976–1980," (Ph.D. dissertation,
University of Toronto, 1992), p. 84.]

December * Vancouver * After the owner of the building housing the ASK
Centre refused to renew the lease, the Centre moved into a former bowling
alley at 1268 E. Hastings Street. In February 1968 the Centre moved again,
to the site of the old Kitsilano Theatre, 2114 W. Fourth Avenue.

[Gary Kinsman (interviewing Douglas Sanders), "Organizing in the Sixties: ASK: Canada's First Gay Rights Organization," *Rites* 3 (October 1986): 11, 15; Norma K. Mitchell, "From the President's Desk," ASK *Newsletter* 5 (January 1968): 1; "We Wish to Announce the New Centre (as of Feb. 17th)" (advertisement), ASK *Newsletter* 5 (February 1968): 5.]

December 21 ✶ Ottawa ✶ Justice Minister Pierre Trudeau introduced an omnibus bill in the House of Commons, Bill C-150, one part of which would allow for the decriminalization of homosexual acts ("gross indecency" and "buggery") in private between two consenting adults twenty-one years of age or older.

["Criminal Code Changes Draw Little Criticism," *Montreal Gazette*, final ed., 23 December 1967, p. 4; "No Place for the State" (editorial), *Vancouver Sun*, four star ed., 22 December 1967, p. 4; Vincent Prince, "Sur deux points particuliers du bill Trudeau" (editorial), *Le devoir*, 29 December 1967, p. 4; Gordon Pape, "Klippert's Case Helped Change the Law, but He Remains in 'Preventive Detention,' " *Montreal Gazette*, final ed., 26 December 1967, p. 7; Gary Ralph, "Law Doesn't Keep the Parasites Away: Homosexuals," *Toronto Telegram*, final ed., 6 January 1968, p. 23; Lewis Seale, "Code Revisions Would Allow Homosexual Acts between Two Consenting Adults," *Globe and Mail*, metro ed., 22 December 1967, p. 5.]

December 22 ✶ Calgary ✶ In response to the proposed Bill C-150, Calgary police chief Ken McIver declared that decriminalizing homosexual acts between consenting adults in private would represent a decay in Canadian society. McIver described homosexuality as "a horrible, vicious and terrible thing. We do not need this in our country."

["Homosexual Law Sign of Decay Says Police Chief," *Toronto Daily Star*, four star ed., 23 December 1967, p. 2; "McIver Opposes Change," *Calgary Herald*, late city ed., 22 December 1967, pp. 1, 2.]

December 28 ✶ Québec, Qué. ✶ Québec Provincial Secretary Yves Gabias declared that Canada was bound to fall into decadence if the Criminal Code was amended to decriminalize homosexual acts.

["Gabias Predicts Bill Will Lead to Decadence," *Globe and Mail*, metro ed., 29 December 1967, p. 31; "Quebecer Hits at New Homosexual Law," *Toronto Daily Star*, four star ed., 29 December 1967, p. 14.]

1968

—— * Montréal * Marie-Claire Blais's novel *Manuscrits de Pauline Archange* was published by Éditions du jour. An English translation (*The Manuscripts of Pauline Archange*) was published in New York in 1970 by Farrar, Straus and Giroux.

[Nicole Bourbonnais, "*Manuscrits de Pauline Archange*," in *Dictionnaire des oeuvres littéraires du Québec*, ed. Maurice Lemire et al., vol. 4 (1960–69) (Montréal: Fides, 1984), pp. 540–44; Mary Kandiuk, *French-Canadian Authors: A Bibliography of Their Works and of English-Language Criticism* (Metuchen, N.J.: Scarecrow Press, 1990), pp. 25, 35.]

—— * Montréal * Paul Chamberland's book of poetry *L'inavouable* was published by Éditions Parti pris.

[André Brochu, "*L'inavouable*," in *Dictionnaire des oeuvres littéraires du Québec*, ed. Maurice Lemire et al., vol. 4 (1960–69) (Montréal: Fides, 1984), pp. 426–28.]

—— * Montréal * Denis Vanier's book of poetry *Pornographic Delicatessen* was published by L'Estérel.

[Roger Chamberland, "*Je* et *Pornographic Delicatessen*," in *Dictionnaire des oeuvres littéraires du Québec*, ed. Maurice Lemire et al., vol. 4 (1960–69) (Montréal: Fides, 1984), pp. 455–58.]

—— * Toronto * Ron Gabe, Jorge Saia, and Michael Tims formed the artistic collective General Idea. They adopted new names — Felix Partz (Gabe), Jorge Zontal (Saia), and A.A. Bronson (Tims) — and proceeded to introduce a satirical and humorous gay sensibility to the Toronto art world. Their early triumphs included The Miss General Idea Pageant (1971), held at the Art Gallery of Ontario, and the creation of FILE magazine (1972). During the late 1970s and early 1980s General Idea garnered an international art following, and in 1984 held the Miss General Idea Pavilion retrospective at the Art Gallery of Ontario. During the late 1980s their art focussed more on the AIDS crisis — their AIDS logo spoofing the famous LOVE sign created by Robert Indiana became internationally famous. General Idea disbanded in 1994, the same year in which both Felix Partz and Jorge Zontal died of AIDS.

["General Idea Artist Partz Dies," *Toronto Star*, metro ed., 7 June 1994, p. B6; Philip Marchand, "The General Idea behind General Idea: Think of Them as Undiscovered Pop Stars Who Play the Media Instead of Guitars," *Toronto Life*, November 1975, pp. 30–32, 35–37; John Bentley Mays, "From the files of General Idea," *Globe and Mail*, metro ed., 21 July 1984, p. E13; John Bentley Mays, "An Idea Whose Time Has Come," *Globe and Mail*, weekend ed., 27 April 1985, p. E15; Roberto Olivo, "Poodle Rampant," *New York Native*, 11–17 November 1985, p. 58; Nik Sheehan, "The Infectious Glamour of General Idea: A.A. Bronson Paints the Final Chapter Alone," *Xtra!*, no. 277 (1995), p. 28; David Vereschagin (interviewing General Idea), "What's the Big Idea?" *Body Politic*, no. 115 (1985), pp. 29–32.]

——— * Vancouver * Helene Rosenthal's book of poetry *Peace Is an Unknown Continent* was published by Very Stone House (Talonbooks).

[Hugh MacCallum, "Letters in Canada: 1968. Poetry," *University of Toronto Quarterly* 38 (July 1969): 352.]

January * Vancouver * ASK hosted a joint seminar with members of the Dorian Society (Seattle) and the Third Name (FEM, Seattle). Speakers included Father James Roberts and Douglas Sanders.

[Norma K. Mitchell, "From the President's Desk," ASK *Newsletter* 5 (February 1968): 2.]

January 13 * Toronto * *The Globe Magazine* published William Johnson's "The Gay World," a feature article on gays.

[William Johnson, "The Gay World," *Globe Magazine*, metro ed., 13 January 1968, pp. 5–8 (reprinted in W.E. Mann, ed., *The Underside of Toronto* [Toronto: McClelland and Stewart, 1970], pp. 322–33, and in W.E. Mann, ed., *Social Deviance in Canada* [Toronto: Copp, Clark, 1971], pp. 380–89).]

January 17 * Toronto * *The Drummer Boy*, an English-language version of Jean Basile's play *Joli tambour*, opened at the Royal Alexandra Theatre. The Theatre Toronto production was directed by Clifford Williams and starred Richard Monette and John Colicos.

[Nathan Cohen, "Beat a Slow Measure of Regret for Drummer," *Toronto Daily Star*, all star ed., 18 January 1968, p. 22; Ralph Hicklin, "Drummer Has First-rate Beat," *Toronto Telegram*, final ed., 18 January 1968, p. 62; Paul Lefebvre, "*Joli tambour*," in *Dictionnaire des oeuvres littéraires du Québec*, ed. Maurice Lemire et al., vol. 4 (1960–69) (Montréal: Fides, 1984), pp. 475–76; Herbert Whittaker, " 'The Drummer Boy' Taps Out a Powerful Tune," *Globe and Mail*, metro ed., 16 January 1968, p. 10.]

February 29 * Vancouver * Douglas Sanders of ASK made a submission to the Royal Commission on Security, arguing against denying homosexuals government employment and security clearance. (See also June 1969.)

["Association for Social Knowledge (ASK)" vertical file, Canadian Lesbian and Gay Archives, Toronto; Gary Kinsman, "Official Discourse as Sexual Regulation: The

Social Organization of the Sexual Policing of Gay Men" (Ph.D. dissertation, University of Toronto, 1989), pp. 396–97; Gary Kinsman, *The Regulation of Desire: Sexuality in Canada* (Montréal: Black Rose Books, 1987), p. 157.]

March 15 * Montréal * Marie-Claire Blais's play *L'exécution* was performed at the Théâtre du Rideau Vert. It was published in 1968 by Éditions du jour.

[Pierre Lavoie and Stéphane Lépine, "Théâtrographie," *Jeu: cahiers de théâtre,* no. 54 (1990), p. 127.]

June * Canada * An anti-gay smear campaign was directed against Prime Minister Pierre Trudeau and the Liberal Party in the weeks leading up to the June 25 federal general election. In letters mailed across Canada Trudeau was labelled a promoter of sexual deviation and a "beast of Sodom" for his government's support of the decriminalization of homosexual acts as presented in Bill C-150. The campaign was co-ordinated by the ultra-conservative groups the Canadian Intelligence Service (Flesherton, Ont.), the Pilgrims of St. Michael (White Berets; Rougement, Qué.), and the Edmund Burke Society (Scarborough, Ont.).

[Dominique Clift, "Quebec Tories Use Crude Whispers about Homosexuality," *Toronto Daily Star,* four star ed., 14 June 1968, p. 8; Robert Miller, "Smear Campaign 'Repugnant': Tories," *Toronto Daily Star,* four star ed., 14 June 1968, pp. 1, 4; "The Ugliest Smear of All" (editorial), *Toronto Daily Star,* four star ed., 20 June 1968, p. 6.]

August * Canada * The Fellowship of Evangelical Baptists, a fundamentalist Christian denomination with more than 100,000 members, protested the proposed legislation that would decriminalize homosexual acts between two consenting adults in private (Bill C-150).

[Allen Spraggett, "Baptists Crusade to Kill Off New Homosexual Law," *Toronto Daily Star,* four star ed., 24 August 1968, p. 13.]

August 11–18 * Chicago, Ill. * Douglas Sanders represented ASK at the fourth annual North American Conference of Homophile Organizations (NACHO), hosted by Mattachine Midwest. A resolution was adopted during the meeting that criticized the age of consent limitations of the proposed reforms to the Canadian Criminal Code (Bill C-150). The resolution was forwarded by Douglas Sanders to Prime Minister Pierre Trudeau on August 24, 1968.

[Gary Kinsman, *The Regulation of Desire: Sexuality in Canada* (Montréal: Black Rose Books, 1987), p. 165.]

September 1 * Montréal * *Le petit journal* reported that the Montréal police had accumulated files on 12,000 known or suspected homosexuals in Montréal alone.

["12,000 homos!" *Le petit journal,* 1 September 1968, p. 12.]

September 5 ∗ Vancouver ∗ A convention of the Canadian Bar Association passed a resolution calling for a further relaxation of gross indecency laws, beyond the changes proposed in Bill C-150. The Bar Association proposed that the age of sexual consent be lowered from twenty-one (as in the proposed bill) to sixteen or eighteen, to reflect the juvenile age limits in each province.

["Lawyers Urge Easing Gross Indecency Law," *Globe and Mail*, metro ed., 6 September 1968, p. 2.]

September 6 ∗ Granby, Ont. ∗ The Canadian Association of Chiefs of Police voted to oppose any changes to the laws concerning homosexuality.

[Rudy Platiel, "Chiefs Oppose Changes in Homosexual Law: Police Meet in Granby," *Globe and Mail*, metro ed., 7 September 1968, p. 3.]

September 10 ∗ Toronto ∗ Ian Young's article "The Problem of Homosexuality" was published in the *Eye Opener*, a student newspaper at Ryerson Polytechnical Institute. The article surveyed the homophobic and generally anti-sexual attitudes present in much of Western Christian society and discussed the work of some scholars (such as Dr. Wainwright Churchill and Dr. Evelyn Hooker) that had presented a more sensible outlook on homosexuality. Young concluded, "The problem is not a problem of 'the homosexual' but of our own attitude to homosexuality in others — and most of all, in ourselves."

[Ian Young, "The Problem of Homosexuality," *Eye Opener* (Ryerson Polytechnical Institute, Toronto), 10 September 1968, pp. 6, 8.]

September–November ∗ Vancouver ∗ *Georgia Straight* published a series of three long articles on lesbians written by Bob Cummings. Norma Mitchell, president of ASK, was interviewed in Part 1, which was an overview of lesbianism. Part 2 dealt with butch-femme relationships, while Part 3 examined legal and psychiatric issues.

[Bob Cummings, "The Lesbians: Part 1," *Georgia Straight*, 13–19 September 1968, pp. 9–12; Bob Cummings, "The Lesbians: Part 2," *Georgia Straight*, 4–10 October 1968, pp. 9–11; Bob Cummings, "The Lesbians: Part 3," *Georgia Straight*, 1–7 November 1968, pp. 9–12.]

Autumn ∗ Toronto ∗ *Sexual Deviations in the Criminal Law: Homosexual, Exhibitionistic, and Pedophilic Offences in Canada*, a study conducted by Alex K. Gigeroff and a research group at the Clarke Institute of Psychiatry, concluded that the proposed changes to the Criminal Code concerning sexual offences (Bill C-150) were inadequate, particularly those sections relating to "gross indecency." The study complained about the vague definition of "gross indecency" and its use to prosecute widely differing offences. Gigeroff had previously written several important studies, including "Sexual

Offences in Relation to Homosexual, Exhibitionistic, and Pedophilic Sexual Offences with Particular Reference to Canadian Legislation and Case Law" (L.L.M. thesis, University of Toronto, 1966) and "The Evolution of Canadian Legislation with Respect to Homosexuality, Pedophilia, and Exhibitionism," *Criminal Law Quarterly*, no. 8 (1965–66), pp. 445–54.

[Alex K. Gigeroff, *Sexual Deviations in the Criminal Law: Homosexual, Exhibitionistic, and Pedophilic Offences in Canada* (Toronto: Clarke Institute of Psychiatry; University of Toronto Press, 1968), pp. 209–14; Gary Kinsman, "Official Discourse as Sexual Regulation: The Social Organization of the Sexual Policing of Gay Men" (Ph.D. dissertation, University of Toronto, 1989), pp. 433–38; Gary Kinsman, *The Regulation of Desire: Sexuality in Canada* (Montréal: Black Rose Books, 1987), p. 161; "Sex Law Revisions to Make Little Change in Practice, Study Says," *Globe and Mail*, metro ed., 14 January 1969, p. 31.]

October 9 * Toronto * In an address to the Ontario College of Family Physicians, University of Toronto professor of psychiatry Daniel Cappon stated that eighty percent of homosexuals who go to psychiatrists and doctors for treatment are helped, and half of these are cured. Cappon declared that homosexuals are never happy, well-adjusted people. He was the author of *Toward an Understanding of Homosexuality* (1965).

[Marilyn Dunlop, "Many 'Homosexuals' Easily Cured: Doctor," *Toronto Daily Star*, four star ed., 10 October 1968, p. 40.]

October 27 * Toronto * Thirty men were charged after police raided the International Steam Bath, 458 Spadina Avenue. Eight men were arrested, and twenty-two others were issued with summonses for being found-ins at a bawdy house.

["Steam Bath Raided, 30 Face Morals Charges," *Toronto Daily Star*, four star ed., 28 October 1968, p. 2.]

October 31 * Toronto * Four thousand spectators lined the sidewalk across from the St. Charles Tavern on Yonge Street to watch men in drag enter the tavern on Halloween. Some members of the crowd hurled insults and bricks; four people were arrested. Police later found several gasoline bombs placed behind the tavern.

["Near-Riot at Drag Contest: Fire-Bombs Found," *Toronto Telegram*, final ed., 1 November 1968, p. 8.]

1969

—— * Montréal * Paul Toupin's memoir *Mon mal vient de plus loin* was published by Le cercle du livre de France.

[Jean-Marcel Paquette, "*Mon mal vient de plus loin*," in *Dictionnaire des oeuvres littéraires du Québec*, ed. Maurice Lemire et al., vol. 4 (1960–69) (Montréal: Fides, 1984), pp. 590–91.]

—— * Toronto * The radical feminist organization New Feminists (NF) was formed by ex-members of the Toronto Women's Liberation Movement (TWLM). The NF, which operated until 1973, failed to adequately address the issue of lesbianism or lesbian oppression. A few lesbian members of NF, such as Holly Devor, protested the group's anti-lesbian stance and were expelled from membership as a result.

[Margaret Fulford, ed., *The Canadian Women's Movement, 1960–1990: A Guide to Archival Resources/Le mouvement canadien des femmes, 1960–1990: guide de ressources archivistiques* (Toronto: Canadian Women's Movement Archives/ECW Press, 1992), entry 447; Becki L. Ross, *The House That Jill Built: A Lesbian Nation in Formation* (Toronto: University of Toronto Press, 1995), p. 25.]

—— * Toronto * Scott Symons's experimental novel *Civic Square* was published by McClelland and Stewart; it was published as an unbound, mimeographed typescript in a Birks box.

[Graeme Gibson, "Gelded and Blue-Boxed MacCanada," *Globe and Mail Magazine*, 18 October 1969, p. 15; Donald Stainsby, "Books and Bookmen" (column), *Vancouver Sun*, 21 November 1969, p. 34A; "Scott Symons," in Charles Taylor, *Six Journeys: A Canadian Pattern* (Toronto: House of Anansi, 1977), pp. 191–243; Charles Taylor, "Scott Symons As Culture Hero: Son of Rosedale, Child of Our Disorder, Brother of Our Decline," *Toronto Life*, July 1977, pp. 50–53, 66–73; Charles Taylor, "The Spy Staying Out in the Cold to Fight Blandman and Methodism-on-the-Make," *Globe and Mail*, metro ed., 28 April 1973, p. 25; Ian Young, "Pigs & Fishes," *Body Politic*, no. 18 (1975), pp. 16–18.]

February 11 * Ottawa * In the House of Commons, Arnold Peters (NDP-Timiskaming) stated that MPs should welcome the proposed amendment of the Criminal Code that would decriminalize certain homosexual acts in private between consenting adults (Bill C-150). Peters made reference to a former (unnamed) Member of Parliament whose political career was ruined because of his homosexuality, and concluded, "I do not think we should build a society that hounds a person for something that he cannot control."

[" 'Ruined' M.P. Cited in Defence of Bill Legalizing Homosexual Acts," *Toronto Daily Star*, four star ed., 12 February 1969, p. 34.]

Spring * Val d'Or, Qué. * The premiere of Michel Tremblay's play *La Duchesse de Langeais*, a monologue of the loves and disillusionments of an aging transvestite, was performed by Les Insolents de Val d'Or. Doris Saint-Pierre starred in the production, which was directed by Hélène Bélanger.

[Pierre Lavoie, "*La Duchesse de Langeais*," in *Dictionnaire des oeuvres littéraires du Québec*, ed. Maurice Lemire et al., vol. 4 (1960–69) (Montréal: Fides, 1984), pp. 277–78.]

April * Scarborough, Ont. * Ian Young's first book of poetry, *White Garland: 9 Poems for Richard*, with an additional poem by Richard Phelan, was published by Cyclops.

[(Ian Young), *Ian Young: A Bibliography 1962–1980*, Canadian Gay Archives Publication no. 3 (Toronto: Pink Triangle Press, 1981), entry A1.]

April 16–May 14 * Ottawa * Bill C-150, the proposed amendment to the Criminal Code, was debated in the House of Commons. During the Commons debate, Justice Minister John Turner declared that Bill C-150 was not intended to condone, endorse, or encourage homosexuality and that "it doesn't even legalize this kind of conduct" but instead lifted " the taint or stigma of the law" from certain sexual acts committed by two consenting adults in private. Such behaviour, Turner concluded, was cause for psychiatric rather than legal intervention. During the debate numerous complaints were raised about the amendments concerning homosexuality, particularly from members of the Progressive Conservative and Créditiste parties. For example, Eldon Woolliams (PC-Calgary North) stated, ". . . I do not want to have this kind of debauchery in our nation," while Walter Dinsdale (PC-Brandon-Souris) declared, "We are bringing the morals and values of skid row into the salons and drawing rooms of the nation." Martial Asselin (PC-Charlevoix) believed that "Homosexuals are mostly inclined to pervert youngsters and the Minister opens the door even wider." The fourteen Créditiste MPs, led by Réal Caouette and all from Québec, were the most critical of the changes introduced by the Bill — especially those relating to homosexuality and abortion — and suggested that communism, socialism, and atheism were behind the changes. André Fortin (Créd.-Lotbinière) declared that the amendments dealing with homosexuality "should be withdrawn pure and simple" while René Matte (Créd.-Champlain) said it was "almost scandalous to see representatives of the people being obliged to discuss these questions." The Créditistes demanded that a public referendum be held on these issues and staged a filibuster of Parliament over the amendments concerning abortion. (See also May 14 and August 26, 1969.)

["Abortion Law Criminal, Say Filibusterers," *Ottawa Citizen*, 6 May 1969, p. 20; George Bain, "A Curious Debate" (column), *Globe and Mail*, metro ed., 18 April 1969, p. 6; "The Criminal Code and 'Morality' " (editorial), *Montreal Star*, final ed., 26 December 1968, p. 10; John Dafoe, "Créditistes Scrap Opposition Plan for Criminal Code Debate Limit," *Globe and Mail*, metro ed., 17 April 1969, p. 10; "Debate Starts on Canadian Sex Laws," *Los Angeles Advocate* 3 (February 1969): 3; Walter Dinsdale, "Now We'll Be for Sin and against Motherhood . . ." ("Opinion" column), *Toronto Daily Star*, four star ed., 5 May 1969, p. 7; "Education in Marriage Preferred to Homosexual Changes: Caouette," *Globe and Mail*, metro ed., 22 April 1969, p. 8; "Homosexuals Not Encouraged, Turner Says,"*Globe and Mail*, metro ed., 18 April 1969, p. 4; "Just What Some Members of Parliament Said about Homosexuality," *Globe and Mail*, metro ed., 19 April 1969, p. 7; Gary Kinsman, *The Regulation of Desire: Sexuality in Canada* (Montréal: Black Rose Books, 1987), pp. 164–72.]

April 19 ∗ Montréal ∗ Gemini I, a private social club for gays and lesbians, opened at 1285, boul. Maisonneuve O. Operated by Paul Bédard, the club was open to members of International Sex Equality Anonymous (ISEA). This was Montréal's first private club for gays and lesbians, but by May 24, 1969, it had closed. (See also September 13, 1969.)

["Homosexuals Form Local Club: Second in Canada," *Montreal Star*, 21 April 1969, p. 17; Gary Kinsman, "Official Discourse as Sexual Regulation: The Social Organization of the Sexual Policing of Gay Men" (Ph.D. dissertation, University of Toronto, 1989), pp. 402–03; Gary Kinsman, *The Regulation of Desire: Sexuality in Canada* (Montréal: Black Rose Books, 1987), p. 159; "Restaurant Replaces Gemini Club," *Montreal Star*, final ed., 24 May 1969, p. 3.]

May 2 ∗ Montréal ∗ Denis Héroux's film *Valérie*, starring Danielle Ouimet, Guy Godin, and Yvan Ducharme, opened at Le Parisien theatre. It included the first lesbian portrayal in a Québécois feature film.

[Prat., "*Valerie*," *Variety*, 4 June 1969, p. 36; D.J. Turner and Micheline Morisset, eds., *Canadian Feature Film Index, 1913–1985/Index des films canadiens de long métrage* (Ottawa: Public Archives, National Film, Television, and Sound Archives, 1987), entry 240; Thomas Waugh, "Nègres blancs, tapettes et 'butch': les lesbiennes et les gais dans le cinéma québécois," *Copie zéro*, no. 11 (1981), pp. 13, 14, 22.]

May 14 ∗ Ottawa ∗ Omnibus Bill C-150, part of which amended the Criminal Code to decriminalize homosexual acts ("gross indecency" and "buggery") between two consenting adults over the age of twenty-one in private, passed third reading in the House of Commons by a vote of 149 (119 Liberals, 18 New Democrats, 12 Progressive Conservatives) to 55 (43 Progressive Conservatives, 11 Créditistes, 1 Liberal). (See also August 26, 1969.)

[Canada. House of Commons, *Hansard,* 1969, pp. 4717–8669 passim; Canada. House of Commons. Committee on Justice and Legal Affairs, *Minutes of Proceedings and Evidence of the Standing Committee on Justice and Legal Affairs,* 1969, pp. 171–668 passim; Thomas Claridge, "Tories Split on 3rd Reading of Code Changes," *Globe and Mail,* metro ed., 15 May 1969, p. 1; "It Was a Great Day" (editorial), *Globe and Mail,* metro ed., 15 May 1969, p. 6; Gary Kinsman, "Official Discourse as Sexual Regulation: The Social Organization of the Sexual Policing of Gay Men" (Ph.D. dissertation, University of Toronto, 1989), pp. 441–64; Gary Kinsman, *The Regulation of Desire: Sexuality in Canada* (Montréal: Black Rose Books, 1987), pp. 164–72; Lyn Pedersen, "Germany, Canada Pass 'Consenting Adults' Laws: U.S., Russia Only Major Nations with Repressive Sex Laws," *Los Angeles Advocate* 3 (June 1969): 3, 31; "Sanity in Sight" (editorial), *Vancouver Sun,* four star ed., 15 May 1969, p. 4; George Smith, "In Defence of Privacy: Or, Bluntly Put, No More Shit," *Action!: A Publication of the Right to Privacy Committee* 3 (1983): 1–3.]

June * Ottawa * Paragraph 100 of the Report of the Royal Commission on Security (The MacKenzie Commission) recommended that homosexuals be allowed to work for the Public Service Commission, but that they "should not normally be granted clearance to higher levels, should not be recruited if there is a possibility that they may require such clearance in the course of their careers and should certainly not be posted to sensitive positions overseas." (See also June 1970.)

[Canada, *Report of the Royal Commission on Security (Abridged)* (Ottawa: Queen's Printer, 1969), p. 36; Charles C. Hill, "Government Guilty!" GO *Info,* no. 6 (1973), pp. 1, 6.]

June 28 * Montréal * Jean-Claude Lord's film *Delivrez-nous du mal,* starring Yvon Deschamps as a homosexual and Guy Godin as his bisexual lover, opened at the Saint-Denis theatre. The film was a faithful adaptation of Claude Jasmin's novel of the same name.

[D.J. Turner and Micheline Morisset, eds., *Canadian Feature Film Index, 1913–1985/Index des films canadiens de long métrage* (Ottawa: Public Archives, National Film, Television, and Sound Archives, 1987), entry 175; Thomas Waugh, "Nègres blancs, tapettes et 'butch': les lesbiennes et les gais dans le cinéma québécois," *Copie zéro,* no. 11 (1981), pp. 16–17.]

June 28–29 * New York, N.Y. * Hundreds of gay street people and drag queens fought back after a routine police raid on a Greenwich Village gay bar at 53 Christopher Street called the Stonewall Inn. Four policemen were injured; thirteen people were arrested. This protest marked the symbolic beginning of the modern gay liberation movement.

[Martin Duberman, *Stonewall* (New York: Dutton, 1993), 330 pp.; "4 Policemen Hurt in 'Village' Raid," *New York Times,* late city ed., 29 June 1969, sec. 1, p. 33; "Police Again Rout 'Village' Youths: Outbreak by 400 Follows a Near-riot over Raid," *New York Times,* late city ed., 30 June 1969, sec. 1, p. 22; Howard Smith, "Full Moon Over the

Stonewall: View from Inside," *Village Voice* 14 (3 July 1969): 1, 25, 29; Lucian Truscott
IV, "Gay Power Comes to Sheridan Square: View from Outside," *Village Voice* 14 (3
July 1969): 1, 18.]

Summer ∗ Winnipeg ∗ The first of a two-part series by Peter Gordge
examining local gay gay life was published in *Winnipeg World*. Part one
described the "Madras" (Mardi Gras) restaurant and bar, a favourite gay
meeting place. Part two discussed cruising and the annual drag ball.

[Peter Gordge, "The Hill Is a Favorite Spot: Part I," *Winnipeg World*, Summer 1969,
pp. 36–41; Peter Carlyle-Gordge, "The Hill Is a Favorite Spot: Part II," *Winnipeg World*,
Winter 1969–Spring 1970, pp. 36–41.]

July 18–27 ∗ Toronto ∗ Toronto's first full-length variety show of female
impersonators was presented at the Global Village theatre, 17 St. Nicholas
Street. *Facad*, a show of mimes, dances, and skits, was directed by Michael
Oscars and featured six impersonators — Sacha (Craig Jeffries), Anita (Rae
Peters), Bodine, Jerry, Riki-Tick (Ricky Sheldon), and Sophie (Richard
Douglas). An expanded version of the show, directed by G.G. Mills, was
presented by Ed Mirvish at the Royal Alexandra Theatre for a two-week run
starting August 21, 1969. Most of these performers also appeared in Michael
Oscars's musical review *She-Rade* during August and September 1969 at the
Theatre-in-the-Dell.

[DuBarry Campeau, "An Evening with the 'Ladies' at The Dell," *Toronto Telegram*,
final ed., 12 August 1969, p. 48; "*Facad* to Play at Royal Alex," *Toronto Daily Star*, four
star ed., 1 August 1969, p. 18; Graham Fraser, "Female Impersonators Go Public: Out
of the Shadows," *Toronto Daily Star*, four star ed., 25 July 1969, p. 23; "Global Village
Has Spawned Two Revues," *Toronto Telegram*, final ed., 2 August 1969, sec. 3, p. 8;
Melinda McCracken, "Boys Bring Les Girls to Life," *Globe and Mail*, metro ed., 19
July 1969, p. 24; "Unisex in Fashion Fine, but 'Drag' on Stage Better," *Tab*, 30 August
1969.]

August 26 ∗ Canada ∗ Amendments to the Canadian Criminal Code passed
in Bill C-150 came into effect, decriminalizing "gross indecency" and "buggery" in private between two consenting adults twenty-one years of age or
older.

[Jack Batten, "The Homosexual Life in Canada: Will Trudeau's Change in the Law
Make Any Difference? An Answer from the Gay World," *Saturday Night*, September
1969, pp. 28–32; "Homosexual, Abortion Laws Effective Aug. 26," *Toronto Daily Star*,
all star ed., 5 August 1969, p. 2.]

September ∗ Vancouver ∗ Roedy Green began to write letters to the people
placing gay personal ads in the *Georgia Straight*. Green's letter-writing
campaign, designed to gather information in order to help people to come
out and to make contacts with various groups within the gay community,

soon grew into a small informational publishing venture. By March 1971, Green's project had grown so large that he was able to publish the fifty-page book *A Guide for the Naive Homosexual*, a guide to coming out and directory of meeting places for gay people in Canada, in an edition of 3,000 copies.

[Roedy Green, *A Guide for the Naive Homosexual*, eleventh revision (Vancouver: The Author, 1971), pp. 33–35.]

September 13 ∗ Canada ∗ A four-page article by William Spencer entitled "Canada's Leading Homosexual Speaks Out" was to appear in the *Weekend* magazine supplement of thirty-nine Canadian newspapers. The article, a profile of Paul Bédard of Montréal, founder of the Gemini 1 club and president of International Sex Equality Anonymous (ISEA), was censored by some of the newspapers; fourteen of the newspapers either tore out the article or refused to include the supplement. In the article, Bédard claimed that ISEA had 4,000 members and that it was affiliated with NACHO; both claims were unlikely. The censorship of the article was raised on March 3, 1970, before the Senate committee on mass media.

[Farrell Crook, "Senators Describe Deletion of *Weekend* Story on Homosexuals as Censorship: 14 Publishers Refused to Distribute Article," *Globe and Mail*, metro ed., 4 March 1970, p. 4; "14 Publishers Tore Out Article: Homosexuality," *Toronto Telegram*, final ed., 4 March 1970, p. 64; Ross Higgins, "Lives, Oral Narratives, Writing the Past," revised version of a paper delivered at the Out of the Archives Conference, Department of History, York University, North York, Ont., 13–15 January 1994, p. 16; "Journalism: Censoring *Weekend*," *Time* (Canadian ed.), 19 September 1969, p. 18; "Papers Object to Story About Homosexuality," *Montreal Star*, final ed., 13 September 1969, pp. 1–2; William Spencer, "Canada's Leading Homosexual Speaks Out," *Weekend Magazine*, 13 September 1969, pp. 6–8.]

Autumn ∗ Toronto ∗ The St. James Bowling League, a mixed-orientation league founded in the mid-1960s, decided to declare itself all gay. Its name was changed to the Judy Garland Memorial Bowling League (JGMBL). Teams with names such as Emerald City, Friends of Dorothy, and Toto Too competed for the Ruby Slippers trophy. The JGMBL, which still exists in 1995, was one of the first and longest-lived gay sports leagues in North America.

[Gerry Keith, "In Pursuit of the Coveted Ruby Slippers," *Body Politic*, no. 83 (1982), p. 13.]

October 15 ∗ Toronto ∗ A four-line advertisement was placed in the *Varsity*, an undergraduate newspaper at the University of Toronto, by Jearld Molden-hauer, asking persons interested in starting a student homophile organization to call him. Moldenhauer, a research assistant at the university, had moved to Canada from the United States in January 1969. He had been an undergraduate at Cornell University when in the spring of 1967 he had

45

helped to form the Cornell Student Homophile League, the second homo-phile group organized at an American university. Moldenhauer's advertise-ment in the *Varsity* was the spark for the first formal meeting on October 24, 1969, of the University of Toronto Homophile Association (UTHA), the first post-Stonewall gay organization in Canada and the first formed at a Cana-dian university. Over the next few years, Moldenhauer would be instrumen-tal in founding several other pioneering Canadian gay organizations, includ-ing *The Body Politic*, Glad Day Bookshop, Toronto Gay Action, and the Canadian Gay Liberation Movement Archives. (See also October 24, 1969.)

[Advertisement, "Classifieds," *Varsity* (Univ. of Toronto), 15 October 1969, p. 13; Gerald Hannon, "Who We Were, Who We Are: Jearld Moldenhauer," *Body Politic*, no. 80 (1982), p. 32; "Jearld Moldenhauer" vertical file, Canadian Lesbian and Gay Archives, Toronto; Jearld Moldenhauer, "Victim of Myopia (or, 'Gerald, Bring Me the Axe')" ("Taking Issue" column), *Body Politic*, no. 82 (1982), p. 7.]

October 24 * Toronto * The first public meeting of the University of Toronto Homophile Association (UTHA) was held at University College. About sixteen people attended. UTHA, the first post-Stonewall gay organization in Canada and the first formed at a Canadian university, was "dedicated to educating the community about homosexuality, working to combat discrim-ination against homosexuality, and bringing about a social and personal acceptance of homosexuality." It sponsored discussion groups, a speaker's bureau, guest lecturers, and dances, and was officially open to all persons of the University of Toronto (although many people from the wider community became involved). Charles Hill, a student at the university, became the first chairman of UTHA; other early influential members included Jearld Molden-hauer and Ian Young. The Community Homophile Association of Toronto (CHAT) grew out of UTHA at the beginning of 1971 and began to undertake many of its activities. UTHA officially ceased operation in 1973.

[Margaret Fulford, ed., *The Canadian Women's Movement, 1960–1990: A Guide to Archival Resources/Le mouvement canadien des femmes, 1960–1990: guide de ressources archivistiques* (Toronto: Canadian Women's Movement Archives/ECW Press, 1992), entry 518; D.F. Hadwin, "Recognition of University Homosexuals Termed a Regressive Move" (letter), *Globe and Mail*, metro ed., 7 January 1970, p. 7; Gerald Hannon, "First Steps," *Xtra!*, no. 134 (1989), p. 5; Charles Hill papers, 82–015, Canadian Lesbian and Gay Archives, Toronto; Charles C. Hill, Ian Young, and William McRae, "Homosex-uality" (letter), *Globe and Mail*, metro ed., 14 January 1970, p. 6; Charles C. Hill, Ian Young, and William McRae, "Homosexuality" (letter), *Globe and Mail*, metro ed., 23 January 1970, p. 6; William Johnson, "Campus Homosexuals Form Association to Discuss Sex," *Globe and Mail*, metro ed., 15 December 1969, p. 2; Jearld F. Molden-hauer, "Homosexuality" (letter), *Globe and Mail*, metro ed., 9 January 1970, p. 6; Jearld Moldenhauer, "Rewriting History?" (letter), *Xtra!*, no. 137 (1989), p. 3; "SAC Supports Homosexuals," *Varsity* (Univ. of Toronto), 5 November 1969, p. 15; Mike Savage,

"Police Harass Homosexuals," *Excalibur* (York Univ., Downsview, Ont.), 1 October 1970, p. 4; University of Toronto Homophile Association (UTHA) papers (82–006) and vertical file, Canadian Lesbian and Gay Archives, Toronto; Thomas Van Dusen, "Homosexuality" (letter), *Globe and Mail*, metro ed., 14 January 1970, p. 6.]

November ∗ Toronto ∗ *The Biblical and Theological Understanding of Sexuality and Family Life*, a report of a study of the Faith and Order Commission of the Canadian Council of Churches, was published. Appendix Four, "Towards a Theological Perspective on Human Sexuality," was the report of the Saskatoon Study Group (pp. 47–75). It addressed homosexuality and Christianity, and stated that the "appropriate Christian response . . . is to dispel all popular misconceptions and grotesque views of homosexual characteristics and behaviour, to alter criminal legislation having to do with this matter, and in general to create a social climate where homosexual men and women can experience some measure of acceptance" (p. 53).

[Canadian Council of Churches. Faith and Order Commission, *The Biblical and Theological Understanding of Sexuality and Family Life* ([Toronto]: Canadian Council of Churches, 1969), 84 pp.]

November ∗ Toronto ∗ Ian Young's book of poetry *Year of the Quiet Sun* was published by the House of Anansi.

[(Ian Young), *Ian Young: A Bibliography 1962–1980*, Canadian Gay Archives Publication no. 3 (Toronto: Pink Triangle Press, 1981), entries A2, A2a, E9–E13, E15, E19.]

1970

—— * Montréal * Nicole Brossard's novel *Un livre* was published by Éditions du jour. It was translated (*A Book*) by Coach House Press in Toronto in 1976.

[Louise Milot, "*Un livre*," in *Dictionnaire des oeuvres littéraires du Québec*, ed. Maurice Lemire et al., vol. 5 (1970–75) (Montréal: Fides, 1987), p. 918.]

—— * Montréal * *L'homme qui se cherchait un fils*, a novel by François Brunante (pseud. of Rolland Lorrain), was published by Le cercle du livre de France.

[Denis Carrier, "*L'homme qui se cherchait un fils*," in *Dictionnaire des oeuvres littéraires du Québec*, ed. Maurice Lemire et al., vol. 5 (1970–75) (Montréal: Fides, 1987), pp. 400–401.]

—— * Montréal * Pierre Dagenais's novel *Le feu sacré* was published by Librairie Beauchemin.

[Gilles De Lafontaine, "*Le feu sacré*," in *Dictionnaire des oeuvres littéraires du Québec*, ed. Maurice Lemire et al., vol. 5 (1970–75) (Montréal: Fides, 1987), pp. 338–39.]

—— * Montréal * *L'homosexuel parmi nous*, an illustrated, thirty-two-page booklet on homosexuality and society, was published by Novalis. It had been written by Claude Picher and others.

[Monograph collection, M85–174, Canadian Lesbian and Gay Archives, Toronto.]

—— * Sackville, N.B. * Evergon (pseud. of Albert Lunt) graduated with a degree in fine arts from Mount Allison University and began to exhibit his photographic artwork. During the 1970s he was well known for sporting radical drag and experimenting with Polaroid photography and, later, colour xerography. Much of Evergon's work contains homoerotic imagery.

[Martha Hanna, *Evergon 1971–1987* (Ottawa: Canadian Museum of Contemporary Photography, 1988); Kathleen Walker, "Art and Radical Drag (Notes on Understanding Evergon)," *Ottawa Citizen*, 22 March 1975, p. 69; Doug Wilson (interviewing Evergon), "Evergon: Queen of High Tech," *Pink Ink* 1 (July 1983): 16–17, 33–34.]

—— * Toronto * Craig Russell (pseud. of Russell Craig Eadie) made his debut as an impersonator of famous female stars in gay establishments such as Club 511 and Club Manatee. By 1972 Russell was touring Canada and the United States with his one-person show. His international stardom was confirmed by 1977 with the release of the film *Outrageous*, which showcased his talents. A sequel, *Too Outrageous*, was released ten years later. Craig Russell died from AIDS-related complications in 1990.

[Martin Knelman, "His Majesty the Queens," *Canadian Magazine*, 15 October 1977, pp. 18, 21; "Craig Russell" vertical file, Canadian Lesbian and Gay Archives, Toronto.]

―――― * Trumansburg, N.Y. * Ian Young's book of poetry *Double Exposure* was published by New Books (The Crossing Press). It was similar in content to *Year of the Quiet Sun*, but with several changes. A revised and enlarged edition of *Double Exposure* was published by The Crossing Press in 1974.

[(Ian Young), *Ian Young: A Bibliography 1962–1980*, Canadian Gay Archives Publication no. 3 (Toronto: Pink Triangle Press, 1981), entries A3, A11, E18, E26, E38, E48.]

―――― * Waterloo, Ont. * *Homosexuality: A Select Bibliography*, compiled by Umesh D. Sharma and Wilfrid C. Rudy, was published by Waterloo Lutheran University. It was the earliest large-scale bibliography on homosexuality published in Canada, containing over 2,000 entries in 114 pages. Sharma and Rudy were librarians at the University.

[Library collection, Canadian Lesbian and Gay Archives, Toronto.]

January 19 * Toronto * Gay activists Charles Hill, Graham Jackson, and Ian Young appeared on Robert Fulford's CBC radio program "This Is Robert Fulford" to discuss gay liberation and the UTHA.

[Charles Hill papers, 82–015, Canadian Lesbian and Gay Archives, Toronto.]

January 22 * Toronto * Dr. Franklin Kameny, founder and president of the Washington, D.C., Mattachine Society, spoke to an audience of 185 people at Cody Hall, University of Toronto, on the theme "The Homosexual Dilemma: What Every Heterosexual Should Know." The talk was sponsored by UTHA.

["Dr. Kameny's Visit," UTHA *Newsletter*, no. 1 (1970), p. 2; Dennis McCloskey, "The Gent Who Prefers Gents Is Not Sick, Says Top Homophile," *Ryersonian* (Ryerson Polytechnical Institute, Toronto), 27 January 1970, p. 1; Mark Wilson, "Kameny: What Makes a Homosexual?" *Varsity* (Univ. of Toronto), 28 January 1970, p. 3.]

February * Edmonton * Club '70, a private social club operated and managed by and for lesbians and gays, opened at 10242 106th Street N.W. The club sponsored bar nights, dances, discussions, and other social events, as well as a newsletter. Club '70, one of the first registered private lesbian and gay clubs in Canada, had 241 members by October 1971. It was active until 1980.

['70 *News*; *Club '70 News*, Canadian Lesbian and Gay Archives, Toronto.]

February 4–7 ✶ Toronto ✶ Graham Jackson's play *To the Hollow*, which portrayed the lives of a group of lesbian and gay students, was performed at Victoria College, University of Toronto.

["*To the Hollow*," UTHA *Newsletter*, no. 1 (1970), p. 2.]

February 18 ✶ Montréal ✶ Michel Tremblay's play *La Duchesse de Langeais* opened at the Théâtre de Quat' Sous. Starring Claude Gai, the production was directed by André Brassard. The play was also published in 1970 by Leméac.

[Pierre Lavoie, "*La Duchesse de Langeais*," in *Dictionnaire des oeuvres littéraires du Québec*, ed. Maurice Lemire et al., vol. 4 (1960–69) (Montréal: Fides, 1984), pp. 277–78.]

March 19 ✶ Calgary ✶ Club Carousel, a private social club owned, operated, and managed by lesbians and gays, officially opened under the umbrella of the Scarth Street Society. The Club became involved in charity and educational work as well as serving as a recreational and social centre for local lesbians and gays. It was immediately popular and had 385 paid members by the end of September 1971. Membership peaked at about 650 in 1972 before beginning a slow decline. Club Carousel closed in 1983.

["Club Carousel: A Brief History," unpublished typescript, 1971, in "Club Carousel" vertical file, Canadian Lesbian and Gay Archives, Toronto; Roy, "President's Report," *Carousel Capers* 4 (September 1973): 7–8; "The Scarth Street Society: An Introduction to Our History and Rules," *Carousel Capers* 5 (April 1974): 17–18.]

March 24 ✶ Toronto ✶ Scott Symons, author of *Combat Journal for Place d'Armes* and *Civic Square*, spoke at a meeting organized by UTHA and held at the Graduate Students Union upstairs lounge, 16 Bancroft Avenue. About fifty members and guests attended.

["Scott Symons," UTHA *Newsletter*, no. 1 (1970), p. 2.]

Spring ✶ Scarborough, Ont. ✶ Catalyst Press was launched as a gay press by Ian Young. Young had been involved with *Catalyst*, a literary magazine produced by graduate English students at the University of Toronto, since early 1969. In the fall of that year, he gained control of the magazine (with Michael Higgins and John Holland). In the wake of Stonewall, Young felt the time was right to transform Catalyst into a small press specializing in books and chapbooks of gay poetry and fiction. Young started the press with no money and virtually no publishing experience. Catalyst's first book publication was *Cool Fire: 10 Poems by Ian Young and Richard Phelan* (1970). Young was able to publish over thirty titles by Canadian, British, and American writers before the press suspended publication in 1980.

[Ian Young, "A Canadian Catalyst Presses for Change," *Advocate* (Los Angeles), no. 315 (1981), pp. 23–26; (Ian Young), *Ian Young: A Bibliography 1962–1980*, Canadian Gay

Archives Publication no. 3 (Toronto: Pink Triangle Press, 1981), 58 pp.; Ian Young, "The Ivory Tunnel: Fodder Runs Out, Cattle List Scratched" (column), *Body Politic*, no. 67 (1980), p. 39; Ian Young papers (which include the files of Catalyst Press), several accessions, Canadian Lesbian and Gay Archives, Toronto.]

May * Toronto * About sixty people attended an inaugural bash held by Spearhead Toronto, the gay leather and denim fraternity. The first issue of Spearhead's newsletter, *Phalia*, was published in June 1970. It is still published in 1995, making it the longest running lesbian or gay publication in Canada.

[K.B., "A Message to the Open-minded," *Phalia*, no. 3 (1970), p. 1; J.J., "Spearhead Inauguration Memorial Day Weekend — 1970," *Phalia*, no. 1 (1970), p. 1.]

May 13 * Hamilton * Charles Hill, chairperson of UTHA, addressed an audience of more than two hundred students about homosexuality and the UTHA during the Westmount Secondary School Day in May lectures. The audience responded sympathetically.

["Homosexuality Said 'Perfectly Normal Thing,' " *Hamilton Spectator*, home ed., 14 May 1970, p. 7.]

June * Toronto * Members of UTHA attempted to find out to what extent the recommendations in Paragraph 100 of the Report of the Royal Commission on Security (The MacKenzie Commission) had been applied. The Report had recommended in June 1969 that homosexuals be allowed to work for the Public Service Commission, but not at higher levels. Canada's Solicitor-General Jean-Pierre Goyer did not reply to letters sent to him by UTHA. Replies from the Ontario and Federal Public Service Commissions stated that there were no set policies, and each case would be judged on its own merits.

[Charles C. Hill, "Government Guilty!," GO *Info*, no. 6 (1973), pp. 1, 6.]

June 3–10 * Vancouver * A gay issues and gossip column entitled "Page 69" debuted in the *Georgia Straight*. It was written by Q.Q. (Kevin Dale McKeown) and ran intermittently in the *Straight* until Q.Q. retired in April 1974. The column was controversial as Q.Q. often feuded with local gay liberation groups. "Page 69" also appeared sporadically throughout the early 1970s in other publications in Vancouver, including *The Gay Canadian, Open Doors*, and *Thrust*.

[Roger Allen, "Spotlight: Kevin McKeown" (interview), *Your Thing* 2 (4 April 1974): 10–11; GLF, "GLF Says Q.Q. Must Go" (letter), *Georgia Straight*, 17–24 March 1971, p. 7; Garrack (pseud. of Dick Rulens), "We Regret to Report," *Your Thing* 2 (4 April 1974): 8–9; Q.Q., "Page 69" (column), *Georgia Straight*, 3–10 June 1970, p. 10; Q.Q., "Page 69" (column), *Georgia Straight*, 13–20 December 1973, p. 22; Q.Q., "Q.Q.'s Last Hurrah!!: Page 69" (column), *Georgia Straight*, 25 April–2 May 1974, pp. 20–21.]

June 18 ∗ New York, N.Y.; Toronto ∗ Jane Rule's novel *This Is Not for You* was published by McCall Publishing Company in New York and Doubleday of Canada in Toronto.

["A Bibliography," *Canadian Fiction Magazine*, no. 23 (1976), pp. 133, 136; Jane Rule, "Jane Rule: The Woman behind *Lesbian Images*" (interview), *Body Politic*, no. 21 (1975), p. 15.]

August ∗ Montréal ∗ Michel Tremblay's musical comedy *Demain matin, Montréal m'attend* was first performed at the Jardin des Étoiles de Terre des Hommes. It was directed by André Brassard and featured music by François Dompierre. *Demain matin, Montréal m'attend* was a musical exploration of the area of boul. Saint-Laurent (the Main), complete with its seedy bars, transvestites, gay men, and prostitutes. A second version of the play was performed in March 1972 at the Théâtre Maisonneuve de la Place des Arts; this version proved to be more popular, and was published in Montréal in 1972 by Leméac.

[Paul Lefebvre, "*Demain matin, Montréal m'attend*," in *Dictionnaire des oeuvres littéraires du Québec*, ed. Maurice Lemire et al., vol. 5 (1970–75) (Montréal: Fides, 1987), pp. 221–23.]

August ∗ Vancouver ∗ In a letter reprinted in the *Georgia Straight*, Huey P. Newton, Minister of Defense of the Black Panther Party, declared that blacks should overcome their "insecurities" about homosexuality and should try to form a working coalition with gay liberation groups.

["A Letter from Huey P. Newton about the Women's Liberation and Gay Liberation Movements," *Georgia Straight*, 19–26 August 1970, p. 12.]

August ∗ Vancouver ∗ A group of gay men and lesbians formed the Gay Action Committee in an attempt to promote gay organizing and activities in Vancouver. The Committee's primary objectives were to form a gay social club as an alternative to the city's night clubs, to form various gay interest groups, and to establish a gay information centre and phone line. The Gay Action Committee was active for only a few months.

[Q.Q., "Page 69" (column), *Georgia Straight*, 19–26 August 1970, p. 21.]

August 17 ∗ Victoria, B.C. ∗ Rev. Troy Perry, founder of the Metropolitan Community Church (MCC) in Los Angeles, spoke at the University of Victoria on "Metropolitan Community Church and the Homosexual Community in America." Perry's talk was at the invitation of the Victoria Youth Council and was part of their annual Youth Week program.

["Perry to Speak in Canadian Youth Week," *Advocate* (Los Angeles) 4 (2–15 September 1970): 24.]

September 24 * Vancouver * The Canadian premiere of Mart Crowley's play *The Boys in the Band* was performed at the Colonial Magic Theatre.

[Nathan Cohen, "A Canadian Debut," *Toronto Daily Star*, three star night ed., 27 August 1970, p. 24; Q.Q., "Page 69"(column), *Georgia Straight*, 30 September–7 October 1970, p. 18.]

October * Montréal * During the October Crisis police used the imposition of the War Measures Act to justify raids and closures of some of the city's gay bars. (See also December 23, 1970.)

["Gay Rights Demo...," *Georgia Straight*, 13–17 August 1971, p. 17.]

October * Montréal * During the October Crisis, the FLQ cell that kidnapped British trade commissioner James Cross deprecatingly referred to Prime Minister Pierre Trudeau as "Trudeau, la tapette (Trudeau, the faggot)" in its Manifesto.

["L'enlèvement du diplomate James R. Cross: Texte intégral du manifeste du Front de Libération du Québec," *La presse*, 9 October 1970, p. D1; "FLQ Manifesto," *Georgia Straight*, 4–11 November 1970, pp. 12–13.]

October * Montréal * The inaugural issue of *Mainmise*, an alternative publication in paperback format, was published. A mouthpiece for the Québécois countercultural movement, *Mainmise* had several openly gay people on staff, including Jean Basile (pseud. of Jean-Basile Bezroudnoff) and Denis Vanier. Translations of American gay liberation articles appeared in its first two issues; the third issue (February 1971) included an article calling for the establishment of a gay liberation front in Montréal. (See also March 26, 1971.)

[Gilles Hughes Yvonne de Maujincourt, "Pour un Front gay à Montréal," *Mainmise*, no. 3 (1971), pp. 186–91; Ed Richer, "Le cinéma, les garçons et le Gay Power," *Mainmise*, no. 1 (1970), pp. 170–81; Carl Wittman, "Manifeste du Front de Libération homosexuelle," *Mainmise*, no. 2 (1970), pp. 86–103.]

October 15 * Montréal * Denis Héroux's film *L'amour humain/The Awakening/Virgin Lovers)*, starring Louise Marleau and Jacques Riberolles, opened at Le Parisien theatre. In the film a priest and a nun leave the religious life to marry, but find that they are incompatible sexually. The man becomes involved briefly with a transvestite singer, who is married to a lesbian.

[Prat., *"L'amour humain (The Awakening),"* *Variety*, 9 June 1971, p. 17; Kenneth Thompson, "Feature Films: *Amour humain L'(Virgin Lovers),"* *Monthly Film Bulletin*, May 1972, p. 91; D.J. Turner and Micheline Morisset, eds., *Canadian Feature Film Index, 1913–1985/Index des films canadiens de long métrage* (Ottawa: Public Archives, National Film, Television, and Sound Archives, 1987), entry 307.]

October 20 * Downsview, Ont. * About thirty people attended the founding meeting of the York University Homophile Association (YUHA), held at

Winters College. Roger Wilkes became the group's first president. This was the second homophile association formed at a Canadian university. YUHA sponsored discussion groups, guest speakers, a speaker's bureau, movie nights, and a newsletter. The group changed its name to Gay Alliance at York (GAY) in 1975.

[Linda Diebel, " 'You're Driven Underground and Then Pursued There': Homosexuals in Toronto," *Toronto Telegram*, metro night ed., 31 March 1971, p. 19; Margaret Fulford, ed., *The Canadian Women's Movement, 1960–1990: A Guide to Archival Resources/Le mouvement canadien des femmes, 1960–1990: Guide de ressources archivistiques* (Toronto: Canadian Women's Movement Archives/ECW Press, 1992), entries 352, 1001; "In the Beginning . . . ," *York University Homophile Association Newsletter*, November 1970, p. 1; "York University Homophile Association (YUHA)" vertical file, Canadian Lesbian and Gay Archives, Toronto; "York University Homophiles Work on Their Future," *Guerilla* 1 (February 1971): 20.]

October 31 * Toronto * More than 8,000 people gathered on Yonge Street to watch men in drag enter the St. Charles Tavern during Halloween. The event was ignored by the mainstream Toronto media.

[Charles C. Hill, "Halloween Non-event" (letter), *Toronto Telegram*, metro night ed., 13 November 1970, p. 19.]

November * Vancouver * The Gay Liberation Front (GLF) formed out of weekly meetings held at the Pink Cheeks commune, 2132 Carolina Street. Gordon Hardy was a key organizer of the group. On December 11, the GLF opened a drop-in centre at 509 Carrall Street, in a building shared with the Youth International Party (Yippies). Formed as an activist, communal collective to combat gay oppression, the almost entirely male membership of GLF held weekly meetings on Sunday nights; the drop-in centre was open Friday nights. A gay switchboard was in operation by January 1971. The group was involved in the production of the gay supplement to the Simon Fraser University student newspaper *The Peak* in March 1971 and published at least one issue of its newsletter *Brite Lite* (April 1971). Also, the Ephemerals, a revolutionary drag group similar to The Cockettes, were associated with the GLF. Formed by Twilight Rose (pseud. of John Forbes) and Ruby Tuesday (pseud. of Ron Whinton), the Ephemerals specialized in street theatre that satirized drag and mocked traditional male-female roles and stereotypes. The GLF was short-lived, disbanding by the autumn of 1971. Its demise was partly due to the secession of Dick Rulens and others from the group to form the Canadian Gay Activists Alliance (CGAA) in February 1971. Many of the remaining members of GLF joined the Gay Alliance toward Equality (GATE), formed in May 1971. (See also February and May 1971.)

["John Forbes" vertical file, Canadian Lesbian and Gay Archives, Toronto; "GLF Changes Perspectives," *Georgia Straight*, 5–8 October 1971, p. 15; Gay Alliance toward

Equality (GATE) (Vancouver) papers, 82–005 and 88–040, Canadian Lesbian and Gay Archives, Toronto; "Gay Liberation Front (GLF)" vertical file, Canadian Lesbian and Gay Archives, Toronto; "Gay Liberation Front: The First in a Two-Part Series on the History and Politics of the Vancouver Gay Liberation Front," *Georgia Straight*, 14–18 May 1971, p. 20 (note: part two was not published); Gerald Hannon, "Who We Were, Who We Are: John Forbes," *Body Politic*, no. 80 (1982), p. 35; Jearld Moldenhauer and Bob Wallace, "History: Toronto & Vancouver," *Gay* (a supplement to *McGill Daily*), 24 November 1972, pp. 3, 6; Q.Q., "Out of the Closets and into the Streets," *Georgia Straight*, 20–27 January 1971, p. 18; Q.Q., "Page 69" (column), *Georgia Straight*, 16–23 December 1970, p. 9; "Street Theatre and the Ephemerals," *Brite Lite: GLF Newsletter* (no. 1) (1971), p. 2; "We ARE the People Our Parents Warned Us About . . . ," *Georgia Straight*, 2–9 December 1970, p. 9.]

November 26 ∗ Toronto ∗ Edward Knight, operator of Le Trique Club, 14 Breadalbane Street, was sentenced to one year in prison for conspiring to burn down a rival gay club, the August Club, above the Parkside Tavern. A fire at the August Club in February 1970 had caused $15,000 damage.

["Club Owner Jailed for Plotting Arson," *Globe and Mail*, metro ed., 27 November 1970, p. 5.]

November 27 ∗ Toronto ∗ The cartoon strip "The Lavender Kid and Butch," featuring a gay superhero and his sidekick, first appeared in *Guerilla*. The strip was written by Richard Jones and drawn by John Perry.

["The Lavender Kid and Butch," *Guerilla* 1 (27 November 1970): 5.]

December ∗ Toronto ∗ Jearld Moldenhauer decided to start Glad Day Bookshop after noticing that Toronto's traditional bookstores were averse to selling the rapidly growing range of lesbian- and gay-positive books and magazines. Moldenhauer started buying stock and sold it out of a knapsack at gay meetings and rallies, at his home at 65 Kendal Avenue, Apt. 8, and through mail order. Over the years Glad Day would grow to become one of the most comprehensive lesbian and gay bookstores in the world. In 1979, Moldenhauer opened a second Glad Day, in Boston, Mass.

[Bernard Courte, "Jearld Moldenhauer: le social capitaliste," *Sortie*, no. 55 (1988), pp. 44–45; Gerald Hannon, "Who We Were, Who We Are: Jearld Moldenhauer," *Body Politic*, no. 80 (1982), p. 32; Jearld Moldenhauer, Letter to the author, 28 November 1993; Jearld Moldenhauer, "Victim of Myopia (or, 'Gerald, Bring Me the Axe')" ("Taking Issue" column), *Body Politic*, no. 82 (1982), p. 7.]

December 5 ∗ Toronto ∗ About ninety-five people attended a gay dance held at the Music Room, Hart House, University of Toronto, sponsored by UTHA. This is believed to be the first public gay dance held in Toronto outside of a gay club.

["UTHA," *Guerilla*, no. 14 (1970), p. 21.]

December 11 ∗ Downsview, Ont. ∗ About a dozen members of YUHA met for drinks at the Winters Pub before attending a dance at McLaughlin College. This was the first "gay-in" held at York University.

["Gay-in at York!" *York University Homophile Association Newsletter*, January 1971, p. 1.]

December 11 ∗ Toronto ∗ During an inaugural meeting held at a private home, a fifteen-person steering committee was formed to set up the Community Homophile Association of Toronto (CHAT). CHAT was established as a spin-off from UTHA. The University of Toronto group had become overwhelmed with people from the general community; CHAT was formed to serve the community-at-large. One of the new group's first objectives was to start a counselling/distress phone line, which became operational January 3, 1971. The steering committee met again on January 4 and 25, 1971, during which it appointed interim officers, with George Hislop as director, and planned the first public meeting, to be held February 1, 1971. (See also February 1, 1971.)

[Community Homophile Association of Toronto (CHAT) papers, 82–001/01, Canadian Lesbian and Gay Archives, Toronto; "We've Arrived!" *Gayokay*, no. 2 (1971), p. 8.]

December 23 ∗ Montréal ∗ Municipal Court judge Herman Primeau upheld a police decision to close two clubs popular with gays, the Chez Paree and the Béret Bleu.

[Michel Auger, "La police ferme les cabarets 'Chez Paree' et le 'Béret Bleu,' " *La presse*, dernière ed., 24 December 1970, p. A3.]

1971

—— * Guelph, Ont. * Paul Maurice's book of poetry *Quem Quaeritis* was published by Alive Press.

[Ian Young, *The Male Homosexual in Literature: A Bibliography*, second ed. (Metuchen, N.J.: Scarecrow Press, 1982), entry 2591.]

—— * Montréal * Paul Chamberland's book of poetry *Éclats de la pierre noire d'où rejaillit ma vie* was published by Éditions Danielle Laliberté.

[Caroline Bayard, "*Éclats de la pierre noire d'où rejaillit ma vie* et *Demain les dieux naîtront*," in *Dictionnaire des oeuvres littéraires du Québec*, ed. Maurice Lemire et al., vol. 5 (1970–75) (Montréal: Fides, 1987), pp. 267–69.]

—— * Montréal * Club Social A & V Enrg., a confidential introduction service for gay men, was operating at 3466, rue St. Denis.

["Confidentiel: Club Social A & V Enrg." (advertisement), *Le tiers*, no. 1 (1971), p. 66.]

—— * Montréal * *Les déviations sexuelles*, a book by Montréal psychiatrist Yvan Léger, was published by Éditions de l'Homme. His discussion of homosexuality was dismissed by some gay critics as being deliberately erroneous.

[André Dion, "Les 'déviations' d'un psychiatre," *Le tiers*, no. 2 (1972), pp. 18–20.]

—— * Montréal * Paul Toupin's memoir *Le coeur a ses raisons* was published by Le cercle du livre de France.

[Jean-Marcel Paquette, "*Le coeur a ses raisons*," in *Dictionnaire des oeuvres littéraires du Québec*, ed. Maurice Lemire et al., vol. 5 (1970–75) (Montréal: Fides, 1987), pp. 159–60.]

—— * New York, N.Y. * *Under the Brightness of Alien Stars*, a novel by Michael Porcsa, was published by Vantage Press. Set in Edmonton and Europe, it was one of the first novels by a Canadian to portray major characters who were gay.

[Ian Young, "Alienation," *Body Politic*, no. 55 (1979), p. 27.]

—— * Scarborough, Ont. * *Lions in the Stream*, a book of poetry by Ian Young and Richard Phelan, was published by Catalyst Press.

[(Ian Young), *Ian Young: A Bibliography 1962–1980*, Canadian Gay Archives Publication no. 3 (Toronto: Pink Triangle Press, 1981), entry A6.]

——— ✴ near Upton, Qué. ✴ Le Domaine Plein Vent, a campground catering to gays, opened along the White River. The gay-owned and operated venture was equipped with tents, private trailers, and cabins.

["Le Domaine Plein Vent" vertical file, Canadian Lesbian and Gay Archives, Toronto; "Quebec's Outdoor Camping Ground," *Montreal Gay Times* 1 (August 1975): 9; Jerry Roberts, "Montreal: A Rich Slice of Gay Life," *Ciao!* 5 (May–June 1977): 33–34.]

——— ✴ Vancouver ✴ Phyllis Webb's *Selected Poems, 1954–1965* was published by Talonbooks. "Naked Poems" and "The Beachcomber" were of particular interest to lesbians.

[Cecilia Frey, "Phyllis Webb: An Annotated Bibliography," in *The Annotated Bibliography of Canada's Major Authors*, ed. Robert Lecker and Jack David, Vol. 6 (Toronto: ECW Press, 1985), entries A5, D24–D36.]

January ✴ Toronto ✴ The influential American article "Notes of a Radical Lesbian," by Martha Shelley, and the Radicalesbian manifesto "The Woman-Identified Woman" were reprinted in the *Toronto Women's Liberation Newsletter*.

[Martha Shelly (sic), "Notes of a Radical Lesbian," *Toronto Women's Liberation Newsletter*, January 1971, pp. 21–24; March Hoffman et al., "The Woman-Identified Woman," *Toronto Women's Liberation Newsletter*, January 1971, pp. 25–26.]

January ✴ Vancouver ✴ The gay motorcycle club The Border Riders was formed.

[CGAA (interviewing Jim Brand), "Border Rider Interview," *Open Doors* 1 (June 1971): 4–6.]

January 13 ✴ Toronto ✴ Charles Hill of UTHA wrote to Otto Lang, federal Minister of Manpower and Immigration, to protest anti-gay clauses in the Immigration Act and request their removal. Lang replied on February 8, 1971, that the immigration legislation was under review and that he could not yet comment on exactly what changes would be made.

["UTHA 2" file, Charles Hill papers, 82–015/04, Canadian Lesbian and Gay Archives, Toronto.]

January 14 ✴ Toronto ✴ Two members of UTHA met with Inspector Wilson, head of the Toronto Morality Squad, to discuss arrests for gross indecency made in public washrooms in the city. At that time, at least six arrests were being made every day.

["Crime and Punishment," *Gayokay*, no. 2 (1971), pp. 4–6.]

January 19–30 * Toronto * Mart Crowley's play *The Boys in the Band* had its Toronto premiere at the Central Library Theatre.

[Urjo Kareda, "*Boys in the Band* Best in Comical Scenes of Bitchery," *Toronto Daily Star*, four star ed., 20 January 1971, p. 44.]

February * Vancouver * The Canadian Gay Activists Alliance (CGAA) was formed and opened an office at 1604–1320 Bute Street. The CGAA was a breakaway group from the Vancouver GLF. Compared to the GLF it was relatively conservative and attempted to work for gay liberation within the existing structure of society. The CGAA sponsored drop-ins, political action, educational projects, a speaker's bureau, a library, and the newsletter *Open Doors*, as well as a twenty-four-hour gayline and a job placement service. The CGAA eventually had numerous committees, including committees on women's issues, transsexuals, transvestites, counselling and referrals, and provincial and federal affairs. Dick Rulens was the chairperson of CGAA. By March 1972, the CGAA's drop-ins had moved to the Gordon House Community Centre, 1068 Davie Street. The CGAA was active until at least May 1973.

["CGAA's New Drop-In," *Open Doors* 2 (March 1972): 2; "Canadian Gay Activists Alliance (CGAA)" vertical file, Canadian Lesbian and Gay Archives, Toronto; Jearld Moldenhauer and Bob Wallace, "History: Toronto & Vancouver," *Gay* (supplement to *McGill Daily*), 24 November 1972, pp. 3, 6; Q.Q., "Page 69"(column), *Georgia Straight*, 3–10 March 1971, p. 7.]

February * Victoria, B.C. * David Wright of Craigdarroch College, University of Victoria, began to place a listing in the *Georgia Straight* advertising a gay liberation group in Victoria. The listing was published until April 1971; no other information has been located on this group. (See also March 1974.)

["Help" (column), *Georgia Straight*, 17–24 February 1971, p. 24.]

February 1 * Toronto * About fifty-five people attended the first public meeting of CHAT, held at Holy Trinity Church. The meeting was chaired by George Hislop, the group's interim director. Hislop gave a general introduction concerning CHAT's immediate goals as a service organization for the homophile movement in Toronto, namely the opening of an office and the operation of an educational and distress phone service. CHAT's aim was to attain gay liberation by working through the existing political system and to sponsor social activities (such as dances) that would be a personal growth alternative to the Toronto gay ghetto. Hislop also introduced the other members of CHAT's steering committee including Pat Murphy, one of the key lesbian organizers. In addition, Charles Hill of UTHA gave a talk about the homophile movement in Toronto. Before the opening of CHAT's community centre in February 1972, CHAT's office was located upstairs at 6

George Hislop, director of CHAT, with his lover Ron Shearer.

Charles Street E.; general meetings and events were held mostly at Holy Trinity Church. CHAT grew to become one of the major lesbian and gay organizations in Canada during the 1970s. It cooperated with various social agencies, sent speakers to high schools, monitored gay-related court cases, provided legal, medical, and psychiatric referrals, and lobbied government and police officials. CHAT officially disbanded at the end of 1977.

[Community Homophile Association of Toronto (CHAT) papers, 82–001, 82–023, plus inventory, Canadian Lesbian and Gay Archives, Toronto; "Community Homophile Association of Toronto (CHAT)" vertical file, Canadian Lesbian and Gay Archives, Toronto; Linda Diebel, " 'You're Driven Underground and Then Pursued There': Homosexuals in Toronto," *Toronto Telegram*, metro night ed., 31 March 1971, p. 19; Val Edwards, "The Time, the Place, and the Person," *Body Politic*, no. 68 (1980), pp. 22–25; Chris Fox, "CHAT: Community Homophile Association of Toronto," *Toronto Women's Liberation Movement Newsletter*, September 1971, p. 7; Margaret Fulford, ed., *The Canadian Women's Movement, 1960–1990: A Guide to Archival Resources/Le mouvement canadien des femmes, 1960–1990: guide de ressources archivistiques* (Toronto: Canadian Women's Movement Archives/ECW Press, 1992), entry 377; "*Guerilla* and Friends: CHAT," *Guerilla* 2 (7 June 1972): 4; George Hislop papers, 94–018, Canadian Lesbian and Gay Archives, Toronto; Penny Kome, "Couples: Portrait of the Homophiles as Just Plain Folks," *Maclean's*, December 1972, pp. 44–45, 62, 64; "Man to Man" (interviewing George Hislop), *Exclusive Male* 1 (January 1972): 30–31; Lanny Nielsen, "CHAT Cheers Homophile Community," *Ryersonian* (Ryerson Polytechnical Institute, Toronto), 15 February 1972, p. 4; Dan Proudfoot, "George Hislop: Straight Talk from the City's Most Out-Front Gay," *Toronto Sunday Sun*, 16 November 1975, pp. M4–M5; "Ron and George Have Been Trying to Get Along for 14 Years, Just Like a Lot of Other Couples," *Canadian Magazine*, 27 May 1972, p. 6; Becki L. Ross, *The House That Jill Built: A Lesbian Nation in Formation* (Toronto: University of Toronto Press, 1995), pp. 34–35; Hartley Steward, "Coming Out in Toronto," *Toronto Life*, March 1972, pp. 41–45; Peter Zorzi, *Queer Catharsis* (Toronto: The Author, 1992), pp. 28–32.]

February 2 * London, Ont. * Twenty students met to discuss the formation of a gay student group at the University of Western Ontario, and to elect officers. Wayne Thompson was appointed the first chairperson of the group. The first general meeting of the UWO Homophile Association (Gay Lib Union) (UWOHA) was held February 8, and was attended by forty people. Subsequent meetings were held weekly during the school year, often at the Grapevine Club, 674 Wellington Road S., and featured guest speakers, discussions, films, and "gay-in" nights at the student pub at Somerville House. By June 1971, official membership in UWOHA stood at almost one hundred, including members from the general community. By late 1973, members from the general community far outnumbered university members. This led in 1974 to the establishment of the Homophile Association of London, Ontario (HALO), an organization for the whole community based off-campus, and the demise of UWOHA. (See also November 1973.)

[Cathie Bartlett, "Gay Libs 'Gratified' by First Meeting Turnout," *Gazette* (Univ. of Western Ontario), 12 February 1971, p. 1; "Gay Lib Union," *Gazette* (Univ. of Western Ontario), 5 February 1971, p. 3; "Gay Lib Union Comes to Western Ontario," *Varsity* (Univ. of Toronto), 8 March 1971, p. 10; "University of Western Ontario Homophile Association (UWOHA)" vertical file, Canadian Lesbian and Gay Archives, Toronto; University of Western Ontario Homophile Association (UWOHA), untitled note, "The Homophile Association Summer Programme: 'Out of the Closets,' June–August 1971," p. 2.]

February 4 * Guelph, Ont. * Four full pages of *The Ontarion*, a student newspaper at the University of Guelph, were devoted to gay liberation, including information on UTHA and YUHA. Also included was an ad announcing the formation of a homophile association on campus. (See also February 23, 1971.)

[*Ontarion* (Univ. of Guelph), 4 February 1971, pp. 5–8.]

February 10 * Toronto * A planning group for a sexual identity educational forum on lesbianism and its relationship to women's liberation held its first meeting at the apartment of Lois McKenzie, 11 Walmer Road, Apt. 207. The group was sponsored by Toronto Women's Liberation Movement. Subsequent meetings were held in collaboration with female members of UTHA. (See also April 15, 1971.)

[Mary Bolton, "Coordinated Political Struggle Minutes: Feb. 22," *Toronto Women's Liberation Newsletter*, February 1971, p. 4; "Lesbian Education Group," *Toronto Women's Liberation Movement Newsletter*, March 1971, p. 4; "Meetings: The Sexual Identity Educational," *Toronto Women's Liberation Newsletter*, January 1971, p. 1.]

February 10 * Toronto * UTHA invited members of the New Feminists and the Toronto Women's Liberation Movement to speak at a UTHA meeting. The meeting attempted to forge closer ties between the women's liberationists and the (mostly male) homophiles. The TWLM representatives were Kathy Keate, Heather Ramsay, and Lyba Spring. Dorothy Curzon spoke for the New Feminists. (See also May 13, 1971.)

[Liz Abraham, "Boys and Girls Together," *Gayokay*, no. 2 (1971), p. 10; Mary Bolton, "Coordinated Political Struggle Minutes: Feb. 22," *Toronto Women's Liberation Newsletter*, February 1971, p. 4; Lyba Spring, "University of Toronto Homophile Association," *Toronto Women's Liberation Newsletter*, February 1971, p. 7.]

February 12–13 * Downsview, Ont. * YUHA and Radio York sponsored a forum on homosexuality that included as speakers Rev. Troy Perry of the Metropolitan Community Church, Los Angeles, and Dr. Franklin Kameny, president of the Washington, D.C., Mattachine Society. About 250 people attended the event, which also included movies and a dance held at Winters College. This was the first large-scale forum on homosexuality held at a

Canadian university. It was ignored by the mainstream Toronto newspapers. (See also February 24, 1971.)

["Canada Forum Draws 250 Despite Snowstorm," *Advocate* (Los Angeles), no. 55 (1971), p. 6; "Dr. Kamaney (sic) for Congress," *Gayokay*, no. 2 (1971), p. 11; "Forum on Homosexuality: A Big First," *YUHA Newsletter*, March 1971, pp. 1–2; "The Homophile Movement in Ontario," *Back Chat Newsletter* 1 (February 1971): 2; Jim Smith, "Homophile Talk a Success: 250 Attend Conference," *Excalibur* (York Univ.), 25 February 1971, p. 3; Ted, "York University Seminar," *Phalia*, no. 5 (1971), p. 6; Roger Wilkes, " 'Homophiles Ignored by Media' " (letter), *Toronto Daily Star*, four star ed., 24 February 1971, p. 7.]

February 23 ✳ Guelph, Ont. ✳ Between forty and fifty men and women attended the inaugural meeting of the University of Guelph Homophile Association (UGHA). Guest speakers at the meeting were Charles Hill of UTHA and Rev. Ritchie McMurray, an Anglican chaplain. The UGHA believed that "morally, socially, physically, psychologically, emotionally, and in every other way the homosexual is not inferior to the heterosexual, and homosexuality is in no way inferior to heterosexuality as a valid way of life." Paul Maurice, editor of the student newspaper the *Ontarion*, became the group's first chairperson. UGHA had problems organizing in its early days and collapsed in late 1971, but was revived in September 1973 with Heather Ramsay and Rick Stenhouse as prominent members. The revived UGHA sponsored a speaker's bureau, dances, and a newsletter. The group received much publicity in the *Ontarion*; the paper ran a regular "Gays at Guelph" column starting in autumn 1973. Late in 1975 UGHA was renamed Guelph Gay Equality.

[Jim D. (Dougan), "Gays at Guelph: What Is the UGHA?" *Ontarion* (Univ. of Guelph), 6 May 1974, p. 17; Bryan Dunlop, "Homosexuals Gather: Valid Way of Life," *Guelph Daily Mercury*, 24 February 1971, p. 17; Peter Leslie, "Gays at Guelph: Clearing Up Misconceptions about U. of G. Homophile Association" (letter), *Ontarion* (Univ. of Guelph), 16 July 1974, pp. 10–11; Sergei, Untitled news item, *YUHA Newsletter*, November 1971, p. 2; Paul Shepherd, "Do Guelph Gays Need the UGHA?" *Gaily Planet* 1 (November 1974): 1; (Rick Stenhouse), "Gays at Guelph" (letter), *Ontarion* (Univ. of Guelph), 12 March 1974, p. 15; "University of Guelph Homophile Association (UGHA)" vertical file, Canadian Lesbian and Gay Archives, Toronto; "Year No. 1 a Success!" *Gaily Planet* 1 (October 1974): 1–2.]

February 24 ✳ Canada ✳ CBC-TV's current affairs programme *Weekday* broadcast a ten-minute report on YUHA, which included interviews filmed during the forum held at York University on February 13.

["T.V. Programme," *YUHA Newsletter*, March 1971, p. 2.]

February 24 ✳ Toronto ✳ Playwright John Herbert, author of *Fortune and Men's Eyes*, spoke at a meeting of the UTHA, attended by about 135 people (125 were male). Herbert urged gay people to come out and to fight society's prejudices against them.

["Meetings," *Gayokay*, no. 2 (1971), pp. 1–2; "Playwright Fights Homosexual Prejudice," *Toronto Star*, four star ed., 25 February 1971, p. 40.]

February (late) ∗ Waterloo, Ont. ∗ The Waterloo Universities' Gay Liberation Movement (GLM) was formed by eight students from the University of Waterloo and Waterloo Lutheran (later Wilfrid Laurier) University. John Dunbar became the first president of the group. The first official meeting of Waterloo GLM was held on March 8, 1971, at Hagey Hall, University of Waterloo. The GLM sponsored speakers, pub nights, discussion groups, film nights, a newsletter (GLM *Newsletter*), a magazine (*Gemini*), and private parties.

["Brief History of Gay Liberation," *Waterloo Universities' Gay Liberation Movement* (Waterloo, Ont.: Waterloo Universities' GLM, 1971), pp. 4–5; "Gay Liberation," *Gemini* II 1 (August–September 1973): 5–6; Robert Rogers, "Gay Group on Campus," *Chevron* (Univ. of Waterloo), 26 February 1971, p. 19; "Gay Lib Comes to Waterloo . . . ," *Cord* (Wilfrid Laurier Univ., Waterloo), 26 February 1971, p. 13.]

March ∗ Burnaby, B.C. ∗ "Homosexuality and the Academy: From Closet Queens to Gay Chauvinists," was published in *The Bridge*, the magazine of the Alumni Association of Simon Fraser University. The unsigned piece was written by a gay graduate of SFU and recalled his experiences there, as well as the activities of the GLF.

["Homosexuality and the Academy: From Closet Queens to Gay Chauvinists," *Bridge* (Simon Fraser Univ.) 3 (March 1971): 8–14.]

March ∗ Burnaby, B.C. ∗ *The Peak*, a student newspaper at Simon Fraser University, published an eight-page gay supplement entitled "Gay Liberation." It included information on the GLF, poetry, a note on revolutionary drag, and Stan Persky's article "Being Homosexual in the World." The supplement was produced by members of GLF, including David Blair, Gordon Hardy, and Persky.

["David Blair" vertical file, Canadian Lesbian and Gay Archives, Toronto.]

March ∗ New York, N.Y.; Toronto ∗ Jane Rule's novel *Against the Season*, which included a female couple amongst its characters, was published by McCall Publishing Company in New York and Doubleday of Canada in Toronto.

["A Bibliography," *Canadian Fiction Magazine*, no. 23 (1976), pp. 133, 136–37.]

March ∗ Toronto ∗ An Indochinese women's conference, organized by TWLM, was held during which divisions emerged over the "lesbian question."

Planned lesbian workshops were cancelled at the last moment, leading lesbian delegates to read a statement at the Plenary Session complaining of mistreatment and demanding that the workshops be rescheduled. This was the first public statement by lesbians in Toronto. Resulting arguments and confusion underscored the importance of holding a lesbian educational forum to help facilitate discussion of lesbianism within TWLM. (See also April 15, 1971.)

[Mary Bolton, "Sisterhood at the Conference," *Toronto Women's Liberation Movement Newsletter*, May 1971, pp. 22–23.]

March 11–13 * Toronto * Graham Jackson's one-act play *Marriage a la Mode* (also called *Balls*), about a young married couple and their same-sex lovers, was performed at Victoria College, University of Toronto.

["Theatre," *Gayokay*, no. 2 (1971), p. 7.]

March 15 * Toronto * Karl John Roestad, thirty-eight, was sentenced by Judge Lloyd Graburn to an indefinite term of preventive detention as a dangerous sexual offender. Roestad had pleaded guilty to twenty counts of indecent assault involving boys between eight and thirteen years old. The Roestad case attracted much attention because it was the first time in ten years that the Crown in Ontario had sought to convict someone as a dangerous sexual offender, liable to life imprisonment. (See also July 30 and September–October, 1974.)

["Pedophile Is Jailed Indefinitely," *Globe and Mail*, metro ed., 16 March 1971, p. 5; Michael Valpy, "The Pedophile Who Faces a Lifetime behind Bars: Diary of a Misspent Life," *Globe and Mail*, metro ed., 9 December 1972, p. 7.]

March 17–18 * Guelph, Ont. * UGHA sponsored its first "gay-ins" at the Campus Pub, Creelman Hall. About forty gay people attended, including members of Waterloo GLM and YUHA.

["Gay-in," *University of Guelph Homophile Association Newsletter*, no. 1 (1971), p. 1; "Gay-in at Campus Pub: Canadian First," *Ontarion* (Univ. of Guelph), 23 March 1971, p. 1; "Two Guelph Gay-ins Successful," *Gemini* 1 (June 1971): 4.]

March 25 * Toronto * Scott Symons, author of *Combat Journal for Place d'Armes* and *Civic Square*, gave the public lecture "Orgasm, Canada, and Us" at the Medical Sciences Auditorium, University of Toronto, sponsored by UTHA.

["Scott Symons Speaks," *Gayokay*, no. 3 (1971), pp. 7–8.]

March 26 * Montréal * Jean Basile (pseud. of Jean-Basile Bezroudnoff) and Georges Khal of the periodical *Mainmise* initiated meetings that led to the formation of the first francophone gay organization in Québec, the Front de libération homosexuelle (FLH). Other early organizers of the group included Normand Bourque, Denis Côté, and Mark Wilson. In its first five months the FLH grew from thirty to 200 members, attracting a wide diversity of men and women with differing goals and ideologies. In November 1971, the more progressive members (including the founders) left when the membership decided to legally incorporate the FLH, and the group became more service-oriented and social. By October the FLH was operating a drop-in centre at 2065, rue St. Denis, which was active until May 1972 when it was closed by order of the City. In June 1972 the centre was reopened at 279, rue Ste. Catherine E. The grand reopening of the centre was raided by the police on June 17–18, 1972. As a result, many FLH members were scared away and the group's executive resigned. By the autumn of 1972 the FLH had collapsed. (See also June 17–18, 1972.)

[Jean Basile, "Le premier soir," *Le berdache*, no. 20 (1981), p. 47; Ron Dayman, "Quebec: Five Years of the Movement," *Body Politic*, no. 29 (1976–77), p. 20; Luc Doré, "Le FLH," *Le berdache*, no. 20 (1981), pp. 47–48; Luc Doré, "History: Montreal — FLH," *Gay* (supplement to *McGill Daily*), 24 November 1972, p. 3; Luc Doré, "La libération des homosexuels" (interview), *Libération*, November 1972, p. 10; "Essai critique sur l'histoire du mouvement gai québécois 1970–1977," in *Contribution sur l'histoire du mouvement gai* ([Montréal ?]: Ligue Ouvrière Revolutionnaire Quatrième Internationale, n.d.), pp. (25–28); "FLH" file, University of Toronto Homophile Association (UTHA) papers, 82–006/01, Canadian Lesbian and Gay Archives, Toronto; Gilles Garneau, "Les militants de la première heure: il y a dix ans naissait le FLH," *Le berdache*, no. 20 (1981), pp. 44–45; Gilles Garneau, "Pour en savoir plus sur le FLH," *Le berdache*, no. 21 (1981), p. 7; Gilles Garneau, "Souvenirs, ô souvenirs . . . ," *Le berdache*, no. 20 (1981), p. 46; Ross Higgins, "Le financement du mouvement gai de Montréal," *Sortie*, no. 34 (1985–86), pp. 21–23; Ross Higgins, "L'impasse linguistique," *Sortie*, no. 25 (1985), p. 12; Jean LeDerff, "FLH: un front de libération des homosexuels à Montréal," *Le tiers*, no. 2 (1972), p. 48; Gérard Pollender, "Un oasis," *Le berdache*, no. 20 (1983), p. 46; Gaétan St-Arnaud, "Le FLH, sept dimensions d'une expérience d'animation socio-culturelle," unpublished student paper, École de service social, Université de Montréal, 8 December 1971, 10 pp. (copy at the Canadian Lesbian and Gay Archives, Toronto); Socrate du Québec, "FLH: un front de libération des homosexuels à Montréal," *Le tiers*, no. 1 (1971), pp. 40–42.]

March 28 ∗ Toronto ∗ Members of CHAT, UTHA, and YUHA chaired an educational meeting on homosexuality at the First Unitarian Church, 175 St. Clair Avenue W. Twenty members of the congregation attended. The meeting was sponsored by the church's Social Action Committee, which had included a subcommittee on homophiles since January 1971.

["Religion and the Homosexual," *Gayokay*, no. 3 (1971), p. 9.]

March 29 ∗ London, Ont. ∗ Dr. Franklin Kameny, president of the Washington, D.C., Mattachine Society, spoke on "The Homosexual Dilemma" before an audience of 200 at the Business Administration Building, University of Western Ontario. The talk had been organized by UWOHA. During his stay in London and Toronto, Dr. Kameny was able to give several other talks and appear on television and radio. (See also March 30, 1971.)

["Coming Events," *Back Chat Newsletter* 1 (March 1971): 2; "Monday 29 March 1971," *University of Western Ontario Homophile Association Newsletter*, no. 8 (1971), p. 1.]

March 30 ∗ Toronto ∗ Dr. Franklin Kameny, president of the Washington, D.C., Mattachine Society, spoke before an audience of 220 at a general meeting of CHAT, held at Holy Trinity Church.

["Dr. Kameny Comes to CHAT," *Back Chat Newsletter* 1 (March 1971): 1; "Speakers," *Back Chat Newsletter* 1 (April 1971): 2.]

Spring ∗ Vancouver ∗ Ted North, one of the owners of the August Club, was appointed the first Empress of Vancouver by the court in Portland, Oregon. The court system, a network of drag performers and their admirers, originated in San Francisco. Its purpose was to generate gay community unity and to support charitable causes within the community through the staging of drag shows and balls. The court was not without its detractors; some activists saw it as an anachronism that promoted sexism and discrimination. The Vancouver court was the first to be established in Canada; it eventually evolved into the Dogwood Monarchist Society and Imperial Dogwood Court.

["Empress & Gay Clubs Promote Sexism & Discrimination," *Open Doors* 2 (June 1972): 6; "Empress Interview" (interviewing Ted North), *Open Doors* 1 (? June 1971): 2, 4; "Sugar Plum Fairies," *Open Doors* 2 (May 1972): 5; Untitled article, *Open Doors* 1 (? June 1971): 13.]

April ∗ Vancouver ∗ Doug Hellquist and Dan Nalbach placed an advertisement in the *Georgia Straight* announcing a new gay group in Saskatoon. Response to the ad eventually resulted in the formation of the Gay Alliance toward Equality (GATE) (Saskatoon), a small group devoted to gay liberation. (See also Autumn 1971 and January 1972.)

["Classifieds: Out-of-Town," *Georgia Straight*, 27–30 April 1971, p. 23; Ed Jackson, "Saskatoon Gay Action: Progress in a Prairie City," *Body Politic*, no. 10 (1973), p. 23; "News of the Gay," *Body Politic*, no. 5 (1972), p. 16; Doug Wilson and Mavis Carleton, "Saskatoon: A Special Place," *Pink Ink*, no. 1 (1983), pp. 25, 28.]

April 1–6 ∗ Vancouver ∗ About 500 women from across North America attended an Indochinese conference, sponsored by the Voice of Women and other groups and held at the University of British Columbia. During the conference, six revolutionary women visiting from Indochina called for unity and resistance in the face of oppression. The final two days of the conference were set aside for women's liberation issues. The delegates included a political grouping of radical lesbians, who called themselves "women-identified women." They declared that "lesbianism is revolution" and that the Indochinese women had as much to learn from the struggle of lesbians as the lesbians had to learn from oppression in Indochina.

[Liz Briemberg and Anne Roberts, "Factions Not Unity at Indochinese Conference," *Georgia Straight*, 16–20 April 1971, pp. 4–5.]

April 15 ∗ Toronto ∗ After two months of preparation, a lesbian educational forum was held at the Graduate Students Union, University of Toronto. The all-female audience heard panellists Linda Jain and Pat Murphy (from UTHA) and radical lesbian-feminists Aline Gregory, Judy Masters, and Susan McEwan discuss various topics including lesbians and childbirth and lesbian separatism. A lesbian collective was formed within the TWLM after the forum and existed until the TWLM's demise in 1972.

[M. Bolton, "Lesbian Educational," *Toronto Women's Liberation Newsletter*, April 1971, pp. 11–13; Becki L. Ross, *The House That Jill Built: A Lesbian Nation in Formation* (Toronto: University of Toronto Press, 1995), pp. 24–25.]

April 16 ∗ Toronto ∗ More than 250 people attended CHAT's first dance, held at Holy Trinity Church. Dances sponsored by CHAT would be popular through the mid-1970s.

["CHAT Dance," *Back Chat Newsletter* 1 (April 1971): 2.]

April 17 ∗ Toronto ∗ Charles Hill (UTHA), Wayne Thompson (UWOHA), and Roger Wilkes (YUHA) debated Dr. Daniel Cappon on the program "Action Set" on CBC radio. Cappon, a professor of environmental studies at York University, was the author of *Toward an Understanding of Homosexuality* (1965). He talked of the "order of nature" and declared that homosexuals were a danger because they attracted others to homosexuality.

["capon, n.: a rooster castrated to improve the flesh for use as food," *Gayokay*, no. 3 (1971), p. 1.]

April 21 ∗ Toronto ∗ An advertisement for Harry Rosen's Men's Wear entitled "Is Hardy Amies Just Another Mad, Gay Designer?" and illustrated with a limp-wristed male hand holding a cigarette holder was published in the *Globe and Mail*. On April 24, in a letter to the editor of the *Globe*, Charles Hill of UTHA complained of the "pure, bigoted stereotyping" of the ad.

[Advertisement, *Globe and Mail*, metro ed., 21 April 1971, p. 3; Charles C. Hill, "Homosexuals" (letter), *Globe and Mail*, metro ed., 24 April 1971, p. 6; "A Slap on the Wrist for Harry," *Marketing*, 3 May 1971, p. 1.]

May ∗ Ottawa ∗ The Club Private opened at 227 Laurier Avenue W. as a private club for gay men and lesbians. Operated by Ron Burridge, it was open to males on Fridays and Saturdays, and to females on Thursdays and Sundays. Activities were restricted to conversation and dancing. By January 1972, the club had five hundred members. On December 16, 1972, Club Private was raided by Ottawa morality detectives, who charged Burridge with selling liquor without a licence. Burridge pleaded guilty and received a suspended sentence.

["Club Not for 'Straights,'" *Ottawa Citizen*, 4 January 1972, p. 13; "Club Private Owner Faces Liquor Charge," *Ottawa Citizen*, 19 December 1972, p. 3; "Club Sold Liquor Illegally," *Ottawa Citizen*, 8 February 1973, p. 16.]

May ∗ Vancouver ∗ The first meetings were held to organize the Gay Alliance toward Equality (GATE). On May 30, 1971, Wayne Thompson was elected chairman and spokesman and Marion Cantie chairwoman. Thompson was succeeded as chair by Roedy Green in August 1971, who was succeeded in July 1972 by Maurice Flood. By September 1971, GATE (Vancouver) had rented office space at 1131 Richards Street, no. 105. GATE (Vancouver) was one of the first Canadian groups to plan gay civil rights strategies, advocating public and political programmes aimed at mobilizing people in mass actions to demand their rights. GATE (Vancouver) became known for its no-compromise positions, several of which were adopted as policy and for discussion by the Canadian gay movement; for example, "No Liaison with the Police," "Self-Determination for Québec," and "Abolish All Age of Consent Laws." GATE (Vancouver) published "The Gateway," an occasional news column, in the *Georgia Straight* between September 1971 and July 1972 and in August 1973 started the influential newspaper *Gay Tide*. GATE (Vancouver) was active until the end of June 1980. (See also June 27, 1971.)

[Margaret Fulford, ed., *The Canadian Women's Movement, 1960–1990: A Guide to Archival Resources/Le mouvement canadien des femmes, 1960–1990: guide de ressources archivistiques* (Toronto: Canadian Women's Movement Archives/ECW Press, 1992), entry 133; Gay Alliance toward Equality (GATE) (Vancouver) papers, 82–005, 88–040, Canadian Lesbian and Gay Archives, Toronto; "Gay Alliance toward Equality (GATE) (Vancouver)" vertical file, Canadian Lesbian and Gay Archives, Toronto; G.K. (Gary Kinsman), "Recovering History: ASK Reunion," *Rites* 3 (November 1986): 6; "New Gay Organization," *Georgia Straight*, 25–29 June 1971, p. 5; Paul Trollope, "GATE Vancouver Passes into History," *Body Politic*, no. 65 (1980), p. 11; "Vancouver Gay Liberation," *Body Politic*, no. 1 (1971), p. 2.]

May 13 ∗ Toronto ∗ UTHA members Danny Gerrard, Alex Goudeketting, and Charles Hill presented an educational on sex-role oppression to members of TWLM at the Graduate Students Union, University of Toronto.

["Educational Report," *Toronto Women's Liberation Movement Newsletter*, May 1971, p. 9.; "Next Educational: Sexual Roles," *Toronto Women's Liberation Newsletter*, April 1971, p. 4.]

May 21–28 ∗ Vancouver ∗ Len Richmond's full-page cartoon "Gay Liberation Presents '2001: A Sex Odyssey'" was published in the *Georgia Straight*.
[*Georgia Straight*, 21–28 May 1971, p. 18.]

June 1–September 24 ∗ Toronto ∗ CHAT received an Opportunities for Youth
grant for $9,000 to help educate the public about homosexuality. The grant,
administered through the Canadian Mental Health Association, allowed
nine people to operate a telephone counselling service and to work on
education programs with church and social groups for a thirteen-week
period. This is believed to be the first time in Canada that a gay organization
received financial assistance from the federal government.

[Community Homophile Association of Toronto (CHAT) papers, 82–001, Canadian
Lesbian and Gay Archives, Toronto; Andrea Merry, "Homosexuals Win Federal Grant
for Service Work," *Toronto Daily Star*, four star ed., 10 August 1971, p. 49.]

June 2 ∗ Edmonton ∗ Edward J. Forsyth's film *I'm Going to Get You . . . Elliot
Boy/Caged Men* was released at the Rialto theatre. Starring Ross Stephanson,
Maureen McGill, and Jeremy Hart, the film was about a thief and his life in
prison, where he encountered violence and homosexuality.

[Adil., "*I'm Going to Get You . . . Elliot Boy*," *Variety*, 6 October 1971, p. 22; D.J. Turner
and Micheline Morisset, eds., *Canadian Feature Film Index, 1913–1985/Index des films
canadiens de long métrage* (Ottawa: Public Archives, National Film, Television, and
Sound Archives, 1987), entry 314.]

June 6–12 ∗ Washington, D.C. ∗ A group of fourteen Unitarians formed a
gay caucus at the annual general assembly of the Unitarian Universalist
(U.U.) Association. One of the leading organizers of the group was Elgin
Blair, of Toronto, who would edit the *U.U. Gay Caucus Newsletter* from the
first issue in September 1971 through June 1973.

[Elgin Blair papers, 84–011, Canadian Lesbian and Gay Archives, Toronto; "Unitarians
Form Own Gay Group," *Advocate* (Los Angeles), 21 July–3 August 1971, p. 15.]

June 9 ∗ Montréal ∗ Claude Fournier's film *Les chats bottés/ The Master Cats*,
starring Donald Pilon and Donald Lautrec, premiered at the Saint-Denis
theatre. It was a comic farce about the sexual adventures of two straight cads.
Jacques Famery played Môman, the gay comic foil.

[D.J. Turner and Micheline Morisset, eds., *Canadian Feature Film Index, 1913–
1985/Index des films canadiens de long métrage* (Ottawa: Public Archives, National Film,
Television, and Sound Archives, 1987), entry 345; Thomas Waugh, "Nègres blancs,
tapettes et 'butch': les lesbiennes et les gais dans le cinéma québécois," *Copie zéro*, no.
11 (1981), pp. 18–20.]

June 24 ∗ Toronto ∗ The film version of John Herbert's play *Fortune and
Men's Eyes*, directed by Harvey Hart and starring Wendell Burton, Michael

Greer, and Zooey Hall, held its Canadian premiere at the New Yorker theatre.
[Gordon Gow, *"Fortune and Men's Eyes," Films and Filming*, April 1972, p. 52; Martin
Knelman, *"Fortune and Men's Eyes*: Earnest Prison Drama," *Globe and Mail*, metro ed.,
24 June 1971, p. 12; Richard McGuinness, "Gay, Yes, but Proud It's Not," *Village Voice*,
1 July 1971, p. 55; Tom Milne, *"Fortune and Men's Eyes," Monthly Film Bulletin*, March
1972, p. 51; D.J. Turner and Micheline Morisset, eds., *Canadian Feature Film Index,
1913–1985 / Index des films canadiens de long métrage* (Ottawa: Public Archives, National
Film, Television, and Sound Archives, 1987), entry 352; Verr., *"Fortune and Men's Eyes,"
Variety*, 9 June 1971, p. 17.]

June 27 * Toronto * The founding meeting of Toronto Gay Action (TGA)
was held. TGA grew out of a proposal for an activist caucus within CHAT and
was "devoted to peaceful confrontation with all elements of sexist oppression." Its activism was directed "toward defeating all legal and social discrimination against homosexuals." TGA was run by a coordinating committee;
Cheri DiNovo, Brian Waite, and John Wilson were early leaders. Its founding project was the August 28, 1971, rally on Parliament Hill in Ottawa. TGA
disbanded early in 1973 and its role was replaced by GATE (Toronto). (See also
August 28, 1971.)
[Margaret Fulford, ed., *The Canadian Women's Movement, 1960–1990: A Guide to
Archival Resources/Le mouvement canadien des femmes, 1960–1990: guide de ressources
archivistiques* (Toronto: Canadian Women's Movement Archives/ECW Press, 1992),
entry 501; Toronto Gay Action collection, 89–058, Canadian Lesbian and Gay
Archives, Toronto; Peter Zorzi, *Queer Catharsis* (Toronto: The Author, 1992), pp. 72–
76.]

June 27 * Vancouver * The first general meeting of the Gay Alliance toward
Equality (GATE) (Vancouver) was held at the Unitarian Centre Hall. The
Burrard Street YMCA had refused to rent a room to GATE for the meeting.
Members of GATE complained about the incident to the British Columbia
Human Rights Commission. John Sherlock, director of the Commission,
responded that it could not act because the province's Human Rights Act did
not protect people from discrimination based on sexual orientation.
["Government Says: Gays Have No Rights" ("The Gateway" column), *Georgia
Straight*, 10–14 September 1971, p. 16; "New Gay Organization," *Georgia Straight*,
25–29 June 1971, p. 5; "YMCA Discriminates against Gays," *Georgia Straight*, 27–31
August 1971, p. 3.]

June 30 * Toronto * The first part of a report by Ernest J. Nagler and Carlton
McEachern, entitled "Male Homosexuality in Toronto: A Sociological and
Social Problems Overview and Perspective. Part I: Socio-economic and
Demographic Description," was published. The survey, based on interviews
of 187 non-patient gay men in Toronto, including members of UTHA, had
been undertaken between December 1969 and June 1971 by the department

of social pathology at the Clarke Institute of Psychiatry. The study was unusual for the time in that it focussed on homosexuals as a legitimate minority group rather than as a deviant culture.

["Clarke Study Sees Homosexuals as Social Minority, Not Deviants," *Toronto Telegram*, metro night ed., 31 March 1971, p. 19; "Homosexuals Treated as Minority, Not Deviants," *Montreal Gazette*, final ed., 7 December 1972, p. 25; Herb Spiers, "Toronto's Gay Males," *Body Politic*, no. 3 (1972), p. 13.]

Summer ∗ Edmonton ∗ The first gay liberation organization in Alberta, Gay Alliance toward Equality (GATE), was formed. GATE (Edmonton) started as a small group of friends around Michael Roberts, Edmonton's first public gay activist, who became GATE (Edmonton)'s regional coordinator. Peter Hall acted as chairperson. During the summer of 1971 Roberts attempted to raise the profile of the group by placing a notice in issues of the *Georgia Straight*. GATE (Edmonton) sponsored drop-ins at the GATE House (located at 11012 86th Avenue from May 1973, moving to 8223 109th Street in April 1974), a twenty-four-hour information and counselling phone line, a speaker's bureau, and a library. The group's early activities included lobbying the Alberta government to amend the Alberta Bill of Rights and the Individual's Rights Protection Act to outlaw discrimination based on sexual orientation and asking candidates about gay rights during the 1972 federal and provincial election campaigns. In mid-1973 Roberts was succeeded as regional coordinator by Don Musbach, and the group began to focus more on social services as opposed to political activity. By October 1973 GATE (Edmonton) had about twenty paid members.

["GATE Drop-ins," *Club '70 News*, February 1974, pp. 4–5; "Gay Alliance toward Equality (GATE) (Edmonton)" vertical file, Canadian Lesbian and Gay Archives, Toronto; "Homosexuals Ask Only for Equality," *Edmonton Journal*, 13 December 1971, p. 49; E. Plawiuk, "GATE: Fighting for Gay Equality," *Poundmaker* (Edmonton), 9–14 October 1973, pp. 12–13; Michael Roberts, "Edmonton Gay Helps Gays" (letter), *Georgia Straight*, 19–22 October 1971, p. 6; Michael Roberts, "Gays . . . Information — Help," *Gateway* (Univ. of Alberta), 20 January 1972, p. 3.]

Summer ∗ Winnipeg ∗ Several people began to meet regularly to plan the formation of a private social club for lesbians and gay men. Monthly meetings/socials were soon held at different locations. The Happenings Club was eventually granted a charter by the provincial government in June 1973, and by October 1973 had permanent premises at 242 Manitoba Avenue. The Club saw itself as strictly a social centre for lesbians and gay men, as opposed to a force for political action, and sponsored many dances, parties, a bowling league, a newsletter, and other activities. By June 1975 the Happenings Club had issued 743 memberships.

["Editorial," *What's Happening!* 3 (March 1974): 1–2; "Editorial," *What's Happening!*, August 1975, pp. 1–2; "Report of the Membership Committee," *What's Happening!*, Summer 1975, p. 10.]

July 1 * Montréal * In their first public action, members of FLH joined in a large anti-Confederation demonstration held at Parc Lafontaine. Denis Côté, president of FLH, addressed the crowd. The gay marchers were subjected to open hostility from other groups, and were condemned by René Lévesque, leader of the Parti Québécois.

[Ives Beaudin and Daniel Rioux, "À la manifestation anti-Canada," *Journal de Montréal*, 2 July 1971, pp. 2–3; Michel Benoit, "Les séparatistes manifestent dans le calme," *Montréal-matin*, 2 July 1971, p. 3; " 'May Day' March Draws Gay Solidarity," *Body Politic*, no. 19 (1975), p. 9; Pierre Richard, "Manifestation pacifique contre la Confédération," *Le devoir*, 2 July 1971, p. 6; Lucien Rivard, "Un 1er juillet paisible dans les rues de Montréal," *La presse*, two star ed., 2 July 1971, p. A3; Paul Waters, "Anti-Canada March Attracts 2,000," *Montreal Gazette*, final ed., 2 July 1971, p. 3.]

July 14, 21 * Toronto * American gay activist Carl Wittman's "A Gay Manifesto" was reprinted in two issues of *Guerilla*.

[Carl Whittman (sic), "Gay Manifesto," *Guerilla* 2 (14 July 1971): 12–13; 2 (21 July 1971): 8–9.]

July 31 * Toronto * A meeting was held between representatives of CHAT, Spearhead, UTHA, UWOHA, and Waterloo GLM regarding cooperation between homophile groups in Ontario and preparations for the August 28 "We Demand" march on Parliament Hill. This was the first of several conferences held during 1971–72 by what would become known as the Ontario Homophile Federation. (See also October 16, 1971.)

[Untitled article, UWOHA *Newsletter*, no. 13 (1971), p. 1.]

August * Toronto * The Central Committee plenum of the League for Socialist Action/Ligue socialiste ouvrière (LSA/LSO) was held, during which gay liberation was first formally raised for discussion. The resulting Plenum Report, written by John Steele, called for the opening of a dialogue with gay liberationists and proposed that the LSA/LSO give educational and propagandistic support to the gay movement. Several LSA/LSO *Discussion Bulletin* papers subsequently examined the League's intervention in gay liberation activities. (See also December 1971.)

[John Bannon, "Some Further Notes on Gay Liberation," *League for Socialist Action/Ligue socialiste ouvrière Discussion Bulletin 1972*, no. 24 (1972), 19 pp.; John Bannon and Brian Bennett, "A Perspective on Gay Liberation," *League for Socialist Action/Ligue socialiste ouvrière Discussion Bulletin 1972*, no. 2 (1972), 40 pp.; Maurice Flood, "For a Full (Not Limited) Intervention in Gay Liberation," *League for Socialist Action/Ligue socialiste ouvrière Discussion Bulletin 1972*, no. 16 (1972), 15 pp.; Randy Notte and Ian

Mackenzie, "Towards Gay Liberation," *Young Socialists/Ligue des jeunes socialistes Discussion Bulletin 1972*, 8, no. 5 (1972), 14 pp.]

August 1 ✳ Toronto ✳ Toronto's first gay picnic was held at Hanlan's Point, Toronto Islands. The event was sponsored by CHAT and TGA, and was attended by about 300 people. Flags and banners were displayed by the picknickers, including an old lace tablecloth bearing the words "Canada the True, North, and Gay."

["A Gay Picnic," *Guerilla* 2 (4 August 1971): 18; Victor Hedworth, "Canadians March on Ottawa: 10 Demands Placed on Parliament," *Advocate* (Los Angeles), no. 69 (1971), pp. 1, 14; Toronto Gay Action collection, 89–058, Canadian Lesbian and Gay Archives, Toronto.]

August 13 ✳ Toronto ✳ Sixty people attended a panel discussion on homosexual people as an oppressed minority in Canadian society and the development of a gay liberation movement in Toronto, held at the Vanguard Forum, 334 Queen Street W. The four panelists were George Hislop and Pat Murphy, representing CHAT, Cheri DiNovo, representing TGA, CHAT, and the Toronto Women's Caucus, and Brian Waite, representing TGA and the League for Socialist Action.

[John Wilson, "Gay Liberation Activists Denounce Discrimination," *Labor Challenge*, 23 August 1971, p. 7.]

August 20 ✳ Toronto ✳ About twelve members of TGA participated in an "On to Ottawa" march to build support for the August 28 rally in Ottawa. This was the first public demonstration by lesbians and gays in Toronto. The marchers met at Queen's Park before heading east on St. Joseph Street to Yonge Street. The group proceeded down Yonge Street to Holy Trinity Square, where they joined in a dance sponsored by CHAT.

["TGA," *Guerilla* 2 (25 August 1971): 18; Toronto Gay Action collection, 89–058, Canadian Lesbian and Gay Archives, Toronto.]

August 21 ✳ Ottawa ✳ "We Demand," a brief prepared by the August 28th Gay Day Committee of TGA and sponsored by Canadian gay groups, was presented to the federal government. The thirteen-page brief contained ten points calling for law reform and changes in public policy relating to homosexuals. It asked that the terms "gross indecency" and "indecent act" be removed from the Canadian Criminal Code and be replaced by a list of specific offences, and that gay people be allowed to serve openly in the Canadian armed forces.

[Toronto Gay Action (TGA) collection, 89–058, Canadian Lesbian and Gay Archives, Toronto; "We Demand," reprinted in the *Body Politic*, no. 1 (1971), pp. 4–7 (reprinted in Ed Jackson and Stan Persky, eds., *Flaunting It!: A Decade of Gay Journalism from The*

A poster for the Canadian Gay Rally on
Parliament Hill, Ottawa, August 28, 1971.

Charles Hill of TGA addresses the crowd during the
demonstration on Parliament Hill, Ottawa, August 28, 1971.

ode (Bill C-150).

Body Politic [Vancouver and Toronto: New Star Books; Pink Triangle Press, 1982], pp. 217–20).]

August 28 ∗ Ottawa; Vancouver ∗ Lesbians and gay men and their supporters assembled on Parliament Hill in support of the brief "We Demand." About one hundred people demonstrated for forty minutes in pouring rain. The crowd was addressed by Charles Hill of TGA, which organized the march, George Hislop and Pat Murphy of CHAT, Pierre Masson of FLH, and John Williams of Cleveland, Ohio. In Vancouver, GATE sponsored a demonstration at the courthouse to show solidarity with the Ottawa marchers. The twenty demonstrators attracted a sympathetic crowd of 150 to 200. Roedy Green, chairperson of GATE, spoke, as did representatives from Vancouver Gay Sisters and the GLF. These were the first large-scale public gay demonstrations held in Canada. They were held on this day to commemorate the second anniversary of the implementation of the amendments to the Canadian Criminal Code (Bill C-150). (See also August 30, 1971.)

["Anti-homosexual Laws Protested," *Vancouver Sun*, four star ed., 30 August 1971, p. 27; "Canada's Gays Join Forces for Rights Rally in Ottawa," *Advocate* (Los Angeles), no. 68 (1971), p. 2; Rick Doucet, "Out of the Closets and into the Streets," *Georgia Straight*, 31 August–3 September 1971, p. 9; "Equality Urged for Homosexuals," *Globe and Mail*, metro ed., 30 August 1971, p. 3; " 'Gay Is Good' Theme of Rally," *Toronto Daily Star*, four star ed., 30 August 1971, p. 28; "Gay Lib Marches on Ottawa: Social Equality Sought," *Montreal Gazette*, final ed., 30 August 1971, p. 33; "Gay Rallies: A Big First Step" ("The Gateway" column), *Georgia Straight*, 10–14 September 1971, p. 17; "Gay Rights Demo . . . ," *Georgia Straight*, 13–17 August 1971, p. 17; Victor Hedworth, "Canadians March on Ottawa: 10 Demands Placed on Parliament," *Advocate* (Los Angeles), no. 69 (1971), pp. 1, 4; "Homosexuals List Grievances in Protest on Hill," *Ottawa Citizen*, 30 August 1971, p. 2; "Les homosexuels manifestent," *Le droit*, dernière ed., 30 August 1971, p. 4; "Homosexuals Rally in Ottawa: Search for Social Equality," *Montreal Star*, final ed., 30 August 1971, p. 45; "In the Pouring Rain," *Guerilla* 2 (8 September 1971): 4; "Nouvelles: le jour gai: 28 août 1971," *Le tiers*, no. 1 (1971), p. 43; John Wilson, "Marchers Demand Full Rights for Gays," *Labor Challenge*, 13 September 1971, p. 6; Lavender Worm, "GLF News: Gays to Protest on Parliament Hill," *Georgia Straight*, 6–10 August 1971, p. 11; Peter Zorzi, *Queer Catharsis* (Toronto: The Author, 1992), pp. 74–76.]

August 30 ∗ Toronto ∗ Dick Smythe, news editor of CHUM radio, delivered an on-air editorial in which he said that the gay march on Parliament Hill on August 28 had been like "a demonstration for equality and acceptance by militant alcoholics, militant lepers, or militant lunatics" and that homosexuality is "a mental and sexual aberration."

[Richard Zorniak, "An Open Reply to Dick Smythe" (letter), *Guerilla* 2 (15 September 1971): 2.]

September ∗ Châteauguay, Qué. ∗ The first issue of *Le tiers: le magazine* *homophile du Québec* was published by Publications Andart. Edited by André Dion, *Le tiers* was the first serious homophile/gay liberation periodical published in Québec. It collapsed after issue two (1972).

[Alain de Valter, "Cet editeur Montréalais lance le premier magazine homophile 'serieux' au Québec," *Montréal flash* 1 (11 October 1971): 4–6; Ross Higgins, "Lives, Oral Narratives, Writing the Past," revised version of a paper delivered at the Out of the Archives Conference, Department of History, York University, North York, Ont., 13–15 January 1994, pp. 20–22.]

September * Toronto * Jearld Moldenhauer announced at a meeting of TGA that a gathering would be held at his home at 65 Kendal Avenue, Apt. 8, concerning the formation of a new gay newspaper. Members of TGA had been mulling over the idea of starting a paper to reflect gay consciousness and community since at least the August 28 march in Ottawa. About ten people attended the meeting, which was the first planning session of what would become *The Body Politic*. (See also October 28, 1971).

[Gerald Hannon, "Who We Were, Who We Are," *Body Politic*, no. 80 (1982), pp. 31–37; Peter Zorzi, *Queer Catharsis* (Toronto: The Author, 1992), pp. 10–11.]

September 8 * Toronto * A group of thirteen gay men and lesbians, most of whom were members of TGA, were thrown out of the Pretzel Bell Public House, 127 Simcoe Street, and were chased and beaten because they had danced with same-sex partners in the pub.

[Chris Podmore, Letter, *Guerilla* 2 (6 October 1971): 20–21; Herb Spiers, Letter, *Guerilla* 2 (15 September 1971): 2; (Peter Zorzi), "Screwd (sic) at the Pretzel," *Guerilla* 2 (15 September 1971): 11.]

September 14 * Ottawa * Maurice Bélanger, Michael Black, Charles Hill, Philip Bianco, Jacques Hoffman, Reg Turcotte, and Terrence Reichey met at Black and Bélanger's home at 270 Somerset Street W., no. 906, to discuss forming a gay organization for the National Capital area. The group contin-ued to meet during September–October in private homes. On October 13, 1971, it adopted the name Gays of Ottawa/Gays d'Ottawa [Gais de l'Outaouais from 1975] (GO); Maurice Bélanger and Paul Wise became GO's first co-chairmen. GO's mandate was to lobby the federal and Ontario provincial governments on behalf of gays and lesbians, to educate the public about homosexuality, and to act as a community organization for gay people in the Ottawa-Hull area. It sponsored many dances and produced the influential newsletter GO *Info*. Charles Hill, a founding member of UTHA, was a member of GO from its early days and succeeded Bélanger as president in April 1973. After November 1971 the group began meeting twice per month at St. George's Anglican Church, 152 Metcalfe Street.

[Don Butler, "Struggle to Overcome 'Dreaded Deviant' Status: Out of the Closet into Street," *Ottawa Citizen*, 12 July 1975, p. 39; Margaret Fulford, ed., *The Canadian Women's Movement, 1960–1990: A Guide to Archival Resources/Le mouvement canadien des femmes, 1960–1990: guide de ressources archivistiques* (Toronto: Canadian Women's Movement Archives/ECW Press, 1992), entries 346, 347, 996, 997; "Gays d'Ottawa," *Body Politic*, no. 2 (1972), p. 19; Gays of Ottawa (GO) papers, 82–017, 88–041, and inventory, Canadian Lesbian and Gay Archives, Toronto; Burt Heward, "Gay Campaign: Homos Push GO Button for Self-Help," *Ottawa Citizen*, 4 January 1972, p. 13; Burt Heward, "Homosexuals Seek Fortune in Men's Eyes," *Ottawa Citizen*, 4 January 1972, p. 13; "History," GO *Info*, no. 1 (1972), p. 2; Susan Stock, "GO," *Charlatan* (Carleton Univ., Ottawa), 8 August 1972, p. 15; Paul-François Sylvestre, "Gais de l'Outaouais: l'âné des organismes homophiles," *Gay Montréal* 1 (25 January 1977): 3.]

September 16 ✻ Toronto ✻ During question period at an orientation festival at the University of Toronto attended by 300 students, two members of UTHA asked Ontario Attorney-General Allan Lawrence whether he would favour an explicit clause in the Ontario Human Rights Code prohibiting discrimination against homosexuals. The minister replied that he believed ". . . a homosexual is a pervert and this perversion should not be legally recognized in any shape or form." (See also October 21, 1971.)

[Raphael Bendahan, "Plato and Allan Lawrence: The Homosexual Controversy," *Varsity Supplement* (Univ. of Toronto), 18 October 1971, p. 18; Jim Hickman, "Bigotry Affects the Boys in the Gay Ghetto" (editorial), *Ryersonian* (Ryerson Polytechnical Institute, Toronto), 3 December 1971, p. 3; "Lawrence Rejects Law on Homosexual Rights," *Toronto Daily Star*, four star ed., 17 September 1971, p. 37; Alexander Schachter, "Lawrence Hits the Gay Boys," *Ryersonian* (Ryerson Polytechnical Institute, Toronto), 28 September 1971, p. 1.]

September 19 ✻ Toronto ✻ Elgin Blair organized the first gay fellowship discussion group held at the First Unitarian Congregation, 175 St. Clair Avenue W. Ten to fifteen people attended subsequent meetings, held on Sunday evenings. The fellowship met until May 1972, by which time Blair's energy was increasingly taken up by the Gay Caucus of the Unitarian Universalist (U.U.) Association.

[Elgin Blair, "Gay Caucus: Unitarian Universalist Gays,"*Body Politic*, no. 2 (1972), pp. 16, 19; Elgin Blair papers, 84–011, Canadian Lesbian and Gay Archives, Toronto; Margaret Fulford, ed., *The Canadian Women's Movement, 1960–1990: A Guide to Archival Resources/Le mouvement canadien des femmes, 1960–1990: guide de ressources archivistiques* (Toronto: Canadian Women's Movement Archives/ECW Press, 1992), entry 513; "News of Gay Activities Across the Continent: Toronto, Ontario," *U.U. Gay Caucus Newsletter* 2 (February 1972): 4.]

Autumn ✻ Don Mills, Ont. ✻ A chapter of YUHA was organized at Glendon College, York University. It was a rap session group that met every second Wednesday under the co-chairmanship of John Henry and Linda Jain.

[Jim Daw, "Homophile Association at Glendon," *Pro Tem* (Glendon College, York Univ.), 23 November 1971, p. 2; Untitled notice, *York University Homophile Association Newsletter*, November 1970, p. 1.]

Autumn ✱ Downsview, Ont. ✱ YUHA organized a gay studies course at McLaughlin College, York University. It was a tutorial with ten people, and was led by Roger Wilkes, a graduate student and chairperson of YUHA. This is thought to be the first gay studies course offered at a Canadian university.

[Roger Wilkes, "York Has Canada's Only Homophile Course," *Excalibur* (York Univ.), 28 October 1971, p. 7; Roger Wilkes, "York Homophile Studies Course," *Body Politic*, no. 2 (1972), p. 12.]

Autumn ✱ Montréal ✱ McGill University instructors Bruce Garside, Linda Page-Hollander, and John Southin initiated a popular course on "Biology and Social Change" that included the examination of gay liberation. By September 1972, a discussion group from this course had formed into GAY (later Gay McGill). (See also September 1972.)

[Ron Dayman, "Quebec: Five Years of the Movement," *Body Politic*, no. 29 (1976–77), p. 21.]

Autumn ✱ New York, N.Y. ✱ Twenty members of FLH spent a few days in New York meeting with members of the Gay Activists Alliance (GAA), visiting, discussing gay liberation, and bar-hopping. They also participated in a demonstration after police raided a women's bar.

["Nouvelles: New York," *Le tiers*, no. 2 (1972), pp. 26–27.]

Autumn ✱ Saskatoon ✱ The Gay Students Alliance (GSA) was formed at the University of Saskatchewan. GSA was campus-oriented, while GATE (Saskatoon) was targeted at the general community. Soon, members of GSA and GATE (Saskatoon) began to plan a new organization that would coordinate social services and activities for the gay community; the Zodiac Friendship Society emerged by January 1972. Many of the same people — Bruce Garman, Doug Hellquist, Dan Nalbach, and Erv (later Tom) Warner — were organizers of all these groups, and were connected to the university as either students or staff. (See also January 1972 and October 1972.)

[Ed Jackson, "Saskatoon Gay Action: Progress in a Prairie City," *Body Politic*, no. 10 (1973), p. 23; "News of the Gay: Saskatoon," *Body Politic*, no. 5 (1972), p. 16; Neil Richards papers and inventory, S-A821, Saskatchewan Archives Board, Saskatoon.]

Autumn ✱ Toronto ✱ Chris John Ayre founded Homophile Information Media (HIM) (later Homophile Information Media of Canada/Centre d'information homophile du Canada [HIMC/CIHC]), which was dedicated to educating about homosexuality. By mail and telephone HIM acted as a referral service for information on social services and the gay social scene across Canada. The Homophile Dating Association was formed as a spin-off of HIM. HIMC/CIHC was dormant by January 1974.

["Homophile Information Media (HIM)" vertical file, Canadian Lesbian and Gay Archives, Toronto.]

October ∗ Kingston, Ont. ∗ George Hislop, director of CHAT, spoke before a crowd of 150 students at Queen's University.

["Getting Around,"*Back Chat Newsletter*, February 1972, p. 4.]

October ∗ Vancouver ∗ The Gay People's Alliance was formed at the University of British Columbia. Its purpose was to provide a nucleus for gay social life on campus. Although it was originally founded by two members of the old Vancouver GLF, the Gay People's Alliance was not initially interested in political action. The group was succeeded by Gay People of UBC in September 1972. (See also September 1972.)

[John Gibbs, "Gay Alliance Struggles for Survival," *Ubyssey* (Univ. of British Columbia), 5 November 1971, p. 3.]

October ∗ Waterloo, Ont. ∗ "Gay Is Good," a weekly radio program coordinated by Waterloo GLM, began broadcasting on Radio Waterloo (94.1 Cable FM) every Friday from 9 to 9:30 p.m.

["Weekly Radio Program," GLM *Newsletter* 1 (30 September 1971): 1.]

October 14 ∗ Hamilton ∗ In an address delivered at the annual meeting of the Canadian Mental Health Association, George Hislop, director of CHAT, declared that requests by homosexuals to become legally married should be taken seriously in order to protect property rights.

[Linda Jain and Pat Murphy, "Tomorrow Is Over!" *Body Politic*, no. 1 (1971), p. 12; Leone Kirkwood, "Legal Marriage Would Enable Homosexuals to Have More Security in Law, CMHA Told," *Globe and Mail*, metro ed., 15 October 1971, p. 12.]

October 16 ∗ Toronto ∗ An informal meeting of representatives of Ontario homophile and gay liberation groups was held at Hart House, University of Toronto. They discussed the possibility of forming a provincial organization, as well as holding a demonstration to demand the inclusion of the term "sexual orientation" in the Ontario Human Rights Code.

[Jim, "Ontario Gay Conference," *Gemini* II 1 (April 1973): 2; "Toronto Conference," *Gemini* 1 (October 1971): 2; Brian Waite, "Strategy for Gay Liberation," *Body Politic*, no. 3 (1972), pp. 4, 19; Richard Zorniak, "Canadian Gays on the Move," *Guerilla* 2 (20 October 1971): 5.]

October 21 * Toronto * Peter Maloney ran as the Liberal candidate in the St. George riding against Ontario Attorney-General Allan Lawrence in the provincial election, held October 21. During the campaign, a group called the Ontario Campaign for Sexual Equality distributed a pamphlet urging lesbians and gays to vote for candidates who advocated sexual equality legislation. Maloney, an advocate of gay rights (but not yet a declared homosexual), waged a vigorous campaign but lost to Lawrence by a wide margin.

[Harry Marsh, "Citizen Profile," *Toronto Citizen*, 2 September 1971, p. 3; Zachs Marshall, "The Liberal Candidate Robert Nixon Didn't Want," *Toronto Citizen*, 11 March 1971, p. 5; "Ontario Campaign for Sexual Equality" vertical file, Canadian Lesbian and Gay Archives, Toronto; "PCs Anathema to Sex Group," *Globe and Mail*, metro ed., 12 October 1971, p. 4; "Toronto Homosexuals Out to Beat Lawrence," *Toronto Daily Star*, four star ed., 12 October 1971, p. 10; Don Walters, "Gay-Backed Candidates Defeated in Toronto," *Advocate* (Los Angeles), no. 72 (1971), p. 6.]

October 28 * Toronto * Five thousand copies of the first issue (November–December) of *The Body Politic* went on sale. Until its demise in February 1987, it was Canada's gay newspaper of record.

[*The Body Politic* papers, several accessions, including "An Inventory of the Records of *The Body Politic* and Pink Triangle Press," compiled by Rick Bébout, Canadian Lesbian and Gay Archives, Toronto; Margaret Fulford, ed., *The Canadian Women's Movement, 1960–1990: A Guide to Archival Resources/Le mouvement canadien des femmes, 1960–1990: guide de ressources archivistiques* (Toronto: Canadian Women's Movement Archives/ ECW Press, 1992), entry 15; Gerald Hannon, "Who We Were, Who We Are," *Body Politic*, no. 80 (1982), pp. 31–37; Stephen MacDonald, "Cold Stone: *The Body Politic*: An Experience of Alternative Press Publishing in Canada in the 70s," unpublished paper, Faculty of Library Science, University of Toronto, 1976, xii, 44 pp.; P.M. (Peter Millard), "Body Politic," *Zodiac Friendship Society* 2 (September 1973): 3; Jearld Moldenhauer, "Victim of Myopia (or, 'Gerald, Bring Me the Axe')" ("Taking Issue" column), *Body Politic*, no. 82 (1982), p. 7; Peter Zorzi, *Queer Catharsis* (Toronto: The Author, 1992), pp. 9–24.]

October 31 * Toronto * Between 5,000 and 8,000 people jammed Yonge Street during Halloween to watch men dressed in drag enter the St. Charles Tavern, 488 Yonge Street. Police closed off the sidewalk for a full block in front of the St. Charles, while members of UTHA passed out leaflets to the crowd, urging understanding of homosexuality.

["Crowds Jam Yonge See 'Gay' Hallowe'en," *Toronto Daily Star*, four star ed., 1 November 1971, p. 59.]

November * Indianapolis, Ind. * Joan Haggerty's novel *Daughters of the Moon* was published by Bobbs-Merrill. It tells the story of two pregnant women who meet and eventually live together as lovers.

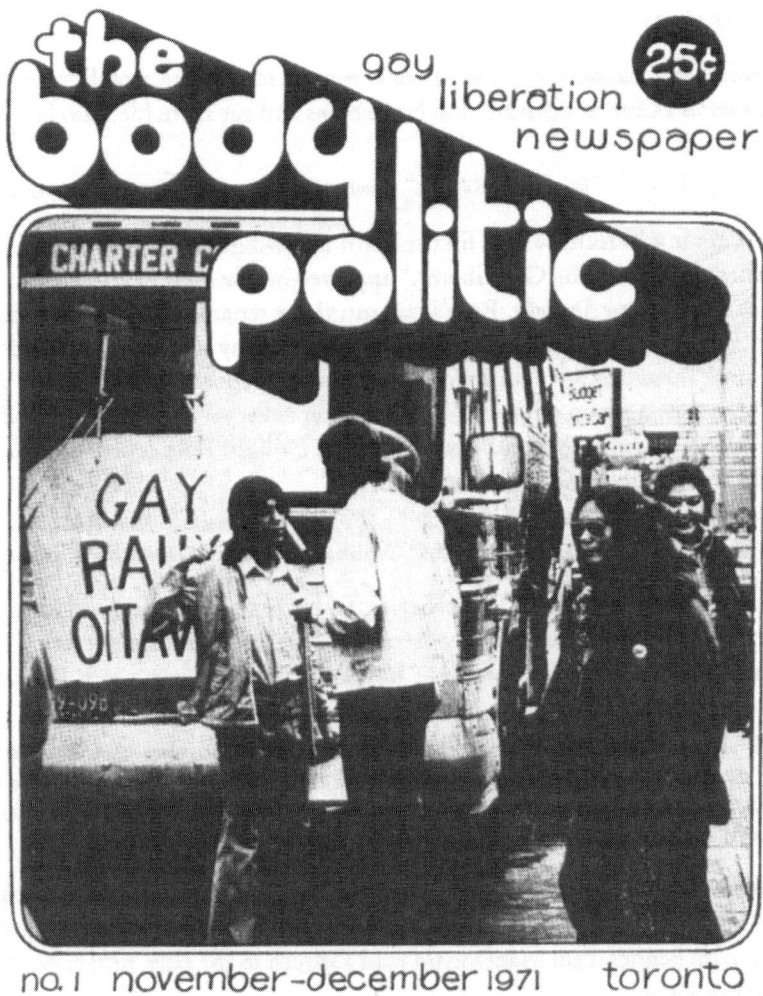

The first issue of *The Body Politic*, November–December 1971.

[Elizabeth Brady, "Voices from the Periphery: First-Generation Lesbian Fiction in Canada," *Resources for Feminist Research* 12 (March 1983): 22–26; A.P.H. (Alice P. Hackett), "Fiction: *Daughters of the Moon*," *Publishers' Weekly*, 13 September 1971, p. 67; Patricia Meyer Spacks, "A Chronicle of Women," *Hudson Review* 25 (Spring 1972): 163–65.]

November ∗ Saskatoon ∗ Initial plans were made for the establishment of the Gemini Club as a private club for lesbians and gay men. (See also January 1972.)

[Doug Hellquist, "President's Report," *Gemini Club News* 1 (13 November 1971): 1–2.]

November ∗ Toronto ∗ The first column by Twilight Rose (pseud. of John Forbes), entitled "The Gay Ghetto," appeared in *The Body Politic*. Reprinted from the *Georgia Straight*, Rose's column (later renamed "Twilight Trails") contained general commentary and gossip on the gay scene in both Vancouver and Toronto. One focus of the column was reports on activities of the Ephemerals, a group of gender-bending drag street revolutionaries founded in Vancouver by Forbes and Ron Whinton. Twilight Rose retired after issue eight of *The Body Politic* (Spring 1973).

[Gerald Hannon, "Who We Were, Who We Are: John Forbes," *Body Politic*, no. 80 (1982), p. 35; "John Forbes" vertical file, Canadian Lesbian and Gay Archives, Toronto.]

November ∗ Toronto ∗ Plans began to be made for the formation of the Women's Place, a drop-in centre and informal meeting place. The Women's Place officially opened in June 1972 at 31 Dupont Street. (See also June 1972.)

[Margaret Fulford, ed., *The Canadian Women's Movement, 1960–1990: A Guide to Archival Resources/Le mouvement canadien des femmes, 1960–1990: guide de ressources archivistiques* (Toronto: Canadian Women's Movement Archives/ECW Press, 1992), entry 566.]

November 6 ∗ Toronto ∗ Members of TGA marched in the Vietnam Mobilization Committee's Amchitka-Vietnam War demonstration under their own banner. Paul MacDonald read a speech to the rally, held at Nathan Phillips Square.

[Paul MacDonald, untitled speech, *Body Politic*, no. 2 (1972), p. 3.]

November 13 ∗ Montréal ∗ The FLH sponsored a party and dance to celebrate the opening of their centre at 2065, rue St. Denis.

["Nouvelles: Montréal," *Le tiers*, no. 2 (1972), p. 26.]

November 15–16 ∗ Waterloo, Ont. ∗ Dr. Franklin Kameny, president of the Washington, D.C., Mattachine Society, was the featured speaker at the "Forum on Homosexuality and Personal Liberation," held at the University of Waterloo on November 15. The next day Kameny visited with members of Waterloo GLM and spoke to a sociology class.

["Forum on Homosexuality and Personal Liberation," GLM *Newsletter* 1 (11 November 1971): 1–4.]

November 18 ∗ London, Ont. ∗ Dr. Franklin Kameny, president of the Washington, D.C., Mattachine Society, spoke on "Sexuality and Homosexuality" at the University of Western Ontario as part of a lecture series sponsored by UWOHA.

["Meeting Held!" UWOHA *Newsletter*, no. 14 (1971), p. 1.]

November 27–28 ∗ Waterloo, Ont. ∗ A conference of the Ontario Homophile Federation was held at the University of Waterloo, sponsored by Waterloo GLM. Its purpose was to improve communications amongst homophile and gay liberation groups in Ontario. Topics for discussion included direct action, publicity, and coming out.

["Joint Meeting of Ontario Homophile Associations," GLM *Newsletter* 1 (21 November 1971): 2–3; Sergei, untitled news item, YUHA *Newsletter*, November 1971, p. 1.]

November 29 ∗ Hamilton ∗ Chris Fox and Brian Waite of TGA presented a talk on gay liberation entitled "Out of the Closets, into the Streets," at Wentworth House, McMaster University. About thirty people attended the event, which was sponsored by the McMaster Women's Liberation Movement.

[Malcolm Gray, "Homosexuals — 'Out of the Closet,'" *Hamilton Spectator*, home ed., 30 November 1971, p. 7; Toronto Gay Action collection, 89–058, Canadian Lesbian and Gay Archives, Toronto.]

November 30 ∗ Toronto ∗ CBC-TV's *Tuesday Night* aired "Nothing to Hide," produced by Jeannine Locke, an hour-long examination of gay life filmed in New York in 1970. It was denounced in the House of Commons as "vulger and distasteful" by Robert Coates (PC-Cumberland-Colchester North) and as "just a fairy tale" by Prime Minister Pierre Trudeau. The film also met with criticism from the gay community. (See also December 9–10, 1971.)

["CBC: Put-Off or Nothing to Hide?: Nothing to Show," *Body Politic*, no. 2 (1972), pp. 1–3; Charles C. Hill, "Homosexuals Not Just Objects" ("Write On" column), *Varsity* (Univ. of Toronto), 8 December 1971, p. 4; "Homosexual Program 'Fairy Tale,' P.M. Says," *Toronto Star*, four star ed., 1 December 1971, p. 80; Blaik Kirby, "No Snickers in CBC's Serious Look at Homosexuality," *Globe and Mail*, metro ed., 1 December 1971, p. 14; Paul Pearce, "Laughing at a Minority Group" (letter), *Toronto Star*, four star ed., 9 December 1971, p. 7; Frank Penn, "Far, but Not Far Enough" (column), *Ottawa Citizen*, 1 December 1971, p. 41; Peter Ward, "Trudeau Quips over T.V. 'Fairy Tale' but Opposition Didn't Think It Funny," *Toronto Sun*, 1 December 1971, p. 2; Roger Wilkes, "CBC Film on Homophiles Is Inaccurate" (letter), *Excalibur*

(York Univ.), 13 December 1971, p. 6; Jim Wright, "'Fairy Tale' Remark Called Destructive" (letter), *Toronto Star*, four star ed., 9 December 1971, p. 7.]

December ★ Toronto ★ A group of lesbian members of CHAT, self-named The Cunts, delivered a written statement to the membership-at-large. They announced that they were starting an independent lesbian group and demanded that the CHAT membership (which was mostly male) confront its own sexism. This issue stemmed from male domination of official positions at CHAT. The Cunts demanded that CHAT adopt an amendment to its proposed constitution that would state "Dykes and faggots in CHAT shall share equally in decision making. This means equalization at *all* official decision making levels, i.e. in the proposed constitution; executive, vice-chair and chair." (See also March 7 and April 6, 1972.)

["Community Homophile Association of Toronto (CHAT)" vertical file, Canadian Lesbian and Gay Archives, Toronto; Peter Zorzi, *Queer Catharsis* (Toronto: The Author, 1992), p. 18.]

December ★ Toronto ★ The editorial "Accept Homosexuals; But Don't Approve Homosexual Acts" was published in the *United Church Observer*.

["Accept Homosexuals; But Don't Approve Homosexual Acts" (editorial), *United Church Observer*, December 1971, p. 11; "Church Magazine Speaks Out on Homosexuals," *Ottawa Citizen*, 27 November 1971, p. 47.]

December ★ Vancouver ★ The CGAA issued a press release denouncing attempts by left-wing groups, particularly the Young Socialist Alliance (YSA), to co-opt the gay movement. The release charged that the YSA "is not for Gay Rights, but is only interested in building up their membership and that of their many front groups."

["GAA Says 'Out Damn Trots,' " *Georgia Straight*, 16–23 December 1971, p. 15.]

December 9–10 ★ Toronto ★ On December 9, CBC radio's *As It Happens* included a discussion between Charles Hill of UTHA and Dr. Lawrence Hatterer concerning "Nothing to Hide." Hatterer, a psychiatrist and author of *Changing Homosexuality in the Male*, had been interviewed in the film. The next day, representatives of the gay community met with CBC officials concerning "Nothing to Hide." Later, fourteen people (mostly members of TGA) protested the "misleading and patronizing" film outside the CBC's offices on Jarvis Street.

[Richard (Zorniak), "Gays Zap & Rap with CBC: Hill Hits Sexist TV Program," *Guerilla* 2 (15 December 1971): 3.]

1972

—— ⋆ Don Mills, Ont. ⋆ Ronald Hambleton's *The Secret of Jalna* was
published by PaperJacks. It examined the connection between Mazo de la
Roche and her literary creation, *Whiteoaks of Jalna*, and was designed as a
tie-in with the popular CBC-TV series *The Whiteoaks of Jalna*. In the book,
Hambleton mentions the seventy-year-long relationship between De la
Roche and her adopted sister Caroline Clement, but is careful to avoid any
discussion of their sexual orientation.

[Morris Wolfe, "The Secrets of Mazo Remain Well Hidden," *Saturday Night*, May
1972, pp. 36–37; Douglas Marshall, "The Dread Canadian Whiteoaks Disease," *Books
in Canada* 1 (February 1972): 12–14; Ian Young, Letter, *Books in Canada* 1 (June 1972): 12.]

—— ⋆ Montréal ⋆ Michel Audy's film *Corps et âme/Body and Soul* was
released. Starring Jacques Pothier, Pierre Héroux, and Danièle Panneton, the
film depicted the close friendship between a young pianist and another man.
The pianist falls into a great depression when his friend is killed in an
accident.

[D.J. Turner and Micheline Morisset, eds., *Canadian Feature Film Index, 1913–
1985/Index des films canadiens de long métrage* (Ottawa: Public Archives, National Film,
Television, and Sound Archives, 1987), entry 354; Thomas Waugh, "Nègres blancs,
tapettes et 'butch': les lesbiennes et les gais dans le cinéma québécois," *Copie zéro*, no.
11 (1981), p. 24.]

—— ⋆ Montréal ⋆ Claude Beausoleil's book of poetry *Intrusion ralentie* was
published by Éditions du jour.

[Bernard Gilbert, "*Intrusion ralentie* et autre recueils de poésies et de textes en prose de
Claude Beausoleil," in *Dictionnaire des oeuvres littéraires du Québec*, ed. Maurice Lemire
et al., vol. 5 (1970–75) (Montréal: Fides, 1987), pp. 436–39.]

—— ⋆ Montréal ⋆ Marie-Claire Blais's novel *Le loup* was published by
Éditions du jour. The work details the life of Sebastien, a gay man who recalls
the abuse of a series of male lovers. An English translation (*The Wolf*) was
published in Toronto by McClelland and Stewart in 1974.

[Nicole Bourbonnais, "*Le loup*," in *Dictionnaire des oeuvres littéraires du Québec*, ed.
Maurice Lemire et al., vol. 5 (1970–75) (Montréal: Fides, 1987), pp. 505–06; Mary

Kandiuk, *French-Canadian Authors: A Bibliography of Their Works and of English-Language Criticism* (Metuchen, N.J.: Scarecrow Press, 1990), pp. 26, 37.]

—— * Montréal * La Fraternité du même sexe, a gay male dating service, was formed.

["Pourquoi la Fraternité du même sexe connaît — elle chez nous un succès grandissant?" *Bisexus* 2, no. 22 (1972): 10.]

—— * Montréal * Denis Vanier's book of poetry *Lesbiennes d'acid* was published by Parti pris.

[Jean-Yves Fréchette, "*Lesbiennes d'acid* et *Le clitoris de la fée des étoiles*," in *Dictionnaire des oeuvres littéraires du Québec*, ed. Maurice Lemire et al., vol. 5 (1970–75) (Montréal: Fides, 1987), pp. 492–95.]

—— * Richmond Hill, Ont. * Leo Orenstein's novel *The Queers of New York* was published by Pocket Books.

[Ian Young, *The Male Homosexual in Literature: A Bibliography*, second ed. (Metuchen, N.J.: Scarecrow Press, 1982), entry 2922.]

—— * Scarborough, Ont. * Graham Jackson's book of short fiction *The Apothecary Jar* was published by Catalyst Press.

[Ian Young, *The Male Homosexual in Literature: A Bibliography*, second ed. (Metuchen, N.J.: Scarecrow Press, 1982), entry 1992.]

—— * Scarborough, Ont. * Ian Young's book of poetry *Some Green Moths* was published by Catalyst Press.

[(Ian Young), *Ian Young: A Bibliography 1962–1980*, Canadian Gay Archives Publication no. 3 (Toronto: Pink Triangle Press, 1981), entries A8, E27, E38.]

—— * Toronto * Several municipal politicians and business interests began to advance proposals to rid the Yonge Street strip of sex trade workers, massage parlours, and visible homosexuals.

[Trent Frayne, "No Crombie Crackdown on Yonge St.," *Toronto Star*, Saturday ed., 13 January 1973, pp. 1, 4; Warren Gerard, "The Strip Has a Pastime to Suit Every Preference," *Globe and Mail*, metro ed., 13 July 1971, p. 27; Gary Kinsman, *The Regulation of Desire: Sexuality in Canada* (Montréal: Black Rose Books, 1987), p. 204.]

—— * Toronto * David Dawson's book of poetry *Ceremonial* was published by Coach House Press.

[Linda Rogers, "Medium or Magician," *Canadian Literature*, no. 62 (1974), pp. 123–24.]

—— * Toronto * Marion Foster's and Kent Murray's (pseuds.) *A Not So Gay World: Homosexuality in Canada*, the first non-fiction book-length study of homosexuality in Canada, was published by McClelland and Stewart. The book received mixed reviews and was seen to be out-of-date and full of factual errors.

[Frank Abbott, "Narrow View Mars Book on Gays," *Varsity* (Univ. of Toronto), 26 January 1973, pp. 14, 15; Kay Alsop, "Gay Doesn't Mean Happy," *Vancouver Province*, 26 October 1972, p. 48; Richard Bébout, "*A Not So Gay World*," *Canadian Reader* 14 (February 1973): 10–11; Chris, "Review," *Zodiac Friendship Society News* 2 (January 1973): 3; Dick Held and Mike Hunt (pseuds.), "*A Not So Gay World*," *Canadian Dimension* 10 (April 1974): 58–59; Ed Jackson, "Canadian Content?" *Body Politic*, no. 7 (1973), p. 7 (reprinted, "Gang Aft A-gay," *Books in Canada* 1 [November–December 1972]: 18); E.W. (Erv Warner), "Book Review," *Zodiac Friendship Society News* 1 (December 1972): 2.]

—— * Toronto * Rebecca Sisler's biography of Canadian sculptors Frances Loring and Florence Wyle, *The Girls*, was published by Clarke, Irwin. For more than fifty years Loring (1887–1968) and Wyle (1881–1968) shared their studio quarters and lives. Although Sisler recognized their life-long, same-sex support structure, she concluded that they were not lesbians.

[Ingrid MacDonald, "Frances Loring and Florence Wyle, Sculptors," *Broadside*, November 1987, pp. 8–9; Frances Rooney, "Loring and Wyle, Sculptors," *Pink Ink* 1 (July 1983): 18–20.]

January * Saskatoon * The Zodiac Friendship Society was officially formed and registered with the provincial government as a non-profit organization. The Society operated the Gemini Club, a weekly dance club, and a drop-in at the Unitarian Centre, 502 Main Street. It soon became an umbrella group for gay social and political activities in Saskatoon. (See also February 11, 1972.)

[Ed Jackson, "Saskatoon Gay Action: Progress in a Prairie City," *Body Politic*, no. 10 (1973), p. 23; "News of the Gay: Saskatoon," *Body Politic*, no. 5 (1972), p. 16; Neil Richards papers and inventory, S-A821, Saskatchewan Archives Board, Saskatoon.]

January * Toronto * *Exclusive Male* began publication. Edited and published by Derek Garlen Travis, *Exclusive Male* was a monthly, general interest magazine aimed at gay men. It ceased publication in October 1972, after ten issues.

[Alan V. Miller, *Our Own Voices: A Directory of Lesbian and Gay Periodicals, 1890–1990, Including the Complete Holdings of the Canadian Gay Archives*, Canadian Gay Archives Publication no. 12 (Toronto: CGA, 1991), p. 168.]

January * Vancouver * A gay women's drop-in was being held at the Vancouver Women's Centre, 511 Carrall Street, by January 7.

["January 1972 Calendar," *Pedestal* 4 (January 1972): 16.]

January 20, 22 * Toronto * Members of TGA handed out leaflets in front of the Parkside Tavern, 530 Yonge Street, one of the city's major gay taverns. TGA was protesting the entrapment of gays in the tavern's downstairs washroom by plainclothes members of Toronto's morality squad. Management of the tavern had allowed the policemen to hide in an adjacent room to peer through holes in the air vents to wait to arrest people for performing sexual acts in public. At least ten people were arrested in the Parkside's downstairs washroom in January 1972. On January 27, during a meeting between Norman Bolter, owner of the Parkside, and George Hislop of CHAT, it was agreed that the police trap would be closed. Hislop later met with Deputy Chief Jack Ackroyd to discuss the ongoing entrapment and arrest of gay men in local parks and subway washrooms. (See also February 4, 1972.)

[" The Parkside Passion Play," *Back Chat Newsletter*, February 1972, pp. 1–3; "The Parkside Passion Play Continued," *Back Chat Newsletter*, March 1972, pp. 4–5; Dave Scott, "Police and Homosexuals Co-operate to Stop Offences in Parks, Subways," *Toronto Star*, four star ed., 6 April 1972, p. 27; "20 'T-Room' Arrests Hit in Toronto," *Advocate* (Los Angeles), no. 80 (1972), p. 10; "UTHA," *Guerilla* 1 (27 November 1970): 5; Pete (Peter Zorzi), "Can Two Morality Dicks Find True Love Behind an Air Vent?" *Guerilla* 2 (2 February 1972): 18–19; (Peter Zorzi), "Piss on Police at Parkside: Gays Unite," *Guerilla* 2 (26 January 1972): 4–5.]

January 21 * Toronto * A dance sponsored by CHAT was picketed by students of a Bible college.

["Fame at Last," *Back Chat Newsletter*, February 1972, p. 4.]

January 22 * Regina * During a private party at the home of Donald J. Murdoch, ten people volunteered to investigate whether it would be worthwhile to organize a formal society to act as a social centre for lesbians and gays in Regina. (See also February 13, 1972.)

[Darrel David Hockley, "A History of the Gay Community of Regina," unpublished typescript, 1993, 93–050, Canadian Lesbian and Gay Archives, Toronto, p. 8.]

January 26 * Charlottetown, P.E.I. * The first Canadian case in which "engagement in a homosexual act" was used as grounds for divorce was heard by Mr. Justice Nicholson of the Prince Edward Island Supreme Court. In the case of M. vs. M., the husband was successful in suing his wife for divorce based on her lesbianism.

[24 *Dominion Law Reports* (3d): 114–26; Chris MacNaughton, "Who Gets the Kids?: Usually Not Lesbian Mothers, at Least Not in the Courts as They Are Being Conducted Today," *Body Politic*, no. 34 (1977), pp. 12–13.]

January 28–29 * Downsview, Ont. * YUHA sponsored the Ontario Homophile Federation conference "Sexuality and Civil Rights" at York University. Forty people (mostly from Ontario and Québec) gathered to discuss strategies for gay liberation. The speakers included Jack Baker and Mike

McConnell of Minneapolis, Minnesota, who talked on same-sex marriages. Baker, a third-year law student, was president of the University of Minnesota Student Association. McConnell, his lover, had been dismissed from his position as a librarian at the University of Minnesota when his homosexuality became known. At that time, they were engaged in a lengthy legal battle for state recognition of their marriage.

[Lars Bjornsen, "Jack, Mike Lose on Job, Marriage," *Advocate* (Los Angeles), no. 72 (1971), pp. 1, 8, 30; "Canada Groups Attend Meet," *Advocate* (Los Angeles), no. 80 (1972), p. 3; Brian Waite, "Strategy for Gay Liberation," *Body Politic*, no. 3 (1972), pp. 4, 19; John Wilson, "Gays Fight Repressive Laws," *Labor Challenge*, 14 February 1972, p. 7; John Wilson, "York Conference," *Body Politic*, no. 3 (1972), p. 8; "The York Conference," *Back Chat Newsletter*, February 1972, p. 3; "York University Homophile Association (YUHA)" vertical file, Canadian Lesbian and Gay Archives, Toronto.]

February ✴ Toronto ✴ CHAT's new community centre officially opened at 58 Cecil Street. The large site, a former synagogue, allowed space for offices as well as dances.

[George Hislop, "For Sale or Rent," *Back Chat* new series 1 (May 1972): 4–5; Pete (Peter Zorzi), "Gay Community Centre," *Guerilla* 2 (19 January 1972): 5.]

February ✴ Toronto ✴ About twenty women of diverse interests and backgrounds — from radical feminists to lesbians to Marxists — attended the first organizational meeting for *The Other Woman* newspaper, held at the *Guerilla* offices. (See also March 11, 1972.)

["Co-ops" (advertisement), *Guerilla* 2 (8 December 1971): 18; "A Herstory: Living with *The Other Woman*," *Other Woman* 3 (Winter 1975): 14–15.]

February ✴ Vancouver ✴ Members of the CGAA protested against two apartment developments from which gays had been illegally evicted.

["News of the Gay," *Body Politic*, no. 3 (1972), p. 9.]

February ✴ Winnipeg ✴ The first gay movement organization in Manitoba, Gays for Equality (GFE), was officially founded by Phil Graham, a student at the University of Manitoba, who had previously been involved with FREE: Gay Liberation of Minnesota at the University of Minnesota. The Manitoba group was known as the Campus Gay Club until early 1973, when it changed its name to reflect an increasingly political stance. By 1973, GFE offered drop-ins, counselling, a speaker's bureau, lectures, political actions, a library, a gayline, and dances.

[Greg Bourgeois and Bob Wallace, "A More Aggressive Stance: Gays in Manitoba," *Body Politic*, no. 9 (1973), pp. 17, 22; Margaret Fulford, ed., *The Canadian Women's Movement, 1960–1990: A Guide to Archival Resources/Le mouvement canadien des femmes, 1960–1990: guide de ressources archivistiques* (Toronto: Canadian Women's Movement Archives/ECW Press, 1992), entry 299; Gays for Equality (GFE) papers (83–024) and vertical file, Canadian Lesbian and Gay Archives, Toronto; George, "Am I an Uncle Tom?" *What's Happening!* 3 (March 1974): 8–9; Bill Lewis and Phil Graham, "A Note by Gays for Equality," *What's Happening!* 2 (April 1973): 5–6; "Prairie Lib a Long, Slow Process," *Advocate* (Los Angeles), no. 133 (1974), p. 14; Susan White, "Struggling On: Winnipeg's Gay Liberation Movement: 2 Years After," *Manitoban* (Univ. of Manitoba), 4 February 1974, p. 7.]

February 4 * Toronto * George Hislop, director of CHAT, was interviewed on CBC radio's *As It Happens* on the topic "Spying on the Public." He discussed recent police entrapment of gay men in the downstairs washroom of the Parkside Tavern.

["Communications," *Back Chat Newsletter*, February 1972, p. 4.]

February 11 * Saskatoon * A Valentine's Day dance was held at the Unitarian Centre, 502 Main Street, as the first public function of the Gemini Club, run by the Zodiac Friendship Society. Membership in the club was still sparse; as of February 1972 the Gemini Club had only fifteen paid members.

[Doug Hellquist, "President's Report," *Gemini News* 1 (February 1972): 1–2.]

February 12 * Ottawa * Peter Maloney, who ran as the Liberal party candidate opposite Ontario Attorney-General Allan Lawrence in the October 1971 Ontario provincial election, announced that he was gay during a policy seminar at the annual Liberal Party convention. Maloney made the announcement during a confrontation with Otto Lang, Canada's new Attorney-General and formerly Minister of Manpower and Immigration. Maloney protested the discrimination against gays posed by the Canadian Immigration Act.

[N. John Adams, "Maloney Tells Liberals of His Homosexuality," *Globe and Mail*, metro ed., 14 February 1972, p. 10; Anthony L. Côté, "Liberals Hear Gay Maloney," *Ryersonian* (Ryerson Polytechnic Institute, Toronto), 15 February 1972, p. 1; Peter Maloney, "Maloney: Coming Out in Politics," *Body Politic*, no. 3 (1972), pp. 7–8; Alexander Ross, "Peter Maloney Publicly Defies Homosexual Myth," *Toronto Star*, four star ed., 25 February 1972, p. 25; J.C. Shepherd, "A New Kind of Politician: Gay, Proud: Toronto's Peter Maloney," *Advocate* (Los Angeles), no. 96 (1972), p. 6; Helen Worthington, "Discrimination Is Very Subtle, Homosexual Says," *Toronto Star*, four star ed., 26 November 1975, p. F3.]

February 13 * Hamilton * Jearld Moldenhauer of *The Body Politic* addressed a session of the New Democratic Party Waffle convention. This was the first time a gay liberation representative had formally addressed a political party conference in Canada.

[Jearld Moldenhauer, "Waffle," *Body Politic*, no. 3 (1972), p. 15.]

February 13 * Regina * The first formal general meeting of the Atropos

Friendship Society was held at the home of Donald J. Murdoch, the group's first president. The Odyssey Club was chosen to be the name of the society's proposed social centre, which started operating on Saturday nights in September 1972. The Atropos Friendship Society was the first lesbian/gay group in Regina.

["Atropos Friendship Society" vertical file, Canadian Lesbian and Gay Archives, Toronto; Darrel David Hockley, "A History of the Gay Community of Regina," unpublished typescript, 1993, 93–050, Canadian Lesbian and Gay Archives, Toronto, pp. 8–9.]

February 26 ✱ Montréal ✱ Singer and journalist Michel Girouard and pianist Réjean Tremblay signed business partnership and personal union contracts in Canada's first widely publicized gay marriage ceremony, held at a downtown discotheque. The couple was married by the Rev. Boniface Grosveld of the Congregation of the Beloved Disciple, Old Catholic. Girouard and Tremblay also travelled to Los Angeles, where their marriage vows were solemnized on March 17, 1972, at the Metropolitan Community Church (MCC) by Rev. Troy Perry.

[Rob Cole, "A Marriage for Liberation," *Advocate* (Los Angeles), no. 83 (1972), pp. 1–3, 34; Rob Cole, " 'Of Course They're Seeking Publicity, but That's Part of Their Way of Life,' " *Advocate* (Los Angeles), no. 83 (1972), p. 3; Eric Devlin, "Michel Girouard: 'Oui, mon mariage a changé quelque chose au Québec" (interview), *Gay Montréal* 1 (7 September 1976): 4–5; Eric Devlin, "Réjean Tremblay: 'J'ai été dépassé par les événements': commentant son mariage avec Michel Girouard" (interview), *Gay Montréal* 1 (19 October 1976): 18–19; "Homosexual Pair Become Partners in Public, Private," *Globe and Mail*, metro ed., 28 February 1972, p. 9; "MCC Coming to Canada, Perry Says in Montreal," *Advocate* (Los Angeles), no. 83 (1972), p. 34; "Le mariage!" *Open Doors* 2 (May 1972): 1–2; "Le 'mariage' Michel Girouard/Réjean Tremblay," *Document flash* 2 (1972): 32 pp.; "Michel Girouard et son ami à la défense des 200,000 homosexuels québécois," *Nouvelles Illustrées* 19 (12 February 1972): 1–4; "Michel: toujours 'star' 15 ans après le scandale," *Sortie*, no. 50 (1987), p. 9; "News of the Gay: Montreal," *Body Politic*, no. 3 (1972), p. 9; "Talk about Gay Weddings . . .: A Legal First in Canada?" *Advocate* (Los Angeles), no. 82 (1972), pp. 1, 15.]

March 1 ✱ Toronto ✱ CHAT was awarded a grant of $14,602 under Canada Manpower's Local Initiatives Program. The money was used to operate CHAT's twenty-four-hour information and counselling telephone service.

["CHAT Grant 'A Step Forward,' " *Globe and Mail*, metro ed., 2 March 1972, p. 37; "Friendly CHAT" (editorial), *Toronto Sun*, 15 June 1972, p. 8; "Government Support," *Back Chat Newsletter*, March 1972, p. 2; "Homosexuals Get Grant from Ottawa for Clinic," *Toronto Star*, four star ed., 2 March 1972, p. 75; "News of the Gay," *Body Politic*, no. 3 (1972), p. 9.]

March 2 ✱ Victoria, B.C. ✱ George Mussallem (SC-Dewdney) rose in the Provincial Legislature and urged British Columbia Minister of Education

Donald Brothers to review the place of sex education in the province's secondary schools. He believed that sex education was "ridiculous non-sense," and that education about gay liberation had no place in the school system. Mussallem was outraged after learning that New Westminster Secondary School had allowed on-site appointments between students and an unnamed "representative of the (gay) liberation movement."

[Iain Hunter, "Gay Liberation Rally in School Shocks Socred MLA: 'We're Spending Too Much, Children Learning Too Much,'" *Vancouver Sun*, four star ed., 3 March 1972, p. 12.]

March 5 * Montréal * The first general assembly of members of FLH was held at the University Settlement. The members adopted a charter and elected a new three-person executive committee: Gilbert Ouellet (president), André Paradis (secretary), and Pierre Masson (treasurer).

[Gilles Garneau, "Les militants de la première heure: il y a dix ans naissait le FLH," *Le berdache*, no. 20 (1981), pp. 44–45.]

March 7 * Toronto * The membership of CHAT elected its first board of directors. Since its inception, CHAT had been directed by a steering commit-tee, and later an interim board. The new board consisted of George Hislop (president), Pat Murphy (vice-president), Clive Bell (treasurer), Kathleen Brindley (secretary), and six general members. Of the ten board members, five were female.

["Meetings," *Back Chat* new series 1 (4 April 1972): 7.]

March 9 * Kingston, Ont. * CHAT members Kathleen Brindley, George Hislop, and Herb Spiers held a forum on homosexuality before second-year medical students at Queen's University.

[Kathleen Brindley, "From a Discussion on Homosexuality to 2nd Year Med Students, Queen's U.," *Back Chat* new series 1 (4 April 1972): 5.]

March 11 * Toronto * Nine women (most of whom were lesbians) attempted to take over the offices of the leftist underground newspaper *Guerilla* for a few days in order to raise publicity for women's liberation and International Women's Day and to use the newspaper's equipment to publish the first issue of *The Other Woman*. When the male members of the *Guerilla* staff were barred entry, they called the police. (See also May 1972.)

[Judy Girard, Letter, *Guerilla* 2 (7 June 1972): 2; "*Guerilla* Tells All" (editorial), *Guerilla* 2 (7 June 1972): 2; "*Guerilla* Theatre," *Other Woman* 1 (May–June 1972): 13; "A Herstory: Living with *The Other Woman*," *Other Woman* 3 (Winter 1975): 14–15; Becki L. Ross, *The House That Jill Built: A Lesbian Nation in Formation* (Toronto: University of Toronto Press, 1995), p. 38; Peter B. Wheatley, Letter, *Guerilla* 2 (7 June 1972): 2.]

March 20 ✷ Montréal ✷ Rev. Troy Perry, founder of the Universal Fellowship of Metropolitan Community Churches (MCC), announced at a press conference that he expected that MCC would be operating in Canada within nine months. (See also June 11, 1972.)

["MCC Coming to Canada, Perry Says in Montreal," *Advocate* (Los Angeles), no. 83 (1972), p. 34.]

Spring ✷ Toronto ✷ Gay Youth Toronto, a social and support group for people under twenty-one years of age, was formed. The group's early organizers included John Powers and John Sullivan. By April they were meeting every Sunday at New College, 40 Willcocks Street, but soon moved to the CHAT Centre.

["Gay Youth," *Back Chat* new series 1 (4 April 1972): 6; "Gay Youth Organizing: Toronto," *Body Politic*, no. 3 (1972), p. 3; "Gay Youth Toronto" vertical file, Canadian Lesbian and Gay Archives, Toronto.]

Spring ✷ Toronto ✷ Plans were made to incorporate the Ontario Alternate Distribution Company to distribute *The Body Politic, Community Schools*, and the *Toronto Citizen*.

[J. Moldenhauer, "News of the Gay," *Body Politic*, no. 3 (1972), p. 9.]

April ✷ Montréal ✷ The Iron Cross M.C. (Motor Club), a gay leather and denim fraternity, was formed.

[Jungle J., "Anniversary of the Iron Cross M.C. — Montreal — April 1973," *Phalia*, no. 18 (1973), pp. 5–6.]

April ✷ Vancouver ✷ The CGAA discovered that some of its outgoing mail had been opened by the Department of National Revenue. Earlier, the CGAA's telephone had been tapped.

["Gay Privacy Invaded," *Open Doors* 2 (May 1972): 7.]

April 6 ✷ Toronto ✷ The first meeting of a Women's Committee was held at CHAT. The eight women present decided that it would be most practical for them to integrate with the other existing committees within CHAT, and the Women's Committee was disbanded.

["Fast Finish," *Back Chat* new series 1 (May 1972): 7; Becki L. Ross, *The House That Jill Built: A Lesbian Nation in Formation* (Toronto: University of Toronto Press, 1995), p. 34.]

April 15 ✷ Ottawa ✷ A contingent of forty gay men and lesbians joined the Vietnam Mobilization Committee demonstration protesting a visit to Canada by American president Richard Nixon. Brian Waite, representing TGA and Gays against the War, made a speech to the demonstrators.

[Brian Waite, " 'Out Now': The Gay Contingent," *Body Politic*, no. 4 (1972), p. 23; Brian Waite, "*Star* Distorted Protest of Gays against the War" (letter), *Toronto Star*, four star ed., 20 April 1972, p. 7.]

May * Québec, Qué. * The idea for establishing a homophile organization in Québec City was first put forward by Patrick Cellier and Father Paul Ouellet, leading to the establishment a year later (May 1973) of the Centre humanitaire d'aide et de libération (CHAL) as a social, service, and organizing centre for gay men and lesbians. Other early members and organizers of CHAL included Claude Bernard, Pierre Falardeau, and Denise Goyette (founder of Tel-Aide). In the early days CHAL held a gay discussion group with a group of heterosexuals at Ouellet's church, Saint-Roch. On June 8, 1973, CHAL was incorporated, and on September 12, 1973, CHAL's centre officially opened in the basement of a Franciscan church at 264, rue des Franciscains. By December 1973, CHAL had 106 registered members. (See also October 6–7, 1973.)

["CHAL Receives Charter," *Body Politic*, no. 9 (1973), p. 6; "Centre humanitaire d'aide et de libération (CHAL)" vertical file, Canadian Lesbian and Gay Archives, Toronto; Ron Dayman, "Quebec: Five Years of the Movement,"*Body Politic*, no. 29 (1976–77), pp. 20–21; "Denise Goyette: ouvrière de la libération gay," *Gay Montréal* 1 (2 November 1976): 4; Gilles Garneau, "Le CHAL au service des québécois depuis 17 [sic] ans," *Le berdache*, no. 3 (1979), p. 20; Lise Guay, "D'hier à demain" (editorial), *Le chaînon* 2 (February 1974): 1–2; Pierre Nadeau, "CHAL" (editorial), *Le chaînon* 1 (December 1973): 1; Paul Ouellet, "Une expérience avec des chrétiens gais," *Le berdache*, no. 4 (1979), p. 32; Don Quichotte, "L'histoire du CHAL: Centre homophile d'aide et de libération," *Gay Montréal* 1 (14 December 1976): 42; "La vraie nature de Denise Goyette" (interview), *Gay Montréal* 1 (25 January 1977): 18, 26.]

May * Toronto * CHAT published the twenty-page "A Selected Bibliography Concerning Male and Female Homosexuality, Consisting of Gay Liberation, Sociological, Psychological and Literary Works," compiled by Chris Fox, Charles Hill, Cil Pinkett, and Ian Young.

[Monograph collection, M95–053, Canadian Lesbian and Gay Archives, Toronto.]

May * Toronto * Two thousand copies of the first issue of *The Other Woman* (May–June 1972) appeared. Produced with the cooperation of the feminist newspapers *Bellyful* and *Velvet Fist*, the new paper contained some material written from a lesbian-feminist viewpoint. It was published until 1977.

["A Herstory: Living with *The Other Woman*," *Other Woman* 3 (Winter 1975): 14–15.]

May * Vancouver * Project Open Doors, many of whose members belonged to the CGAA, received an Opportunities for Youth grant for $9,329 to study social services for gays in the greater Vancouver area. Project Open Doors existed from May 29 to September 15 and produced the eighty-two-page

Open Doors: A Manual on the Prejudice and Discrimination against Gay People,
by John Greenfield, Dick Rulens, and Dieter Grapp. Other participants in
the project included Cathy Nittolo and Debie Zazubeck. During the course
of the project, several Vancouver radio personalities and columnists attacked
Project Open Doors. Jack Webster of CJOR, for example, described *Open
Doors* as a project "to provide a bilingual handbook for French Canadian
queers in Vancouver."

["$9,329 to Gay Research," *Open Doors* 2 (June 1972): 1, 5 (reprinted in *Gay Canadian*
1 [7 September 1972]: 5, 6); "OFY Grant," *Body Politic*, no. 5 (1972), p. 18; "*Open Doors*,"
Open Doors 2 (December 1972): 15; Q.Q., "Page 69" (column), *Georgia Straight*, 15–22
June 1972, p. 13.]

May 2 ∗ Toronto ∗ CHAT persuaded the co-owners of Momma Cooper's club
(above the Parkside Tavern) to sign a document declaring that they would
no longer practise discrimination against lesbians on the basis of appearance,
dress, or admission prices.

[Ed Jackson, "Spring Cleaning at 'Momma Cooper's,' " *Body Politic*, no. 4 (1972), p. 5;
"Murray, Golda, & David," *Back Chat* new series 1 (June 1972): 6–7.]

May 4 ∗ Toronto ∗ A community forum entitled "Homosexuality: Myth and
Reality," held at the St. Lawrence Centre Town Hall, was disrupted when
two members of the right-wing group Western Guard (formerly the Edmund
Burke Society) sprayed the crowd of 450 people with tear gas. The meeting
was sponsored by CHAT. The two members of the Western Guard were later
found guilty of spraying a volatile substance and were sentenced to sixty days
in jail. The same evening, someone attempted to firebomb a house next door
to CHAT's Community Centre on Cecil Street. The intended target was
probably the CHAT centre. Indeed, the next night someone threw a Molotov
cocktail through a window into the Centre; the resulting fire was quickly
extinguished.

["Fascists Gas Gays," *Body Politic*, no. 4 (1972), p. 4; Donald Grant, "Bomb Thrown
at Teacher's Home Shatters on Ground and Burns," *Globe and Mail*, metro ed., 5 May
1972, p. 4; J. Proos, "Western Guard Smashes Homosexual Propaganda Show," *Straight
Talk!* (Western Guard, Toronto) 4 (May–June 1972): 4–5; Becki L. Ross, *The House
That Jill Built: A Lesbian Nation in Formation* (Toronto: University of Toronto Press,
1995), p. 34; "Tear Gas Spray Disrupts Meeting on Homosexuality," *Toronto Star*, four
star ed., 5 May 1972, p. 27; "Western Guard in Jail," *Body Politic*, no. 6 (1972), p. 11.]

May 10 ∗ Ottawa ∗ Bill C-206, which would have amended the Canada
Labour Code and the Public Services Act concerning discrimination based
on age, sex, and marital status, received first reading in the House of
Commons. The Bill's amendments were intended to reinforce the Canada
Fair Employment Act (1953) and would affect the federal public service and

industries under federal jurisdiction. The amendments, however, did not specifically add sexual orientation as an area of prohibited discrimination. The Bill was not passed before the House adjourned on July 7, 1972.

[Gaston Charpentier, "Bill C-206 Is Dead," GO *Info*, no. 2–3 (1972): 6; Dennis Foley, "Govt. Tightens Guard against Employee Discrimination," *Ottawa Citizen*, 11 May 1972, p. 13; "Will 'Bill C-206' Help End Employment Discrimination?" GO *Info*, no. 1 (1972), p. 6.]

May 18 ✳ Toronto ✳ Australian gay activist Dennis Altman, author of *Homosexual: Oppression and Liberation*, was the guest speaker at a public forum organized by *The Body Politic*. One hundred fifty people attended the event, held at the CHAT centre.

["Altman Visits Toronto," *Body Politic*, no. 5 (1972), p. 18.]

May 19 ✳ Ottawa ✳ Representatives of groups from Vancouver, Ontario, Montréal, Québec City, and Halifax met to discuss strategies for gay liberation. During the meeting it was proposed that an official pan-Canadian conference of gay organizations be held; the first such gathering was eventually held in Québec City, October 6–7, 1973. (See also October 6–7, 1973.)

[Merv Walker, " 'Many Faces, One Focus': 4th Annual Conference Planned for Toronto," *Body Politic*, no. 26 (1976), p. 6.]

May 20, 27 ✳ Vancouver ✳ Members of GATE (Vancouver) boycotted and picketed the newly renovated Castle Hotel pub after an attempt was made by the management to exclude "obviously gay" men from the premises. The pub had hosted a large gay clientele for twenty years but had shown insensitivity to its gay patrons. During 1971, members of GLF had demonstrated outside the pub and had confronted the owner-manager but were unsuccessful. During the GATE picket, one local taxi company refused to pick up fares at the hotel in a show of solidarity with the demonstrators. The protest was opposed by Dick Rulens and members of the CGAA, who crossed the picket line.

["Cab Drivers Honour Homosexual Picket in Vancouver," *Zodiac Friendship Society/Gemini Club Newsletter* 1 (June 1972): 3; "Castle Pub: 'Incredible Lack of Sensitivity,' " *Georgia Straight*, 2–6 July 1971, p. 2; "GATE Calls for Gay Boycott of Castle Hotel" ("The Gateway" column), *Georgia Straight*, 27 April–4 May 1972, p. 10; "Gays to Picket Castle Hotel" ("The Gateway" column), *Georgia Straight*, 18–25 May 1972, p. 9; "Government Anti-gay?" *Georgia Straight*, 10–17 August 1972, p. 4; Garry Ker, "Castle Anti-gay" (letter), *Georgia Straight*, 27 April–4 May 1972, p. 7; Jearld Moldenhauer and Bob Wallace, "History: Toronto & Vancouver," *Gay* (supplement to *McGill Daily*), 24 November 1972, pp. 3, 6; "News of the Gay: Vancouver," *Body Politic*, no. 5 (1972), p. 16; "Partial Pregnancy" (letter), *Georgia Straight*, 18–25 May 1972, p. 8; "Partial Victory at the Castle Pub" ("The Gateway" column), *Georgia Straight*, 11–18 May 1972, p. 15; Photo, *Gay Canadian* 1 (7 September 1972): 3; "Total Win Possible in Castle

Dick Rulens, chairman of the Canadian Gay
Activists Alliance (CGAA), Vancouver.

Maurice Flood, chairman of the Gay Alliance toward Equality (GATE)
(Vancouver), with his successor to the position, Stephen Sherriffs.

Boycott" ("The Gateway" column), *Georgia Straight*, 8–15 June 1972, p. 17; Untitled article with photo, *Georgia Straight*, 25 May–1 June 1972, p. 4.]

May 23 ⋆ Toronto ⋆ CHAT and the Association for Canadian Transsexuals (ACT) sponsored a forum on transsexuality, held at the CHAT centre. Between 100–150 people attended.

["How about You?" *Back Chat* new series 1 (June 1972): 1, 12.]

June ⋆ Toronto ⋆ The Women's Place officially opened at 31 Dupont Street. It was a feminist organizing drop-in centre whose activities and groups included liberation workshops, rap sessions, consciousness-raising groups, speaking engagements, a library, and lesbian drop-ins. The Women's Place was administered by the Women's Information Centre of Toronto. It disbanded about 1975.

[Margaret Fulford, ed., *The Canadian Women's Movement, 1960–1990: A Guide to Archival Resources/Le mouvement canadien des femmes, 1960–1990: guide de ressources archivistiques* (Toronto: Canadian Women's Movement Archives/ECW Press, 1992), entry 566; Becki L. Ross, *The House That Jill Built: A Lesbian Nation in Formation* (Toronto: University of Toronto Press, 1995), pp. 44–45.]

June 4 ⋆ Halifax ⋆ Following several informal meetings beginning in March 1972, the Gay Alliance for Equality (GAE) was officially formed. Early organizers of the group included Nils Clausson and Anne Fulton. In the first few months of its existence, GAE formed an executive and established GAELine, a telephone counselling service. Meetings were held at the Unitarian Universalist Church, 5500 Inglis Street, every second Wednesday, and later at the Green Lantern Building, 1585 Barrington Street, Suite 207. GAE operated a drop-in centre (Thee Klub) for a few months in 1973. GAE's office closed in June 1974 and the group ceased formal operation in December 1974. GAE reorganized and was in operation again by October 1975.

[Margaret Fulford, ed., *The Canadian Women's Movement, 1960–1990: A Guide to Archival Resources/Le mouvement canadien des femmes, 1960–1990: guide de ressources archivistiques* (Toronto: Canadian Women's Movement Archives/ECW Press, 1992), entry 664; Gay Alliance for Equality (GAE) papers, 84–018, Canadian Lesbian and Gay Archives, Toronto; Marci Landry-Milton, "GAE Gives 'Liberation through Pride: Gay Lib Comes to Halifax,'" *Dalhousie Gazette* (Dalhousie Univ.), 2 February 1973, p. 3; John L. Marr, "From the Armchair of the Public Relations Officer" (letter), GAE *Monitor Newsletter*, January 1974, p. 3.]

June 7 ⋆ Burnaby, B.C. ⋆ CGAA members Tom Durrie and Dick Rulens spoke on homosexuality before 150 students of kinesiology during a "Contemporary Health Issues" program sponsored by Simon Fraser University.

["CGAA at Simon Fraser," *Open Doors* 2 (June 1972): 2.]

June 11 * Vancouver * Thirty people attended the first religious service for gays held in Vancouver. The service was led by Rev. Bob Sirico, a local missionary for the Metropolitan Community Church (MCC).

["God's Gay Liberation," *Open Doors* 2 (June 1972): 3 (reprinted, Canadian Gay Activists Alliance, "Gay Unity: God's Gay Liberation," *Exclusive Male*, September 1972, p. 10; and "God's Gay Liberation," *Gay Canadian* 1 [7 September 1972]: 3).]

June 17 * Ottawa * GO sponsored Ottawa's first public gay dance, held at Pestalozzi College. Over 100 people attended the event. The GO dances became very popular, but were discontinued in January 1975 after the Liquor Licensing Board of Ontario refused to continue to grant liquor permits for events held at Pestalozzi College, which they had decided was a residence.

["$$$ GO Needs HELP!" GO *Info* 2 (March 1975): 3; "News of the Gay: Ottawa," *Body Politic*, no. 5 (1972), p. 16; "Ottawa Comes Out," GO *Info*, no. 1 (1972), p. 5; Dave Rand, "Some Thoughts on the GO Dance," *içi* (Pestalozzi College, Ottawa), 7 July 1972, p. 4.]

June 17–18 * Montréal * FLH held a dance to celebrate the opening of its new gay centre at 279, rue Ste. Catherine E. Police raided the event and charged forty people with being found in an establishment that was selling liquor without a permit. Although all charges were later dropped on a technicality, attendance at the centre fell. The executive of the FLH resigned and the group collapsed by the autumn of 1972.

[Ron Dayman, "Quebec: Five Years of the Movement," *Body Politic*, no. 29 (1976–77), p. 20; Luc Doré, "History: Montreal — FLH," *Gay* (supplement to *McGill Daily*), 24 November 1972, p. 3; "News of the Gay: Montreal," *Body Politic*, no. 5 (1972), p. 16.]

June 19 * Vancouver * Members of GATE (Vancouver) delivered a sixty-five-foot-long petition demanding the repeal of anti-gay sections in the Immigration Act to the Vancouver office of the Department of Manpower and Immigration.

["The Gateline" ("The Gateway" column), *Georgia Straight*, 22–29 June 1972, p. 13; "Gay Alliance toward Equality (GATE) (Vancouver)" vertical file, Canadian Lesbian and Gay Archives, Toronto.]

June 29 * Toronto * About twenty-five members of CHAT and TGA demonstrated at the Ontario Legislature to protest the omission of a sexual orientation clause from Bill 199, an amendment to the Ontario Human Rights Code then being considered by the Legislature. On June 27, 1972, CHAT had sent a brief to all members of the Legislature asking them to end discrimination based on sexual orientation in employment, housing, and other areas. This was the first public gay action in Ontario that centred on rights code reform.

[Hugh Brewster, "OHRC: Ontario Human Rights Code," *Body Politic*, no. 5 (1972), pp. 11, 18; "Homophile Body Raps Prejudice," *Toronto Star*, four star ed., 28 June 1972, p. 50; Patricia Murphy, "Gay Pride Hurt" (letter), *Globe and Mail*, metro ed., 8 July 1972, p. 7.]

June 30–July 2 ∗ Vancouver ∗ Gay Pride celebrations were held, including a debate between Rev. Bob Sirico of MCC and an anti-gay minister (June 30), a gala dance (June 30), and a gay rally in Ceperly Park (July 1).

["Gay Alliance toward Equality (GATE) (Vancouver)" vertical file, Canadian Lesbian and Gay Archives, Toronto.]

July 24 ∗ Toronto ∗ Gay activist Peter Maloney announced that he planned to run for a seat on the Toronto School Board in response to a petition that sought to prevent homosexual activists from addressing students in Toronto high schools. The petition had been organized by Rev. J.R. Armstrong of the Mount Pleasant Road Baptist Church.

["Rev. J.R. Armstrong" vertical file, Canadian Lesbian and Gay Archives, Toronto; "Ban Sought in Schools on Homosexual Talks," *Toronto Star*, four star ed., 24 July 1972, p. 25; "Homosexual Plans to Run for Seat on School Board," *Toronto Star*, four star ed., 25 July 1972, p. 51; "News of the Gay," *Body Politic*, no. 6 (1972), p. 10.]

July 24 ∗ Vancouver ∗ A lesbian resource centre was operating at A Woman's Place, 1766 W. Broadway. It carried a large collection of Canadian and American lesbian and feminist publications and was used by lesbians as a place to hold meetings. In October 1972 it moved to 130 W. Hastings Street, and in late 1973 to 804 Richards Street. By that time, a lesbian drop-in/rap group was being held on Monday nights.

["Happenings at Women's Place," *Pedestal* 4 (July 1972): 14–15.]

August ∗ Ottawa ∗ GO opened an education and counselling centre at Pestalozzi College, 160 Chapel Street, Suite 601. The centre acted as the headquarters for GO and as a clearinghouse for information on homosexuality, and included a telephone counselling service and a library.

["CBC & CTV Coverage," GO *Info*, no. 2–3 (1972), p. 7; "The GO Centre," GO *Info*, no. 2–3 (1972), pp. 1–2; "GO Centre Opens," *Body Politic*, no. 6 (1972), p. 14; "Gay Centre Opens," *Centretown News* (Ottawa), 27 August 1972, p. 3.]

August 9 ∗ Vancouver ∗ When questioned by members of GATE (Vancouver) about rights for homosexuals, all seven Vancouver-Burrard candidates who attended a rally for the August 30 provincial election supported equality for gays. (See also August 23, 1972.)

[Scott Honeyman, "Politicians Woo Gay Liberationists: Candidates Support Equality," *Vancouver Sun*, four star ed., 10 August 1972, p. 13.]

August 17 * Ottawa * Four representatives of GO met with MPP Michael Cassidy (NDP-Ottawa-Centre) to discuss the NDP's position on gay issues.
["NDP Meet," GO *Info*, no. 2–3 (1972), p. 4.]

August 19–27 * Toronto * Toronto's first annual Gay Pride Week was organized by CHAT, TGA, and *The Body Politic*. It was held in late August to celebrate the first anniversary of the "We Demand" march on Ottawa and the third anniversary of the implementation of the changes to Canada's criminal code (Bill C-150). George Hislop, director of CHAT, opened the festival and read letters of support from Ontario NDP leader Stephen Lewis and Toronto alderman William Kilbourn. Toronto mayor William Dennison had refused to declare Gay Pride Week in Toronto. Several events were planned for the week, and on August 20 more than 400 people held a gay pride picnic on Ward's Island.
["Former Church Becomes Centre of Gay Festival," *Globe and Mail*, metro ed., 21 August 1972, p. 5; "Gay Pride Week: Pride and Prejudice!" *Body Politic*, no. 6 (1972), pp. 12–13.]

August 22 * Toronto * Three hundred people attended a seminar entitled "The Open Society," held at the Cecil Street Community Centre as part of Gay Pride Week. Moderated by Kathleen Brindley, the panel included Madeleine Davis, Barbara Gittings, Don Goodwin, Gerald Hannon, and George Hislop.
["Homosexuals to Seek Acceptance by Public," *Toronto Star*, four star ed., 23 August 1972, p. 54.]

August 23 * Vancouver * Bert Price, the Social Credit incumbent in Vancouver-Burrard riding and a candidate in the August 30 provincial election, caused an uproar amongst gays and their supporters at an all-candidates meeting. Although Price said that he would help gays "as much as I can" to gain equal rights, he said that people who belong to gay liberation organizations are in a dangerous situation because "one day society will want to castrate the lot of you to stop you reproducing your kind."
["Castration in Vancouver," *Zodiac Friendship Society/Gemini Club Newsletter* 1 (September 1972): 1; "The Gateway," *Gay Canadian* 1 (7 September 1972): 3; "Mrs. McCarthy Ducks Out on Gay Lib, Docker's Queries," *Vancouver Sun*, four star ed., 25 August 1972, p. 34; "Price's Theory Paid Off in Boos: 'Castration' of Homosexuals," *Vancouver Sun*, four star ed., 24 August 1972, p. 10.]

August 23–28 * Toronto * Toronto's daily newspapers were in an uproar over the publication of Gerald Hannon's article "Of Men and Little Boys" in the July–August issue of *The Body Politic*. Although criminal charges against the paper were threatened, none were laid. An article by Kenneth Bagnell in the

Globe and Mail on August 23, entitled "Gay Liberation," in turn raised the ire of some members of the gay community. Bagnell suggested that a federal grant given to CHAT to operate a distress centre had been used to fund *The Body Politic*, which, he claimed, counselled the seduction of young boys. Two hundred people picketed the *Globe and Mail* to protest the article. (See also August 25, 1972.)

[Kenneth Bagnell, "Gay Liberation," *Globe and Mail*, metro ed., 23 August 1972, p. 29; "Body Politic" (editorial), *Toronto Sun*, final ed., 28 August 1972, p. 8; Maurice Flood, "Toronto Paper Slanders Gays," *Grape* (Vancouver), 30 August–5 September 1972, p. 2; Gerald Hannon, "Men and Little Boys" (letter), *Globe and Mail*, metro ed., 26 August 1972, p. 6; George Hislop, "Gay Liberation" (letter), *Globe and Mail*, metro ed., 25 August 1972, p. 6; Ed Jackson, "Notes from the Bagnell Closet," *Body Politic*, no. 6 (1972), p. 10; Jearld Moldenhauer, "Men and Little Boys" (letter), *Globe and Mail*, metro ed., 26 August 1972, p. 6; "Multiply or Divide," *Body Politic*, no. 6 (1972), p. 2; "No Open Season on Children" (editorial), *Toronto Star*, four star ed., 24 August 1972, p. 6; "Pederasty in Toronto," *Zodiac Friendship Society/Gemini Club Newsletter* 1 (September 1972): 1; David Rand, "*Body Politic* Article Evokes Hysterical & Explosive Reaction," GO Info, no. 2–3 (1972), pp. 3–4; "Sexual Rights for Youth" (editorial), *Gay Tide* 1 (October 1973): 2; "Within the Law?" (editorial), *Globe and Mail*, metro ed., 24 August 1972, p. 6.]

August 25 ✶ Toronto ✶ George Hislop, director of CHAT, declared that the organization dissociated itself from the views expressed in Gerald Hannon's article "Of Men and Little Boys," published in the July–August issue of *The Body Politic*.

[George Hislop, "Gay Liberation" (letter), *Globe and Mail*, metro ed., 25 August 1972, p. 6; "Homosexual Group Disclaims Magazine," *Toronto Star*, Saturday ed., 26 August 1972, p. 98.]

August 26 ✶ Toronto ✶ A rally and march of 200 people representing Canadian and American gay groups made its way from the Ontario Legislature down University Avenue to Toronto City Hall to mark Gay Pride Week. The event was sponsored by CHAT and TGA. Gays and their supporters sang songs, including "We are here because we're queer / because we're queer / because we're here / 2, 4, 6, 8 / gay is just as good as straight / 3, 5, 7, 9 / lesbians are mighty fine / 2, 4, 6, 8 / is your husband (wife) really straight / . . . ." Other chants included "Hey, hey, what do you say / try it on the other way."

["Homosexual Paraders Cry 'Justice,'" *Toronto Star*, four star ed., 28 August 1972, p. 25; "Queen's Park Demonstration," GO Info, no. 2–3 (1972), p. 2; Richard Zorniak, "Toronto Gays in Action," *Guerilla* 3 (2 September 1972): 4.]

August 30 ✶ British Columbia ✶ A provincial election was held. This was the first Canadian provincial election in which gays took a visible role, and homosexuality became an issue through calls for gay civil rights. During the election campaign, gay activists (mostly members of CGAA and GATE) attended seven all-candidates meetings, sent questionnaires to all candidates, and distributed several thousand leaflets.

["GATE and the B.C. Elections: Successful Campaign!" *Body Politic*, no. 6 (1972), p. 7; "GATE — Votes," *Georgia Straight*, 3–10 August 1972, p. 7; "The Gateway," *Gay Canadian* 1 (7 September 1972): 3; "Gay Alliance toward Equality (GATE) (Vancouver)" vertical file, Canadian Lesbian and Gay Archives, Toronto; "Gays Plunge into Canadian Politics," *The Advocate* (Los Angeles), no. 94 (1972), p. 2.]

September ∗ Canada ∗ On the suggestion of Maurice Flood of GATE (Vancouver), the National Gay Election Coalition (NGEC) was formed by sixteen groups in five provinces to intervene in the October 30 federal election. Coordinated by TGA, the member groups sent questionnaires to candidates and had representatives ask questions at public meetings.

["Gay Rights Election Coalition," *Zodiac Friendship Society News* 1 (October 1972): 1; "National Gay Election Coalition," *Body Politic*, no. 6 (1972), p. 11; "National Gay Election Coalition," *Club '70 News*, June 1974, pp. 8–9; "National Gay Election Coalition (1972)" vertical file, Canadian Lesbian and Gay Archives, Toronto; Mike Pasternak, "Smile, Your Policies Are on Camera," *Ottawa Citizen*, 24 October 1972, p. 2.]

September ∗ Edmonton ∗ Members of Edmonton Lesbian Feminists (ELF) were instrumental in establishing a Women's Centre, first at 9623 103A Avenue, and after December 1972 at 11812 95th Street. Lesbian drop-ins began to be held regularly at the Centre.

["Women's Centre," *On Our Way: An Edmonton Women's Newspaper* 2 (May–June 1974): 19.]

September ∗ Montréal ∗ The first anglophone gay organization in Québec, GAY (later called Gay McGill), was formed at McGill University. About 150 people attended the founding meeting. The group had emerged out of popular gay-consciousness discussions offered by instructors Bruce Garside, Linda Page-Hollander, and John Southin in the course "Biology and Social Change," dating back to the 1971–72 school year. James Young became the first president of GAY, and Patrick Ormos acted as liaison officer. The movement by gay students to organize at McGill was opposed from the start, particularly by a group known as the Society for the Repression of Homosexuality (SRH). The SRH's flyers, distributed on campus, described homosexuality as a "repugnant mental illness"; the group's aim was to "oppose (by peaceful means) the passive acceptance of homosexuality by today's lax society" and "to encourage psychiatric treatment as a viable alternative for homosexuals." GAY was originally devoted to study groups, consciousness raising, and discussion, and soon attracted anglophone members from outside the university. Community services became a focus, with the establishment of a gayline information service (active until November 1973), a women's committee, a speaker's bureau, a newsletter, drop-in nights, and community dances (to summer 1973). Many of these community services and activities were taken over by the Centre d'accueil homophile/Gay Community Centre and by the AHM/GMA after their formation in June 1973. Gay McGill's activities were focussed around the school year, but for most of 1975 it was not active at all. In the autumn of 1975 Gay McGill attempted to revive the McGill dances but was ultimately unsuccessful. (See also June 27, 1973.)

[Scott Bowness, "McGill Gays Organize," *McGill Daily*, 19 October 1972, p. 5; Ron Dayman, "Quebec: Five Years of the Movement," *Body Politic*, no. 29 (1976–77), p. 21; "Gay McGill" vertical file, Canadian Lesbian and Gay Archives, Toronto; "Gay McGill Dances Cancelled: News in Brief," *Montreal Gay Times* 2 (Spring 1976): 6; "Gay McGill Starts Up After One Year Hiatus," *Montreal Gay Times* 1 (November 1975): 20; "Gayline. Part 1: History," *Association homophile de Montréal/Gay Montreal Association Bulletin/Newsletter*, June 1974, pp. 1–6; Ross Higgins, "L'Androgyne: 10 ans d'histoire," *Sortie*, no. 11 (1983), pp. 30, 36; "Some of the Whys; Some of the Ways," *Long Time Coming* 1 (October–November 1973): 2–6; "University Apathy — Who Needs Gay McGill?" (editorial), *Gay News* 2 (Xmas 1973): 2.]

September ★ Vancouver ★ Gay People of UBC (University of British Columbia) was formed as a successor to the Gay People's Alliance. Maurice Flood and other members of GATE (Vancouver) helped to establish the group, which was devoted to gay liberation, to eliminating anti-gay content in courses and textbooks, and to proposing a gay studies programme. By November 1972, Gay People of UBC held meetings every week, and social events every second Friday that attracted up to eighty men and women.

["Campus Gays," *Gay Tide* 1 (October 1973): 3; "Gay People of UBC," *Gay Canadian* 1 (November 1972): 6; "New Gay University Group," *Body Politic*, no. 6 (1972), p. 14; Randy Notte, "Gay" (letter), *Ubyssey* (Univ. of British Columbia), 3 October 1972, p. 4.]

September 7 ★ Vancouver ★ The first issue of *The Gay Canadian* newspaper appeared. Published by Kevin D. McKeown (also known as Q.Q.) and edited by Jack R. Dowhy, *The Gay Canadian* attempted to include news of interest to gays across Canada. It folded after issue two (November 1972).

["*Gay Canadian*" vertical file, Canadian Lesbian and Gay Archives, Toronto.]

September 9 ★ Regina ★ The Odyssey Club, the community centre operated by the Atropos Friendship Society, opened at 2242 Smith Street. The Club was open only on Wednesday, Friday, and Saturday evenings, and eventually offered music, dancing, an information and counselling telephone line, a library, and the bi-monthly newsletter *The Odyssey News*. The Odyssey Club operated until August 1980.

[Darrel David Hockley, "A History of the Gay Community of Regina," unpublished typescript, 1993, 93–050, Canadian Lesbian and Gay Archives, Toronto, pp. 9–11.]

September 11 ∗ Toronto ∗ "Coming Out," Canada's first regularly scheduled television progamme produced by and for gay people, premiered on Metro Cable Channel 10. The thirteen-episode series, shown on Monday nights, was produced by CHAT and featured Sandra Dick and Paul Pearce as moderators.

["Coming Out," *Back Chat Newsletter* 2 (5 October 1972): 1; "Gay Television Series," *Body Politic*, no. 6 (1972), p. 22.]

September 16 ∗ Toronto ∗ The Association for Canadian Transsexuals (ACT) held its semi-annual Transsexual Seminar at the CHAT centre.

["Association for Canadian Transsexuals (ACT)" vertical file, Canadian Lesbian and Gay Archives, Toronto; "Transsexual Seminar," *Body Politic*, no. 6 (1972), p. 11.]

September 23 ∗ Vancouver ∗ Prime Minister Pierre Trudeau was met by about forty members of CGAA picketing in front of the Georgia Hotel, where Trudeau was scheduled to appear on an open-line radio show. The picketers were opposed to anti-gay laws. After the show, Trudeau came back onto the street and talked briefly to Dick Rulens, chairperson of CGAA, who gave Trudeau some literature published by the CGAA. Later that evening members of GATE (Vancouver) demonstrated outside of the Showmart at the Pacific National Exhibition, where Trudeau gave a speech.

["Canadian Gay Activists Alliance (CGAA)" vertical file, Canadian Lesbian and Gay Archives, Toronto; "Gays & PET," *Gay Canadian* 1 (November 1972): 3, 5; Bob Hunter, Column, *Vancouver Sun*, four star ed., 27 September 1972, p. 45.]

September 26 ∗ Vancouver ∗ Progressive Conservative leader Robert Stanfield spoke before an audience of 1,500 University of British Columbia students as part of his campaign leading up to the October 30 federal election. During question period Maurice Flood, chairperson of GATE (Vancouver), asked where Stanfield stood on the passage of a common age of consent for homosexuals and on the removal of gays from among the list of persons prohibited from immigrating to Canada. Flood's questions were both hissed and cheered by the students. Stanfield replied, "I just have to tell you very frankly, very bluntly, that I want to leave the laws where they are."

["Election Campaign," *Publication of the Gay People of* UBC 1 (1 December 1972): 1; Maurice Flood, "Gay Rights" (letter), *Ubyssey* (Univ. of British Columbia), 29 September 1972, p. 2; Mike Sasges, "Tory Leader Leaves Students Cold," *Ubyssey* (Univ. of

British Columbia), 29 September 1972, p. 1; "Stanfield on Gay Rights," *Zodiac Friendship Society News* 1 (October 1972): 4.]

September 27 ∗ Ottawa ∗ The first meeting of Carleton University's Gay Club was held. The organization was a branch of GO and was coordinated by Meris Gava and Ron Smyth. As with many other university-based organizations, activities were centred around the school year. With a constantly changing membership it was difficult to keep the club going. It had collapsed by 1975, but Chris Morden attempted to revive it in the autumn of that year.

["GO Goes to Carleton U.," GO *Info*, no. 2–3 (1972), p. 7; Elske Kuiper, "Gays Discuss 'Human Sexuality,'" *Charlatan* (Carleton Univ.), 20 October 1972, p. 9; Chris Morden, "Gays of Carleton," GO *Info* 2 (November–December 1975): 6; Susan Stock, "GO," *Charlatan* (Carleton Univ.), 8 August 1972, p. 15.]

September 28 ∗ Montréal ∗ About fifty people met at Sir George Williams (later Concordia) University to consider setting up an anglophone Gay Liberation Front.

["News of the Gay: Montreal," *Body Politic*, no. 6 (1972), p. 14.]

Autumn ∗ Saint-Laurent, Qué. ∗ David Jacobs and Stephen Searle organized the group Gay Vanier at Vanier College. The group set up an office and drop-in centre, a library, and sponsored guest lectures. Gay Vanier may have been the earliest gay group to be established at a CEGEP. It collapsed in 1973 when Jacobs moved away. Jacobs was later active in Gay People of SFU.

["The CEGEPs and Gay Liberation: A Slow Start," *Gay-Zette* (Coming Out Edition), November–December 1974, p. 10.]

October ∗ Edmonton ∗ Michael Roberts of GATE (Edmonton) mailed a brief to members of the Alberta legislature requesting that sexual orientation be included in the proposed anti-discrimination legislation Bill 2, The Individual's Rights Protection Act. The Alberta Bill of Rights and The Individual's Rights Protection Act became law on January 1, 1973, but without a clause outlawing discrimination based on sexual orientation.

["Gay Alliance toward Equality (GATE) (Edmonton)" vertical file, Canadian Lesbian and Gay Archives, Toronto; "Press Release for Immediate Publication," *Club '70 News* 3 (8 November 1972): 4; "Rights Protection Sought in Alberta," *Advocate* (Los Angeles), no. 100 (1972), p. 23.]

October ∗ Saskatoon ∗ Gay Alliance toward Equality (GATE) (Saskatoon) and the Gay Students Alliance (GSA) merged to form Saskatoon Gay Action, under the umbrella of the Zodiac Friendship Society. Saskatoon Gay Action was organized to coordinate the educational, political, and civil rights activities of the Society. Bruce Garman was the first chairman of the group.

["Gay Action Committee," *Zodiac Friendship Society Information* 2 (February 1973): 5; "News of the Gay: Saskatoon," *Body Politic*, no. 7 (1973), p. 19; "Saskatoon Gays Merge 3 Groups for Better Effect," *Advocate* (Los Angeles), no. 99 (1972), p. 20; "Zodiac Friendship Society" vertical file, Canadian Lesbian and Gay Archives, Toronto.]

October 1–November 12 ✳ Vancouver ✳ The CGAA, in cooperation with Open Doors Research Program and the British Columbia Department of Health, sponsored a six-week seminar series on homosexuality, held on Sunday evenings at the Gordon House Community Centre. Lectures covering such topics as gays and venereal disease, gay public space, homophobia, transvestism, and gay liberation were delivered by CGAA members, including Dieter Grapp and Dick Rulens. This is believed to be one of the first times that Canadian gays presented their own seminars on homosexuality.

["Canadian Gay Activists Alliance (CGAA)" vertical file, Canadian Lesbian and Gay Archives, Toronto; "Canadian Gays Begin Seminars," *Advocate* (Los Angeles), no. 97 (1972), p. 18; "Gay Action in Vancouver," *Zodiac Friendship Society News* 1 (November 1972): 4.]

October 12 ✳ Vancouver ✳ During a campaign stop at the University of British Columbia, federal Urban Affairs minister Ron Basford was questioned by Maurice Flood of GATE (Vancouver) concerning the Liberal party's stance on age of consent and immigration laws relating to homosexuals. Basford replied that the party would not support lowering the age of consent for homosexuals from twenty-one to eighteen years, the age of consent for heterosexuals.

["Basford Rapped on 'Disregard' for Homosexuals," *Vancouver Sun*, four star ed., 13 October 1972, p. 23; Michael Merrill and Randy Notte, "Gay Rights" (letter), *Ubyssey* (Univ. of British Columbia), 17 October 1972, p. 4.]

October 31 ✳ Montréal ✳ George Hislop and Pat Murphy of CHAT spoke to more than sixty members of GAY at McGill University, mostly about CHAT but also about gay liberation and organizing in general.

[Sue Tobin, "CHAT Meets GAY," *McGill Daily*, 1 November 1972, p. 1.]

October 31 ✳ Toronto ✳ About 5,000 people gathered along Yonge Street to watch men in drag enter the St. Charles Tavern on Halloween.

[Hugh Brewster, "The Halloween Phenomenon," *Body Politic*, no. 6 (1972), p. 21; "Oct. 31, 1972," *Body Politic*, no. 7 (1973), p. 20.]

November 5 ✳ Vancouver ✳ Gay People Together, a social drop-in group that met Saturday evenings, was established by Ray Horton.

[Ray Horton, "Gay Ray Today" (letter), *Georgia Straight*, 11–18 January 1973, p. 6; Raymond Larry Horton, "GPT," *Georgia Straight*, 22–28 March 1973, p. 4; Q.Q., "Page 69" (column), 19–25 October 1973, p. 22.]

November 11–12 ∗ Saskatoon ∗ The first Western Canada Gay Clubs Conference was held, hosted by the Gemini Club. Over forty representatives from five private clubs in the three prairie provinces (Club '70, Edmonton; Club Carousel, Calgary; Happenings Social Club, Winnipeg; Odyssey Club, Regina; Gemini Club, Saskatoon) met to discuss ways to cooperate on gay issues and how to form gay political organizations.

["Gay Convention at Saskatoon," *Zodiac Friendship Society News* 1 (November 1972): 1; D.H. (Doug Hellquist), "Western Gay Clubs Conference," *Zodiac Friendship Society News* 1 (December 1972): 1–2; "News of the Gay: Saskatoon," *Body Politic*, no. 7 (1973), p. 19; "Western Canadian Gay Clubs Conference at Saskatoon," *Club '70 News* 3 (1972): 2.]

November 15 ∗ Hamilton ∗ George Hislop and Cil Pinkett of CHAT addressed about fifty students at McMaster University on the subject of homosexuality and gay liberation. The meeting was seen as a step towards organizing a gay group at the university but no one in the audience admitted to being gay or came forward to start a local group. Although attempts had been made to start a homophile group at McMaster from at least March 1971, they had been unsuccessful. Later, stimulated by this visit, Dr. John Stewart and Susan Rosenthal decided to form a gay liberation organization at McMaster University. Several meetings followed and the Hamilton-McMaster Gay Liberation Movement (GLM) emerged in January 1973. (See also January 1973.)

["Epidemicus Homophilius," *Gayokay*, no. 2 (1971), pp. 2–3; "Hamilton-McMaster GLM Founded," *Body Politic*, no. 8 (1973), p. 20; "No Offers to Organize McMaster Homosexual Club," *Hamilton Spectator*, home ed., 16 November 1972, p. 14; S.S. Que Hee, "The Chronology of Events during the Existence of the Hamilton McMaster and McMaster Homophile Associations 1972–1977," unpublished typescript, September 1977, 82–013, Canadian Lesbian and Gay Archives, Toronto, p. 2.]

November 18 ∗ Montréal ∗ GAY (later Gay McGill) held the first of what were to become the most successful community dances in the city. Gay McGill sponsored the dances until the summer of 1973, after which time they were sponsored by AHM/GMA (although still held at McGill). By 1973–74 the McGill dances had become so popular that they may have been the largest regularly held gay dances in the world, attracting up to two thousand people each. Although very successful, the dances were discontinued in April 1975 after the Québec liquor permit board withdrew the group's liquor licence. Gay McGill attempted to revive the dances in the autumn of 1975 but was ultimately unsuccessful.

["Clarification on Dances: Miscellany," *Gay News* 2 (Xmas 1973): 2; "Dances — What Are We Paying For?" (editorial), *Gay News* 2 (12 December 1973): 1; "'Dancing the Gay Lib Blues,'" *Gay-Zette* 2 (June 1975): 2; Ron Dayman, "Quebec: Five Years of the

Movement," *Body Politic*, no. 29 (1976–77), p. 21; "Gay Montreal Answers *News Editorial*" (letter), *Gay News* 2 (January 1974): 3; "Montreal: Gay," *Body Politic*, no. 7 (1973), p. 20; "No Liquor: McGill Dance Cancelled," *Gay Times* 1 (May 1975): 3.]

November 18 ✳ Vancouver ✳ Maurice Flood, chairperson of GATE (Vancouver), addressed about 150 demonstrators at a rally organized by the Vietnam Action Committee. Flood declared that homosexuals and the Vietnamese "share a common oppressor" — the United States.

[Jay Melmer, "GATE Slams the War," *Georgia Straight*, 23–30 November 1972, p. 3; Berton Woodward, "Rally Told War Causes Port Losses," *Vancouver Province*, 20 November 1972, p. 37.]

November 21 ✳ Toronto ✳ All five of CHAT's social service counsellors (Sandra Dick, Linda Jain, Ed Jackson, Pat Murphy, and Paul Pearce) officially resigned from CHAT in protest over the organization's limiting structure and conservative goals. The move followed a policy convention meeting during which the counsellors lost a resolution that would have created a shared power structure in CHAT, with more autonomy going to the social services section.

["CHAT Moves," *Body Politic*, no. 7 (1973), p. 20; "Gone 'Fission,'" *Body Politic*, no. 7 (1973), p. 2; Peter Zorzi, *Queer Catharsis* (Toronto: The Author, 1992), p. 28.]

November 23 ✳ Windsor, Ont. ✳ The organizational meeting of the Windsor Homophile Association was held. Steve Lough was the group's key organizer. At first it was focussed around rap sessions, then dances, community education, and a gayline. In January 1973 it was renamed Windsor Gay Unity (WGU). By early 1974 WGU had collapsed, but it reorganized as a more formal organization in November 1974. Eventually WGU would sponsor gaylines, a speaker's bureau, dances, a newsletter, and a drop-in centre.

[Jim Monk, "To Learn from Your Mistakes You Have to Make Them," *Windsor Gay Unity Newsletter* 1 (October 1975): 1–3; "Windsor: New Group," *Body Politic*, no. 7 (1973), p. 20; "Windsor Gay Unity (WGU)" vertical file, Canadian Lesbian and Gay Archives, Toronto.]

November 24 ✳ Montréal ✳ A special eight-page supplement entitled "Gay" appeared in the *McGill Daily*. It had been assembled by a five-member collective (F. Brayton, M. Galan, B. Peck, W. Aitken, and K. Kelley). "Gay" included articles by Bruce Garside on the politics of gay liberation, Jearld Moldenhauer and Bob Wallace on the history of gay organizing in Toronto and Vancouver, Luc Doré on the FLH, Martha Shelley on radical lesbianism, and Will Aitken on his reaction to the film version of *The Boys in the Band*.

[*Gay* (supplement to *McGill Daily*), 24 November 1972, included the following: Will Aitken, "Boys in the Back, Or How a Movie Made Me Come Out," p. 6; Luc Doré,

"Montreal — FLH," p. 3; Bruce Garside, "The Politics of Gay Liberation: Reform or Revolution?," pp. 2, 6; Jearld Moldenhauer and Bob Wallace, "History: Toronto and Vancouver," pp. 3, 6; Martha Shelley, "We Are Women First and Foremost: Notes of a Radical Lesbian," pp. 4–5.]

December ∗ Saskatoon ∗ An independent Gay Women's Group was formed and began holding regular meetings to discuss issues of interest to lesbians. Many of its members were drawn from the Gemini Club and from women's liberation groups in the city. By February 1973 the group had thirteen members, but by March 1973 its formal meetings were discontinued.

[K.V.P., "Women," *Zodiac Friendship Society Information* 2 (February 1973): 3; "Women," *Zodiac Friendship Society Information* 2 (March 1973): 3.]

December 1 ∗ Vancouver ∗ Maurice Flood, chairperson of GATE (Vancouver), sent a letter to B.C. Minister of Labour William King asking for amendments to the British Columbia Human Rights Act to outlaw discrimination based on sexual orientation. King replied on December 12, 1972, that "I find it rather difficult to conceive of a situation where a homosexual would be discriminated against unless his tendencies were a matter of public knowledge. As one who believes that personal matters of this nature are one's own business, and should not be flaunted publicly, I cannot accept that a wide problem exists in this regard. I am personally of the opinion that homosexuality, although apparently quite widespread, should not receive the benefit of legal sanction."

[Gay Alliance toward Equality (GATE) (Vancouver) papers, 82–005/08, Canadian Lesbian and Gay Archives, Toronto; "Labour Minister Responds," *Body Politic*, no. 7 (1973), p. 19; "Minister Criticized by Gays," *Vancouver Province*, final home ed., 20 December 1972, p. 7.]

December 1, 8 ∗ Vancouver ∗ Members of GATE (Vancouver) and Gay People of UBC picketed Jiffy Print at 1179 Richards Street after the printing shop refused to print a leaflet advertising a dance sponsored by Gay People of UBC.

[Robert Cook, "Jiffy Print Demo," *Body Politic*, no. 7 (1973), p. 19; Barbara Coward, "Local Publisher Thinks Homosexuals Should Be Shot," *Grape* (Vancouver), 13–19 December 1972, p. 4; "Gay Group Pickets Print Plant," *Vancouver Sun*, four star ed., 2 December 1972, p. 19; "How Sick Are You?: Gays Threatened," *Georgia Straight*, 14–21 December 1972, p. 5; "In a Jiffy . . . ," *Publication of the Gay People of* UBC 1 (1 December 1972): 1.]

December 4 ∗ Toronto ∗ In the City of Toronto elections, Peter Maloney was defeated in his bid to become a Toronto Board of Education school trustee in Ward 6. Two trustees were elected for the Ward; Maloney was a close third.

["Pete's Defeat," *Body Politic*, no. 7 (1973), p. 20.]

December 5 ∗ Winnipeg ∗ The Manitoba provincial government denied private club charters to two gay groups because it didn't want to encourage the proliferation of homosexuality. Attorney-General A.H. Mackling stated that "our concern is that such groups ought not to be clothed with the same rights and respectability as other groups." One of the groups was Happenings, a gay social club operated by the Mutual Friendship Society. Happenings was eventually granted a charter in June 1973.

[["Editorial," *What's Happening!* 3 (March 1974): 1–2; "Manitoba Homosexuals Denied Club Charters," *Toronto Star*, four star ed., 6 December 1972, p. 52; Susan White, "Struggling On: Winnipeg's Gay Liberation Movement 2 Years After," *Manitoban* (Univ. of Manitoba), 4 February 1974, p. 7.]

December 7 ∗ Montréal ∗ Linda Diebel's survey article on lesbians and gays in Montréal, "Homosexuals Speak," was published in the *Gazette*. Denise Cassidy, manager of the lesbian bar Baby Face, was one of the people interviewed in the piece.

[Linda Diebel, "Homosexuals Speak: 'We Are People Too,' " *Montreal Gazette*, final ed., 7 December 1972, p. 25.]

December 9 ∗ Vancouver ∗ In a speech before a meeting of about fifty representatives of twenty-three human rights groups, MLA Rosemary Brown (NDP-Vancouver-Burrard) recognized homosexuals as an oppressed group seeking human rights. This is believed to be the first occasion in Canada that an elected politician made unsolicited remarks on gay rights, and tied gays in with other groups engaged in civil rights struggles.

[["Still Plenty of Work, Human Right (sic) Groups Told," *Vancouver Province*, 11 December 1972, p. 20.]

December 25 ∗ Montréal ∗ The gayline operated by GAY was inaugurated during the Christmas weekend. It was active until November 1973.

[["Gayline 'Hotline' Inaugurated," *Gay: A Newsletter* 1 (1 January 1973): 1; "Gayline Report," *Gay: A Newsletter* 1 (16 January 1973): 1.]

December 31 ∗ Montréal ∗ GAY sponsored a New Year's Eve dance, which was attended by between 600 and 1000 people.

[R.J.B., "New Year's Eve Dance Wildly Wonderful!!!!" *Gay: A Newsletter* 1 (16 January 1973): 1.]

1973

—— ✳ Montréal ✳ Claude Beausoleil's book of poetry *Les bracelets d'ombre: poésies* was published by Éditions du jour.

[Bernard Gilbert, "*Intrusion ralentie* et autre recueils de poésies et de textes en prose de Claude Beausoleil," in *Dictionnaire des oeuvres littéraires du Québec*, ed. Maurice Lemire et al., vol. 5 (1970–75) (Montréal: Fides, 1987), pp. 436–39.]

—— ✳ Montréal ✳ Marie-Claire Blais's novel *Un joualonais sa joualonie* was published by Éditions du jour. An English-language edition (*St. Lawrence Blues*) was published in 1974 in New York by Farrar, Straus and Giroux. One of the characters is a gay man who works as a female impersonator; brief mention is also made of a lesbian couple.

[Gabrielle Frémont, "*Un joualonais sa joualonie*," in *Dictionnaire des oeuvres littéraires du Québec*, ed. Maurice Lemire et al., vol. 5 (1970–75) (Montréal: Fides, 1987), pp. 916–17; Mary Kandiuk, *French-Canadian Authors: A Bibliography of Their Works and of English-Language Criticism* (Metuchen, N.J.: Scarecrow Press, 1990), pp. 26, 37.]

—— ✳ Montréal ✳ Ron Hallis's film *Toni, Randi and Marie* was released. It was an intimate portrait of three characters leading parallel lives: Toni, a transvestite, and Randi and Marie, prostitutes.

[D.J. Turner and Micheline Morisset, eds., *Canadian Feature Film Index, 1913–1985/Index des films canadiens de long métrage* (Ottawa: Public Archives, National Film, Television, and Sound Archives, 1987), entry 413; Thomas Waugh, "Nègres blancs, tapettes et 'butch': les lesbiennes et les gais dans le cinéma québécois," *Copie zéro*, no. 11 (1981), p. 19.]

—— ✳ Montréal ✳ Jean LeDerff's book about gay men and urban gay life, *Homosexuel? Et pourquoi pas!*, was published by Ferron Éditeur. This was one of the first positive books on gay liberation published in Canada.

[Jean-François Courcelles, "Pour Jean LeDerff, l'homosexuel irrite la société, car il ne joue pas le jeu du dominateur," *Gay Montréal* 1 (10 August 1976): 18; Ron Dayman, "Quebec: Five Years of the Movement," *Body Politic*, no. 29 (1976–77), p. 22; Ken Popert, "The Best Yet," *Body Politic*, no. 11 (1974), p. 10; Jean-Guy Prince, "Les carnets de Jean-Guy Prince" (column), *Gay Montréal* 1 (14 December 1976): 29.]

—— ✳ Richmond Hill, Ont. ✳ Simon and Schuster published *The Happy*

Hairdresser, an autobiography by Nicholas Loupos. Some reviewers dismissed it as being aggressively anti-gay.

["Publishers Parade Prejudice," *Body Politic*, no. 12 (1974), p. 24.]

—— * San Francisco, Ca. * *The Gay Liberation Book*, edited by Len Richmond and Gary Noguera, was published by Ramparts Press. A collection of articles and photographs on gay oppression and liberation, *The Gay Liberation Book* included five photographs by Jearld Moldenhauer of Toronto.

[Len Richmond and Gary Noguera, eds., *The Gay Liberation Book* (San Francisco: Ramparts Press, 1973), pp. 21, 92, 128, 137, 164.]

—— * Trumansburg, N.Y. * *The Male Muse: A Gay Anthology*, edited by Ian Young, was published by The Crossing Press. This was the first contemporary anthology of poetry in English with gay male themes. (See also Spring 1974.)

[(Ian Young), *Ian Young: A Bibliography 1962–1980*, Canadian Gay Archives Publication no. 3 (Toronto: Pink Triangle Press, 1981), entries A9, E29–E33, E35–E37, E40–E42, E44, E47, E49; Ian Young, "Pigs and Fishes," *Body Politic*, no. 18 (1975), pp. 16–18.]

—— * Vancouver * Bertrand Lachance's book of poetry *Air 13* was published by Air (A Bryte Raven Production).

[Ian Young, *The Male Homosexual in Literature: A Bibliography*, second ed. (Metuchen, N.J.: Scarecrow Press, 1982), entry 2201.]

—— * Vancouver * Bertrand Lachance's book of poetry *Cock Tales* was published by Talonbooks.

[Antony Lorraine, "*Cock Tales*," *Georgia Straight*, 10–17 May 1973, p. 16; Ian Young, *The Male Homosexual in Literature: A Bibliography*, second ed. (Metuchen, N.J.: Scarecrow Press, 1982), entry 2202.]

—— * Vancouver * David Watmough's *Ashes for Easter and Other Monodramas* was published by Talonbooks. This collection of brief autobiographical fictions included musings on homosexual identity that had been performed by the author on stage, television, and record throughout North America and Europe.

[Robert Fulford, "Thinking Changed on Homosexuality" (column), *Ottawa Citizen*, 4 August 1973, p. 60; Geoff Hancock, "Interview with David Watmough," *Canadian Fiction Magazine*, no. 20 (1976), pp. 65–83; Beth Jankola, "A Magnificent Bad Trip," *Georgia Straight*, 3–7 September 1971, p. 20; Andrew Parkin, "A Double Exile," *Canadian Literature*, no. 59 (1974), pp. 108–09.]

January * Calgary * The People's Liberation Coalition (PLC) was officially formed from a University of Calgary encounter group, with Allan Zdurich as one of the key organizers. The PLC was able to secure office space at the old YMCA, 223 12th Avenue, S.W., where it established a drop-in and a phoneline to provide information and counselling for lesbians and gays. The PLC dissolved by 1975 and was succeeded by Gay Information and Resources Calgary (GIRC). (See also June 1975.)

["News of the Gay: Calgary New Group," *Body Politic*, no. 8 (1973), p. 19; "People's Liberation Coalition (PLC)" vertical file, Canadian Lesbian and Gay Archives, Toronto.]

January * Hamilton * The Hamilton-McMaster Gay Liberation Movement (GLM) was officially founded. By March 6, the group had organized an executive with Allan Masters and Bruce Kyle acting as the first co-chairs. The group was based at McMaster University and held bi-monthly meetings at first. By the end of its first year it had sponsored dances, advertisements, and lectures, established a library and a newsletter (*Dialogue*), and published the twelve-page booklet "Learning Together." By September 1974 the Hamilton-McMaster GLM had about sixty regular members. The group was renamed the McMaster Homophile Association (MHA) in January 1976; MHA was active until September 1977.

[Margaret Fulford, ed., *The Canadian Women's Movement, 1960–1990: A Guide to Archival Resources/Le mouvement canadien des femmes, 1960–1990: guide de ressources archivistiques* (Toronto: Canadian Women's Movement Archives/ECW Press, 1992), entry 434; McMaster Homophile Association (MHA) papers, 82–013, Canadian Lesbian and Gay Archives, Toronto; S.S. Que Hee, "The Chronology of Events during the Existence of the Hamilton McMaster and McMaster Homophile Associations 1972–1977," unpublished typescript, September 1977, 82–013, Canadian Lesbian and Gay Archives, Toronto, 12 pp.]

January * Toronto * Allen Ginsberg's book of poetry *Iron Horse* was published by Coach House Press. The first American issue was published in San Francisco in March 1974 by City Lights Books.

[Michelle P. Kraus, *Allen Ginsberg: An Annotated Bibliography, 1969–1977*, Scarecrow Author Bibliographies no. 46 (Metuchen, N.J.: Scarecrow Press, 1980), entries 14, 1205–07.]

January * Toronto * Graduate students Herb Spiers and Robert Wallace submitted briefs to the University of Toronto's New Program Review Committee requesting a course on and research into homosexuality. At that time the university still had not instituted either a credit or a non-credit course on homosexuality. York University had offered a non-credit tutorial in 1972, and McGill University and Vanier College offered similar courses in 1973.

[Heather-Jane Sanguins, "Want Gay Courses and Research," *Varsity* (Univ. of Toronto), 26 January 1973, p. 6.]

January * Vancouver * Zodiac M.C. (Motor Club), a gay leather and denim fraternal organization, was formed. The group provided social space for gays interested in leather and s/m and was also very active in organizing community fundraising events. The Zodiacs disbanded in 1990.

["News: Historic Leather Group Zodiac Disbands," *Rites* 6 (April 1990): 6.]

January 8 * Montréal * *Gay*, a program of "free expression" produced by local gays and bisexuals, premiered on Radio McGill (91.5 on Cable FM). The program aired every Monday at 7:30 p.m.

["Gay Radio Talk Show," *Gay: A Newsletter* 1 (16 January 1973): 1.]

January 10 * Toronto * Daniel Cappon's article "The Homosexual Hoax: This Aberration Is Not a Right" appeared in the *Toronto Star*. Cappon was a professor of environmental studies at York University and the author of *Toward an Understanding of Homosexuality* (1965). This article generated much (mostly negative) public response. (See also January 13 and January 14, 1973.)

[David Berger, "Homosexuality: An Attempt to Set the Record Straight," *Toronto Star*, four star ed., 22 February 1973, p. 6; Daniel Cappon, "The Homosexual Hoax: This Aberration Is Not a Right," *Toronto Star*, four star ed., 10 January 1973, p. 6; Clifford Collier, "York Homophiles Disagree with Prof" (letter), *Excalibur* (York Univ.), 18 January 1973, p. 7; George Hislop, " 'Homosexuality Shouldn't Be Cured' " (letter), *Toronto Star*, four star ed., 23 January 1973, p. 7; Sandra Porter, Tom Philbrook, Eric Zachon, and fifty-four others, "York Faculty Group Disagree with Cappon," *Toronto Star*, four star ed., 23 January 1973, p. 7; Claudia Wuppermann, "Cappon Feels Homosexuality 'Is Not a Right': In the *Toronto Star*," *Excalibur* (York Univ.), 18 January 1973, p. 7; "Zappin' Cappon," *Body Politic*, no. 7 (1973), p. 3.]

January 13 * Toronto * George Hislop of CHAT was interviewed by Peter Gzowski on CBC radio in response to Daniel Cappon's article "The Homosexual Hoax: This Aberration Is Not a Right," published January 10 in the *Toronto Star*.

["Toronto: Roast Cappon," *Body Politic*, no. 7 (1973), p. 24.]

January 14 * Toronto * Herb Spiers of *The Body Politic* was interviewed by Larry Solway on CBC-TV's "Weekday" in response to Daniel Cappon's article "The Homosexual Hoax: This Aberration Is Not a Right," published January 10 in the *Toronto Star*. The interview was broadcast January 15.

["Toronto: Roast Cappon," *Body Politic*, no. 7 (1973), p. 24.]

January 19–20 * Montréal * GAY co-sponsored (with the McGill Student Society Social Entertainment Committee) a "Moveable Feast" at the McGill Ballroom, as part of the Montreal Folk Festival.

["Folk Festival Success — Social Director Upset," *Gay: A Newsletter* 1 (23 January 1973): 1–2.]

February * Montréal * Trident M.C. (Motor Club), a fraternal club for gays interested in leather and denim, was formed at the Taverne Neptune, 121, rue de la Commune O.

["Trident (Montréal)" vertical file, Canadian Lesbian and Gay Archives, Toronto.]

February * Regina * The University of Saskatchewan Homophile Association (USHA) was officially formed at the university's Regina campus. During 1972, Ann Tarjanne, a graduate student in psychology, had tried to promote gay awareness on campus and attempted to establish Gay Alliance toward Equality (GATE) (Regina). When USHA was formed, the organizers Gary McDonald and Bev Siller had great difficulty in attracting other members to the group.

["Gays on Campus," *Odyssey News* 1 (14 May 1975): 7; Darrel David Hockley, "A History of the Gay Community of Regina," unpublished typescript, 1993, 93–050, Canadian Lesbian and Gay Archives, Toronto, pp. 23–24; "News of the Gay: Regina," *Body Politic*, no. 8 (1973), p. 19; Bev Siller, "University Homophile Association" (letter), *Carillon* (Univ. of Saskatchewan, Regina), 9 February 1973, p. 2; "University of Saskatchewan Homophile Association (USHA)" vertical file, Canadian Lesbian and Gay Archives, Toronto.]

February 5 * Toronto * ANIK (meaning "brotherhood" in Inuktitut) held its first meeting at Holy Trinity Church. This social, non-political gay charitable foundation was the first gay organization in Ontario to receive a charter as a non-profit group.

["ANIK" (advertisement), *Metro Community News* 1 (1 December 1973): 6; "ANIK," *Metro Community News* 1 (4 October 1974): 4; "ANIK Charitable Foundation" vertical file, Canadian Lesbian and Gay Archives, Toronto; "News of the Gay: ANIK," *Body Politic*, no. 8 (1973), p. 20.]

February 9 * Montréal * The Women's Committee of GAY sponsored a women-only dance, "Your Mother Wears Army Boots," held at the Student Union, McGill University. (See also March 1973.)

[Advertisement, *Gay: A Newsletter* 1 (30 January 1973): 5.]

February 9 * Windsor, Ont. * WGU held its first dance at the University Centre, during which a group of straight men came up from the pub downstairs and attacked several dancers.

["Struggle in Windsor . . . ," *Gemini* 11 1 (April 1973): 4; "Windsor Gay Unity (WGU)" vertical file, Canadian Lesbian and Gay Archives, Toronto.]

February 12 * Montréal * Dr. Franklin Kameny, founder of the Mattachine Society of Washington, D.C., spoke on gay liberation movements at the Leacock Building, McGill University, in an event sponsored by GAY and the McGill Debating Union.

[Advertisement, *Gay: A Newsletter* 1 (30 January 1973): 8.]

February 14 ∗ Toronto ∗ Five people attended the inaugural meeting of the Gay Alliance toward Equality (GATE) (Toronto). Jearld Moldenhauer was a key force in its formation. Other influential early members included Michael Lynch, Ken Popert, and Tom Warner. GATE (Toronto) was the successor to TGA in organizing around civil rights issues and became a major force in gay liberation activities in Ontario, fighting for legal reform and championing the cause of John Damien. GATE (Toronto) also sponsored numerous lectures and dances; its activities were documented in the newsletter *Gay Rising*. GATE (Toronto) was active until 1980.

[Margaret Fulford, ed., *The Canadian Women's Movement, 1960–1990: A Guide to Archival Resources/Le mouvement canadien des femmes, 1960–1990: guide de ressources archivistiques* (Toronto: Canadian Women's Movement Archives/ECW Press, 1992), entry 393; Gay Alliance toward Equality (GATE) (Toronto) papers, 82–029, Canadian Lesbian and Gay Archives, Toronto; "News of the Gay: GATE Formed," *Body Politic*, no. 8 (1973), p. 19; Peter Zorzi, *Queer Catharsis* (Toronto: The Author, 1992), p. 35.]

February 15 ∗ Toronto ∗ The *Toronto Star* refused to publish a classified ad soliciting subscriptions for *The Body Politic*. The entire ad read: "*The Body Politic*, Gay Liberation Journal, $2 for six issues. 4 Kensington Ave., Toronto, Ont. M5T 2J7." The *Star* declared that it was not its policy "to accept advertising which would identify or tend to identify a person as a homosexual or to carry advertisements relating to homosexual activity." *The Body Politic* lodged a complaint of discrimination against the *Star* with the Ontario Press Council. (See also April 11 and April 30, 1973.)

["Why 8's Late," *Body Politic*, no. 8 (1973), p. 5.]

February 20 ∗ Vancouver ∗ GATE (Vancouver) submitted a brief to B.C. Labour Minister William King requesting that the provincial Human Rights Act be amended to prohibit discrimination on the basis of sexual orientation. The minister, whose department administered the Act, had said that a commission would be appointed to consider changes to the Human Rights Act. (See also August 29, 1973.)

[Gay Alliance toward Equality (GATE) (Vancouver) papers, 82–005/08, Canadian Lesbian and Gay Archives, Toronto; "Sexual Freedom Sought," *Vancouver Province*, final home ed., 22 February 1973, p. 11.]

February 24 ∗ Saskatoon ∗ Doug Hellquist and Bruce Garman of Saskatoon Gay Action met with the board of the Saskatchewan Human Rights Commission to discuss sexual orientation and the provincial Bill of Rights Act. They were encouraged to submit a brief to the Commission, which they did in March 1973. (See also August 25, 1973.)

["Breakthrough with Human Rights," *Zodiac Friendship Society Information* 2 (March 1973): 3; "Saskatoon Gay Action," *Zodiac Friendship Society Information* 2 (May 1973): 3.]

February 25–April 8 * Vancouver * At a general meeting of GATE (Vancouver) held February 25, the membership decided to launch a formal protest against the *Georgia Straight*'s cavalier attitude towards gay liberation, its mutilation of material submitted by GATE, and the overt sexism and homophobia that sometimes appeared in its editorials and cartoons. A series of charges and countercharges soon emerged from both sides. The *Straight* claimed that GATE was a "Trotskyist Front." GATE threatened to picket the offices of the *Straight*, which it finally did on March 29 and 30, 1973, but to no avail. On April 8, GATE called for a boycott of the paper.

[(Walter Blumenthal), "Indeed, Sir!" (letter), *Georgia Straight*, 5–11 April 1973, p. 8; Maurice J. Flood, "GATE to Picket *Straight*" (letter), *Grape* (Vancouver), 29 March–10 April 1973, p. 6; Maurice J. Flood, "Gay Pompousity (sic)" (letter), *Georgia Straight*, 22–28 March 1973, p. 10; "GATE Withdraws" (letter), *Georgia Straight*, 10–17 August 1972, p. 7; Haslett, "GATE Pickets *Straight*," *Georgia Straight*, 29 March–5 April 1973, p. 8; Michael Merrill, Maurice Flood, and Fred Thomson, "Gay Troika Replies" (letter, with response by Dan McLeod), *Georgia Straight*, 29 March–5 April 1973, p. 6; "News of the Gay: Vancouver," *Body Politic*, no. 8 (1973), p. 19; Herbert Spiers, "Further Revelations" (letter, with response by Dan McLeod), *Georgia Straight*, 5–11 April 1973, p. 4.]

February 27 * Toronto * A discussion on radical lesbianism was held at the University of Toronto as part of the interdisciplinary course "Women: Oppression and Liberation."

["News of the Gay: Lesbian Panel," *Body Politic*, no. 8 (1973), p. 20.]

March * Montréal * The Women's Committee of GAY sponsored a second dance for lesbians, after which members of the Committee decided to leave GAY. These women found GAY to be overwhelmingly male in membership and outlook, and were determined to start an independent lesbian organization in Montréal. They continued holding social evenings and consciousness-raising groups, which were the basis for the formation of the group Montreal Gay Women. Some of the members of the Committee were also involved in organizing the Women's Centre, which opened at 3764, boul. St. Laurent on May 1, 1973. (See also July 1973.)

["Some of the Whys; Some of the Ways," *Long Time Coming* 1 (October–November 1973): 3–6.]

March 4 * Toronto * CHAT sponsored an all-candidates meeting for the provincial by-election to be held in St. George riding. All three major candidates (Margaret Campbell [Lib.], Roy McMurtry [PC], and Ellen

Adams [NDP]) attended, and gave cautious and mostly negative responses to questions regarding gay rights.

["News of the Gay: Toronto By-election," *Body Politic*, no. 8 (1973), p. 19; Norman Webster, "St. George Candidates Meet Homophiles, and Tread a Cautiously Negative Line," *Globe and Mail*, metro ed., 5 March 1973, p. 5.]

March 5 * Halifax * GAE presented a five-page brief to the Nova Scotia Legislature recommending that a clause concerning sexual orientation be included in the provincial Human Rights Act. The brief had been drawn up by the Legal Reform Committee of GAE, under the direction of Nils Clausson. During the same week, representatives of GAE were in contact with Dr. William Gillis, minister in charge of the Human Rights Act, with Dr. McCurdy, director of the Human Rights Commission, and with the provincial Health and Welfare Committee. (See also March 28, 1973.)

[G.F./B.B., "The Brief and Its Progress," GAE/Y *Information Services* 1 (March 1973): 1; "News of the Gay: Halifax: Human Rights Act and NGEC," *Body Politic*, no. 8 (1973), p. 19.]

March 6 * Edmonton * A lecture entitled "Lesbian Feminism" was given as part of the "Talking about Women — 1973" course, sponsored by the Women's Programme Centre, University of Alberta.

["Talking about Women — 1973," *On Our Way: A Monthly Women's Newspaper* 1 (January 1973): 4.]

March 8 * Ottawa * Before a meeting of the Senate Committee on Legal and Constitutional Affairs, Senator Lionel Choquette (Lib.-Ontario) said that he had been told that lesbianism was "rampant" among both prisoners and guards at the prison for women in Kingston, Ontario. He asked for comments on this from a delegation from the Elizabeth Fry Society that was testifying before the Committee. A suggestion was made that the introduction of more male staff would counteract lesbianism at the institution.

["Male Staff for Prison Suggested: 'Lesbians,'" *Vancouver Sun*, final ed., 8 March 1973, p. 2.]

March 17 * Saskatoon * A dance was held to celebrate the opening of the Zodiac Friendship Society's new centre (which included the Gemini Club) at 124A 2nd Avenue N. The centre provided social activities and services for gay people, as well as information about homosexuality to the general community. Drop-ins were held Tuesday and Wednesday evenings; lesbian drop-ins were held Friday evenings.

["At Last! A Place of Our Own," *Zodiac Friendship Society Information* 2 (March 1973): 1; "Do You Find Homosexuals Revolting? . . . You Bet Your Sweet Ass We Are," *Sheaf* (Univ. of Saskatchewan), 25 September 1973, p. 5; Doug Hellquist, "The Club," *Zodiac*

Friendship Society Information 2 (April 1973): 2; "News of the Gay: Saskatoon: Gay Centre Opens," *Body Politic*, no. 8 (1973), p. 19.]

March 17 ∗ Toronto ∗ UTHA sponsored a conference of the Ontario Homophile Federation, held at Hart House, University of Toronto. About twelve groups were represented, half of which were from Toronto. The discussion included accounts of attempts to introduce gay studies courses into Ontario's universities and colleges.

[C. Hill, "Ontario Homophile Conference," GO *Info*, no. 6 (1973), p. 8; Jim, "Ontario Gay Conference," *Gemini* II 1 (April 1973): 2.]

March 21 ∗ Toronto ∗ A meeting sponsored by Canadians against a Racist Immigration Policy was addressed by Mark MacGuigan, parliamentary secretary to the federal Minister of Manpower and Immigration. A *Body Politic* reporter was able to ask about discrimination against homosexuals in immigration.

["News of the Gay: Immigration Policy," *Body Politic*, no. 8 (1973), p. 19.]

March 22 ∗ Kitchener-Waterloo, Ont. ∗ Three members of Waterloo GLM, as well as Pat Murphy of CHAT, appeared on a one-and-a-half-hour, live, open-line talk show about homosexuality, broadcast locally on Grand River Cable (Cable 12).

["Zap," *Gemini* II 1 (April 1973): 6.]

March 28 ∗ Halifax ∗ Five representatives of GAE met with the Nova Scotia Human Rights Commission to discuss the brief that they had presented to members of the Nova Scotia Legislature on March 5, which concerned the inclusion of sexual orientation in the provincial Human Rights Act. The Commission decided not to recommend that the Act be changed at that time, citing several reasons but particularly because the Commission was not aware of enough cases of discrimination against gays to warrant immediate action. The Legal Reform Committee of GAE immediately undertook a campaign to document cases of discrimination against lesbians and gay men in Nova Scotia.

[Nils Clausson, "GAE Appears before Human Rights Commission," GAE/Y *Information Services* 1 (April 1973): 1; Nils Clausson, "A Letter to the Gay Community" (letter), GAE/Y *Information Services* 1 (April 1973): 1–2; "What's Happening: Halifax, N.S.," *U.U. Gay Caucus Newsletter* 3 (June 1973): 6.]

March 29 ∗ Toronto ∗ An editorial in the *Toronto Sun* discussed the state of the women's liberation movement and decided that it had become "so serious, so nasty, so intolerant" and was "in danger of being dominated by Marxist *lesbians* — which is a scarey (sic) thought."

["Dear Lovely Ladies" (editorial), *Toronto Sun*, final ed., 29 March 1973, p. 8.]

Spring ✷ Ottawa ✷ Four members of GO (David Ireland, Peter Lancastle, Terry Reichey, and Susan Tilley) were awarded an Opportunities for Youth grant of $6,325 to make a series of four half-hour videotape television programmes to be called "Breaking the Ice." The programmes were to concern "Sexuality, Discrimination, Oppression, and Prejudice."

[" 'Breaking the Ice,' " GO *Info*, no. 7 (1973), p. 8; " 'Breaking the Ice' — Gay Media Grant," *Body Politic*, no. 9 (1973), p. 7.]

Spring ✷ Toronto ✷ The spring meeting of the Ontario Teacher's Federation passed a resolution concerning disciplinary action for a teacher "found guilty of a homosexual offence involving another adult." A second resolution pointing out that homosexual acts between consenting adults were legal in Canada was referred to the Executive and to the Relations and Discipline Committee for study.

["Union Threatens Gays," *Body Politic*, no. 9 (1973), p. 7.]

Spring ✷ Waterloo, Ont. ✷ Waterloo GLM published the fourteen-page pamphlet *I Am a Humansexual.*

[Monograph collection, M95–050, Canadian Lesbian and Gay Archives, Toronto.]

April ✷ Montréal ✷ The Northern Lights M.C. (Motor Club), a leather and denim fraternal organization for gay men, was formed.

[Ken B., "A Baker's Dozen: 4) A New Montreal Club," *Phalia*, no. 18 (1973): 1.]

April 6 ✷ Toronto ✷ *August and July*, a film about a lesbian couple who spend the summer on an isolated farm, began a week's run at Cinecity. Starring Sharon Smith and Alexa De Wiel, it was directed by Murray Markowitz and produced by Crawley Films.

[Adil., "*August and July*," *Variety*, 11 April 1973, p. 61; Sheila Ascroft, "The Mad Adventures of Crawley Films," *Ottawa Citizen*, 14 April 1973, p. 65; "*August and July*: A Review," *Other Woman* 1 (April–May 1973): 8; D.J. Turner and Micheline Morisset, eds., *Canadian Feature Film Index, 1913–1985/Index des films canadiens de long métrage* (Ottawa: Public Archives, National Film, Television, and Sound Archives, 1987), entry 422.]

April 11 ✷ Ottawa ✷ In response to a request by *The Body Politic* to examine the *Toronto Star*'s refusal on February 15 to publish their classified advertisement, the Ontario Press Council announced that it agreed that the *Star* could refuse to run ads, although there had been "discrimination" in this case. (See also April 16 and April 30, 1973.)

["Press Council Says *Star* 'Discriminated' in Refusing Ad for Homosexual Paper," *Toronto Star*, four star ed., 11 April 1973, pp. 1, 3; "Why 8's Late," *Body Politic*, no. 8 (1973), p. 5.]

April 16 ∗ Toronto ∗ Three members of *The Body Politic* collective met with *Toronto Star* officials concerning the *Star*'s refusal to print their ad.

["Why 8's Late," *Body Politic*, no. 8 (1973), p. 5.]

April 30 ∗ Toronto ∗ Representatives of *The Body Politic* and GATE (Toronto) met with Daniel Hill, chairperson of the Ontario Human Rights Commission. Hill suggested that they prepare a brief documenting cases of discrimination against gays in employment and housing.

["The Ontario Human Rights Omission: A Chronology," in Gays of Ottawa, *Cleaning Up the Acts: Selected Discrimination Issues Affecting the Gay Minority* (Ottawa: GO, 1983), p. 25.]

April 30 ∗ Toronto ∗ Newsweb Enterprises, a printing company controlled by the *Toronto Star*, refused to print issue eight of *The Body Politic* following the paper's battle with the *Star* over classified ads. (See also May 2, 1973.)

["*Body Politic* and *The Toronto Star*," *Zodiac Friendship Society Information* 2 (May 1973): 4; Jon Caulfield, "Fighting a Corporate Octopus," *Toronto Citizen*, 18 May 1973, pp. 1, 5; "Firm Quits Printing Paper in Wake of Ad Ban, Protest," *Advocate* (Los Angeles), no. 114 (1973), p. 20; Rowena (Hunnisett), "*Body Politic, Star* Affair," *Other Woman* 1 (July–August 1973): 6–7; "*Toronto Star* Out to Get *Body Politic*," GO *Info*, no. 7 (1973), p. 6; "Why 8's Late," *Body Politic*, no. 8 (1973), p. 5.]

April–May ∗ Toronto ∗ "The Pig, the Prick, and the Dyke Patrol," a comic by Kathy Ross, appeared in the April–May issue of *The Other Woman*.

[Kathy Ross, "The Pig, the Prick, and the Dyke Patrol," *Other Woman* 1 (April–May 1973): 7.]

May ∗ Vancouver ∗ Secretary of State Hugh Faulkner personally rejected an application for an Opportunities for Youth grant to fund a gay service centre in Vancouver after it had already been approved at several government levels. The plan for the Service and Information Centre project had been developed by Ian Mackenzie of GATE (Vancouver).

["OFY Application Turned Down," *Body Politic*, no. 9 (1973), p. 7; George Stanley, "Gay Center Shot Down," *Grape* (Vancouver) 2 (6–19 June 1973): 4.]

May ∗ Vancouver ∗ The Gay Transient Referral and Information Centre (Gay TRIC) was established as a collective to help provide free temporary housing, emergency meals, job referrals, and referrals to community and social services to the constant influx of gay transients arriving in Vancouver. Gay TRIC's centre was located at 752 E. 17th Avenue and was coordinated by Dieter Grapp. The service collapsed in March 1974 and was succeeded by the Have a Gay Stay Transient Housing and Gay Information Service. (See also March 1974.)

["Gay Transient Referral and Information Centre (Vancouver)" vertical file, Canadian Lesbian and Gay Archives, Toronto; Dieter Grapp and Warren Reid, "Transients," *Gay Tide* 1 (October 1973): 6; Q.Q., "Page 69" (column), *Georgia Straight*, 7–13 September 1973, p. 20.]

May 2 ∗ Toronto ∗ Demonstrations sponsored by *The Body Politic* and GATE (Toronto) were held in front of the *Toronto Star* building to protest the paper's refusal to publish an advertisement for *The Body Politic*. The ad was refused because "*The Star* considers itself to be a family newspaper."

[George Addison, "Gay Activists Protest Newspaper Censorship," *Labor Challenge*, 7 May 1973, p. 3; " 'Gay Lib' Protesters Picket *Star* for Refusing to Run Their Ad," *Toronto Star*, four star ed., 2 May 1973, p. 4; "*Toronto Star* Out to Get *Body Politic*," GO *Info*, no. 7 (1973), p. 6; "Why 8's Late," *Body Politic*, no. 8 (1973), p. 5.]

May 2 ∗ Toronto ∗ Representatives of *The Body Politic* and GATE (Toronto) met with members of the New Democratic Party caucus at the Ontario Legislature. The meeting was seen as an opportunity to educate politicians about their gay constituents. Five of the nineteen caucus members attended.

["News of the Gay: 'Gays Meet . . . NDP Caucus,' " *Body Politic*, no. 8 (1973), p. 20.]

May 4 ∗ Toronto ∗ Gerald Hannon, a *Body Politic* reporter, attended a reception at the Royal York Hotel for Prime Minister Pierre Trudeau and welcomed Trudeau to Toronto on behalf of the gay community, and informed him about the paper.

["News of the Gay: Gays Meet . . . Trudeau," *Body Politic*, no. 8 (1973), p. 20.]

May 10 ∗ Montréal ∗ Michel Tremblay's play *Hosanna*, about a transvestite and his biker boyfriend, premiered at the Théâtre de Quat' Sous. Hosanna's ambition is to dress up as Elizabeth Taylor in the movie *Cleopatra*; his illusions are shattered after he attends a party at which everyone has dressed as Cleopatra. *Hosanna* was published by Éditions Leméac in 1973; an English translation was published in Vancouver by Talonbooks in 1974.

[Roch Turbide, "*Hosanna*," in *Dictionnaire des oeuvres littéraires du Québec*, ed. Maurice Lemire et al., vol. 5 (1970–75) (Montréal: Fides, 1987), pp. 410–14.]

May 19–20 ∗ Ottawa ∗ A meeting of representatives of Canadian homophile and gay liberation organizations was held at Pestalozzi College, sponsored by GO. Although many of the sixty delegates were from Ontario, representatives were also sent by groups in Vancouver, Saskatoon, Montréal, Québec City, and Halifax. Workshops were held to discuss political action and organization, the reestablishment and role of the NGEC, the publication of the booklet *Homosexuals: A Minority without Rights/Les homosexuels: une minorité sans droits*, and a national gay pride week to be held August 17–26,

1973. A dance was held on the final day. (See also June 30–July 1, 1973.)

["Canada: Watch Out," *Gemini* 11 1 (May–June 1973): 6; "Canada Election Coalition Formed," *Advocate* (Los Angeles), no. 114 (1973), p. 20; Gays of Ottawa (GO) papers, 82–017, Canadian Lesbian and Gay Archives, Toronto; "Gays," *Gemini* 11 1 (May–June 1974): 2; "Gays Establish Election Coalition," GO *Info*, no. 7 (1973), p. 3; C. Hill, "Ontario Homophile Conference," GO *Info*, no. 6 (1973), p. 8; Michael Merrill, "NGEC to Set Strategy," *Gay Tide* 1 (August 1973): 1, 4; "National Gay Election Coalition: What It's All About," *Body Politic*, no. 14 (1974), p. 8; "Ottawa Meeting," *Back/Chat Newsletter* 3 (13 June 1973): 2; Joe Young, "Gays Map Cross-Country Actions," *Labor Challenge*, 11 June 1973, p. 11.]

May 29–June 3 ✱ Toronto ✱ The Unitarian-Universalist Association held its twelfth General Assembly at the Royal York Hotel, with 1,300 delegates from across North America attending. The U.U. Gay Caucus was able to have a resolution to establish an Office of Gay Affairs placed on the agenda. After some discussion, the resolution was passed, by a three-to-two margin, with two amendments.

[Elgin Blair, "UUA Delegates Vote Approval for OGA!!!!" *U.U. Gay Caucus Newsletter* 3 (June 1973): 1–2; "Unitarian Church Establishes Gay Office," GO *Info*, no. 7 (1973), pp. 5, 8; "Unitarians Establish Gay Office," *Body Politic*, no. 9 (1973), p. 5.]

May–June ✱ Winnipeg ✱ Members of GFE attended all-candidates meetings and polled candidates concerning their stand on rights for homosexuals in Manitoba, leading up to the June 28 provincial election. (See also June 19, 1973.)

[Greg Bourgeois and Bob Wallace, "A More Aggressive Stance: Gays in Manitoba," *Body Politic*, no. 9 (1973), pp. 17, 22; Susan White, "Struggling On: Winnipeg's Gay Liberation Movement 2 Years After," *Manitoban* (Univ. of Manitoba), 4 February 1974, p. 7.]

June ✱ Toronto ✱ CHAT's social centre moved to a permanent location at 201 Church Street. The new centre was described as "probably the most modern of all homosexual association premises in all of North America." Administration and counselling offices moved to 223 Church Street.

["CHAT Moves," *Body Politic*, no. 9 (1973), p. 7; "It's New! It's Permanent! It's Ours!," *Back/Chat Newsletter* 3 (13 June 1973): 1; "Our New Home," *Back/Chat Newsletter* 3 (July 1973): 1; "Year One at 201," *Metro Community News* 1 (31 May 1974): 6.]

June 7 ✱ Ottawa ✱ Representatives of GO met with Anna Whitley, an officer with the Ontario Human Rights Commission, to stress the need for legislative protection for sexual orientation. Whitley was supportive and asked for documented cases of discrimination against lesbians and gay men.

["Commission Needs Documented Cases: Discrimination," GO *Info*, no. 7 (1973), pp. 1–2; "OHRC Representative Backs Gay Civil Rights Struggle," *Body Politic*, no. 9 (1973), p. 6.]

June 19 ✶ Winnipeg ✶ During an all-candidates meeting in Point Douglas constituency, leading up to the June 28 Manitoba provincial election, Independent candidate Joe Borowski stated that "homos and perverts" were taking over the NDP. When asked about rights for homosexuals, Borowski replied, "I don't regard homos as human beings." The other candidates also made negative remarks about homosexuality, and derided women's liberation.

[" 'Homos and Perverts' Running NDP: Borowski," *Winnipeg Tribune*, final ed., 20 June 1973, p. 12.]

June 27 ✶ Montréal ✶ An open house was held to mark the official opening of the Centre d'accueil homophile/Gay Community Centre at 3439, rue St. Denis. The Centre, founded by Tony Farebrother and several other members of Gay McGill, offered a drop-in, social functions, counselling, and a gayline. At about the same time the Association homophile de Montréal/Gay Montreal Association (AHM/GMA) was formed and took offices at the Gay Community Centre. Although it took over operation of the McGill dances in the summer of 1973 and its members were involved in speaking engagements during the rest of the year, the AHM/GMA didn't really get moving until January 1974, after it had incorporated and when it held its first general meeting. (See also January 11, 1974.)

["Association homophile de Montréal/Gay Montreal Association (AHM/GMA)" vertical file, Canadian Lesbian and Gay Archives, Toronto; "Centre to Help 'Gays' Live in Straight World," *Montreal Gazette*, final ed., 28 June 1973, p. 4; "Clarification on Dances: Miscellany," *Gay News* 2 (Xmas 1973): 2; Ron Dayman, "Quebec: Five Years of the Movement," *Body Politic*, no. 29 (1976–77), p. 21; "Gay Centre Opens," *Body Politic*, no. 9 (1973), p. 5; "3439 St-Denis: Centre d'accueil homophile de Montréal," *Omnibus* 2 (July 1973): 21.]

June 29 ✶ Vancouver ✶ Police raided the Hampton Court Club, a gay discotheque at 1066 Seymour Street, for selling liquor without a licence. They smashed down the front door and photographed patrons, but made no arrests; similar heterosexual establishments were not harassed in this way. This was part of a campaign of police harassment of gays in Vancouver that continued throughout the summer of 1973.

["Gay Bar Raided," *Body Politic*, no. 9 (1973), p. 6; Ray Gundersen, " 'We're Not Doing This Just Because You're Queer,' " *Gay Tide* 1 (October 1973): 1, 6; Stan Persky, "GATE Protests Gay Club Raid," *Grape* (Vancouver) 2 (18 July–1 August 1973): 4; "It's Curtains for Hampton Court!" *Your Thing* 1 (5 July 1973): 8–9.]

June 30 ✶ Toronto ✶ The first exclusively lesbian conference in Canada was held at the YWCA, 21 McGill Street. The Gay Women's Festival included discussion groups on legal rights, relationships, lesbian mothers, lesbians and employment, and lesbian feminism. A dance and picnic were also held.

Proposals were put forth to attempt to form new groups, including a lesbian bar-club in Toronto, as well as a group of radicalesbians. About fifty women attended, some from as far away as Vancouver and Montréal.

["Coming Events," *Back/Chat Newsletter* 3 (13 June 1973): 4; "Gay Women's Festival (Toronto, 1973)" vertical file, Canadian Lesbian and Gay Archives, Toronto; Guthrie, "A Letter and a Reply," *Other Woman* 2 (September–October 1973): 1; "In Toronto," *Gemini* 11 1 (July 1973): 4–5; "Lesbian Conference First in Canada," *Body Politic*, no. 9 (1973), p. 7; Jackie (Manthorne), "Lesbians Together," *Long Time Coming* 1 (August 1973): 6–10; Becki L. Ross, *The House That Jill Built: A Lesbian Nation in Formation* (Toronto: University of Toronto Press, 1995), pp. 46–47.]

June 30–July 1 * Toronto * Representatives of Ontario homophile and gay liberation organizations met at the CHAT Centre, 201 Church Street, to plan stategy concerning Gay Pride Week (August 17–26) activities in Ontario, as well as activities of the reestablished NGEC. Participation in the meeting was overwhelmingly male (only one woman attended).

["In Toronto," *Gemini* 11 1 (July 1973): 4–5.]

Summer * Waterloo, Ont. * *Operation Socrates Handbook*, one of the first education-information publications of the Canadian gay movement, was published by the Waterloo GLM. Seven people (Dennis Findlay, Nancy Hills, Ana MacNeil, Peter McDonald, Margaret Murray, Ed Phillips, and Bob Williams) had worked on the project, which was funded by an Opportunities for Youth grant of $9,290. The *Handbook* included answers to common questions about homosexuality, several interviews, information on venereal disease, and a reading list. About 4,000 copies of the forty-page booklet were printed and were distributed to high school guidance departments. Several articles and letters appeared later in the *Kitchener-Waterloo Record* disputing the use of government funds (the OFY grant) to support such projects. (See also November 21, 1973.)

["Editorial," *Gemini* 11 1 (July 1973): 2; "Homosexual Survey Brings 'Negative, Obscene' Replies," *Toronto Star*, four star ed., 18 June 1973, p. 10; "Metro Schools May Receive 'Textbook' on Homosexuality," *Toronto Sun*, final ed., 19 June 1973, p. 10; "Operation: Socrates," *Gemini* 11 1 (July 1973): 5–6; "Students' Gay Lib Handbook Sent to Kitchener Schools," *Toronto Star*, Saturday ed., 17 November 1973, p. A5; Merv Walker, "Pleasing Predictability," *Body Politic*, no. 10 (1973), p. 9; "Youth Grant to Bankroll Gay Survey," *Globe and Mail*, metro ed., 5 May 1973, p. 10.]

Summer * Winnipeg * A Lesbian Resource Centre was being planned by A Woman's Place, in conjunction with Winnipeg Women's Liberation.

["Around Town," *What's Happening!* 2 (Summer 1973): 5.]

Summer–early Autumn * Vancouver * The B.C. NDP constituency organi-zations for Vancouver-Burrard and Vancouver-Centre passed resolutions

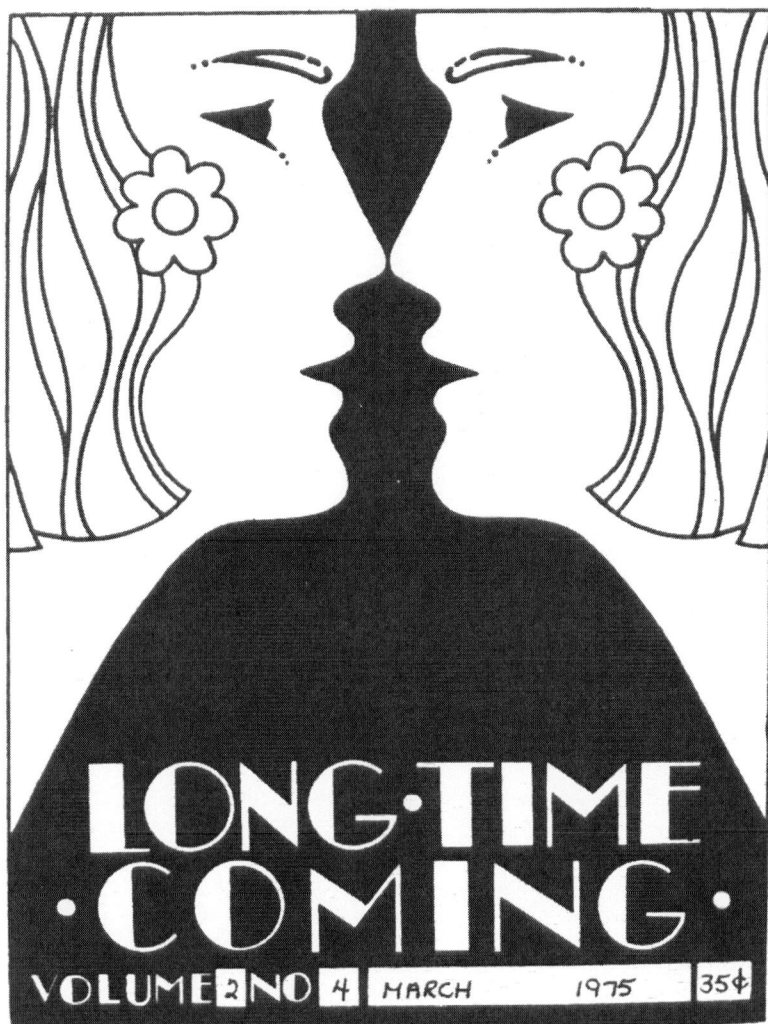

An issue of *Long Time Coming*, the first lesbian journal
in Canada, published by Montreal Gay Women.

favouring the inclusion of a sexual orientation clause in the provincial Human Rights Act.

["Gays Pressure NDP in B.C.," *Body Politic*, no. 10 (1973), p. 4; "NDP Locals Back Changes," *Gay Tide* 1 (October 1973): 3.]

July ∗ Montréal ∗ The first issue of *Long Time Coming* was published by Montreal Gay Women. Edited by Jackie Manthorne, this was the first lesbian journal published in Canada. *Long Time Coming* contained news, poetry, opinion pieces, book reviews, advertisements, and listings. It ceased publication in April–May 1976, after twenty issues.

[Margaret Fulford, ed., *The Canadian Women's Movement, 1960–1990: A Guide to Archival Resources/Le mouvement canadien des femmes, 1960–1990: guide de ressources archivistiques* (Toronto: Canadian Women's Movement Archives/ECW Press, 1992), entry 618.]

July ∗ Toronto ∗ In response to requests from gays in Toronto, Troy Perry of the Universal Fellowship of Metropolitan Community Churches granted Toronto the first official MCC mission in Canada. Rev. Robert Wolfe was sent by MCC from Sacramento, Ca., to be MCC Toronto's first minister. Wolfe conducted his first service in Toronto on July 22, 1973, in offices at 501 Yonge Street. Ten people attended. Within two weeks, the group began holding services at Holy Trinity Church, 20 Trinity Square. (See also March 9, 1974.)

[Gary Curtis, "Gays Pray on Sunday, Just Like 'Normal People,' " *Eyeopener* (Ryerson Polytechnic Institute, Toronto), 17 October 1974, p. 16; Margaret Fulford, ed., *The Canadian Women's Movement, 1960–1990: A Guide to Archival Resources/Le mouvement canadien des femmes, 1960–1990: guide de ressources archivistiques* (Toronto: Canadian Women's Movement Archives/ECW Press, 1992), entry 442; Wayne Hagan papers, 82–035, Canadian Lesbian and Gay Archives, Toronto; "MCC Toronto Mission Opens," *Body Politic*, no. 9 (1973), p. 6; "Praise the Lord," *Metro Community News* 1 (12 July 1974): 1, 3.]

July ∗ Vancouver ∗ During the national convention of the New Democratic Party, delegate Maurice Flood of GATE (Vancouver) was unable to introduce a discussion of gay rights. Cynthia Flood spoke out for same-sex couples supporting children in a resolution on family life.

["British Columbia New Democrats Hear Rights Plea," *Advocate* (Los Angeles), no. 119 (1973), p. 23; "NDP Conference," *Body Politic*, no. 9 (1973), p. 7.]

July 7 ∗ Saskatoon ∗ Representatives of Saskatoon Gay Action, the USHA (Regina campus), and the Atropos Friendship Society met to discuss areas of common interest and ways to work together for gay rights in Saskatchewan. They also discussed the brief concerning the addition of sexual orientation to the Saskatchewan Bill of Rights Act that they were to present to the provincial government. (See also August 14, 1973.)

["Prairie Gays Prepare Brief," *Body Politic*, no. 9 (1973), p. 7; R.W. (Richard Wood-ford), "Saskatoon Gay Action," *Zodiac Friendship Society Information* 2 (June–July 1973): 3.]

July 11 ∗ Ottawa ∗ Prime Minister Pierre Trudeau confirmed in the House of Commons that suspected homosexuality was one of the factors considered by the government before clearing any federal employee to handle classified documents. Trudeau made the disclosure in response to a series of questions on security asked earlier by Erik Nielsen (PC-Yukon). Gay groups across Canada opposed this policy and sent letters of protest to local members of Parliament, Solicitor-General Warren Allmand, and Prime Minister Trudeau.

["Canada Gays Protest Admitted Bias Policy," *Advocate* (Los Angeles), no. 119 (1973), p. 9; Charles C. Hill, "Security Rule Seen as Unfair to Homosexuals" (letter), *Ottawa Citizen*, 17 July 1973, p. 6; George Hislop, "From the President's Pen," *Back/Chat Newsletter* 3 (August 1973): 2; "Homosexuals, Unstable Kept from Secrets: P.M.," *Toronto Star*, four star ed., 12 July 1973, p. 77; Michael Merrill, "Discrimination Canada," *Gay Tide* 1 (October 1973): 4.]

July 18 ∗ Windsor, Ont. ∗ WGU tried to place a classified advertisement for a gay dance in the *Windsor Star* and was refused. The entire ad read: "Gay Dance / Saturday / 8 p.m. / Alumni Lounge / University of Windsor." J. Patrick O'Callaghan, publisher of the *Star*, said that the ad had been rejected because it "exploited sex," that it discriminated against heterosexuals, and that it was offensive. WGU filed a complaint with the Windsor Press Council on July 27, 1973. (See also July 20 and September 25, 1973.)

["Press Council Rules against the *Star*," *Windsor Star*, final ed., 27 September 1973, pp. 3–4.]

July 20 ∗ Toronto ∗ When the *Windsor Star* refused to print a classified ad for *The Body Politic*, the gay paper filed a formal complaint with the Ontario Press Council, which accepted the complaint for consideration. (See also October 23, 1973.)

["*Star* Continues Ban," *Body Politic*, no. 9 (1973), p. 5.]

August ∗ Montréal ∗ André Roy's book of poetry *N'importe quelle page* was published by Les Herbes rouge.

[Roger Chamberland, "*N'importe quelle page* et autres recueils de poésies d'André Roy," in *Dictionnaire des oeuvres littéraires du Québec*, ed. Maurice Lemire et al., vol. 5 (1970–75) (Montréal: Fides, 1987), pp. 594–96.]

August ∗ Toronto ∗ Mayor David Crombie refused to proclaim August 17–26 Gay Pride Week. (See also August 17–26, 1973.)

["Crombie Rejects Gay Pride Week," *Body Politic*, no. 9 (1973), p. 5.]

August * Vancouver * GATE (Vancouver) opened new offices at 1982 W. 6th Avenue, which included work space as well as rooms for meetings and drop-ins.

[Michael Merrill, "GATE Opens New Quarters," *Gay Tide* 1 (August 1973): 1, 4.]

August * Vancouver * The first issue of *Gay Tide* was published by GATE (Vancouver) to celebrate Gay Pride Week 1973. *Gay Tide* became one of the most influential Canadian gay publications of the 1970s; it was published until February–March 1980. (See also December 2, 1973.)

["Who We Are" (editorial), *Gay Tide* 1 (November 1973): 2.]

August (mid) * Toronto * Police raided the International Steam Bath, 458 Spadina Avenue, and arrested four men on charges of gross indecency.

["Toronto Police Raid Bath," *Body Politic*, no. 10 (1973), p. 7.]

August 14 * Saskatoon * Representatives of Saskatoon Gay Action presented a brief to Ned Shillington, executive assistant to Attorney-General Roy Romanow. The brief called for changes to the Saskatchewan Bill of Rights Act, the Fair Accommodations Practices Act, the Fair Employment Practices Act, and the Saskatchewan Human Rights Commission Act, to outlaw discrimination based on sexual orientation. (See also August 25, 1973.)

[B.G. (Bruce Garman), "The Brief: Another First for Sask.?" *Zodiac Friendship Society* 2 (September 1973): 1; "Sask. Attorney-General Stalls," *Gay West*, no. 2 (1975), p. 10; "Saskatchewan Attorney-General Favors Gay Rights Amendment," *Body Politic*, no. 10 (1973), p. 7.]

August 17 * Montréal * Members of Montreal Gay Women participated in a press conference in support of Dr. Henry Morgentaler. Police had raided his clinic on August 15 and arrested Morgentaler, his staff, and patients, charging them with performing or conspiring to perform illegal abortions.

["Why Gay Women Should Support Dr. Morgentaler," *Long Time Coming* 1 (October–November 1973): 11.]

August 17–26 * Vancouver; Saskatoon; Toronto; Ottawa; Montréal; Halifax * The second annual Gay Pride Week became a national celebration, with a political theme: to express pride in gay sexuality, to bring to the attention of the general public the existence of homosexuals in Canadian society, to work towards the end of discrimination against homosexual people, and in particular to petition for a clause regarding sexual orientation in provincial human rights codes. (See also October 1–6, 1973.)

[Robert Cook, "Festive Solidarity Marks Gay Pride Week," *Gay Tide* 1 (October 1973): 1, 7; J. de Y. (J. de Young), "Announcing, Gay Pride Week in Canada!" GAE/Y *Monitor* 2 (24 August 1973): 1–2; Maurice Flood, "Gays Organize Week of Celebration and

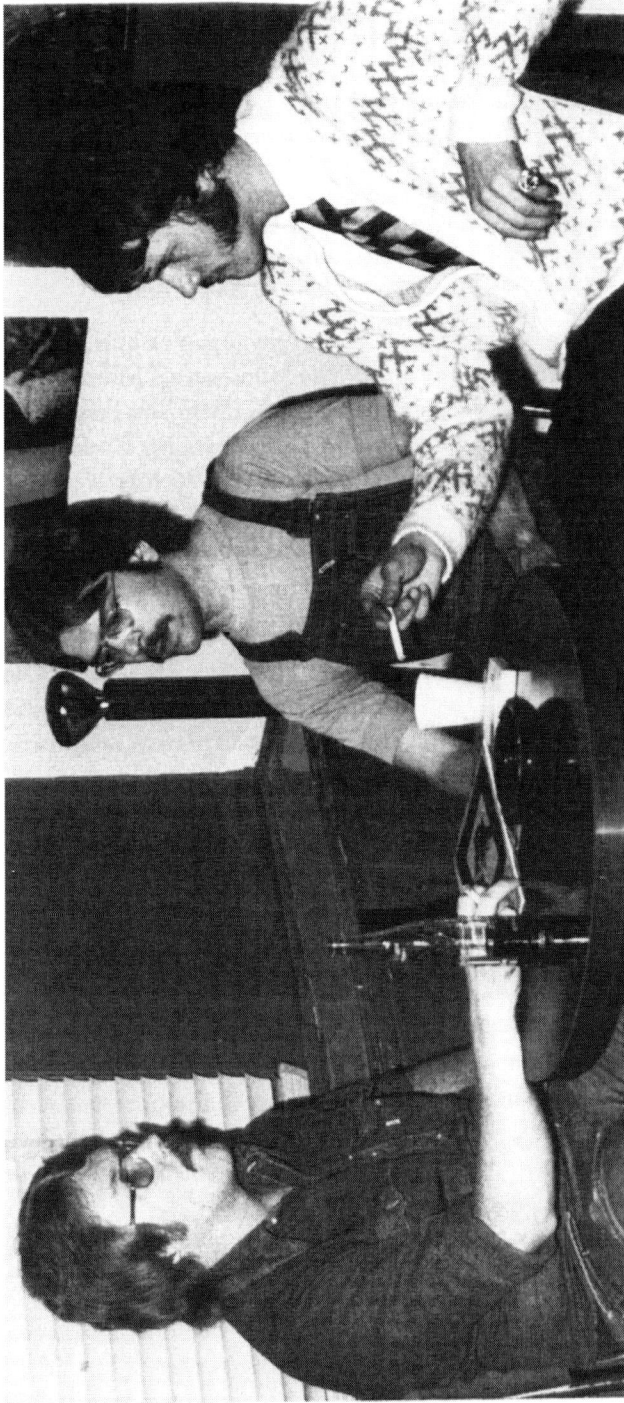

Doug Hellquist, Bruce Garman, and Tim LeMay, members of Saskatoon Gay Action, 1973. Photo by John MacLean Cook.

Solidarity," *Grape* (Vancouver) 2 (14–28 August 1973): 17; "Gay Arts Festival and Dance Will Open Gay Pride Week," *Gay Tide* 1 (August 1973): 3; "Gay Pride Week," *Gemini* 11 1 (August–September 1973): 3–4; George Hislop, "Address by George Hislop, President of CHAT, Given on Saturday, August 18, 1973," in *Gay Directions: Gay Pride Week August 17–26, 1973* (Toronto: CHAT, 1973), pp. 27–35; Rowena Hunnisett, "Gay Pride Week," *Other Woman* 2 (September–October 1973): 18–19; "1973's Gay Pride Week: A National Event . . . ," *Body Politic*, no. 10 (1973), p. 7; "Saskatoon Won't Be Gay," *Saskatoon Star-Phoenix*, 14 August 1973, p. 4; Nancy Walker, "Address by Nancy Walker, Vice-President of CHAT, Given Saturday, August 18, 1973," in *Gay Directions: Gay Pride Week August 17–26, 1973* (Toronto: CHAT, 1973), pp. 3–9.]

August 21 ∗ Toronto ∗ A coalition of Ontario gay organizations, represented by GATE (Toronto), presented the brief "The Homosexual Minority and the Ontario Human Rights Code" to Ontario Labour Minister Fern Guindon, calling for an amendment to the Ontario Human Rights Code to outlaw discrimination based on sexual orientation. Copies of the brief were also sent to Ontario Human Rights Commission representatives in Hamilton, Kitchener-Waterloo, Ottawa, and Windsor. (See also February 18, 1974.)

["Homosexual Group Tells Guindon Law Should Support Their Rights," *Toronto Star*, four star ed., 22 August 1973, p. A7.]

August 24 ∗ Toronto ∗ The brief "Ontario Homosexuals and the Ontario Human Rights Commission" was presented by members of GO on behalf of all gay groups in Ontario to Daniel Hill, chairperson of the Ontario Human Rights Commission, asking that the Commission recommend to the Ontario cabinet that discrimination based on sexual orientation be outlawed in the province. Dr. Hill promised a response within six weeks. (See also February 18, 1974.)

["Brief to Be Presented," *Back/Chat Newsletter* 3 (August 1973): 2; "Homosexuals Seeking Protection of Rights in Commission Brief," *Ottawa Citizen*, 24 August 1973, p. 3.]

August 25 ∗ Saskatoon ∗ The Saskatchewan Human Rights Commission decided to recommend the expansion of anti-discrimination legislation and equal opportunity programs in Saskatchewan, including the outlawing of discrimination based on sexual orientation. This was the first time that a Human Rights Commission in Canada had called for the inclusion of sexual orientation in human rights legislation.

["Rights Commission Decides Priorities: Anti-discrimination," *Saskatoon Star-Phoenix*, 25 August 1973, p. 3.]

August 25 ∗ Vancouver; Toronto ∗ Simultaneous demonstrations for the inclusion of a sexual orientation clause in provincial human rights codes took place as part of Gay Pride Week. In Vancouver, about 100 people (mostly male) attended the rally at the courthouse. Few women took part in the demonstration because many lesbians felt that the protest was geared towards fighting gay male oppression and ignored the concerns of women.

[‘‘Claim Our Rights,’’ *Body Politic*, no. 9 (1973), p. 1; Robert Cook, ‘‘Festive Solidarity Marks Gay Pride Week,’’ *Gay Tide* 1 (October 1973): 1, 7; Maurice Flood, ‘‘Gay Rights Rally Will Demand ‘Sexual Orientation’ Protection,’’ *Gay Tide* 1 (August 1973): 1; ‘‘Gays Converge on Ontario House,’’ *Gay Tide* 1 (October 1973): 3; Rowena Hunnisett, ‘‘Gay Pride Week,’’ *Other Woman* 2 (September–October 1973): 18–19; Adrienne Potts, ‘‘Adrienne Potts’ Speech for Gay Pride March,’’ *Other Woman* 2 (September–October 1973): 20; Pat Smith, ‘‘Why I Didn’t Go to the Gay Pride Rally,’’ *Pedestal* 6 (January 1974): 15 (reprinted in *Long Time Coming* 1 [May–June 1974]: 20–22); ‘‘Vancouver Rally Marks Canada Gay Pride Week,’’ *Advocate* (Los Angeles), no. 121 (1973), p. 14.]

August 28 * Vancouver * ‘‘The Struggle for Gay Rights,’’ a half-hour documentary about gay liberation, was shown on Channel 10 (Cablevision). Produced by members of GATE (Vancouver) in cooperation with Metro Media, this was the first documentary shown on television to deal with gay liberation in Vancouver.

[Robert Cook, ‘‘Festive Solidarity Marks Gay Pride Week,’’ *Gay Tide* 1 (October 1973): 1, 7; ‘‘T.V. to Document Gay Struggle,’’ *Gay Tide* 1 (August 1973): 3.]

August 29 * Victoria, B.C. * Maurice Flood and Fred Gilbertson of GATE (Vancouver) and George Nicola, a gay activist from Oregon, met with B.C. Minister of Labour William King to discuss civil rights for gays, and protection from discrimination based on sexual orientation as an addition to the provincial Human Rights Act. The minister rejected the group’s requests and declared that homosexuality should not have explicit legal sanction. (See also November 7, 1973.)

[‘‘B.C. Gays Meet Labour Minister,’’ *Body Politic*, no. 10 (1973), p. 6; Maurice Flood, ‘‘King Says No to Civil Rights,’’ *Gay Tide* 1 (October 1973): 1, 6; ‘‘Gay Alliance to Meet King on Rights for Homosexuals,’’ *Vancouver Province*, final ed., 27 August 1973, p. 40; ‘‘King Agrees to Meet with GATE,’’ *Body Politic*, no. 9 (1973), p. 6; ‘‘No Progress in British Columbia Talks,’’ *Advocate* (Los Angeles), no. 121 (1973), p. 17.]

August 30 * Montréal * The Association of Gay Psychologists was organized during the eighty-first annual convention of the American Psychological Association, held in Montréal. The group’s first meeting drew about 100 people (twenty were women) to discuss fighting oppression within their profession.

[Donna Gabeline, ‘‘Abolishing Fear of the Gay a Future Psychological Goal,’’ *Montreal Gazette*, final ed., 28 August 1973, p. 16; ‘‘Gay American Psychologists Come Out at Montreal Meeting,’’ *Body Politic*, no. 10 (1973), p. 5; ‘‘New Gay Role Felt as Psychologists Convene,’’ *Advocate* (Los Angeles), no. 122 (1973), p. 5.]

August 31 ✱ Halifax ✱ Thee Klub, the drop-in centre run by GAE at 1585 Barrington Street, Suite 207, was officially closed. In operation for only a few months, the centre provided a library, music, games, and a personal message board, as well as a coffee house on Tuesday nights. Thee Klub closed due to internal squabbling over finances.

[J. de Young, "Drop-in Centre News," GAE/Y *Monitor* 2 (21 September 1973): 3.]

September ✱ Ottawa ✱ The Coral Reef, 30 Nicholas Street, was the only gay club in Ottawa that allowed both drinking and dancing and as a result was very popular. In September, the club's management decided to turn the Coral Reef into a bar for students. "Obvious" gays were banned and admission was restricted to students with an identification card. This new policy did not last long, and by February 1974 the Coral Reef was gay again.

[Jay, "Lesson to the Gay Community," GO *Info*, no. 8 (1973), p. 10; Jay, "The New Coral Reef," GO *Info*, no. 9 (1974), p. 5.]

September ✱ Toronto ✱ The Canadian Gay Liberation Movement Archives was founded as a spin-off from *The Body Politic*, with the newspaper's back files serving as the original core of the collection. Jearld Moldenhauer was instrumental in getting the Archives started, and Ron Dayman served as the Archives' first volunteer archivist. Over the next twenty years, the (renamed) Canadian Lesbian and Gay Archives would grow to become one of the largest repositories of gay and lesbian materials in the world.

["Archives to Preserve, Index Gay Canadiana," *Metro Community News* 1 (15 December 1973): 3; Rick Bébout, "Stashing the Evidence," *Body Politic*, no. 55 (1979), pp. 21–22, 26; "Gay Archives" (editorial), *Body Politic*, no. 10 (1973), p. 2.]

September ✱ Toronto ✱ The newly renovated Carriage House, 306 Jarvis Street, opened as Toronto's first hotel catering to gays.

["The Carriage House," *Gemini* 11 2 (February 1974): 5.]

September ✱ Toronto ✱ The Club Baths, the first of the modern gay-operated bathhouses in Canada, opened at 231 Mutual Street. Owned by Peter Maloney and associates, the operation was affiliated with the Club Baths chain in the United States. Over the next few years, the Club chain would spread to other cities in Canada, from Montréal to Vancouver.

[Advertisement, *Metro Community News* 1 (18 October 1974): 19; "The Club," *Body Politic*, no. 9 (1973), p. 22; Nails (interviewing Peter Maloney), "Interesting Human Beings," *Metro Community News* 2 (18 July 1975): 14; Larry Ryan, Letter (with reply from Peter Maloney), *Metro Community News* 2 (15 August 1975): 6.]

September 20 ✱ Victoria, B.C. ✱ Rosemary Brown (NDP-Vancouver-Burrard) reaffirmed her support for the inclusion of a sexual orientation clause in the provincial Human Rights Act in a speech in the British Columbia Legislature.

["Legislator Supports B.C. Gay Rights," *Body Politic*, no. 10 (1973), p. 6; "MLA Re-affirms Gay Rights Stand," *Gay Tide* 1 (October 1973): 3.]

September 25 ⋆ Windsor, Ont. ⋆ The Windsor Press Council ruled that the *Windsor Star* had discriminated against WGU on July 18 by refusing to print their advertisement for a gay dance. *The Star* said they had rejected the ad because "We have no intention of lowering our standards on good taste."

["Press Council Rules against the *Star*," *Windsor Star*, final ed., 27 September 1973, pp. 3–4; "Windsor Paper Discriminates," *Body Politic*, no. 10 (1973), p. 4; "*Windsor Star* Discriminates (Still)," *Windsor Gay Unity Newsletter* 1 (August 1975): 7.]

September 27 ⋆ Toronto ⋆ A resolution protecting civic workers from discrimination based on sexual orientation was passed by the City of Toronto's Committee on Urban Renewal, Housing, Fire and Legislation. Members of GATE (Toronto) attended the meeting and had presented a brief to Committee members on September 7. (See also October 10, 1973.)

[Gay Alliance toward Equality (GATE) (Toronto) papers, 82–029, Canadian Lesbian and Gay Archives, Toronto; "GATE Lobbies Toronto Council," *Body Politic*, no. 9 (1973), p. 5; "New City Policy Would Bar Bias against Homosexuals," *Toronto Star*, four star ed., 28 September 1973, p. A7.]

September 29 ⋆ Vancouver ⋆ A workshop on discrimination and the B.C. Human Rights Act was held by the B.C. Civil Liberties Association. Representatives from thirty organizations, including two gay/lesbian groups — Gay Alliance toward Equality (GATE) (Vancouver) and Gay People of UBC — formulated recommendations for improving the B.C. Human Rights Act. The resolutions, which included extending the Act to protect people from discrimination based on sexual orientation, were sent to the provincial government. (See also November 7, 1973.)

[Gay Alliance toward Equality (GATE) papers, 82–005/08, Canadian Lesbian and Gay Archives, Toronto.]

September–October ⋆ Toronto ⋆ A seventeen-point lesbian-feminist statement was published in a special lesbian issue of *The Other Woman*.

["On a Queer Day . . . We Can See Forever: A Lesbian-Feminist Statement," *Other Woman* 2 (September–October 1973): 26–27.]

Autumn ⋆ Halifax ⋆ The Student's Council of St. Mary's University adopted an entertainment policy that denied students the right to take people of their own sex as guests to campus social functions. The action was protested by GAE, and was later changed.

["Still Hassled," *Body Politic*, no. 12 (1974), p. 7; "Students Hinder Same-Sex Dating," *Body Politic*, no. 11 (1974), p. 4.]

Autumn ✶ Montréal ✶ The lesbian and gay student group Egaylity was formed at Loyola College. Its early membership was almost entirely female.

["Gay Women," *Gay News* 2 (21 November 1973): 2.]

Autumn ✶ Ottawa ✶ A gay caucus was established at the First Unitarian Church of Ottawa.

["Community News: Ottawa, Canada," *U.U. Gay World* 4 (August 1975): 7.]

Autumn ✶ Saskatoon ✶ The group Lesbian Feminists was established, with Erin Shoemaker as a key organizer.

["Lesbian Feminists (Saskatoon)" vertical file, Canadian Lesbian and Gay Archives, Toronto.]

Autumn ✶ Toronto ✶ George Hislop, president of CHAT, was elected to the Administrative Committee of Project '73 (later Project '74), a coalition of youth services agencies in Metropolitan Toronto.

["CHAT President Elected to Post," *Body Politic*, no. 11 (1974), p. 4; George Hislop, "From the President's Pen," *Back/Chat Newsletter*, December 1973, p. 1; "Non-gay Group Votes Known Gay to Board," *Metro Community News* 1 (15 December 1973): 3.]

October ✶ Kingston, Ont. ✶ The Queen's University Homophile Association (QUHA) was formed. The first leader of the group was Terry Watson (pseud.). In addition to holding meetings and parties, the QUHA ran the Gay Rap Line, a telephone information service. By the spring of 1974 membership numbered about fifty. By March 1975 the group had become dormant, but it revived again in September–October 1975.

[Ron Dayman, "Little Rock, Ont.?" *Body Politic*, no. 12 (1974), p. 23; Jim Finn, "New Group at Queen's," *GO Info*, no. 9 (1974), p. 4; "Queen's Homophiles Uniting," *Queen's Journal* (Queen's Univ.), 2 November 1973, p. 4; J.P. Wilmshurst, "Where's Terry Watson?" *Queen's Journal* (Queen's Univ.), 29 May 1975, p. 5.]

October ✶ Montréal ✶ Several members of Gay McGill, including Will Aitken, Bruce Garside, and John Southin, opened Androgyny Books, specializing in gay and feminist titles, at 1225A, rue Crescent. Over the next twenty years Androgyny (L'Androgyne) would establish itself as the premier lesbian and gay bookstore in Québec.

[Ron Dayman, "Quebec: Five Years of the Movement," *Body Politic*, no. 29 (1976–77), p. 21; Margaret Fulford, ed., *The Canadian Women's Movement, 1960–1990: A Guide to Archival Resources/Le mouvement canadien des femmes, 1960–1990: guide de ressources archivistiques* (Toronto: Canadian Women's Movement Archives/ECW Press, 1992), entries 1125, 1126; Ross Higgins, "L'Androgyne: 10 ans d'histoire," *Sortie*, no. 11 (1983), pp. 30, 36; Yves Lafontaine, "Lawrence Boyle: L'Androgyne," *Fugues* 11 (May 1994): 58–59; Louis-Michel Noël, "Lawrence Boyle: d'amour et de livres," *Sortie*, no. 51 (1987), pp. 32–33.]

October ✳ Ottawa ✳ The Law Reform Committee of GO published the nineteen-page booklet *Gays and the Law*, a guidebook to Canadian laws governing gay sexual activities.

[Monograph collection, M86–050, Canadian Lesbian and Gay Archives, Toronto.]

October 1–6 ✳ Winnipeg ✳ GFE sponsored Winnipeg's first Gay Pride Week, held at the University of Manitoba. Events included lectures, films, a coffee house, folk singing, and a dance. More than 100 people (mostly students) attended a symposium entitled "Homosexuality: A Contemporary View." Gay Pride Week was the first major project undertaken by GFE.

[Maurice Flood, "Gay Pride Celebrated in Buffalo Country," *Gay Tide* 1 (November 1973): 3; "Gay Panel Sparks Biblical Debate," *Winnipeg Free Press*, 6 October 1973, p. 6; B. Vogel and B. Wallace, "Gay Pride Week," *Manitoban* (Univ. of Manitoba), 4 October 1973, p. 12; Susan White, "Struggling On: Winnipeg's Gay Liberation Movement 2 Years After," *Manitoban* (Univ. of Manitoba), 4 February 1974, p. 7.]

October 5–8 ✳ Edmonton ✳ The second annual Western Canada Gay Clubs Conference was held, during which representatives from five organizations met to discuss common goals.

["Conference," *Zodiac Friendship Society* 2 (December 1973): 4; Marlene M., "Western Gay Conference," *Carousel Capers* 4 (November 1973): 12; "West Clubs Meet," *Body Politic*, no. 11 (1974), p. 5.]

October 6–7 ✳ Québec, Qué. ✳ The first pan-Canadian conference of gay organizations was hosted by CHAL. More than eighty delegates from twenty groups attended. Workshops were held on the NGEC questionnaire, relationships between gay men and lesbians, homosexuality and the Catholic church, gay pride week, and homosexuality and aging. During the proceedings divisions within CHAL surfaced when a dissident group gathered to protest CHAL's representation of Québec's gays, complaining that its approach was too conservative. Most of the progressive members left CHAL soon after the conference, but CHAL continued to flourish with a large male and female membership, under the leadership of Denise Goyette.

[Eleanor Anstruther, "CHAL Gay Conference," *Dialogue*, no. 2 (1973), pp. 11–12; Marcel Charland, "Les homosexuels 'envahissent' Québec pour un congrès mixte," *Journal de Québec*, 8 October 1973, p. 14; Ron Dayman, "Quebec: Five Years of the Movement," *Body Politic*, no. 29 (1976–77), pp. 20–21; "The Gay National Assembly," *Long Time Coming* 1 (October–November 1973): 6; "National Conference Meets in Quebec City," *Body Politic*, no. 10 (1973), p. 6; "Quebec City Conference," GO *Info*, no. 8 (1973), p. 3; Merv Walker, " 'Many Faces, One Focus': 4th Annual Conference

A poster advertising the Centre d'accueil homophile/
Gay Community Centre, Montréal, 1973.

Planned for Toronto," *Body Politic*, no. 26 (1976), p. 6; "What Comes Out of a Conference?" GAE *Monitor* 2 (25 October 1973): 6–7.]

October 10 ✱ Toronto ✱ By a vote of 15–1, the Toronto City Council passed a resolution banning discrimination on the basis of sexual orientation in city employment. The vote came after a six-month lobbying effort by GATE (Toronto). This was the first time in Canada that any legislative body had recognized gay people as a legitimate minority, with a right to equal opportunity in employment. The event was called "our first win" by *The Body Politic*.

["Breakthrough," *Zodiac Friendship Society* 2 (December 1973): 2; "City Bars Job Discrimination," *Body Politic*, no. 10 (1973), p. 5; Gay Alliance toward Equality (GATE) (Toronto) papers, 82–029, Canadian Lesbian and Gay Archives, Toronto; "Gay Rights," *Metro Community News* 1 (15 November 1973): 7; "Gays Win Real Victory," GO *Info*, no. 8 (1973), p. 1; George Hislop, "From the President's Pen," *Back/Chat Newsletter*, November 1973, p. 1; "In Brief: Resolution Opposes Discrimination against Gays," *Labor Challenge*, 22 October 1973, p. 10; "Toronto Bans Anti-gay Bias in City Jobs," *Advocate* (Los Angeles), no. 125 (1973), p. 3; "Toronto City Council Backs Gay Rights," *Gay Tide* 1 (November 1973): 1; "Toronto Resolution: Powerful Precedent" (editorial), *Gay Tide* 1 (November 1973): 2.]

October 23 ✱ Ottawa ✱ The Ontario Press Council announced it would not hear a complaint of discrimination against the *Windsor Star* relating to the *Star*'s refusal to print a classified ad for *The Body Politic*. The Council stated that it had already ruled in April on a similar complaint against the *Toronto Star* and did not, as a general rule, consider complaints identical to those on which it has already ruled.

["Ad Refused, Press Body Won't Hear Complaint," *Toronto Star*, four star ed., 23 October 1973, pp. A1, A2; "No: Council," *Body Politic*, no. 10 (1973): 6.]

October 25–November 10 ✱ Toronto ✱ Louis Del Grande's play *So Who's Goldberg?* was performed at the Theatre Upstairs, 11 Trinity Square. It was also published in Toronto in 1973 by Fineglow Plays.

[Louis Del Grande, "*So Who's Goldberg?*" in Connie Brissenden, ed., *Now in Paperback: Six Canadian Plays of the 1970s* (Toronto: Fineglow Plays, 1973), pp. 11–30.]

October 31 ✱ Montréal ✱ On Halloween, members of WITCH (War in the Interest of Terrorizing Corporate Hedonists), including feminists and members of Montreal Gay Women, converged on The Sex Machine nightclub, the first topless waitress club in Montréal, to demonstrate against sexism. The demonstrators wore masks and costumes.

["A WITCH Action" (advertisement), *Long Time Coming* 1 (October–November 1973): 14.]

November ✱ London, Ont. ✱ A petition signed by seventy-seven people asking that the UWOHA extend the hours of its dances was the catalyst for considering moving UWOHA off-campus into a building that could be used as a general lesbian-gay community centre. This was the first move towards the formation of the Homophile Association of London, Ontario (HALO). (See also March 1974.)

[Executive Committee, "Dear Members" (letter), UWOHA *Newsletter* 2 (December 1973): 3.]

November 3 ∗ Toronto ∗ About thirty people attended a day-long conference sponsored by GATE (Toronto). The meeting was held to set priorities for the group and to elect an Administrative Committee to oversee GATE's operations. Walter Blumenthal, Don Brant, Michael Lynch, Ken Popert, and Tom Warner were elected to the Committee.

["GATE Meeting," *Metro Community News* 1 (15 November 1973): 5; "Toronto GATE Decides Goals," *Body Politic*, no. 11 (1974), p. 5.]

November 7 ∗ Victoria, B.C. ∗ The provincial NDP government passed a revised Human Rights Act that did not include specific protection against discrimination based on sexual orientation. Labour Minister William King stated that gays were not protected in the Act specifically because he did not want to give homosexuality legal sanction. King did believe, however, that gays would be protected from discrimination by the "reasonable cause" section of the new Act. (See also November 8, 1973.)

[Rick Gordon, "King Tagged Out on Code Discrepancies," *Western Voice*, 21 November–4 December 1973, p. 4; "Homosexuals Protected, Says King," *Vancouver Sun*, three star ed., 10 November 1973, p. 14; "Human Rights Code Rips-off Biggest Group," *Gay Tide* 1 (November 1973): 1; "Human Rights Code Still Ignores Gays," *Body Politic*, no. 11 (1974), p. 5; "Rights Code Protects Homos, Says Minister," *Vancouver Province*, four star ed., 10 November 1973, p. 8.]

November 8 ∗ Victoria, B.C. ∗ Nine members of GATE (Vancouver) demonstrated on the steps of the B.C. Legislature to protest the exclusion of a sexual orientation clause from the revised provincial Human Rights Act.

[Maurice Flood, "Bill Sneaks Through; Ferries Go to Victoria," *Gay Tide* 1 (January 1974): 4–5; "Gay Group Protests," *Vancouver Sun*, four star ed., 9 November 1973, p. 42; "Gay Protest Made No Points," *Victoria Times-Colonist*, 9 November 1973, p. 16; "Human Rights Code Rips-off Biggest Group," *Gay Tide* 1 (November 1973): 1.]

November 11 ∗ Vancouver ∗ A lesbian and seven of her friends were verbally and physically assaulted by staff and thrown out of Champagne Charlie's, 612 Davie Street, after they complained about sexist remarks that had been made to them. At that time, Champagne Charlie's was one of the major lesbian and gay clubs in Vancouver.

[Dave Rand, "Sexism Strikes Again," *Gay Tide* 1 (January 1974): 9.]

November 16 ∗ Toronto ∗ Toronto police charged Reg Hartt, director of the Rochdale College Cinema Archives, with possession of obscene material for distribution, after seizing three sex films in a raid on his home. Two of the films were gay classics (*Bijou* and *The Boys in the Sand*); the third was *Deep Throat*.

["Toronto Police Confiscate Films," *Body Politic*, no. 11 (1974), p. 6.]

November 19 ∗ Halifax ∗ GAE was incorporated as a non-profit organization under the Nova Scotia Societies Act.

[Gay Alliance for Equality (GAE) papers, 84–018, Canadian Lesbian and Gay Archives, Toronto.]

November 21 ∗ Ottawa ∗ In a speech before the Senate Finance Committee, Senator Raymond Perrault (Lib.-British Columbia) demanded an investigation be made into government funding of the *Operation Socrates Handbook*. The *Handbook*, produced by Waterloo GLM during the summer of 1973, had been funded by an Opportunities for Youth grant of $9,290.

["Perrault Demands Justification," *Gay Tide* 1 (January 1974): 3; "Senator Attacks Waterloo Grant," *Body Politic*, no. 11 (1974), p. 4.]

November 23–24 ∗ New York, N.Y. ∗ The first conference of the Gay Academic Union was held at the City University of New York. A number of Canadian academics and students attended, including Edgar Z. Friedenberg of Dalhousie University, who was interviewed there by a *Body Politic* reporter.

[Greg Lehne, "An Interview: Edgar Z. Friedenberg," *Body Politic*, no. 11 (1974), pp. 17–19.]

November 27 ∗ Montréal ∗ An unauthorized, altered version of Edward Albee's play *Who's Afraid of Virginia Woolf?* opened, in which the lead characters were two gay lovers. Albee stopped the production before a second performance could be presented.

["Author Halts Montreal Production," *Body Politic*, no. 11 (1974), p. 4.]

December ∗ Edmonton ∗ The Unitarian Church established an Office of Gay Affairs, which sponsored open discussions on a variety of topics concerning lesbians and gays. By March 1974, the Church was sponsoring a Gay Evening Out each Sunday.

["Gay Symposium Committee to Open 'Gay Evening Out,'" *Club '70 News*, March 1974, p. 5.]

December ∗ Toronto ∗ A counselling service for lesbians and gays was inaugurated at MCC. (See also January 15, 1974, and July 1975.)

["Counselling Services Available at Church," *Metro Community News* 1 (1 December 1973): 3.]

December 2 * Montréal * Twenty people attended the first service of L'Église communautaire de Montréal/Montreal Community Church (ECM/MCC), held at the Gay Community Centre, 3439, rue St. Denis. Rev. Bob Wolfe of MCC (Toronto) conducted the first service. In 1974, Rev. Rainier became the group's first pastor. By February 1975 ECM/MCC was meeting regularly on Sundays at the YMCA Chapel, 1441, rue Drummond, was providing counselling services, and had started a newsletter (*Montréalités*). By December 1975 the church had about ninety members.

[John Blacklock, "Local Church Group Is Two Years Old," *Montreal Gay Times* 1 (December 1975): 8; "The Chaplain's Corner: What Is MCC?" *Gay News* 2 (January 1974): 4; "The Church on the Move," *Metro Community News* 1 (13 September 1974): 1; "Church Opens in Montreal," *Body Politic*, no. 11 (1974), p. 5; "Editorial," *Montréalités* 1 (November 1975–January 1976): 3; "L'Église communautaire de Montréal/ Montreal Community Church (ECM/MCC)" vertical file, Canadian Lesbian and Gay Archives, Toronto; "L'Église communautaire de Montréal — Montreal Community Church Moves to New Home," *Montréalités* 1 (February 1975): 1, 3; "Gays at 'Y'?: Why Not!" *Gay-Zette* 2 (June 1975): 3; "MCC Services Begin in Montreal Sunday," *Metro Community News* 1 (1 December 1973): 3.]

December 2 * Vancouver * After the *Vancouver Sun* refused to print a classified subscription ad for *Gay Tide* in November, GATE (Vancouver) organized a demonstration of fifteen people outside the Pacific Press Building, 2250 Granville Street. The proposed ad read "Subs. to *Gay Tide*, Gay Lib Paper. 6 monthly issues, $1. Box 6572, Station G, Van 8." The *Sun* had a standing rule not to print any ad containing the words "gay" or "homophile." In October 1973 the *Sun* had refused to print an ad for Gay People Together, for the same reason. (See also October 23, 1974.)

["GPT Meet WECC" (letter), *Georgia Straight*, 19–25 October 1973, p. 7; Rick Gordon, "The *Vancouver Sun* Charged with Bias," *Western Voice*, 4–17 December 1973, p. 5; "Group Pickets Newspaper Office," *Vancouver Sun*, four star ed., 3 December 1973, p. 36; "Group Raps Ad Rejection," *Vancouver Province*, 3 December 1973, p. 8; Q.Q., "Page 69" (column), *Georgia Straight*, 19–25 October 1973, p. 22; "Sun Discriminates: No Ads for Gays," *Gay Tide* 1 (January 1974): 1; "Vancouver Paper Turns Down Ad: GATE Protests, Demands Justice," *Body Politic*, no. 11 (1974), p. 6; "*Vancouver Sun*" vertical file, Canadian Lesbian and Gay Archives, Toronto.]

December 3 * London, Ont. * Ed Blake, a supporter of gay rights, was elected to London's Board of Control for a one-year term.

["London Elects Rights Supporter," *Body Politic*, no. 11 (1974), p. 6.]

December 10 * Waterloo, Ont. * Six members of GATE (Toronto) and *The*

Body Politic attended a meeting of Waterloo GLM to discuss the activities and organization of the NGEC.

["GLM Meetings," *Gemini* 11 2 (January 1974): 3.]

December 13 * Montréal * *La presse* refused to print an ad for a gay New Year's Eve dance to be held at McGill University.

["*La presse*: Bull on the Stands but Chicken in the Office," *Gay News* 2 (Xmas 1973): 1.]

December 15 * Washington, D.C. * Following three years of lobbying by members of the gay liberation movement, the American Psychiatric Association removed homosexuality from its official list of mental disorders. The trustees of the 20,000-member Association also urged an end to private and public discrimination against gays in employment, housing, and other areas, and recommended that state legislatures repeal their "irrational" laws against sodomy or "unnatural" sex acts. Homosexuality, however, would still be classified as a "sexual orientation disturbance (homosexuality)" for people who were dissatisfied with their condition. (See also January 16, 1974.)

["APA: Good News from Washington," *Gay News* 2 (Xmas 1973): 1; Victor Cohn, "Doctors Rule Homosexuals Not Abnormal," *Washington Post*, 16 December 1973, pp. A1, A21; "Homosexuality Not a Mental Disease, U.S. Psychiatrists Say," *Globe and Mail*, metro ed., 17 December 1973, p. 11; "Homosexuality Off Psychiatrists' List of Mental Illnesses," *Dialogue*, no. 5 (1974), pp. 1–2; Sidney Katz, "Homosexuals: Sick or Not? Canadian Psychiatrists Expect Debate," *Toronto Star*, four star ed., 10 April 1974, p. B3; Gary Kinsman, *The Regulation of Desire: Sexuality in Canada* (Montréal: Black Rose Books, 1987), p. 180; "Nomenclature Changed — but Not Much Else: U.S. Shrinks Reverse Policy" (editorial), *Gay Tide* 1 (April 1974): 2; "U.S. Psychiatry Now Echoing Dr. Freud," *Body Politic*, no. 11 (1974), p. 7; "U.S. Shrinks Shrink from Stand," GO *Info*, no. 9 (1974), p. 3.]

December 17 * Montréal * The AHM/GMA was granted a provincial charter as a non-profit organization. (See also January 11, 1974.)

["Gay Montreal: General Assembly Elects Officers," *Gay News* 2 (January 1974): 1.]

December 19 * Toronto * ANIK sponsored a dance at the St. Lawrence Centre to raise money to buy Christmas gifts for the occupants of a predominantly gay ward at the Clarke Institute of Psychiatry.

["A Christmas Tradition in the Making Dec. 19," *Metro Community News* 1 (15 December 1973): 4; "Society's Victims Get Community Help," *Body Politic*, no. 11 (1974), p. 4.]

1974

—— ∗ Montréal ∗ Three books of poetry by Claude Beausoleil were published this year: *Avatars du trait*, by Éditions de l'Aurore; *Deadline*, by Éditions Danielle Laliberté; and *Journal mobile*, by Éditions du jour.

[Bernard Gilbert, "*Intrusion ralentie* et autres recueils de poésies et de textes en prose de Claude Beausoleil," in *Dictionnaire des oeuvres littéraires du Québec*, ed. Maurice Lemire et al., vol. 5 (1970–75) (Montréal: Fides, 1987), pp. 436–39.]

—— ∗ Montréal ∗ Nicole Brossard's novel *French Kiss* was published by Éditions du jour.

[Max Roy, "*French Kiss*," in *Dictionnaire des oeuvres littéraires du Québec*, ed. Maurice Lemire et al., vol. 5 (1970–75) (Montréal: Fides, 1987), pp. 354–56.]

—— ∗ Montréal ∗ Paul Chamberland's book of poetry *Demain les dieux naîtront* was published by Éditions de l'Hexagone.

[Caroline Bayard, "*Éclats de la pierre noire d'où rejaillit ma vie* et *Demain les dieux naîtront*," in *Dictionnaire des oeuvres littéraires du Québec*, ed. Maurice Lemire et al., vol. 5 (1970–75) (Montréal: Fides, 1987), pp. 267–69.]

—— ∗ Montréal ∗ Jean LeDerff's book *Homolibre*, a theoretical analysis of gay liberation from a progressive viewpoint, was published by Ferron Éditeur.

[Jean-François Courcelles, "Pour Jean LeDerff, l'homosexuel irrite la société, car il ne joue pas le jeu du dominateur," *Gay Montréal* 1 (10 August 1976): 18; Ron Dayman, "Quebec: Five Years of the Movement," *Body Politic*, no. 29 (1976–77), p. 22; Eric Devlin, "Le deuxième livre de Jean LeDerff: libérer l'homosexuel," *Gay Montréal* 1 (15 June 1976): 8.]

—— ∗ Montréal ∗ André Roy's books of poetry *En image de ça* and *L'espace de voir* were published by Éditions de l'Aurore.

[Roger Chamberland, "*N'importe quelle page* et autres recueils de poésies d'André Roy," in *Dictionnaire des oeuvres littéraires du Québec*, ed. Maurice Lemire et al., vol. 5 (1970–75) (Montréal: Fides, 1987), pp. 594–96.]

—— ∗ Scarborough, Ont. ∗ E.A. Lacey's book of poetry *Path of Snow: Poems 1951–1973* was published by Catalyst Press and The Ahasuerus Press.

[Fraser Sutherland, "Muy Hombre," *Canadian Literature*, no. 65 (1975), pp. 104–07.]

—— * Scarborough, Ont. * Wayne McNeill's book of poetry *Pantomime* was published by Catalyst Press.

[Ian Young, *The Male Homosexual in Literature: A Bibliography*, second ed. (Metuchen, N.J.: Scarecrow Press, 1982), entry 2629.]

—— * Toronto * S.S. Smith's experimental novel *Fox Lore: A Journal by Day and Night*, which employed a lesbian narrator, was published by Coach House Press.

[Elizabeth Brady, "Voices from the Periphery: First-Generation Lesbian Fiction in Canada," *Resources for Feminist Research* 12 (March 1983): 22–26.]

—— * Toronto * Ian Young's book of poetry *Invisible Words* was published by Missing Link Press.

[(Ian Young), *Ian Young: A Bibliography 1962–1980*, Canadian Gay Archives Publication no. 3 (Toronto: Pink Triangle Press, 1981), entry A10.]

—— * Vancouver * Stan Persky's book of poetry *Slaves* was published by New Star Books.

[Ian Young, *The Male Homosexual in Literature: A Bibliography*, second ed. (Metuchen, N.J.: Scarecrow Press, 1982), entry 3010.]

—— * Vancouver * Scott Watson's book of short fiction *Stories* was published by Talonbooks.

[Michael O. Nowlan, "Stories," *Quill & Quire*, March 1975, p. 21; Merv Walker, "Stories," *Body Politic*, no. 18 (1975), p. 25.]

January * Canada * Jearld Moldenhauer of *The Body Politic* undertook a cross-country tour in an effort to consolidate and coordinate the activities of the NGEC and to initiate the formation of gay liberation groups in centres where there were none. Moldenhauer spoke to gays in Windsor, Thunder Bay, Winnipeg, Edmonton, Calgary, and Vancouver. (See also January 24, 1974.)

[Jearld Moldenhauer, Letter to the author, 28 November 1993.]

January * Québec, Qué. * The Service d'accueil, d'information et de référence du CHAL Inc. began operation under the direction of Denise Goyette. This counselling and referral service was so popular that it became an independent body (SEHQ) in January 1975. (See also January 1975.)

[Denise Goyette, "Information: Service d'accueil, d'information et de référence du CHAL Inc.," *Le chaînon* 2 (January 1974): 13–19; "Denise Goyette: ouvrière de la libération gay," *Gay Montréal* 1 (2 November 1976): 4; "La vraie nature de Denise Goyette" (interview), *Gay Montréal* 1 (25 January 1977): 18, 26.]

January * Thunder Bay, Ont. * Lakehead Gay Liberation was formed at

The Brunswick Four (left to right: Adrienne Potts, Pat Murphy, Sue Wells, Heather [Beyer] Elizabeth), 1974.

Lakehead University after Jearld Moldenhauer of *The Body Politic* visited the campus. Dave Belrose was the coordinator of the group, which had eight to twelve members and was active for only six months, after which gay activities in Thunder Bay centred around the private membership Backstreet Athletic Club, which existed until January 1980.

["Lakehead Gay Liberation" vertical file, Canadian Lesbian and Gay Archives, Toronto; "Thunder Bay Group Organizes," *Body Politic*, no. 13 (1974), p. 6.]

January 5 * Toronto * During amateur night at the Brunswick House Tavern Adrienne Potts and Pat Murphy sang "I Enjoy Being a Dyke," a revised version of the *South Pacific* tune "I Enjoy Being a Girl," after being insulted and abused by a male customer. The tavern's management objected, and when the women and their friends Sue Wells and Heather Beyer refused to leave, police were called. Eight policemen dragged the women out of the bar and then detained and harassed them. The women were released from custody and when they returned to the Brunswick House to find witnesses they were again ejected and arrested. Three of the women (Beyer, Murphy, and Potts) were charged with creating a disturbance and obstructing the police. The group became known as the Brunswick Four. Their arrest generated anger and concern throughout Toronto's lesbian and gay community. (See also January 10, March 4, May 31, July 16, November 1, 1974, and April 1975.)

["Brunswick Four" vertical file, Canadian Lesbian and Gay Archives, Toronto; "The Brunswick Tavern Dyke Bust" (interview with Heather Beyer), *Long Time Coming* 1 (April 1974): 2–9; "The Brunswick Tavern Dykes," *Long Time Coming* 1 (May–June 1974): 6; Margaret Fulford, ed., *The Canadian Women's Movement, 1960–1990: A Guide to Archival Resources/Le mouvement canadien des femmes, 1960–1990: guide de ressources archivistiques* (Toronto: Canadian Women's Movement Archives/ECW Press, 1992), entry 357; Jay, "Women Harassed by Toronto Police: Ugly Incident," GO *Info*, no. 9 (1974), p. 6; Agnes Kruchio, "4 Women Charge Brutality: Kicked Out of Bar," *Excalibur* (York Univ.), 21 March 1974, p. 2; "Police Harass Toronto Women," *Gemini* 11 2 (February 1974): 3; Becki L. Ross, *The House That Jill Built: A Lesbian Nation in Formation* (Toronto: University of Toronto, 1995), pp. 47–48; "Toronto Cops Assault Women," *Gay Tide* 1 (April 1974): 6; "Uppity Women," *Body Politic*, no. 12 (1974), p. 1; "Women Doused with Beer, Then Busted — Man Goes Free," *Advocate* (Los Angeles), no. 132 (1974), p. 17; "Women Harassed and Arrested," *Other Woman* 2 (February 1974): 17.]

January 6, 13 * Edmonton * The first Metropolitan Community Church (MCC) services held in Edmonton were conducted at the Unitarian Church by gay activist Michael Roberts, who was a student in the MCC ministry. Fifteen people (all male) participated in the services. The Unitarian Church later passed a resolution positive to gays, and offered to make their facilities available to the gay community. By August, however, the MCC was still struggling to develop a presence in Edmonton. (See also June 1975.)

["Church Passes Strong Resolution," *Body Politic*, no. 12 (1974), p. 7; "Edmonton?" *Metro Community News* 1 (23 August 1974): 6; "MCC in Edmonton," *Club '70 News*, February 1974, p. 6.]

January 8 ∗ Toronto ∗ The *Toronto Star* refused to print a service advertisement submitted by CHAT.

["*Star* Refuses CHAT Service Ad," *Body Politic*, no. 12 (1974), p. 4.]

January 10 ∗ Toronto ∗ A public meeting of about twenty-five people at Holy Trinity Church heard the Brunswick Four recount details of their arrest. This meeting led to the formation of HASP (Heather, Adrienne, Sue, Pat), a legal defence committee for the Brunswick Four. (See also October 1974.)

["Defense Committee for the Brunswick Four," *Metro Community News* 1 (25 January 1974): 3; "Four Women Claim Police Harassment in Arrest," *Metro Community News* 1 (11 January 1974): 1; "HASP Defence Committee," *Metro Community News* 1 (4 October 1974): 4; "Uppity Women," *Body Politic*, no. 12 (1974), p. 1.]

January 11 ∗ Montréal ∗ The Association homophile de Montréal/Gay Montreal Association (AHM/GMA) held its first general assembly. The AHM/GMA was organized out of the Centre d'accueil homophile/Gay Community Centre, which had wanted to expand into the social, service, and political spheres, and to involve more people. About ninety percent of the group's charter members attended, many of whom were women. Robert Vallée was elected president; the other officers were Danielle Dahan (vice-president), Tony Farebrother (secretary), and Felicity Stevens (treasurer). The AHM/GMA was anxious from the start to balance francophone/anglophone and male/female elements in the organization but was ultimately unsuccessful — eventually most members were male anglophones. It sponsored a variety of activities: the large drop-in centre located at 3439, rue St. Denis, counselling services, a gayline, a coffee house, a newsletter (*Gay-Zette*), a civil liberties committee, and the McGill dances. Financial problems fueled by the cancellation of the McGill dances, and internal divisions, led to a series of collapses. The demise of AHM/GMA occurred by February 1976, although a few members were able to continue to operate the gay information phone line Gay Info. (See also May 6, 1974, and July 1975.)

["Association homophile de Montréal/Gay Montreal Association (AHM/GMA)" vertical file, Canadian Lesbian and Gay Archives, Toronto; "Charter Granted," *Body Politic*, no. 12 (1974), p. 24; Bernard Courte, "1983: les dix ans de Gay Info," *Sortie*, no. 4 (1983), p. 45; Ron Dayman, "Quebec: Five Years of the Movement," *Body Politic*, no. 29 (1976–77), p. 21; Tony Farebrother, "What Went Wrong with GMA," *Gay Times* 1 (June 1975): 7; "The Finances of Gay Montreal," *Montreal Gay Times* 1 (August 1975): 8, 14;

"Gay Montreal: General Assembly Elects Officers," *Gay News* 2 (January 1974): 1; "Gay Montreal: Going Down for the Third Time," *Montreal Gay Times* 1 (December 1975): 6; "Gay Montreal Association, Inc." vertical file, Canadian Lesbian and Gay Archives, Toronto; "Gay Montreal Association Is Dead: News in Brief," *Montreal Gay Times* 2 (Spring 1976): 6; Ross Higgins, "Le financement du mouvement gai de Montréal," *Sortie*, no. 34 (1985–86), pp. 21–23; Ross Higgins, "L'impasse linguistique," *Sortie*, no. 25 (1985), p. 12; Eric Hill, "Death of Gay Montreal" (letter), *Montréalités* 2 (February 1976): 3; Eric Hill, Letter, *Montreal Gay Times* 1 (December 1975): 18; Charles H. Thorpe, "Gay Montreal Is Dead. Why?" *Montréalités* 2 (February 1976): 7.]

January 11 ∗ Vancouver ∗ Stephen Morris's article "Clubbing It: Safe and Secure," an extended commentary on gay clubs in the city, was published in the *Ubyssey*. Morris's tour guide was the gay columnist Q.Q. (pseud. of Kevin Dale McKeown).

[Stephen Morris, "Clubbing It: Safe and Secure," *Ubyssey* (Univ. of British Columbia), 11 January 1974, pp. 4–5, 8.]

January 12 ∗ near Victoria, B.C. ∗ Two members of GATE (Vancouver) were refused access to visit a gay male prisoner at William Head, a federal penitentiary near Victoria. The inmate wished to make a public statement about conditions for gays at the prison. Although the visitors had met all the required formalities, they were turned back at the gate because they were journalists for *Gay Tide* and thus required special permission to visit.

[Terry Phillips, "Document: Gays behind Bars," *Gay Tide* 3 (November 1975): 5.]

January 15 ∗ Toronto ∗ Rev. Bob Wolfe of MCC went to Toronto City Hall and persuaded a sixteen-year-old youth he had been counselling not to commit suicide by jumping from the roof of the building's east tower. (See also January 31 and February 6, 1974.)

[Donald Grant, "Youth Threatens City Hall Jump, Fire Chief, Minister Talk Him Down," *Globe and Mail*, metro ed., 16 January 1974, p. 5; J.L., "Near Suicide at City Hall Gives Gays a Second Chance," *Metro Community News* 1 (25 January 1974): 1, 4; "Minister and Fireman Rescue Boy from Suicide on City Hall Roof," *Toronto Star*, four star ed., 16 January 1974, p. C1.]

January 16 ∗ Ottawa ∗ Radio station CJOH devoted fifteen minutes to an investigation by GO that the Lord Elgin Hotel bars discriminated against gays.

[Norman Hay, "CJOH Show on L.E. Bars 'Supercilious,'" *GO Info*, no. 9 (1974), p. 2.]

January 16 ∗ Toronto ∗ George Hislop, director of CHAT, debated Dr. Daniel Cappon of York University on the Channel 19 television program "Background." The discussion centred on reactions to the American Psychiatric Association's removal of homosexuality from the official list of mental disorders in December 1973.

["George and Dr. Cappon: A Real Talk Show," *Metro Community News* 1 (28 December 1973): 6.]

January 19–20 * Montréal * A two-day national conference for lesbians, sponsored by Montreal Gay Women, was held at the Women's Centre, 3764, boul. St. Laurent. More than 200 lesbian feminists attended, which to that time was the largest gathering of its kind ever held in Canada. The event included workshops, films, a book display, and planning for a future national conference.

["Conference," *Long Time Coming* 1 (February 1974): 2–8; "Conference: Lesbian Conference, Montreal, January 19–20, 1974" vertical file, Canadian Lesbian and Gay Archives, Toronto; Lorna, "Dykes Unite," *Other Woman* 2 (February 1974): 6; "Montreal Gay Women: Lesbian Conference Held Here," *Gay News* 2 (January 1974): 1; "Montreal Hosts Lesbian Meeting," *Body Politic*, no. 12 (1974), p. 7; Betty Shapiro, "Lesbian Conference a 'Step into the Open,'" *Montreal Gazette*, final ed., 24 January 1974, p. 22; "Sisterhood," *Gemini* 11 2 (February 1974): 8; Germain Tardif, "Les lesbiennes se disent à l'avant-garde du mouvement d'emancipation de la femme," *La presse*, 23 January 1974, p. E8.]

January 23 * Saskatoon * The Zodiac Friendship Society and Saskatoon Gay Action launched an educational program with a debate entitled "Gay Is Good for God and Man." Peter Millard and Beth Foster spoke for the motion, Rev. Michael Horban and Hetty Clews against. About 250 people attended the event, which was sponsored by the University of Saskatchewan Students' Debating Society.

["Debate Opens Sask. Campaign," *Body Politic*, no. 12 (1974), p. 6; Diana Rogers and Doug Bird, "Gay, God, Man (and Woman) in Sexual Battle," *Sheaf* (Univ. of Saskatchewan), 29 January 1974, p. 3.]

January 24 * Vancouver * Approximately 150 people attended a symposium entitled "Contemporary Society and the Gay Struggle," sponsored by GATE (Vancouver) and Gay People of UBC and held at the University of British Columbia. Jearld Moldenhauer of *The Body Politic* was one of five panelists who spoke on a variety of issues, including social services for gays, civil rights issues, lesbian concerns, and youth sexuality. This was the first gay liberation symposium held at the University of British Columbia.

["B.C. Forum Weighs Movement Strategy," *Body Politic*, no. 12 (1974), p. 7; "Gay Liberation Symposium: Youth Sexuality Key Issue," *Gay Tide* 1 (April 1974): 3, 6.]

January 25 * Montréal * The Centre homophile urbain de Montréal (CHUM) was formed at a meeting of twelve people organized by Lionel Quessy. This conservative group offered pastoral-style counselling, social functions, a Roman Catholic religious service, and an Alcoholics Anonymous group. The CHUM drop-in centre was located at 5223, rue St. Denis and was open six days per week. By May 1975, CHUM had 150 members, mostly francophone, of whom forty were women. In December 1975, the CHUM centre moved to a larger space at 6581, boul. St. Laurent.

["Centre homophile urbain de Montréal (CHUM)" vertical file, Canadian Lesbian and Gay Archives, Toronto; "CHUM Centre a Friendly Gay Space," *Gay Times* 1 (May 1975): 6; "CHUM — c'est un vrai ami," *Montreal Gay Times* 1 (December 1975): 10; Ron Dayman, "Quebec: Five Years of the Movement," *Body Politic*, no. 29 (1976–77), p. 21; Gilles Garneau, "Une église qui acceuille les gais," *Le berdache*, no. 9 (1980), pp. 23–24.]

January 29 * Toronto * Roman Catholic scholar Father Gregory Baum of St. Michael's College, University of Toronto, spoke to about fifty-five people at the CHAT Centre on the topic "Homosexuality and Human Dignity." (See also February 15, 1974.)

[M.R., "Father Baum to CHAT: Fulfill God's Calling — Be Gay," *Metro Community News* 1 (8 February 1974): 4–5.]

January 29–31 * Hamilton * Seven members of the Hamilton-McMaster GLM participated in the Sexuality Awareness Programme workshop "What Is Normal?," sponsored by the Sexual Education Centre at McMaster University.

["Hamilton Gays Join Sex Panel," *Body Politic*, no. 11 (1974), p. 4; S.S. Que Hee, "The Chronology of Events during the Existence of the Hamilton McMaster and McMaster Homophile Associations 1972–1977," unpublished typescript, September 1977, 83–013, Canadian Lesbian and Gay Archives, Toronto, p. 4.]

January 31 * Toronto * Rev. Bob Wolfe submitted a brief classified advertisement for the MCC to the *Toronto Star*. The ad read: "Gay Christians are invited to worship with Metropolitan Community Church, Sundays at 8 p.m. at the Holy Trinity Church, 364–9799." It was rejected by the *Star* as being "distasteful to our readership in general." (See also February 6, 1974.)

[" 'Baloney,' Templeton Says of *Star* Letter on City-TV," *Metro Community News* 1 (8 February 1974): 6; "Gay Ad 'Distasteful,' Says *Star*," *Metro Community News* 1 (8 February 1974): 3.]

February * Fredericton * Keith Sly made an initial attempt to form Gay Friends, the first organization for lesbians and gays in New Brunswick, by placing ads in *The Body Politic* and by corresponding with other groups in Canada. Progress was very slow; by February of 1975, Gay Friends had only three active members. The group devoted itself to writing letters and distributing pamphlets such as the *Operation Socrates Handbook* and *With Downcast Gays*. Gay Friends collapsed in August 1975 when Sly moved to Montréal.

["Gay Friends" vertical file, Canadian Lesbian and Gay Archives, Toronto.]

February ★ Milton, Ont. ★ Rev. Ken Campbell refused to pay a portion of his school tax bill to protest "moral pollution" in the public education system. This protest was triggered, in part, by the visit during January 1974 of four members of Hamilton-McMaster GLM to address a grade twelve health class at M.M. Robinson High School in Burlington, attended by Campbell's daughters. George Hislop of CHAT and Campbell later discussed the issue on the CTV program *Canada A.M.* At this time Campbell was an evangelist with the Campbell-Reese Evangelistic Association, Inc., whose motto was "Global Evangelism Beginning at Home." He used the gays in schools controversy to form the Halton Renaissance Committee, which in turn grew to become Renaissance Canada, a registered charitable organization with branches across the country. Renaissance Canada was one of the sponsoring groups of Anita Bryant's Canadian tour in 1978.

[Tom Alderman, "Saving the Children: Ken Campbell Rises with the Dawn to Liberate Them from Filth, Immorality, and Bad Spelling," *Canadian Magazine*, 15–16 September 1979, pp. 14–15; "Ken Campbell" vertical file, Canadian Lesbian and Gay Archives, Toronto; "Evangelist Fights School 'Sex Fascism,'" *Toronto Star*, four star ed., 13 March 1974, p. C11; Rob Joyce, "Rebirth of Bigotry," *Gay Tide*, no. 19 (1978), pp. 1, 3; "'Moral Pollution' Sparks School Taxes Holdback," *Hamilton Spectator*, home ed., 26 February 1974, p. 10; Rudy Platiel, "Parson Withholds School Taxes as Protest over 'Moral Pollution,'" *Globe and Mail*, metro ed., 12 March 1974, p. 2; S.S. Que Hee, "The Chronology of Events during the Existence of the Hamilton McMaster and McMaster Homophile Associations 1972–1977," unpublished typescript, September 1977, 82–013, Canadian Lesbian and Gay Archives, Toronto, p. 4.]

February ★ Montréal ★ In an address to the Advertising and Sales Executive Club, federal Solicitor-General Warren Allmand declared that acts classified as crimes because they offend the moral standards of legislators should be deleted from the Canadian Criminal Code.

["Federal Minister Would Drop Laws," *Body Politic*, no. 13 (1974), p. 4.]

February ★ Ottawa ★ Minister of Justice Otto Lang announced that the federal government was considering forming a federal Human Rights Commission. Tom Warner of GATE (Toronto) wrote to the minister and was informed that sexual orientation was to be excluded from the functions of the Commission. (See also July 21, 1975.)

["Federal Human Rights Code Excludes Gays," *Body Politic*, no. 13 (1974), p. 4; Ken Popert, "Phoney Privacy Law Won't Protect Gays," *Body Politic*, no. 20 (1975), p. 7.]

February ★ Saskatoon ★ Saskatoon Gay Action sent a brief to members of the Saskatchewan Legislature that was accompanied by a questionnaire concerning the members' position on including sexual orientation in the provincial Human Rights Code.

["Sexual Orientation Raised in Saskatchewan Legislature," *Body Politic*, no. 13 (1974), p. 5.]

February ✶ Toronto ✶ Gay Media, an independent producer and distributor of slides, video and audio tapes, and films on gay themes, was formed by Michael Roberts.

["Gay Media Announces . . ." (advertisement), *Metro Community News* 1 (8 February 1974): 10; "Media Group to Circulate Films," *Body Politic*, no. 12 (1974), p. 5; "N.Y. Gay Show," *Metro Community News* 1 (23 August 1974): 7.]

February ✶ Toronto ✶ Students at Oakwood Collegiate invited a speaker from CHAT to address them. The principal referred the matter to a joint parent-teacher-student advisory group. Nine people voted to allow the speaker (seven parents and two students); twelve voted against (twelve teachers).

[Evelyne Pytka, "Student Rights at Oakwood," *Community Schools* 4 (March 1974): 16–17; "Student Poll O.K.'s Gay Educationals," *Metro Community News* 1 (5 April 1974): 3; "Teachers Deny Request for Gay Speaker," *Body Politic*, no. 13 (1974), p. 6.]

February 5–7 ✶ Montréal ✶ A symposium on sexuality held at the McGill University Student Union ballroom heard several panelists discuss aspects of homosexuality. The speakers included Dr. John Southin (on the 1969 Criminal Code amendments), Deborah Thomas, president of Gay McGill, and Dr. Alan Bell of the Institute for Sex Research, Bloomington, Indiana. On February 7, American psychologist Bruno Bettelheim was verbally attacked by members of the audience for his statements regarding homosexuality. Bettelheim told the audience of 500 that "Homosexual relations are always narcissistic — they involve an unconscious search for the self, instead of the other," and that ". . . homosexuality is based on fear of the other sex."

[Gerry Sparrow, "Anti-gay Stand Shouted Down: McGill Symposium on Sex," *Montreal Gazette*, final ed., 8 February 1974, p. 3; Mark Wilson, "Homosexuals Still Oppressed under Law, Symposium Told," *Montreal Star*, 6 February 1974, p. B7.]

February 6 ✶ Toronto ✶ Toronto City Council officially honoured Rev. Bob Wolfe of the MCC for his role in persuading a young man not to jump from the roof of City Hall on January 15. Wolfe used the occasion to raise the matter of the *Toronto Star*'s refusal in January to print an advertisement for the MCC. The *Star* printed the ad on February 7.

["Blasts Bias at Award Ceremony: Cited for Bravery," *Advocate* (Los Angeles), no. 133 (1974), p. 14; "Civic Recognition Forces Newspaper to Print Ad," *Body Politic*, no. 12 (1974), p. 4; "Clergyman Gets Award, Criticizes the *Star*," *Toronto Star*, four star ed., 7 February 1974, p. B7; J.L., "City Council Honours Gay Pastor," *Metro Community News* 1 (8 February 1974): 1, 3; "Paper Prints Ad," *Metro Community News* 1 (22 February 1974): 3.]

February 7 ∗ Winnipeg ∗ Maurice Flood, chairperson of GATE (Vancouver), addressed the annual Festival of Life and Learning at the University of Manitoba. Flood spoke on the problems faced by gay students on campus, the importance of coming out, and gay political activism. The talk was well received by the almost 1,000 (mostly heterosexual) students in attendance.

[“Group's Main Goals Explained at Festival,” *Winnipeg Tribune*, final ed., 8 February 1974, p. 29; “Liberationist Addresses Students,” *Body Politic*, no. 12 (1974), p. 6; Susan White, “Struggling On: Winnipeg's Gay Liberation Movement 2 Years After,” *Manitoban* (Univ. of Manitoba), 4 February 1974, p. 7.]

February 11 ∗ Toronto ∗ The *Toronto Star* again refused to print a classified ad for *The Body Politic*.

[“*Star* — 'No Again,' ” *Body Politic*, no. 13 (1974), p. 7.]

February 11 ∗ Winnipeg ∗ Richard North, twenty-two, and Chris Vogel, twenty-six, were married by Rev. Norman Naylor of the Unitarian Universalist Fellowship. This was the second time a gay couple sought legal sanction in Canada. The marriage was not recognized by the province when North and Vogel attempted to have the union recorded as a vital statistic. The province's refusal to recognize the marriage was publicly supported by the executive committee of the Canadian section of the Lutheran Church in America. (See also December 17, 1974.)

[“Activists Wed, Test Equality,” *Body Politic*, no. 12 (1974), p. 6; “Couple Foresees No Legal Barriers,” *Winnipeg Tribune*, final ed., 13 February 1974, p. 3; “Homosexual Marriage Ruling Held: Registration Bid Was Rejected,” *Globe and Mail*, metro ed., 22 November 1974, p. 8; “Homosexuals Are Married in Winnipeg,” *Dialogue*, no. 6 (1974), p. 4; “LCA Praises Marriage Ban,” *Advocate* (Los Angeles), no. 142 (1974), p. 20.]

February 14 ∗ Toronto ∗ Professor John Alan Lee appeared as a guest on the Valentine's Day edition of the *Judy LaMarsh Show*, broadcast on TVO, Channel 19. Lee discussed his sociological research on the subject of romantic love. He emphasized that his respondents included romances among gay men, and declared that he himself was gay. Lee was the first Canadian professor to so publicly declare his homosexuality.

[John Alan Lee, Letter to the author, 25 October 1993.]

February 15 ∗ Toronto ∗ Roman Catholic scholar Father Gregory Baum of St. Michael's College, University of Toronto, published a gay-positive feature article entitled “Catholic Homosexuals” in *Commonweal*.

[Gregory Baum, “Catholic Homosexuals,” *Commonweal* 99 (15 February 1974): 481; Letters and a reply, *Commonweal* 100 (22 March 1974): 51, 70; and *Commonweal* 100 (12 April 1974): 123, 141–42; “R.C. Theologian Takes Favourable Stand,” *Body Politic*, no. 13 (1974), p. 7.]

February 15 ✳ Winnipeg ✳ Barbara Love, a member of the boards of the National Gay Task Force and the New York National Organization for Women and co-author of *Sappho Was a Right-on Woman*, spoke on "Feminism and Lesbian Liberation" at the University of Manitoba. The talk was sponsored by GFE.

[Susan White, "Struggling On: Winnipeg's Gay Liberation Movement 2 Years After," *Manitoban* (Univ. of Manitoba), 4 February 1974, p. 7.]

February 16 ✳ Edmonton ✳ The all-male membership of GATE (Edmonton) organized a meeting with representatives of Edmonton Lesbian Feminists (ELF) to talk about areas of separate and collective concern. At the meeting it was concluded that women would decide themselves what role, if any, they wished to play in GATE (Edmonton). Over the next few months, a working relationship was established between the two groups.

["Edmonton GATE, Lesbians Hold Forum," *Body Politic*, no. 13 (1974), p. 6; "GATE (Edmonton): Outline of Activities, September 1973 through August 1974," flyer in the "GATE (Edmonton)" vertical file, Canadian Lesbian and Gay Archives, Toronto; Don Musbach, "Summary of GATE Lesbian Drop-in — Feb. 16, 1974," *Club '70 News*, March 1974, pp. 6–7.]

February 18 ✳ Toronto ✳ Thirty-five men and women picketed the offices of the Ontario Human Rights Commission (OHRC) on University Avenue in a demonstration organized by GATE (Toronto). They were protesting the Commission's failure to respond to the brief "The Homosexual Minority and the Ontario Human Rights Code," submitted in August 1973, which called for the inclusion of sexual orientation in the Ontario Human Rights Code. Eight of the protesters were able to meet directly with Robert McPhee, director of the Commission. The picket also led to a meeting with the full Commission on March 1, 1974. (See also March 1, 1974.)

["Board Refuses to Set Gay Rights Pace: Only for Heterosexuals?" *Advocate* (Los Angeles), no. 134 (1974), p. 19; Don Brant,"Our Task," *Body Politic*, no. 12 (1974), p. 2; "Gays Protest Stalling by Human Rights Commission," *Varsity* (Univ. of Toronto), 27 February 1974, p. 15; "Gays Screwed by OHRC: In Ontario," *Gay Tide* 1 (April 1974): 3, 6; "Pickets Demand Equal Gay Rights," *Metro Community News* 1 (22 February 1974): 1, 3; "Rights Commissioners Renege: GATE Demo Wins Meeting," *Body Politic*, no. 12 (1974), p. 5.]

February 23 ✳ St. Catharines, Ont. ✳ Police raided the Twilight Villa Social Club, 117 Chetwood Street, and arrested the manager, ten lesbians, and sixty-one gay men on liquor offences.

["Club Raid Nets 72 on Liquor Charges," *Hamilton Spectator*, 25 February 1974, p. 1; "News from St. Catherines [sic]," *Other Woman* 2 (April 1974): 5; "News Tidbits," *Long Time Coming* 1 (May–June 1974): 19.]

February 28 ∗ Montréal ∗ André Brassard's film *Il était une fois dans l'est/Once Upon a Time in the East* premiered at the Fleur-de-Lys theatre. Starring Denise Filiatrault, Michelle Rossignol, and Frédérique Collin, the film's screenplay was by Brassard and Michel Tremblay. Adapted from some of Tremblay's works, the film presented connected stories of a working-class housewife and a bar populated by lesbians and gays. Some of Tremblay's greatest characters appeared in the work, including Hosanna, Cuirette, and the Duchess de Langeais. *Il était une fois dans l'est* was shown in competition at the Cannes Film Festival on May 21, 1974.

> [M. Bélair, "D'un oratorio sacré ou peut-être profane," *Cinéma Québec* 3 (April–May 1974): 39–42; "Face à face cannois: Brassard-Tremblay s'expliquent" (interview), *Cinéma Québec* 3 (June–July 1974): 21–23; Martin Knelman, "The World of Michel on the Screen," *Globe and Mail*, metro ed., 3 May 1975, p. 31; Mark Miller, "*Il était une fois dans l'est*: Dreams and Despair on the Main," *Cinema Canada*, no. 20 (1975), pp. 65–66; (G.) Mosk(owitz)., "*Il était une fois dans l'est (Once Upon a Time in the East)*," *Variety*, 15 May 1974, p. 24; J.-P. Tadros, "André Brassard: comment passer de théâtre au cinéma," *Cinéma Québec* 3 (February–March 1974), pp. 28–32; D.J. Turner and Micheline Morisset, eds., *Canadian Feature Film Index, 1913–1985/Index des films canadiens de long métrage* (Ottawa: Public Archives, National Film, Television, and Sound Archives, 1987), entry 489; Thomas Waugh, "Nègres blancs, tapettes et 'butch': les lesbiennes et les gais dans le cinéma québécois," *Copie zéro*, no. 11 (1981), pp. 19, 25–27.]

March ∗ Halifax ∗ GAE conducted a civil rights campaign prior to the April 2 Nova Scotia provincial election. Twenty-two candidates replied to a GAE poll concerning legislation to protect lesbians and gays against discrimination in the province.

> ["Halifax Gays Conduct Poll," *Body Politic*, no. 13 (1974), p. 5.]

March ∗ London, Ont. ∗ The general membership of UWOHA chose the name Homophile Association of London, Ontario (HALO) for the new community association. HALO was officially incorporated on July 16, 1974.

> ["Announcements," HALO *Newsletter* 1 (September 1974): 2; "Announcements and Notices," UWOHA *Newsletter* 3 (April 1974): 2.]

March ∗ Montréal ∗ Two lesbians (Sandra and Lise) were verbally and physically abused by male employees of the Lime Light disco, 1254, rue Stanley, after they complained that women were being charged a higher admission price than men. Police arrived on the scene and charged the women with disturbing the peace; they spent the night and most of the next day in jail. In May 1974, they were found not guilty of the charge. The Lime Light's management soon reverted to an equal admission policy when it was threatened with a boycott and picketing by the gay community.

["The Gay Bar and the Montreal Gay Community," *Gay-Zette* 1 (September 1974): 3; "Gay McGill" vertical file, Canadian Lesbian and Gay Archives, Toronto; "Limelight Discotheque Discriminates against Women," *Long Time Coming* 1 (March 1974): 16; "News: Not Guilty of Disturbing the Peace," *Long Time Coming* 1 (May–June 1974): 23.]

March ∗ Vancouver ∗ The Have a Gay Stay Transient Housing and Gay Information Service was established as a successor to the Gay Transient Referral and Information Centre (Gay TRIC). It was operated by the Vancouver Gay Information Service (Van-Gay) and was coordinated by David Lewis. (See also September 26, 1974.)

["B.C. Gays Offer Visitor Low Cost Housing," *Metro Community News* 1 (19 April 1974): 3; "Have a Gay Stay," *Gay Tide* 1 (August 1974): 11; "Have a Gay Stay" vertical file, Canadian Lesbian and Gay Archives, Toronto; Q.Q., "Page 69" (column), *Georgia Straight*, 28 March–4 April 1974, p. 22; "Vancouver Gay Information Service" vertical file, Canadian Lesbian and Gay Archives, Toronto.]

March ∗ Victoria, B.C. ∗ A leaflet commenting on the sad state of gay liberation in Victoria was distributed by Randy Notte. It stated, in part, that "In Victoria . . . gay people have few places to be with one another. If such places are not basically straight, they are patrolled extensively by the police. As a result, most gays in this city are lonely and isolated." The leaflet caused a sensation. Notte was threatened by a number of closeted gays and was called by the RCMP. This incident was the impetus for the formation on April 17, 1974, of the Gay People's Alliance, the first gay liberation group in Victoria. (See also April 17, 1974.)

["Gay People's Alliance" vertical file, Canadian Lesbian and Gay Archives, Toronto; Randy Notte papers, 90–081, Canadian Lesbian and Gay Archives, Toronto.]

March 1 ∗ Toronto ∗ Representatives of GATE (Toronto) and other groups met with the entire membership of the Ontario Human Rights Commission (OHRC). The OHRC continued to refuse to take a comprehensive stand on anti-gay discrimination, but offered to investigate and mediate individual, well-documented incidents of anti-gay bias. (See also Summer 1974 and September 1975.)

["Audience with Commission Brings No Progress on Rights," *Advocate* (Los Angeles), no. 137 (1974), p. 22; Jody Campbell, "Gays Want Rights," *Ryersonian* (Ryerson Polytechnical Institute), 13 March 1974, p. 3; "Crocodile Tears," *Metro Community News* 1 (8 March 1974): 1; GATE (Toronto), "To the Employees of the Ministry of Labour" (letter), *Dialogue*, no. 6 (1974), pp. 6–8; "Human Rights Legislation: Gay Alliance Gathers Support," *Body Politic*, no. 13 (1974), p. 5; "Ontario Human Rights Commission Rejects Requests from Homosexuals," UWOHA *Newsletter* 3 (March 1974): 1; "Rights Agency Failing on Promise," *Advocate* (Los Angeles), no. 146 (1974), p. 21.]

Members of *The Body Politic* collective, early 1974 (back row, left to right: Walter Bruno, Ron Dayman, Paul MacDonald, James Steakley, Ed Jackson, Herb Spiers, Ken Popert, Gerald Hannon, Robert Trow; front, left to right: Tom Warner, Merv Walker, Jearld Moldenhauer).

March 4 * Toronto * Judy LaMarsh, women's advocate and former federal Cabinet minister in the Pearson government, defended the Brunswick Four as their trial opened at Old City Hall. (See also May 31, 1974.)

["Lawyer Former Cabinet Member," *Advocate* (Los Angeles), no. 133 (1974), p. 14; "Uppity Women," *Body Politic*, no. 12 (1974), p. 1.]

March 4–24 * Toronto * Darryl Tonkin, a twenty-two-year-old artist from Brantford, Ont., exhibited his "gay art" at the Kensington Art Association Gallery, 4 Kensington Avenue.

["Controversial Art Exhibit Opens," *Body Politic*, no. 12 (1974), p. 4; Ed Jackson, "Pictures at a Gay Exhibition," *Body Politic*, no. 13 (1974), p. 13.]

March 6 * Toronto * Radical Lesbians held a public meeting at which Judy, one of their members, spoke on what it means to be a radical lesbian feminist. She told the exclusively female audience that "All women carry within them the potential for lesbianism, and this must be realized whether or not it is acted upon."

[Heather Sanguins, "Lesbian Equality," *Varsity* (Univ. of Toronto), 8 March 1974, p. 8.]

March 6 * Vancouver * Paul Krasny's film *Christina* opened at the Capitol theatre. Starring Barbara Parkins, the film also featured the Canadian drag artists The Fabulous Freaks as a group of transvestites.

[D.J. Turner and Micheline Morisset, eds., *Canadian Feature Film Index, 1913–1985/ Index des films canadiens de long métrage* (Ottawa: Public Archives, National Film, Television, and Sound Archives, 1987), entry 474.]

March 6–24 * Toronto * The National Touring Company's production of A.J. Kronengold's *Tubstrip* was performed at the Global Village Theatre, 17 St. Nicholas Street. The play was set in a steambath and had an all-male cast.

[Urjo Kareda, "Play Set in Steam-Bath Aims at Special Audience," *Toronto Star*, four star ed., 7 March 1974, p. E8; P.S.L., "*Tubstrip*," *Metro Community News* 1 (22 March 1974): 6; "*Tubstrip*," *Body Politic*, no. 13 (1974), p. 13.]

March 7 * New York, N.Y. * The film *Montreal Main* was released with a showing at the Whitney Museum. Its co-author, co-producer, editor, director, and star was Frank Vitale, a twenty-eight-year-old Florida-born photographer. *Montreal Main* chronicled the close, Platonic friendship between a man and a thirteen-year-old boy. Their relationship is cut short due to social restrictions and the difference in their age. *Montreal Main* was one of the first English-Canadian films to give a positive portrayal of homosexuality. It was released in Canada on April 14, 1974, at the City Nights threatre and in Montréal (with French subtitles) on October 18, 1974, at the Elysée.

[Martin Auty, "*Montreal Main*," *Monthly Film Bulletin*, November 1978, p. 222; David Beard, "*Montreal Main*," *Cinema Canada* 2 (April–May 1974): 32–33; Ron Dayman, "Our Image: *Montreal Main*," *Body Politic*, no. 16 (1974), p. 18; Michel Euvrard, "*Montreal Main*," *Cinéma Québec* 4 (December 1974): 45–46; Mari Maler, "*Straight Woman Meets Montreal Main* Man Frank Vitale" (interview), *Georgia Straight*, 25 April–2 May 1974, pp. 12–13, 22; David Mole, "Mainlining," *Body Politic*, no. 54 (1979), p. 33; "*Montreal Main*," *Maclean's*, May 1974, p. 96; D.J. Turner and Micheline Morisset, eds., *Canadian Feature Film Index, 1913–1985/Index des films canadiens de long métrage* (Ottawa: Public Archives, National Film, Television, and Sound Archives, 1987), entry 438; Thomas Waugh, "Négres blancs, tapettes et 'butch': les lesbiennes et les gais dans le cinéma québécois," *Copie zéro*, no. 11 (1981), p. 27.]

March 8 ✷ Brandon, Man. ✷ Rev. Bruce McLeod, moderator of the United Church of Canada, said in an interview that Christians should not prejudge homosexuals. "Some of the great people in the earth's history from Michelangelo on have been homosexuals. We would all be poorer without them," McLeod said.

["Don't Prejudge Homosexuals, Moderator Says," *Toronto Star*, Saturday ed., 9 March 1974, p. H4.]

March 8 ✷ Montréal ✷ At a general meeting of the AHM/GMA, over one-third (predominantly francophone) of the members present voted in favour of a non-confidence resolution and asked that the group's leadership resign immediately. This was a manifestation of frustrations that had been growing within the group. Some members raised questions of financial irregularities related to the proceeds from the monthly McGill dances, sponsored by the AHM/GMA. Others questioned the perceived inertia and timidity of the group's leadership. More explosive still were accusations by francophone members that their concerns were being ignored in the officially bilingual, but predominantly anglophone, organization. These problems led to a split in the AHM/GMA and the formation of the francophone-dominated Front homosexuel québécois de libération (FHQL) by March 18, 1974. (See also March 18, 1974.)

["Front homosexuel québécois de libération (FHQL)" vertical file, Canadian Lesbian and Gay Archives, Toronto.]

March 9 ✷ Boston, Mass. ✷ The Board of Elders of the Universal Fellowship of Metropolitan Community Churches approved the petition of MCC Toronto for recognition as a fully chartered church of the Fellowship. On June 7–9, 1974, Rev. Troy Perry, the founder of MCC, visited Toronto to present the charter. (See also June 7–9, 1974.)

["MCC Founder to Visit," *Metro Community News* 1 (22 March 1974): 1; "MCC Toronto Chartered," *Metro Community News* 1 (22 March 1974): 1.]

March 12 * Calgary * Five members of Club Carousel went to the Pastoral Institute to discuss gay life and the Club with a group of ministers and counsellors, and were well received.

[Bob, "President's Report," *Carousel Capers* 5 (April 1974): 4.]

March 12 * Saskatoon * *The Western Producer*, a weekly farm newspaper, refused to print a classified ad for the Zodiac Friendship Society/Saskatoon Gay Action. The same ad had been printed weekly in the *Star-Phoenix* and *The Commentator* for almost two years without incident. The Society filed a complaint with the Saskatchewan Human Rights Commission, and the complaint was investigated. The Commission ruled that refusal of the ad was not a breach of the Human Rights Code because sexual orientation was not included in the Code. This is believed to be the first time that a Canadian Human Rights Commission actively investigated a complaint of discrimination based on sexual orientation. (See also Summer 1974.)

["Prairie Paper Won't Print Ad," *Body Politic*, no. 14 (1974), p. 4; "Sask. Commission Investigates Discrimination," *Gay West*, no. 1 (1974), p. 3; "Zodiac Fights Discrimination," *Saskatonian*, 8 August 1974, p. 3.]

March 14–16 * Waterloo, Ont. * Three one-act plays by gay Canadian playwright John Burgess were presented at the University of Waterloo.

[Robert Trow, "John Burgess," *Body Politic*, no. 13 (1974), p. 13.]

March 18 * Montréal * The Front homosexuel québécois de libération (FHQL) was formed by gay francophones as an independent organization to counter the perceived inertia of the anglophone-dominated AHM/GMA. Peter Amyot, Patrick Cellier, and Gui Lavoie-Goyette were the early coordinators of FHQL. The group was interested in legal reform; its members appeared on television and in the press and gave public lectures. An associated collective worked on producing the publication *Le coup-de-poing*, which never appeared due to lack of funds. The FHQL failed by the end of 1974.

[Ron Dayman, "Quebec: Five Years of the Movement," *Body Politic*, no. 29 (1976–77), p. 22; "Front homosexuel québécois de libération," *Long Time Coming* 1 (April 1974): 33; "Front homosexuel québécois de libération (FHQL)" vertical file, Canadian Lesbian and Gay Archives, Toronto; "New Francophone Group Formed," *Body Politic*, no. 13 (1974), p. 7.]

March 18 * Québec, Qué. * About twenty CEGEP students visited the offices of CHAL, where they viewed CHAL's audio-visual presentation "Un être que tu ignores" and participated in a question-and-answer period with about ten members.

[R.R., "Recontre . . . avec un groupe d'étudiants en technique d'assistance sociale," *Le chaînon* 2 (April 1974): 14.]

March 20 * Toronto * Jean LeDerff, author of *Homolibre* and *Homosexuel? Et pourquoi pas!*, was to have been the guest speaker at a meeting entitled "Toward a Sexual Revolution," sponsored by GATE (Toronto) and held at the Ontario Institute for Studies in Education (OISE). The event was cancelled after OISE's Board of Governors reportedly withdrew the group's room booking because it did not want OISE to be associated with "undesirables." GATE (Toronto) protested the move, and OISE agreed to reschedule the event on April 17, 1974. (See also April 17, 1974.)

["Homosexual Author Banned from the Ontario Institute for Studies in Education," *Long Time Coming* 1 (March 1974): 15–16.]

March 23, 30 * London, Ont. * "It's a Queer Thing," a series of readings from literature by gay writers, was performed at the Mini Theatre by David Marriage and Bill Mitchell.

[Dik Yake, "Here's a Queer Thing: Readings from the Literature of the Gay Subculture," *UWOHA Newsletter* 3 (May 1974): 6.]

Spring * England * A shipment of copies of Toronto poet Ian Young's anthology of gay poetry *The Male Muse*, sent to England by the book's American publisher, was seized and burned by British customs officials.

["U.K. Bans Poetry," *Body Politic*, no. 14 (1974), p. 7.]

Spring * Québec, Qué. * The Liberal government of Robert Bourassa announced that a Québec Charter of Human Rights would be introduced. Lesbians and gays in the province began to lobby for the inclusion of a clause guaranteeing protection from discrimination based on sexual orientation. An informal coalition of members of AHM/GMA, CHAL, CHUM, and individuals was established to lobby the government. Known as the Civil Liberties Committee, the group was led by Roger Bellemare, a law student at Laval University. Working hard as behind-the-scenes lobbyists during the next several months, the Committee wrote briefs and collected letters of support. AHM/GMA, CHAL, and CHUM also prepared briefs concentrating on the legal arguments for gay civil rights protection. (See also January 23, 1975.)

[Ron Dayman, "Quebec: Five Years of the Movement," *Body Politic*, no. 29 (1976–77), pp. 21–22; "Gay Montreal Prepares Brief," *Body Politic*, no. 13 (1974), p. 6; "The Quebec Charter of Human Rights," *Nous nous préparons/Getting Ready*, May 1974, pp. 11–13.]

Spring * Québec * Guy Roy, an inmate at Leclerc Penitentiary, complained to prison director J.P. Dugas and Solicitor-General Warren Allmand of discrimination based on his sexual orientation. Roy claimed that he had been allowed to telephone his lover of two years, Steven Hannah, only once in ten months.

[Walter Bruno, "Stone Walls and Prejudice Indeed a Prison Make: Lament of a Gay Inmate," *Body Politic*, no. 15 (1974), pp. 1, 24; " 'Gay' Convict Asks Right to Phone," *Toronto Sun*, 28 April 1974, p. 15; "Prisoner Wants Phone Rights," *Body Politic*, no. 13 (1974), p. 7; Peter Zorzi papers, 88–031/01, file 29, Canadian Lesbian and Gay Archives, Toronto; Peter Zorzi, *Queer Catharsis* (Toronto: The Author, 1992), pp. 67–70.]

Spring ∗ Toronto ∗ The Eglinton New Democratic Party Riding Association passed a resolution in support of the inclusion of sexual orientation in the Ontario Human Rights Code.

["NDP Support," *Body Politic*, no. 14 (1974), p. 5; "Rights Coalition to Form," *Metro Community News* 1 (17 May 1974): 1.]

Spring ∗ Toronto ∗ GATE (Toronto), coordinating the NGEC, had 2,000 copies of the booklet *Homosexuals: A Minority without Rights/Les homosexuels: une minorité sans droits* printed in preparation for the July 8 federal election campaign. (See also July 8, 1974.)

["NGEC Booklet Completed," *Body Politic*, no. 13 (1974), p. 4.]

Spring ∗ Toronto ∗ The Institute of Professional Librarians of Ontario (IPLO) supported the inclusion of sexual orientation in the Ontario Human Rights Code.

["Human Rights," *Metro Community News* 1 (5 April 1974): 3; "Human Rights Legislation: Gay Alliance Gathers Support," *Body Politic*, no. 13 (1974), p. 5.]

Spring ∗ Toronto ∗ Members of the Society of Friends (Quakers) wrote to Ontario Minister of Labour Fern Guindon to support the inclusion of sexual orientation in the Ontario Human Rights Code.

["Church Group Endorses Gay Rights," *Metro Community News* 1 (5 April 1974): 5; "Human Rights," *Metro Community News* 1 (5 April 1974): 3; "Quakers Support Gay Rights," *Body Politic*, no. 13 (1974), p. 4.]

Spring ∗ Waterloo, Ont. ∗ Jackie Thomas (pseud.), a female impersonator, won second prize in a "Thigh High" contest for the shortest hemline, sponsored by the University of Waterloo Engineering Undergraduate Society. When it was discovered "she" was a man, Thomas was stripped of the prize.

["Jocks Reject Drag Queen," *Body Politic*, no. 14 (1974), p. 5.]

April 1974–August 1975 ∗ Burnaby, B.C. ∗ When Michael Eliot-Hurst came out publicly, joining the struggle for gay rights, he had to fight to keep his position as chairperson of the Department of Geography at Simon Fraser University. In March of 1975, Eliot-Hurst was briefly hospitalized and was placed on a medical leave-of-absence by Pauline Jewett, the university's president. An acting department chair was appointed. By May, however,

Eliot-Hurst had recovered and was ready to return to work, but was not allowed to by the university. It was then that he uncovered an attempt to replace him as chairperson for the rest of his term (to August 31, 1975) because the department had "lost confidence" in him. Eliot-Hurst suspected the real reason behind his medical "suspension" was the university administration's disapproval of his open homosexuality and Marxist politics. After much wrangling, Eliot-Hurst was reinstated as chairperson of the Department of Geography effective August 15, 1975, only two weeks before his term was to expire.

[Robert Cook, "Michael Eliot-Hurst" (interview), *Gay Tide* 2 (March 1975): 6–9; Michael E. Eliot-Hurst, "Coming Out in One's Mid-Thirties: Reflections from an Ivory Tower," *Peak* (Simon Fraser Univ.) (*Gay Supplement*), 9 July 1975, p. 3 (reprinted as "Coming Out in a Liberal University," *Montreal Gay Times* 1 [September 1975]: 3–5); "Michael Eliot-Hurst" vertical file, Canadian Lesbian and Gay Archives, Toronto; Joann Kronquist, "Eliot-Hurst Refuses to Give Up," *Peak* (Simon Fraser Univ.), 18 June 1975, p. 3; Tim McCaskell, "Out Gay Teacher Fights Administration," *Body Politic*, no. 20 (1975), pp. 6–7.]

April 17 * Toronto * Jean LeDerff, author of *Homolibre* and *Homosexuel? Et pourquoi pas!*, spoke on the topic "Toward a Sexual Revolution" at the Ontario Institute for Studies in Education (OISE). Sixty-five people attended the talk, which was sponsored by GATE (Toronto).

["Jean LeDerff," *Metro Community News* 1 (19 April 1974): 3, 10; "Noted Writer Speaks in Toronto," *Body Politic*, no. 13 (1974), p. 4.]

April 17 * Victoria, B.C. * Six men and women officially formed the Gay People's Alliance (GPA) to promote lesbian and gay pride, equality, and liberation in Victoria. Randy Notte became the group's first chairperson. GPA became affiliated with the NGEC and its first political actions involved questioning local candidates about gay civil rights issues during the campaign leading up to the federal election of July 8, 1974. The GPA collapsed in the autumn of 1974 when Notte moved to Toronto. (See also June 18, 1974.)

["Candidates Have Say about Gay," *Victoria Daily Colonist*, 29 June 1974, p. 17; "Gay People's Alliance (GPA)" vertical file, Canadian Lesbian and Gay Archives, Toronto; "New Hope for Victoria's Gay Population" ("Ask Alice" column), *Victorian*, 19 June 1974, p. 36; Randy Notte, Letter, *Long Time Coming* 1 (May–June 1974): 16; Randy Notte papers, 90–081, Canadian Lesbian and Gay Archives, Toronto; "Victoria Gays Organize," *Gay Tide* 1 (August 1974): 8; "Victoria Gets New Group," *Body Politic*, no. 14 (1974), p. 5.]

April 24 * Toronto * Ontario Minister of Labour Fern Guindon declared in a letter to GATE (Toronto) that she did not intend to recommend to Cabinet any changes in the Ontario Human Rights Code with regard to sexual orientation.

["The Ontario Human Rights Omission: A Chronology," in Gays of Ottawa, *Cleaning Up the Acts: Selected Discrimination Issues Affecting the Gay Minority* (Ottawa: GO, 1983), p. 25.]

April 25 * Regina * MLA John Richards (Ind. Soc.-Saskatoon-Centre) presented a petition to the Saskatchewan legislature calling for the inclusion of a sexual orientation clause in all provincial human rights legislation. During question period the next day, Mr. Richards asked Attorney-General Roy Romanow about the government's intentions. Romanow replied that the government was considering the matter but had not reached a decision. Mr. Richards's actions were spurred by the lobbying of members of Saskatoon Gay Action. (See also Spring 1975.)

["Gay Rights in Legislature," *Gay West*, no. 1 (1974), p. 4.]

April 27 * Toronto * GATE (Toronto) held its second semi-annual conference, during which a new constitution was adopted and GATE's political and educational functions were enhanced. A new executive board was elected, which included Don Brant as chairperson, Ron Dayman as public spokesperson, and John Wilson as provincial affairs coordinator.

["GATE Conference," *Metro Community News* 1 (3 May 1974): 6.]

May * St. John's * The Community Homophile Association of Newfoundland (CHAN) was founded as a social and political group for lesbians and gays in Newfoundland. CHAN's first meeting was held in late May 1974 after Norman Hay of GO appeared on an open-line radio program on CJON. Thirteen people (seven women, six men) met with Hay and decided to establish a social group that would meet Thursday nights in members' homes. CHAN published the newsletter *Aboutface*, and established a branch in Corner Brook by 1975. CHAN was active until 1980.

["Community Homophile Association of Newfoundland" (CHAN) vertical file, Canadian Lesbian and Gay Archives, Toronto; Gays and Lesbians Together, " 'Here to Stay!' Lesbians and Gays in Newfoundland and Labrador Fighting for Our Rights," St. John's, June 1991, pp. 14–15; "History of CHAN . . . ," *Aboutface* 2 (May 1976): 2; L. Murphy, "Frustration in Newfoundland" (letter), *Body Politic*, no. 75 (1981), p. 4; Ken Popert, "Gays Find Organization Means Better Life," *Body Politic*, no. 26 (1976), p. 5.]

May * Saskatoon * Saskatoon Gay Action and the Zodiac Friendship Society established a Legal Defence Fund to help with legal expenses in cases involving sexual orientation. The Darlene Case child custody battle was one of the first cases supported by the Fund. (See also July 25, 1974.)

["Defence Fund Established," *Gay West*, no. 1 (1974), p. 1.]

May * Toronto * The Lanyards, a gay leather and denim fraternity and travel club, was formed.

["Lanyards" vertical file, Canadian Lesbian and Gay Archives, Toronto.]

May ∗ Toronto ∗ The *Toronto Star* refused to accept an advertisement for Glad Day Bookshop, stating that the ad tended to "proselytise for the homosexual movement." Glad Day lodged a complaint against the *Star* with the Ontario Press Council. Later, the *Star* declared that it would reconsider printing the ad if the word "gay" was changed to "homosexual." Glad Day refused this request. (See also October 12, 1974.)

["OHRC Will Look into Complaints," *Metro Community News* 1 (31 May 1974): 15.]

May 1 ∗ Ontario ∗ Cora, a women's bookmobile and resource centre, began its travels around rural and small-town Ontario. Funded by an Opportunities for Youth grant, Cora was named after E. Cora Hind, a pioneer suffragist, and was stocked with much material on feminism and lesbianism. Its aim was to help women in smaller centres overcome their isolation from the women's movement. The project was so popular that it was revived in the summer of 1975. (See also Summer 1975.)

["Cora the Travelling Bookmobile," *Other Woman* 3 (Fall 1974): 14–15.]

May 3 ∗ Halifax ∗ Members of GAE presented a brief to the Nova Scotia Human Rights Commission.

[Gay Alliance for Equality, "Human Rights and the Nova Scotia Homophile Community: A Brief Presented to the Nova Scotia Human Rights Commission by the Gay Alliance for Equality, May 3, 1974," Canadian Lesbian and Gay Archives, Toronto.]

May 4 ∗ New York, N.Y. ∗ Two delegates from UWOHA attended a conference entitled "Gay Couple Counselling," sponsored by the Homophile Community Counselling Center (HCCC). A series of panels and discussions focussed on long-term gay relationships.

[Untitled article, UWOHA *Newsletter* 3 (June 1974): 9–10.]

May 6 ∗ Montréal ∗ The AHM/GMA Centre moved to 3664, rue Ste. Famille. This new, three-floor, ten-and-a-half-room Centre was shared with Montreal Gay Women. The basement was reserved for social activities and the Au Naturel coffeehouse; the main floor contained the offices and drop-in centre of Montreal Gay Women; the upper floor was occupied by AHM/GMA. By May 1975 the Centre was forced to move again due to harassment and high rental costs; by July it had relocated in a three-and-a-half-room apartment at 6–3425, rue Peel. (See also July 1975.)

[Felicity, "Womanspace," *Long Time Coming* 1 (February 1974): 18–19; Randy Fisher, "Gay Montreal Drop-in Centre Now Open," *Montreal Gay Times* 1 (September 1975): 13; "Gay Montreal Association, Inc. . . ./Association homophile de Montréal, Inc. . . . ," *Gay-Zette* Christmas edition (December 1974–January 1975): 4–7, 8–12; "Gay

Montreal Centre: What's in It for You?" *Gay-Zette* Christmas edition (December 1974–January 1975): 11; "Gay Montreal Moving," *Gay-Zette* 2 (July 1975): 7; "Information: Gay Montreal Association . . . ," *Long Time Coming* 1 (May–June 1974): 33; "Information: Montreal Gay Women . . . ," *Long Time Coming* 1 (May–June 1974): 32; "The New Centre," *Nous nous préparons/Getting Ready*, May 1974, pp. 8–11; "New Gay Montreal Center," *Montreal Gay Times* 1 (August 1975): 7.]

May 13–August 16 ✶ Winnipeg ✶ An Opportunities for Youth grant of $5,000 was awarded to GFE's Project Understanding to compile and publish the twenty-four-page newsprint booklet *Understanding Homosexuality*. The booklet contained excerpts from academic research and religious publications and was aimed at people working in the professions and social services. The project had been initiated and led by Richard North, and was assisted by Gregory Bourgeois, Brent McKinstry, Donald Morden, and Susan White. (See also July 2, 1974.)

["News: Project Understanding," *Long Time Coming* 2 (July–August 1974): 5; "OFY Programme Funds 2 Groups," *Body Politic*, no. 14 (1974), p. 4.]

May 15–June 30 ✶ Toronto ✶ Michel Tremblay's play *Hosanna* was performed in English at the Tarragon Theatre. The production featured Richard Monette as Hosanna, the transvestite hairdresser, and Richard Donat as Cuirette, his biker lover. The Tarragon production was revived and played at the Global Village Theatre, September 11–October 6, 1974. (See also October 14, 1974.)

[Gerald Hannon and Jean LeDerff, "*Hosanna*: Two Views," *Body Politic*, no. 14 (1974), p. 12; Agnes Kruchio, "*Hosanna* Explores the Politics of Love: Leaving the Stereotypes," *Excalibur* (York Univ.), 19 September 1974, p. 11; "The Pastor Sees *Hosanna*," *Metro Community News* 1 (20 September 1974): 7, 12; E. Donnell Stoneman, "Special Report — Theatre: *Lying in State* in Washington; *Hosanna* in Toronto," *In Touch* 2 (1974): 44–45, 80–81; "Upcoming Events," *Body Politic*, no. 13 (1974), p. 13.]

May 18–19 ✶ Saskatoon ✶ Saskatoon Gay Action hosted the first conference of Prairie gay activists. More than twenty delegates from organizations in Winnipeg, Edmonton, and Saskatoon attended. Topics for discussion included the NGEC, lesbians and the gay movement, funding, counselling, and community relations.

["Conference: Prairie Gay Activist Conference, 1st. Saskatoon, May 18–19, 1974" vertical file, Canadian Lesbian and Gay Archives, Toronto; "First Prairie Conference," *Gay West*, no. 1 (1974), p. 1; "Prairie Conference in Saskatoon," *Body Politic*, no. 13 (1974), p. 7; "Western Gays Hold Conference," *Body Politic*, no. 14 (1974), p. 4.]

May 18–20 ✶ Waterloo, Ont. ✶ About seventy people from Ontario gay organizations, as well as representatives from Saskatoon and Montréal, attended a conference at the University of Waterloo entitled "Gay Liberation and Human Growth." Several workshops were held, covering topics such as lesbians, gay politics (only one woman attended), and gay counselling. (See also May 20, 1974.)

["Conference at Waterloo," *Metro Community News* I (19 April 1974): 4; "Conference: Gay Liberation and Human Growth Conference, Waterloo, May 18–20, 1974" vertical file, Canadian Lesbian and Gay Archives, Toronto; "Ontario Groups Gather in K-W," *Body Politic*, no. 14 (1974), p. 4; "A Report on the Conference of Gay Liberation and Human Growth Held 18–20 of May, 1974 at the University of Waterloo, Waterloo-Kitchener (sic), Ontario, Canada," HALO *Newsletter* I (September 1974): 5; Charlie Thorpe, "Report of the Gay Liberation and Human Growth Conference at Waterloo U., May 18, 19, & 20," *Association homophile de Montréal/Gay Montreal Association (AHM/GMA) Bulletin/Newsletter*, June 1974, pp. 17–18.]

May 19 ✳ Hamilton ✳ The Canadian Unitarian Council voted sixteen to five (with seventeen abstentions) against a resolution recommending changes in federal and provincial human rights codes and the Canadian Immigration Act to provide equal treatment and protection for homosexuals. Members of the Gay Caucus were shocked as they had expected the resolution to pass easily.

["Canadian Unitarian Council Defeats Gay Rights Resolution," *Unitarian Universalist Gay Caucus Newsletter* 4 (June 1974): 12–13; "Frustration and Anger," *Metro Community News* I (31 May 1974): 11; "News: Canadian Unitarian Council Denies Gays Their Rights," *Long Time Coming* I (May–June 1974): 24; "Unitarians Balk at Rights Move," *Body Politic*, no. 14 (1974), p. 7.]

May 20 ✳ Waterloo, Ont. ✳ A GATE (Toronto) proposal for the formation of the Coalition for Gay Rights in Ontario (CGRO) was endorsed at the plenary session of the "Gay Liberation and Human Growth" conference at the University of Waterloo. CGRO was formed to coordinate the efforts of thirteen Ontario gay groups lobbying to amend the Ontario Human Rights Code to include sexual orientation. (See also January 18–19, 1975.)

["Coalition Endorsed at Waterloo," *Metro Community News* I (31 May 1974): 11; "Ont. Coalition Formed," *Body Politic*, no. 14 (1974), p. 5.]

May 24 ✳ Montréal ✳ The AHM/GMA ratified a new constitution that removed the executive as the organizing and decision-making power, making the group a collective.

["Information: Gay Montreal Association . . . ," *Long Time Coming* I (May–June 1974): 33.]

May 27 ✳ Toronto ✳ Ron Dayman and Walter Klinger, members of GATE (Toronto), were harassed and physically attacked by rally organizers at the Etobicoke Liberal Riding Association nomination meeting of Alastair Gillespie, held in preparation for the July 8 federal election. The meeting was addressed by Prime Minister Pierre Trudeau. Attempts were made to evict Dayman and Klinger from the rally because they carried gay rights signs and distributed leaflets calling for gay rights as advocated by the NGEC.

["Activists Beaten," *Body Politic*, no. 14 (1974), p. 7; "Gays Attacked at Rally," *Metro Community News* 1 (31 May 1974): 13; "Two Gay Men Attacked at Liberal Rally," NGEC *Newsletter*, no. 1 (1974), p. 1.]

May 29 ★ Toronto ★ Fifteen gays, including members of GATE (Toronto) and GATE (Vancouver), attended the York Riding nomination meeting of David Lewis, leader of the New Democratic Party, held in preparation for the July 8 federal election. The gays leafleted the crowd. After Lewis delivered his acceptance speech, he was questioned from the floor about his thoughts on federal laws, such as the Immigration Act, which discriminated against gays. Mr. Lewis replied that he would favour the repeal of legislation that discriminated against any minority, including homosexuals, and that anti-gay laws should be repealed.

["Lewis Favours Rights," *Metro Community News* 1 (31 May 1974): 13; "NDP Leader Supports Civil Rights for Gays," NGEC *Newsletter*, no. 1 (1974), p. 1.]

May 31 ★ Toronto ★ Judgement was handed down in the trial of the Brunswick Four. Adrienne Potts was convicted of causing a disturbance and was sentenced to three months probation. Pat Murphy and Heather Beyer were acquitted of the same charge; Sue Wells was never charged. (See also July 16 and November 1, 1974.)

["The Brunswick Four Minus One: The Trial," *Other Woman* 2 (June 1974): 2; "Lesbian Found Guilty; Harassment No Defense," *Advocate* (Los Angeles), no. 143 (1974), p. 21; "Partial Win for Brunswick 4," *Body Politic*, no. 14 (1974), p. 6; "3 Women Claim Police Abused Them in Garage," *Toronto Star*, four star ed., 28 May 1974, p. A4; "Woman Guilty, 2 Cleared in Disturbance: Obstruction Charges Withdrawn," *Globe and Mail*, metro ed., 1 June 1974, p. 26.]

May 31 ★ Toronto ★ Gays picketed Manny's delicatessen, 494 Yonge Street, after several "street gays" were expelled. Fifteen people marched in the afternoon, and twenty-five in the evening.

["Gays Hold Impromptu Picket," *Body Politic*, no. 14 (1974), p. 6.]

May–June ★ Edmonton ★ A special lesbian issue of *On Our Way: An Edmonton Women's Newspaper* (vol. 2, no. 3) was published. The twenty-page paper was edited by members of Edmonton Lesbian Feminists (ELF) and included articles on lesbian feminism, lesbian motherhood, lesbians and the church, as well as news, poetry, art, and a short story.

May–June ★ Toronto ★ An exhibition of photographs by Raphael Bendahan entitled "Children of the Drag Ritual" was shown at Café LaBarge. Many of the images were of performers at the Club Manatee.

[Raphael Bendahan photographs, 82–014, Canadian Lesbian and Gay Archives, Toronto.]

June ∗ Guelph, Ont. ∗ *The Ontarion* reported on June 18 that four members of UGHA had recently attended a Liberal party meeting at which Prime Minister Pierre Trudeau was present. The four carried signs and managed to ask Trudeau about civil rights for gays. Trudeau was on a campaign tour leading up to the July 8 federal election.

["Guelph Group Pickets Trudeau," *Body Politic*, no. 14 (1974), p. 8; Heather (Ramsay), "Gays at Guelph," *Ontarion* (Univ. of Guelph), 18 June 1974, p. 12; "Trudeau Confronted in Guelph," NGEC *Newsletter*, no. 3 (1974), pp. 1–2.]

June ∗ Montréal ∗ A group of six gay men and lesbians were awarded an $8,000 Opportunities for Youth grant to organize a counselling service at the AHM/GMA Centre during the summer. The proposal had been submitted by Jackie Manthorne and Robert Vallée.

["Gay Group Gets Backing from Ottawa," *Globe and Mail*, metro ed., 25 June 1974, p. 9; "Information: Montreal Homophile Counselling," *Long Time Coming* 1 (May–June 1974): 35; "OFY Programme Funds 2 Groups," *Body Politic*, no. 14 (1974), p. 4; Betty Shapiro, "OFY Grant a First for Lesbians and Homosexuals," *Montreal Gazette*, final ed., 20 August 1974, pp. 35, 36.]

June ∗ Saskatoon ∗ The first issue of *Gay West* was published by Saskatoon Gay Action. It survived for two issues.

["New Paper on Prairies," *Body Politic*, no. 14 (1974), p. 4.]

June ∗ Toronto ∗ *The Body Politic* and GATE (Toronto) moved to new storefront premises at 193 Carlton Street.

["*Body Politic* and GATE Share New Premises," *Body Politic*, no. 14 (1974), p. 5; "GATE and *Body Politic* Open Office," *Metro Community News* 1 (31 May 1974): 13.]

June 7–9 ∗ Toronto ∗ Rev. Troy Perry, founder of MCC and moderator of the Universal Fellowship of Metropolitan Community Churches, was the special guest of MCC (Toronto). A discussion forum, dinner, and dance were held in celebration. On June 9, MCC (Toronto) received its charter and membership in the Universal Fellowship of Metropolitan Community Churches from Rev. Perry in a special service held at Holy Trinity Church. By June 1974, MCC (Toronto) was attracting about seventy men and women regularly to its Sunday services.

["Big Weekend for Troy Perry," *Metro Community News* 1 (17 May 1974): 3; "Church Chartered," *Body Politic*, no. 14 (1974), p. 4; "Five Years L.A. to Toronto," *Metro Community News* 1 (31 May 1974): 7; "MCC Gets Province O.K.," *Metro Community News* 1 (17 May 1974): 3; *Metro Community News*, Special Issue, June 1974, 4 pp.; "Spreading the Word," *Metro Community News* 1 (14 June 1974): 2; "Troy Perry's Visit," *Metro Community News* 1 (31 May 1974): 1.]

June 10 ∗ Vancouver ∗ On CKNW-AM's "Investigators Programme," Bob Cook of GATE (Vancouver) was able to ask NDP leader David Lewis whether he and the NDP supported the inclusion of a sexual orientation clause in the Canadian Bill of Rights. Lewis declared that he believed the Bill of Rights was not the proper place for that provision but that statutes that discriminated against people because of their sexual orientation were unjustified. Lewis was on a campaign tour leading up to the July 8 federal election.

["Lewis Questioned for Fourth Time," NGEC *Newsletter*, no. 2 (1974), pp. 1–2; "Lewis Repeats Stand," *Metro Community News* 1 (28 June 1974): 7.]

June 13 ∗ Toronto ∗ GATE (Toronto) sponsored a public all-candidates meeting at Ryerson Polytechnical Institute, leading up to the July 8 federal election. Only six candidates (three NDP, two Communists, and one Revolutionary Marxist) came to address a crowd of 75–100 people. All the candidates expressed their general support of gay rights.

["GATE Toronto All Candidates Meeting," NGEC *Newsletter*, no. 2 (1974), p. 2; "Liberals, Conservatives Boycott Meeting," *Body Politic*, no. 14 (1974), p. 5.]

June 15 ∗ Toronto ∗ The predominantly lesbian-run Amazon Workshop held a grand opening party at 12 Kensington Avenue. It was an umbrella organization for community services such as the Women's Self-Defense Centre, Amazon Press (formerly Women's Liberation Type Press), and the Toronto Women's Bookstore (formerly Let Us Out Bookstore) that had formerly been located at the Women's Place on Dupont Street.

["Ads: Amazon Press," *Other Woman* 3 (Fall 1974): 22; "Amazon Workshop: Announcing the Opening of a New Feminist Centre," *Other Woman* 2 (June 1974): 2; Becki L. Ross, *The House That Jill Built: A Lesbian Nation in Formation* (Toronto: University of Toronto Press, 1995), pp. 46–47; "Toronto Women's Bookstore," *Other Woman* 3 (August 1974): 2.]

June 15 ∗ Victoria, B.C. ∗ GPA organized its first social evening, which was attended by nearly fifty people. This was seen as an enormous success in a city that until that time had no gay bars or clubs.

["Gay People's Alliance (GPA)" vertical file, Canadian Lesbian and Gay Archives, Toronto.]

June (mid) ∗ Winnipeg ∗ During a question-and-answer session with students at Red River Community College, NDP leader David Lewis was asked whether it was NDP policy to end discrimination against homosexuals. Lewis replied, "Let me tell you this. I believe, and I say with complete confidence that my wife and my family also believe, that discrimination against anyone because of how they are made is totally unacceptable in a modern society." Lewis was on a campaign tour leading up to the July 8 federal election.

[Richard Gwyn, "The Anger in Lewis Frightens Strangers," *Toronto Star*, four star ed., 11 June 1974, p. B6; "Lewis Questioned for Fourth Time," NGEC *Newsletter*, no. 2 (1974), pp. 1–2.]

June 18 * Ottawa * Members of GO attended a town hall meeting sponsored by John Turner (Lib.-Ottawa Centre), who was campaigning for reelection July 8. When asked where he stood on the issue of including sexual orientation in the Canadian Bill of Rights, Turner replied that doing so would not alleviate discrimination against gays. He later spoke informally with the GO members.

["Questions in Ottawa," NGEC *Newsletter*, no. 4 (1974), p. 2.]

June 18 * Sooke, B.C. * During an all-candidates meeting for the July 8 federal election, Randy Notte of the GPA asked Tommy Douglas, former leader of the NDP and the incumbent for Nanaimo-Cowichan-The Islands, about gross indecency and buggery in the Criminal Code and about the inclusion of sexual orientation in the Canadian Bill of Rights. Douglas replied, "I do not feel that heterosexuals should oppose a minority but questions of freedom should be confined to adults only and I feel that a minority has no right to induce seduction."

["Tommy Douglas on Gay Rights?" NGEC *Newsletter*, no. 3 (1974), p. 2.]

June 25 * Winnipeg * The question of protection from discrimination based on sexual orientation was raised during an all-candidates town hall meeting in St. Boniface constituency, leading up to the July 8 federal election. The Progressive Conservative candidate, Dr. John Hare, advised the questioner to " 'go back to where you came from,' because homosexuality 'doesn't belong in a political discussion.' "

["Issue Flusters Candidates," *Winnipeg Tribune*, final ed., 27 June 1974, p. 21.]

June 26 * London, Ont. * Four members of the executive committee of UWOHA/HALO met with London's police chief Walter Johnson to inform him of the existence of HALO as well as its objectives. They were well received.

["Announcements," UWOHA *Newsletter* 3 (July 1974): 3.]

Summer * Don Mills, Ont. * Cheryl Freeman was harassed by neighbours and by the Ontario Housing Corporation because she was a lesbian.

["Lesbian Mother Harassed," *Body Politic*, no. 14 (1974), p. 6.]

Summer * Regina * Saskatchewan Attorney-General Roy Romanow upheld a decision by the Saskatchewan Human Rights Commission that the *Western*

Producer's refusal to print an ad for the Zodiac Friendship Society/Saskatoon Gay Action was not a violation of the provincial Human Rights Code because sexual orientation was not covered under the Code.

["Sask. Human Rights Commission Refuses to Take Action," *Body Politic*, no. 15 (1974), p. 6.]

Summer ∗ Toronto ∗ The Brown Breast Brigade (BBB) was formed by several lesbians to protest that women could be fined for gross indecency for baring their chests while at the same time sexist strip joints flourished on Yonge Street. Several topless members of the Brigade, complete with BBB banner, were featured in photographs published in *The Other Woman*.

["BBB," *Other Woman* 2 (July 1974): 10–11; Linda, "BBB," *Other Woman* 3 (August 1974): 4.]

Summer ∗ Toronto **∗** Although representatives of the Ontario Human Rights Commission (OHRC) had agreed to investigate and mediate well-documented cases of discrimination based on sexual orientation, early complaints filed with the OHRC received little attention.

["OHRC Will Look into Complaints," *Metro Community News* 1 (31 May 1974): 15; "OHRC Yawns at Discrimination," *Body Politic*, no. 14 (1974), p. 6.]

July ∗ Toronto **∗** Bill Ert and Tony Molina filed a request with the Ontario Health Insurance Plan (OHIP) that they be recognized as a family unit in order to qualify for medical coverage under OHIP's family plan. Ert and Molina had been legally married at the MCC in Houston, Texas, on October 5, 1972. They had moved to Toronto in 1973, were enrolled with OHIP, and had paid the family premium. When Ert was hospitalized, OHIP refused to pay expenses because the couple were both male. Ert and Molina eventually accepted a compromise proposal from OHIP.

[Sidney Katz, "Homosexual Couple Battles for OHIP Family Benefits," *Toronto Star*, four star ed., 19 July 1974, p. A4; "OHIP Compromise Robs Gay Couple of 'Family Rates,'" *Body Politic*, no. 15 (1974), p. 7; "They Took Their Premiums, but Won't Pay Benefits," *Advocate* (Los Angeles), no. 145 (1974), p. 19.]

July 2 ∗ Steinbach, Man. **∗** Eleven members of GFE and A Woman's Place in Winnipeg picketed Derksen Printers, who on June 25 had refused to print Project Understanding's booklet *Understanding Homosexuality* because it presented homosexuality favourably. The marchers were met by Mennonite clergymen who preached about the evils of homosexuality.

["Canadian Printer Continues His Private War: Mennonites Confront Gays," *Advocate* (Los Angeles), no. 145 (1974), p. 18; "Gays Picket Printer," *Winnipeg Tribune*, 2 July 1974, p. 3; "Homosexuals Plan to Picket Publisher," *Winnipeg Free Press*, 29 June 1974, p. 9; David Lee, "Steinbach Protest Ends in Standoff," *Winnipeg Free Press*, 3 July 1974, pp. 1, 5; Bill Lewis, "Forcing the Issue," *Body Politic*, no. 17 (1975), p. 9; "Prairie Gays Combat Prejudice" (editorial), *Gay Tide* 1 (August 1974): 2; "Printer Refuses OFY Publication," *Body Politic*, no. 14 (1974), p. 4; "Rejected by Printer, Manitoba Gays Want Law Changed: Seek Protection against 'Discrimination,'" *Globe and Mail*, metro ed., 4 July 1974, p. 9.]

July 8 ∗ Canada ∗ The federal election marked the culmination of more than a year's work by the NGEC, a concerted effort by twenty gay organizations across Canada to make gay civil rights an issue in federal elections. Questionnaires regarding positions on gay issues were sent to all candidates, as was the booklet *Homosexuals: A Minority without Rights/Les homosexuels: une minorité sans droits*. Results of the questionnaires were reported in the NGEC *Newsletter*.

["Candidates Polled Favor Immigration Law Change," *Body Politic*, no. 15 (1974), p. 8; "Cross-Country Campaign 74," *Gay Tide* 1 (August 1974): 6; Gays of Ottawa (GO) papers and inventory, 82–017/05(03), Canadian Lesbian and Gay Archives, Toronto; "Homosexuals Mobilize for Federal Election," UWOHA *Newsletter* 3 (June 1974): 11; "How the Candidates Responded," *Gay Tide* 1 (August 1974): 7, 8, 9; "Legal Reform: Gay McGill Goes Ahead with NGEC," *Gay News* 2 (Xmas 1973): 4–6; "National Gay Election Coalition," *Club '70 News*, June 1974, pp. 8–9; "National Gay Election Coalition," *Gay West*, no. 1 (1974), p. 5; "National Gay Election Coalition: What It's All About," *Body Politic*, no. 14 (1974), p. 8; "National Gay Election Coalition Questionnaire," *Club '70 News*, July 1974, pp. 2–3; "No Small Accomplishment" (editorial), *Body Politic*, no. 14 (1974), p. 2; Stan Persky, "Gay Election Coalition Demands Answers," *Western Voice*, 12–25 June 1974, p. 5; "Some Answers to NGEC Questionnaire," *Metro Community News* 1 (14 June 1974): 3; Tom Warner, "NGEC: Model for a National Movement," *Body Politic*, no. 15 (1974), pp. 16–17.]

July 16 ∗ Toronto ∗ Police Constable Robert Hall went on trial, charged by Adrienne Potts with common assault in connection with the Brunswick Four incident. (See also November 1, 1974.)

July 25 ∗ Saskatoon ∗ Darlene Case, a lesbian, lost custody of her two children to her ex-husband. She had been granted custody in 1973; this decision was reversed after her ex-husband appealed the case on the basis of the mother's lesbianism. At this time there was no Canadian precedent for a self-declared lesbian or gay man gaining or retaining child custody. In making his ruling, Justice Murdoch MacPherson stated: "It seems to me that homosexuality on the part of a parent is a factor to be considered along with all of the other evidence in the case. It should not be considered a bar in itself to a parent's right to custody." Darlene Case was supported by the Saskatoon Women's Centre, Saskatoon Gay Action, and the Zodiac Friendship Society, among others.

[Christine Boyle, "Custody, Adoption and the Homosexual Parent," *Reports of Family Law* 23 (1976): 129–45; "Case v. Case," *Reports of Family Law* 18 (1975): 132–38; "Defence Fund Established," *Gay West*, no. 1 (1974), p. 1; "Ex-husband Steals Kids from

Lesbian: She Had Won Custody," *Advocate* (Los Angeles), no. 146 (1974), p. 20; "Lesbian Mother," *Gay Tide* 2 (Autumn 1974): 11; Chris MacNaughton, "Who Gets the Kids?: Usually Not Lesbian Mothers, at Least Not in the Courts as They Are Being Conducted Today," *Body Politic*, no. 34 (1977), pp. 12–13; "News: Lesbian Mother May Lose Children," *Long Time Coming* 1 (May–June 1974): 23; Terry Martiniuk, Letter, *Club '70 News*, July 1974, p. 9; "Mother Fights for Children in Court," *Body Politic*, no. 14 (1974), p. 5; "Saskatoon Gay Action" vertical file, Canadian Lesbian and Gay Archives, Toronto; "Saskatoon Mother Loses Children," *Body Politic*, no. 15 (1974), p. 5.]

July 30 ∗ Toronto ∗ The Ontario Court of Appeal dismissed an appeal by Karl John Roestad to end his indefinite term in penitentiary as a dangerous sexual offender. Roestad had been convicted in March 1971 of sexually assaulting twenty boys. (See also September–October 1974.)

["Given Life, Sex Offender Loses Appeal," *Globe and Mail*, metro ed., 31 July 1974, p. 5; "Pedophile Indefinitely Jailed Suffers Aversion Therapy," *Body Politic*, no. 15 (1974), p. 7.]

July 31 ∗ Ottawa ∗ The Vanier Institute of the Family announced that homosexual couples who live together for long periods should be viewed as a family.

[True Davidson, "Vanier Institute" (column), *Toronto Sun*, final ed., 8 August 1974, p. 11; "Family Folly" (editorial), *Toronto Sun*, final ed., 14 August 1974, p. 10; "Family Institute Recognizes Gay Couples," *Body Politic*, no. 15 (1974), p. 5; "Institute Sees a Family Life for Homosexuals," *Toronto Star*, four star ed., 1 August 1974, p. A6; Bill Terry, ". . . And the Sun Stood Still!" *Metro Community News* 1 (23 August 1974): 9; "The Vanier Institute Speaks . . . Et True, Too!" *Metro Community News* 1 (9 August 1974): 6–7.]

August ∗ Toronto ∗ The Barracks bathhouse officially opened at 56 Widmer Street.

[Advertisement, *Metro Community News* 1 (18 October 1974): 19.]

August ∗ Toronto ∗ Police officers visited the offices of *The Body Politic* to order that a window display be removed. A compromise was reached when erections in the offending drawing (from issue 14) were covered.

["Politicians Overexposed: Morals Squad Mobilizes," *Body Politic*, no. 15 (1974), p. 7.]

August ∗ Toronto ∗ Toronto Public Library employees who were members of CUPE Local 1582 failed to secure a clause in their contract barring discrimination based on sexual orientation. Management did agree to include the clause in a Letter of Intent that was to be appended to the contract.

["Union Wins 'Partial Victory,' " *Body Politic*, no. 16 (1974), p. 8.]

August ✱ Windsor, Ont. ✱ The Human Rights Committee of Local 195 of the United Auto Workers recommended that all plant units review the non-discrimination clause in their contracts and broaden its scope to include sexual orientation.

[Harold Desmarais, "Union Action Protects Gays," *Body Politic*, no. 19 (1975), p. 7.]

August 17 ✱ Toronto ✱ More than 100 people participated in a march from Allan Gardens to Queen's Park and back to launch Gay Pride Week (August 17–25). The march was organized to focus attention on efforts to include sexual orientation in the Ontario Human Rights Code. The parade was covered by the *Toronto Sun* and the *Globe and Mail*; this was the first time that major mainstream newspapers covered a Gay Pride march in Toronto.

[Gillean Chase, "Gay Pride? Week," *Other Woman* 3 (August 1974): 16 (reprinted in *Long Time Coming* 2 [December 1974]: 28–29); "Gays, Greeks Demonstrate at Legislature," *Globe and Mail*, metro ed., 19 August 1974, p. 5; "Gays March to Queen's Park," *Toronto Sun*, final ed., 16 August 1974, p. 2; Terry Phillips, "Toronto Gay Pride," *Gay Tide* 2 (Autumn 1974): 10; K.D. Popert, "Civil Rights Marchers" (letter), *Globe and Mail*, metro ed., 30 August 1974, p. 6; "Spirited March Launches Gay Pride Week," *Body Politic*, no. 15 (1974), p. 6.]

August 17–25 ✱ Canada ✱ The third annual Gay Pride Week was held to reaffirm the goals set in the "We Demand" demonstration on Parliament Hill in Ottawa on August 28, 1971, and to celebrate the fifth anniversary of the Criminal Code amendments. Political, cultural, and social events were held in larger gay centres across the country.

["Gay Pride Week," *Metro Community News* 1 (26 July 1974): 13; "Gay Pride Week August 17–25, 1974: 50 Were They," *Metro Community News* 1 (23 August 1974): 1.]

August 20 ✱ Montréal ✱ Nigel Gibson's article "Gay Bars: The Boulevard of Broken Dreams. Loves Lost and Found" was published in the *Gazette*. Its melodramatic tone stereotyped the gay world as furtive and depressing.

[Nigel Gibson, "Gay Bars: The Boulevard of Broken Dreams. Loves Lost and Found," *Montreal Gazette*, final ed., 20 August 1974, p. 35; "Homosexuality As It Is?" *Gay-Zette* 1 (September 1974): 4.]

August 20 ✱ Toronto ✱ Three members of GATE (Toronto) met with John MacBeth, the new Ontario Minister of Labour, to discuss inclusion of sexual orientation in the Ontario Human Rights Code. MacBeth stated that public opinion against homosexuals would not support any move by the government to introduce such an amendment to the Code.

[" 'Public Opinion' Invoked to Stall GATE Demands," *Body Politic*, no. 15 (1974), p. 8.]

August 25–29 * Montréal * The annual meeting of the American Sociological Association included a discussion entitled "Theoretical Perspectives on Homosexuality," during which Edward Sagarin (a.k.a. Donald Webster Cory), professor of sociology at the City College of New York and author (as Cory) of such classics as *The Homosexual in America: A Subjective Approach* (1951) and *The Homosexual and His Society: A View from Within* (1963), urged homosexuals to go straight. Sagarin's view was opposed by four discussants, including Laud Humphries, who declared his own homosexuality. On August 27, a gay caucus of the ASA was founded by Barry Adam and Ron Lawson.

["Homosexual Label Rapped by New York Sociologist," *Montreal Gazette*, final ed., 27 August 1974, p. 4; "Sociologists Form Gay Caucus," *Body Politic*, no. 15 (1974), p. 6.]

August 26 * Niagara Falls, Ont. * American gay activist John Kyper was turned back at the Canadian border because he had admitted to Canadian immigration officials that he was gay. Kyper was a member of Boston's *Fag Rag* collective and also a staff member at *Gay Community News*. Copies of *Gay Community News* were found in his possession. Homosexuals were excluded from entering Canada as a prohibited class of person, as described in paragraph 5(e) of the Immigration Act. This action was protested by GATE (Toronto), and through their help Kyper was able to sneak into the country on September 19. In March 1975, after months of protests on his behalf by members of GATE (Toronto) and GO, Kyper was allowed to visit Canada officially after being granted a special Minister's Permit by the Department of Manpower and Immigration. (See also October 15, 1974.)

["Deported Homosexual Allowed to Re-enter Canada," *Metro Community News* 2 (7 February 1975): 1; "Deported Homosexual Sneaks into Canada," *Globe and Mail*, metro ed., 21 September 1974, p. 58; "A Deported U.S. Gay Reentered Canada in March," *Body Politic*, no. 18 (1975), p. 6; "Gay Deportee Gains Reentry," *Body Politic*, no. 17 (1975), p. 7; "Gay Refused Entry," *Gay Tide* 2 (Autumn 1974): 10; Carol Goar, "Homosexual Seeks Law Changes: Border Ban Brought Fame," *Ottawa Citizen*, 26 March 1975, p. 2; Tom Hurley, "Canada Deports GCN Staffer," *Gay Community News* (Boston), 7 September 1974, pp. 1–2; "Immigration: Kyper Gets Permit," *Gay Tide* 2 (March 1975): 5; "John Kyper" vertical file, Canadian Lesbian and Gay Archives, Toronto; "John Kyper in Ottawa," GO *Info* 2 (April–May 1975): 7; "Kyper Speaks to GO," GO *Info* 2 (March 1975): 7; "Liberationist Defies Immigration Act," *Body Politic*, no. 15 (1974), pp. 5–6; "Official Says Ban on U.S. Homosexual 'First I've Seen,' " *Toronto Star*, four star ed., 12 September 1974, p. A10; "U.S. Gay Refused Entry," *Gay-Zette* 2 (April 1975): 4; "U.S. Hiker Admits Homosexuality, Deported by Immigration Official," *Globe and Mail*, metro ed., 7 September 1974, p. 2.]

August 31–September 2 * Winnipeg * The second annual national gay conference was attended by seventy-five delegates representing two dozen organizations. Sponsored by GFE and held at the University of Manitoba, the conference included workshops, discussions, and plenary sessions. Some tension was evident between representatives of gay clubs and social organizations who supported low-key events, and the gay liberationists, who favoured public demands for gay rights. During a plenary session, Ron Dayman presented a proposal on behalf of GATE (Toronto) suggesting that the NGRC/CNDH be established as the permanent successor to the NGEC. On August 31, about eighty people took part in the National Gay March from the Richardson Building to the Manitoba Legislature; this was the first such march and rally held on the Prairies. (See also June 28–July 1, 1975.)

[Jim Dougan, "The Second Annual National Gay Conference," *Gaily Planet* 1 (October 1974): 4–5; Maurice Flood, "2nd National Conference: Winnipeg," *Gay Tide* 2 (Autumn 1974): 3–5; Gays of Ottawa (GO) papers and inventory, 82–017/05(38), Canadian Lesbian and Gay Archives, Toronto; Vernon Hern, "Report on the Second Annual National Gay Convention Held in Winnipeg on Labour Day Weekend," *Homophile Association of London, Ontario Newsletter* 1 (October 1974): 3–6; "Homosexuals Seek More Freedom," *Winnipeg Tribune*, two star final ed., 3 September 1974, p. 4; "Marchers Get Mixed Response," *Winnipeg Free Press*, 3 September 1974, p. 3; Leslie Orchard, "The Second Annual National Gay Conference," *Long Time Coming* 2 (December 1974): 2–6; Stan Persky, "Homosexuals Break Gay Barrier in Winnipeg," *Western Voice*, 11–24 September 1974, p. 3; "2nd National Conference Produces Broad Consensus," *Body Politic*, no. 15 (1974), p. 5; Merv Walker, " 'Many Faces, One Focus': 4th Annual Conference Planned for Toronto," *Body Politic*, no. 26 (1976), p. 6; "Winnipeg Rights March First in Prairie Provinces," *Body Politic*, no. 15 (1974), p. 5; R.W. (Robert Wolfe), "A Kind of Liberation," *Metro Community News* 1 (26 July 1974): 1.]

September * London, Ont. * HALO leased a two-storey building at 649 Colborne Street. This new centre became London's headquarters for lesbian and gay activities, including meetings, dances, social services, a coffee house, and a library. With more than 10,000 square feet of space, the HALO centre became the largest gay community centre in Canada.

["London Group Makes Plans for New Centre," *Body Politic*, no. 16 (1974), p. 8; "Members of HALO," *Homophile Association of London, Ontario Newsletter* 1 (October 1974): 1–3.]

September * Montréal * A resolution declaring homosexuality "subversive of the family and contrary to divine law" was adopted during the twenty-ninth annual convention of the Antiochian Orthodox Church in North America.

[" 'Homosexuality Is Subversive,' " *Advocate* (Los Angeles), no. 148 (1974), p. 17.]

September 15 * Hamilton * Twelve people attended the first MCC service held in Hamilton, which was conducted by Rev. Bob Wolfe of MCC (Toronto).

["MCC Hamilton," *Metro Community News* 1 (20 September 1974): 1.]

September 20 * Montréal * Claude Fournier's film *La pomme, la queue . . . et les pépins!/The Apple, the Stem . . . and the Seeds!* opened at the Papineau and twelve other theatres. This sex comedy about a playboy politician's attempts to restore his virility starred Donald Lautrec.

[D.J. Turner and Micheline Morisset, eds., *Canadian Feature Film Index, 1913–1985/Index des films canadiens de long métrage* (Ottawa: Public Archives, National Film, Television, and Sound Archives, 1987), entry 523; Thomas Waugh, "Nègres blancs, tapettes et 'butch': les lesbiennes et les gais dans le cinéma québécois," *Copie zéro*, no. 11 (1981), pp. 18, 20, 22.]

September 22 * Ottawa * A congregation of the MCC held its first service (at the Club Private), which was conducted by Rev. Philip Speranza. The church soon moved to a hall at the Church of St. Alban the Martyr on King Edward Street, where it remained until December 1975 when it moved to the second floor of an office building at 69 Sparks Street.

[Denis LeBlanc, "MCC Loses Home," GO *Info* 2 (November–December 1975): 10; "MCC Is Being Called, Ottawa Is in It's (sic) Sights," *Metro Community News* 1 (23 August 1974): 15; "Mission to Ottawa," *Metro Community News* 1 (13 September 1974): 1; Angela Pelly, "Ottawa Church for Homosexuals Proves Beacon of Hope and Help," *Ottawa Citizen*, 10 May 1975, p. 86; "What We're Up To . . . ,"*New Beginnings* 1 (30 May 1975): 1.]

September 26 * Hamilton * Dr. Charles Socarides, a psychiatrist at the Albert Einstein Centre in New York and the author of *The Overt Homosexual* (1968), was challenged by members of the audience during a taping of the CBC television programme *Under Attack*, held at McMaster University. Socarides was one of the prime defenders of the "homosexuals are sick and should be treated" school of psychiatry, and was known for his statement "There is no such thing as a happy homosexual." The program was broadcast on CHCH-TV on December 21, 1974.

[Paul C., "Members Attend 'Under Attack' Taping," *Gaily Planet* 1 (October 1974): 5–6; Orvin Millett, "Gays Are Sick: Dr. Socarides," *Back/Chat* 4 (25 October 1974): 1; "Socarides Slammed, Skips Second Session," *Body Politic*, no. 15 (1974), p. 7; "Under Attack," *Dialogue*, no. 8 (1974), pp. 5–9; "Watch For," *Metro Community News* 2 (13 December 1974): 8.]

September 26 * Vancouver * Representatives of the Vancouver Gay Information Service (Van-Gay) appeared before City Council's Standing Committee on Social Services to seek a grant for $26,720 to help support Van-Gay's programs, which included the Have a Gay Stay Transient Housing and Gay Information Service, a twenty-four-hour crisis centre, a drop-in centre, a drug counselling program, a consciousness-raising seminar, and a speaker's bureau. The group's proposal was sent to the Social Planning Department for study and comment. Van-Gay had been seeking funding assistance from the City since July 1974, but could not get a substantive response. Its quest for funding had been ridiculed by *Vancouver Sun* columnist Jack Wasserman, who in his August 20 column published a scornful poem written by Senior Social Planner Jonathan Baker, a city official to whom Van-Gay's report had been referred. This event led to gay protests against Wasserman and Baker. Vancouver's Director of Social Planning turned down the request for funding on November 4, 1974.

["City Aid Asked by 'Gays,' " *Vancouver Province*, four star ed., 25 September 1974, p. 13; The Editors, "Gays Confront City Hall," *Gay Tide* 2 (Autumn 1974): 1; "Gay Aid Dynamite — Marzari," *Vancouver Province*, four star final ed., 27 September 1974, p. 9; "Gays Seeking City Money: Aldermen Seek More Data," *Vancouver Sun*, four star ed., 27 September 1974, p. 11; "Manager's Report," *Gay Tide* 2 (March 1975): back cover; "Vancouver Gay Information Service (Van-Gay)" vertical file, Canadian Lesbian and Gay Archives, Toronto; "Vancouver Groups Seek City Council Funding," *Body Politic*, no. 16 (1974), p. 8; Jack Wasserman, Column, *Vancouver Sun*, four star ed., 20 August 1974, p. 35; Jack Wasserman, Column, *Vancouver Sun*, four star ed., 7 September 1974, p. 43.]

September 27 ⋆ Guelph, Ont. ⋆ President Paul Shepherd and other representatives of UGHA met with Mark Shopian, editor of *The Daily Bastphuque*, the Mills Hall dormitory newsletter that had printed anti-gay, racist, and sexist material in its September 6 edition. Also present at the meeting were representatives of other groups maligned in the paper. Shopian printed an apology in the *Ontarion* on October 1, but when the next issue of the *Bastphuque* was published, it included similar offensive material. Comments on the incident, both pro and con, were printed in the *Ontarion* throughout November 1974.

["*Bastphuque* Editor Retracts Apology," *Ontarion* (Univ. of Guelph), 22 October 1974, p. 1; "Newsletter Disgusts Ethnic Groups, Women, Gays," *Ontarion* (Univ. of Guelph), 1 October 1974, pp. 1, 2; "Student Group Strikes Back at Guelph Campus Bigotry," *Body Politic*, no. 16 (1974), pp. 6, 8; "University of Guelph Homophile Association (UGHA)" vertical file, Canadian Lesbian and Gay Archives, Toronto.]

September 27 ⋆ Winnipeg ⋆ GFE presented the brief "Manitoba Homosexuals: A Minority without Rights" to Attorney-General Howard Pawley, urging the provincial government to amend its Human Rights Act to protect gay people from discrimination. Pawley replied that "no change will be made to the Act." Although he admitted that protection for homosexuals was needed, Pawley thought that the vast majority of the NDP caucus would be against it.

["Gays for Equality Present Demands to Manitoba NDP Government," *Labor*

Challenge, 10 February 1975, p. 10; Bill Lewis, "Forcing the Issue," *Body Politic*, no. 17 (1975), p. 9; "Manitoba Gays Demand Change," *Body Politic*, no. 16 (1974), p. 6; "Pawley, Gays to Talk," *Winnipeg Tribune*, 16 July 1974, p. 3.]

September–October ✳ Toronto ✳ Gerald Hannon's opinion piece "Outrage" was published in the September–October issue of *The Body Politic*. Hannon urged the gay community to lobby for the release of Karl John Roestad, a convicted homosexual pedophile who had been imprisoned in March 1971 for an indefinite term of detention as a dangerous sexual offender. The article generated much reaction (mostly negative) in both the gay community and the local mainstream press. (See also October 19, 22, and October–November 1974.)

[Gerald Hannon, "Outrage" (opinion column), *Body Politic*, no. 15 (1974), p. 10; M.J. McReavy, "Pedophile Is 'Dangerous' " (letter), *Body Politic*, no. 16 (1974), p. 3; Bob Wolfe, "Church Editorial," *Metro Community News* 1 (1 November 1974): 1, 3; Ian Young, "An Issue of Prime Importance" (letter), *Body Politic*, no. 16 (1974), p. 3.]

Autumn ✳ Burnaby, B.C. ✳ Gay People of SFU was formed at Simon Fraser University. Dr. Michael Eliot-Hurst of the Department of Geography was involved in establishing the group. Although it was formed with the intent of including both men and women, at first Gay People of SFU was almost exclusively male. Weekly meetings were held, as were various social gatherings. One of the early events was a talk by Del Martin and Phyllis Lyon, co-founders of the pioneering American lesbian organization The Daughters of Bilitis.

["Gay People of SFU," *Peak* (Simon Fraser Univ.), *Gay Supplement*, 9 July 1975, p. 1.]

Autumn ✳ Guelph, Ont. ✳ A lesbian drop-in began to be held on Thursday nights at the UGHA office, University Centre, University of Guelph.

["Women's News," *Gaily Planet* 1 (November 1974): 7.]

Autumn ✳ Montréal ✳ A gay studies course entitled "The Other Face of Love — Studies in Gay Male Literature" was offered at Concordia University by Prof. Robert K. Martin and Will Aitken of Androgyny Books.

["Gay Studies Survive Obstacles, Others Appear," *Body Politic*, no. 16 (1974), p. 7.]

Autumn ✳ Montréal ✳ An anonymous donor provided funds in memory of a relative to the Loyola campus of Concordia University to finance a $200 bursary to be awarded annually to a third-year lesbian or gay student of superior academic achievement. This is believed to be the first scholarship at a Canadian educational institution restricted to lesbians or gay men.

["Gay Bursary Established," *Body Politic*, no. 16 (1974), p. 8; "Gay Scholarship at Loyola," *Gay-Zette* Coming Out Edition (November–December 1974): 12.]

Autumn ∗ Ottawa ∗ Newly elected MPP Paul Taylor (Lib.-Carleton-East) sent a letter to GO in which he supported the inclusion of sexual orientation in the Ontario Human Rights Code.

["MLA (sic) Supports Gay Civil Rights," *Body Politic*, no. 17 (1975), p. 7; "Paul Taylor Supports Gay Rights," GO *Info* 2 (March 1975): 3.]

Autumn ∗ Toronto ∗ The Carriage House Motor Hotel, 306 Jarvis Street, which catered to gay people, introduced new regulations that discriminated against women by preventing them from using the downstairs bars and by not allowing them to wear blue jeans upstairs. *The Body Politic* dropped their ads in protest.

["*The Body Politic* Refuses Ad for Toronto Bar," *Body Politic*, no. 16 (1974), p. 8.]

Autumn ∗ Toronto ∗ The formation of the Labyris Collective was announced in *The Other Woman*. The short-lived group attempted to provide a relaxed place for lesbians to meet.

["Women Are Opening the Labyris and It's About Time!" *Other Woman* 3 (Fall 1974): 22.]

Autumn ∗ Toronto ∗ A weekly gay studies course entitled "New Perspectives on the Gay Experience" was offered by the University of Toronto School of Continuing Studies. The first class was held October 7. It was taught by Prof. Michael Lynch; guest speakers included Prof. John Alan Lee, Prof. Phyllis Grosskurth, Dr. David Berger, and Father Gregory Baum.

[Lawrence Clarke, "Gay Course Overrides Obstacles," *Varsity* (Univ. of Toronto), 30 October 1974, p. 1; "Gay Studies Survive Obstacles, Others Appear," *Body Politic*, no. 16 (1974), p. 7; "Low Enrolment Threatens Gay Studies Course," *Body Politic*, no. 15 (1974), p. 6; Ken Popert, "Gay Studies Course Faces Cancellation over Low Enrolment," *Varsity* (Univ. of Toronto), 27 September 1974, p. 1; "Understanding the 'Gay' Life," *Metro Community News* 1 (20 September 1974): 12.]

October ∗ Ottawa ∗ Although the Department of the Secretary of State had invited more than seventy Canadian women's groups to participate in the International Women's Year Consultation, not one lesbian group was invited to the conference. The conference had been called to set priorities for Canadian celebrations during International Women's Year (1975). The women's organizations became upset with the government's plans, complaining of misdirected initiatives and inadequate funding for grass-roots organizing.

[Letters, *Long Time Coming* 2 (December 1974): 23; "News: Statement of Policy re: International Women's Year from Women's Information and Referral Centre," *Long Time Coming* 2 (March 1975): 30–31; "News: Women Protest International Women's Year," *Long Time Coming* 2 (March 1975): 30.]

October ∗ Toronto ∗ Gary Curtis's four-part series on gay life in Toronto was published in the Ryerson Polytechnical Institute's student newspaper *The Eyeopener*. The series interviewed gay men and examined gay living conditions, relations with the police, and community institutions and facilities.

[Gary Curtis, "Gays Talk Straight," *Eyeopener*, 3 October 1974, p. 12; Gary Curtis, "Cops on Top of Gays," *Eyeopener*, 10 October 1974, p. 20; Gary Curtis, "Gays Pray on Sunday, Just Like 'Normal People,' " *Eyeopener*, 17 October 1974, p. 16; Gary Curtis, "A Gay Guide to Toronto," *Eyeopener*, 24 October 1974, pp. 14–16.]

October ∗ Toronto ∗ The HASP Defence Committee, formed in reaction to the Brunswick Four case, resolved to form a Women's Defence Fund.

["HASP Defence Committee," *Metro Community News* 1 (4 October 1974): 4; "Women's Defence Fund," *Back/Chat* 4 (11 October 1974): 4.]

October ∗ Toronto ∗ The *Toronto Star* decided to ban the use of the word "gay" in display advertising; the word "homosexual" was to be used instead. (See also October 19, 1974.)

[Lawrence Clarke, "The *Star* Bans Use of 'Gay' in Ads," *Varsity* (Univ. of Toronto), 30 October 1974, p. 1.]

October ∗ Toronto ∗ The Wages Due Lesbians collective was formed. The group was composed of lesbians who were trying to integrate a class analysis into lesbian-feminism. They became heavily involved in the International Wages for Housework movement, which linked various aspects of women's oppression to unpaid labour in the home. Wages Due Lesbians was interested in the rights of lesbian mothers and produced several position papers on lesbians and wages for housework, including "Why Lesbians Want Wages for Housework" and "Fucking Is Work."

[Ellen Agger, Letter, *Long Time Coming* 3 (September 1975): 13–14; Connie Beaulieu, "Wages for Housework: A Comment," *Long Time Coming* 2 (April 1975): 25; Margaret Fulford, ed., *The Canadian Women's Movement, 1960–1990: A Guide to Archival Resources/Le mouvement canadien des femmes, 1960–1990: guide de ressources archivistiques* (Toronto: Canadian Women's Movement Archives/ECW Press, 1992), entry 527; Becki L. Ross, *The House That Jill Built: A Lesbian Nation in Formation* (Toronto: University of Toronto Press, 1995), pp. 53–54; Wages Due Collective, "Lesbian and Straight," in Wendy Edmond and Suzie Fleming, eds., *All Work and No Pay: Women, Housework, and the Wages Due* (Bristol, England: Power of Women Collective/Falling Wall Press, 1975), pp. 21–25; Wages Due Lesbians papers, Canadian Women's Movement Archives, University of Ottawa, Ottawa; "Wages Due Lesbians" vertical file, Canadian Lesbian and Gay Archives, Toronto; "Wages for Housework: 'Strike While the Iron Is Hot' " (editorial), *Other Woman* 4 (December 1975–January 1976): 1; Ellen Woodsworth, "Lesbians Want Wages for Housework Too," in *Wages for Housework: Women Speak Out* (Toronto: Amazon Press, 1975), pp. 22–24.]

October ∗ Toronto ∗ Robert Wallace's play *'67* was published by Playwrights Co-op.

[Alexander Leggatt, "Letters in Canada 1974: Drama," *University of Toronto Quarterly* 44 (Summer 1975): 348–49.]

October ∗ Vancouver ∗ During the founding convention of the British Columbia Federation of Women a Rights of Lesbians Subcommittee was formed to undertake a feminist analysis of the rights of lesbians. The Subcommittee's first meeting was held at the Ms. Club, a lesbian bar. (See also October 31–November 1, 1975.)

["B.C. Lesbian Caucus Advances Feminist Analysis," *Body Politic*, no. 20 (1975), p. 11; "BCFW Lesbian Caucus," *Gay Tide* 2 (June 1975): 4; M. Julia Creet, "A Test of Unity: Lesbian Visibility in the British Columbia Federation of Women," in Sharon Dale Stone, ed., *Lesbians in Canada* (Toronto: Between the Lines, 1990), pp. 183–97; "Lesbian Caucus," BCFW *Newsletter* 1 (November 1974): 9; "Lesbian Caucus," *Pedestal: Lesbian-Feminist Newspaper* 7 (June–July 1975): 7.]

October ∗ Vancouver ∗ Policemen and city inspectors harassed gay bars and clubs during raids to check for liquor law violations. This harassment led directly to the formation of the Society for Education Action Research and Counselling on Homosexuality (SEARCH) on November 20, 1974. (See also November 17, 20, 23, and December 17, 1974.)

["A Brief History of SEARCH," *SEARCHLight* 1 (April 1978): 4; Maurice Flood, "Double Standard, Double Dealing," *Gay Tide* 2 (March 1975): 3–4; Don Hann and Rob Joyce, "City Police Record: Smash Hit!" *Gay Tide*, no. 16 (1977), p. 4; "Society for Education Action Research and Counselling on Homosexuality (SEARCH)" vertical file, Canadian Lesbian and Gay Archives, Toronto; Jack Wasserman, Column, *Vancouver Sun*, four star ed., 5 November 1974, p. 35.]

October 8 ∗ Canada ∗ "The Outrage," an episode of the series *Marcus Welby, M.D.*, was shown on ABC-TV affiliate stations across the country. The episode dealt with the rape of a fourteen-year-old male high school student by his male teacher, and triggered protests across North America for its stereotypical depiction of gays as child molesters and psychopaths.

["*Marcus Welby*: An Outrage," *Gay Tide* 2 (Autumn 1974): 10; "*Marcus Welby* Show Protested," *Metro Community News* 1 (20 September 1974): 1; Herb Spiers, "Outrage," *Body Politic*, no. 16 (1974), Our Image section, p. 19.]

October 11–14 ∗ Winnipeg ∗ The Happenings Club hosted the third annual Western Canada Gay Clubs Conference. Eighteen delegates from clubs in Edmonton, Regina, Saskatoon, and Winnipeg attended.

["Convention 1974," *What's Happening!* 4 (September–October 1974): 3; "Editorial," *What's Happening!* 4 (September–October 1974): 2; "Minutes of Meeting, Western Gay Clubs Convention . . . ," *What's Happening!* 4 (November 1974): 7–8.]

October 12 ✳ Toronto ✳ The Ontario Press Council ruled that the *Toronto Star* had discriminated against Glad Day Bookshop in May 1974 when it refused to print their classified ad. Jearld Moldenhauer, proprietor of Glad Day, then filed a complaint against the *Star* with the Ontario Human Rights Commission (OHRC). The OHRC ruled that its jurisdiction did not extend to discrimination based on sexual orientation. (See also October 19, 1974.)

["Ad Refused, OHRC Passes Buck," *Body Politic*, no. 17 (1975), p. 7; "Found Guilty of Bias, Newspaper Retaliates with Smear Campaign," *Body Politic*, no. 16 (1974), pp. 5, 7; "Press Council Says *Star* Entitled to Name Nationalist's Employer," *Toronto Star*, Saturday ed., 12 October 1974, pp. A1, A10.]

October 14 ✳ New York, N.Y. ✳ Michel Tremblay's play *Hosanna*, starring Richard Monette and Richard Donat, opened on Broadway at the Bijou Theatre. This was the first Canadian production of any play to reach Broadway since the 1950s. It closed after thirty performances.

["Our Image: Upcoming Events," *Body Politic*, no. 15 (1974), p. 19; Lawrence Sabbath, "No '*Hosanna*' on Broadway: Tremblay Play Folds," *Montreal Star*, final ed., 5 November 1974, p. B12.]

October 15 ✳ Ottawa ✳ Ron Dayman, Charles Hill, and Denis LeBlanc of GO met with T.B. Sheehan, acting director-general of the Department of Manpower and Immigration. Manpower and Immigration Minister Robert Andras was reported to be in favour of repealing sections of the Immigration Act that prohibited the entry of gay people into Canada. On the same day, twelve picketers distributed leaflets in front of the Manpower and Immigration building. This was to protest government inaction as well as the barring from Canada of American gay activist John Kyper on August 26, 1974. (See also October 23, 1974.)

[" 'Borders Closed to Gays . . . ,' " *Gay-Zette* Christmas Edition (December 1975–January 1976): 4–5; "Gays Picket Immigration," *Metro Community News* 1 (1 November 1974): 3; "Gays Protest Immigration Law," *Ottawa Journal*, 16 October 1974, p. 37; "Government May End Ban on Immigrants," *Body Politic*, no. 16 (1974), pp. 5, 6; "Homosexuals Allege Foul Play," *Ottawa Citizen*, 16 October 1974, p. 2; "Official Says Andras Favors Letting Homosexuals into Canada," *Toronto Star*, four star ed., 16 October 1974, p. A9; "Ottawa May Lift Gay Ban: Immigrants," *Globe and Mail*, metro ed., 17 October 1974, p. 9; "Restriction to End?" *Advocate* (Los Angeles), no. 155 (1975), p. 23.]

October 19 ✳ Toronto ✳ The *Toronto Star* published the editorial "Homosexuals: Where the *Star* Draws the Line," which outlined the paper's attitude and policy towards homosexuality and condemned the "aggressive recruitment propaganda" of *The Body Politic* and other gay groups. The *Star*'s editorial was triggered in part by its disapproval of Gerald Hannon's opinion piece "Outrage," published in the September–October 1974 issue of *The Body Politic*, in which Hannon urged the gay community to call for the release of Karl John Roestad, an imprisoned homosexual pedophile. (See also October 22, October 30, October–November, and November 8, 10, 1974.)

[M.C., "An Open Reply" (letter), *Metro Community News* 1 (1 November 1974): 14; "Found Guilty of Bias, Newspaper Retaliates with Smear Campaign," *Body Politic*, no. 16 (1974), pp. 5, 7; Gerald Hannon, "Outrage" (opinion column), *Body Politic*, no. 15 (1974), p. 10; "Homosexuals: Where the *Star* Draws the Line" (editorial), *Toronto Star*, Saturday ed., 19 October 1974, p. B2; Gary Kinsman, "Defeat Sexual Reaction! In Canada: Mass Media Attacks Gays," *Old Mole* (RMG, Toronto), no. 15 (1974), p. 7; "Open Forum: Homosexuality and SIECCAN. An Exchange on Gay Liberation, the Editorial Policy of the *Toronto Star* and SIECCAN's Role in Public Education about Homosexuality," *SIECCAN Toronto Newsletter* 10 (Summer 1975): 9–20; Terence Phillips, "Gays Smeared by Toronto Press," *Pro Tem* (Glendon College, York Univ.), 30 October 1974, p. 2; Bob Wolfe, "Church Editorial," *Metro Community News* 1 (1 November 1974): 1, 3.]

October 22 ∗ Toronto ∗ The *Toronto Sun* printed an editorial that called for "toleration" of homosexuality, even though it is "unnatural and abnormal," an "aberration." (See also October 26, 1974.)

["Homosexuals" (editorial), *Toronto Sun*, final ed., 22 October 1974, p. 10; Terence Phillips, "Gays Smeared by Toronto Press," *Pro Tem* (Glendon College, York Univ.), 30 October 1974, p. 2.]

October 23 ∗ Ottawa ∗ Robert Andras, federal minister of Manpower and Immigration, wrote to GO to say that he favoured the removal of prohibitions against homosexuals from Canadian immigration law.

["Andras Reaffirms Support for Immigration Law Change," *Body Politic*, no. 16 (1974), p. 6.]

October 23 ∗ Vancouver ∗ Maurice Flood, chairperson of GATE (Vancouver), attempted to advertise the group's publication *Gay Tide* in the classified advertising section of the *Vancouver Sun*. The ad read: "Subs. to GAY TIDE, gay lib paper. $1.00 for 6 issues. 2146 Yew St., Vancouver." The *Sun* refused to publish the ad. When it failed to reconsider, Flood filed a complaint against the *Sun* with the B.C. Human Rights Commission on November 15. On November 16, twenty gays picketed the *Sun*'s Pacific Press building, 2250 Granville Street, in protest. This was the beginning of one of the most famous Canadian legal cases involving gay rights: *Gay Alliance toward Equality* vs. *The Vancouver Sun*. (See also November 20, 1974, and February 28, 1975.)

[Gay Alliance toward Equality (GATE) (Vancouver) papers, 82–005 and 88–040, Canadian Lesbian and Gay Archives, Toronto; " 'Gay' Protest Cites *Sun*," *Vancouver Sun*, four star ed., 18 November 1974, p. 10; "Newspaper Rejects Gay Ad, Human Rights Notified," *Vancouver Province*, four star final ed., 18 November 1974, p. 10;

"Paper Refuses Ad, Rights Code Invoked," *Body Politic*, no. 16 (1974), p. 7; Jeff Richstone and J. Stuart Russell, "Comment: Shutting the Gate: Gay Civil Rights in the Supreme Court of Canada," *McGill Law Journal* 27 (1981): 92–117; "*Sun* Picket," *Gay Tide* 2 (March 1975): 11; "*Vancouver Sun*" vertical file, Canadian Lesbian and Gay Archives, Toronto.]

October 23 * Winnipeg * Brenda Dineen, running under the League for Socialist Action banner, placed a distant second in the Winnipeg mayoralty race. Dineen had supported civil and human rights for gay people.

["Rights Supporter Wins 6,000 Votes," *Body Politic*, no. 16 (1974), p. 6.]

October 26 * Toronto * About thirty-five people demonstrated in front of the *Toronto Sun* building to protest the October 22 *Sun* editorial "Homosexuals." The protest was organized by GATE (Toronto).

["Metro Homosexuals Picket *Sun*," *Toronto Sun*, 27 October 1974, p. 2; "Picketers Hit Newspaper Slanders," *Body Politic*, no. 16 (1974), p. 7.]

October 29 * Québec, Qué. * During a press conference concerning a bill to establish a provincial Human Rights Commission, Québec Justice Minister Jérôme Choquette suggested that gays might be protected through amendments to the bill at the committee stage.

[Hubert Bauch, "Quebec Bill to Enshrine Rights Laws," *Globe and Mail*, metro ed., 30 October 1974, p. 8; "Quebec Committee Studies Civil Rights," *Body Politic*, no. 16 (1974), p. 5.]

October 30 * Toronto * The Committee for Media Fairness to Gays was formed to combat anti-gay comments published in a *Toronto Star* editorial on October 19. Terence Phillips acted as chairperson. The Committee sponsored pickets against the *Star* on November 8 and 10. (See also November 8, 10, 1974.)

["Media Fairness Committee Challenges *Star* Slanders," *Body Politic*, no. 16 (1974), p. 7.]

October–November * Toronto * Peter Maloney, manager of the Club Baths and part-owner of the Barracks steambath, withdrew ads for the baths from *The Body Politic* after negative editorials appeared in Toronto newspapers concerning Gerald Hannon's opinion piece "Outrage," which had been published in the September–October issue of the magazine. The Roman Baths and the Library steambath followed suit.

["Advertisers Desert *The Body Politic*," *Body Politic*, no. 16 (1974), p. 7.]

November * Montréal * The Encore Cinema (formerly the Cinéma du Vieux Montréal), 136, rue St. Paul E., began to show erotic films aimed at a gay audience. By June 1975 the theatre was under new management and had stopped showing gay films.

["Encore's Last Encore," *Gay-Zette* 2 (June 1975): 4; Martin Malina, "Now City Gays Have Own Cinema," *Montreal Star*, final ed., 5 November 1974, p. B13.]

November ∗ Montréal ∗ Thirty to forty lesbians formed a demonstration line outside of Madame Arthur's, 2170, rue Bishop, for three nights after the Madame Arthur's Riot, during which lesbian customers had rebelled against a long series of incidents of sexism and physical violence on the part of male waiters and management of the club. At that time, Madame Arthur's was one of the major lesbian bars in Montréal. The picketing of the club was the beginning of an organized boycott; within six months Madame Arthur's had closed.

[Ross Higgins, "Repression et resistance gaie," unpublished typescript, ca. 1982, Canadian Lesbian and Gay Archives, Toronto, p. 15; "Montreal Gay Bars," *Other Woman* 3 (Winter 1975): 25; Leslie Orchard, "Fighting Back," *Long Time Coming* 2 (December 1974): 31–33; P. Tavormina, "Le bar Madame Arthur et le mouvement des lesbiennes de 1970 à 1975/Madame Arthur and the Lesbian Movement 1970–75," *Amazones d'hier lesbiennes d'aujourd'hui* (Montréal), no. 22 (1991), pp. 104–23.]

November ∗ Montréal ∗ A gay synagogue was organized, patterned after the gay synagogue in New York City. Meetings were initially held Friday evenings at 407–7461, rue Kingsley, in Côte St. Luc. Originally there were only four members but by June 1975 it had evolved into a Jewish discussion group that attracted between ten and fifteen people (mostly men) every week. This was the beginning of the gay Jewish group Naches.

[Ron Dayman, "Quebec: Five Years of the Movement," *Body Politic*, no. 29 (1976–77), p. 21; Margaret Fulford, ed., *The Canadian Women's Movement, 1960–1990: A Guide to Archival Resources/Le mouvement canadien des femmes, 1960–1990: guide de ressources archivistiques* (Toronto: Canadian Women's Movement Archives/ECW Press, 1992), entries 625, 626; Gilles Garneau, "Naches, groupe gai juif de Montréal," *Le berdache*, no. 2 (1979), pp. 20–21; "Gay Synagogue," *Gay-Zette* Coming Out Edition (November–December 1974): 15; "Group for Jewish Gays," *Gay Times* 1 (June 1975): 10; Untitled news item, *Body Politic*, no. 17 (1975), p. 7.]

November ∗ Montréal ∗ The erotic boutique Priape, specializing in items for gay men, opened at 1661, rue Ste. Catherine E.

[Jean-Denis (Lubrik), "Bernard Rousseau: Priape," *Fugues* 11 (May 1994): 54–55.]

November ∗ Toronto ∗ A group of lesbians decided to open Clementyne's, a café for women, at 342 Jarvis Street. A lease was signed and a number of women, including Heather Elizabeth (Beyer), Holly Devor, Pat Murphy, Chris Lawrence, and Eve Zaremba, worked hard to renovate the three-storey Victorian property. Plans for the café were set aside, however, when city zoning by-laws hampered the opening of a commerical venture in the residential space. Clementyne's never opened, but the space was not wasted.

By Spring 1975, 342 Jarvis Street housed several feminist organizations and businesses, some run by lesbians, including *The Other Woman* newspaper, Wages Due Lesbians, and the Women's Information Centre (WIC). Early in 1977 it also became the headquarters for the Lesbian Organization of Toronto (LOOT), Toronto's foremost lesbian institution of the late 1970s.

[Becki L. Ross, *The House That Jill Built: A Lesbian Nation in Formation* (Toronto: University of Toronto Press, 1995), pp. 49–51; "Women's Cafe," *Other Woman* 3 (Winter 1975): 27.]

November 1 ✳ Toronto ✳ Constable Robert Hall, a police officer accused of common assault by Adrienne Potts, one of the Brunswick Four, was acquitted. Potts and four of her friends were in turn found in contempt of court for refusing to stand. Pat Murphy chose to go to jail for three days rather than pay a $25 fine. (See also April 1975.)

[John Beaufoy, "Constable Is Acquitted of Common Assault, 5 Women in Contempt," *Globe and Mail*, metro ed., 2 November 1974, p. 2; "Five Fined for Contempt, One Takes Jail," *Globe and Mail*, metro ed., 5 November 1974, p. 5; "Justice Denied: Assailant Acquitted, Victim Convicted," *Body Politic*, no. 16 (1974), p. 6.]

November 1–14 ✳ Montréal ✳ A collection of photographs by Jacques Lafond entitled "Le gai Montréal" was exhibited at the Véhicule Art Gallery, 61, rue Ste. Catherine O.

["Jacques Lafond" vertical file, Canadian Lesbian and Gay Archives, Toronto.]

November 2 ✳ Hamilton ✳ Dr. William Marra, a professor of philosophy at Fordham University and anti-gay activist, was debated by a panel of seven Toronto gay activists in an hour-long session of *Under Attack*, broadcast on CHCH-TV.

["Under Attack: Them for a Change, Not Us," *Metro Community News* 1 (1 November 1974): 5.]

November 8, 10 ✳ Toronto ✳ Forty picketers representing the Committee for Media Fairness to Gays demonstrated in front of the *Toronto Star* building to protest the paper's October 19 anti-gay editorial. Two days later, about twenty people demonstrated in front of the home of Beland Honderich, president and publisher of the *Star*, at 6 Bluejay Place.

["Homosexuals Picket the *Star* Building," *Toronto Star*, Saturday ed., 9 November 1974, p. C23; "Media Fairness Committee Challenges *Star* Slanders," *Body Politic*, no. 16 (1974), p. 7; Gilda Oran, "Gays Demonstrate to Protest *Star* Policy," *Varsity* (Univ. of Toronto), 11 November 1974, p. 1.]

November 10–16 ✳ Winnipeg ✳ Gay Pride Week was held, sponsored by GFE. Activities included a coffeehouse, four panel discussions, and a dance.

[Gays for Equality (GFE) papers, 83–024, Canadian Lesbian and Gay Archives, Toronto.]

November 11–29 ∗ Toronto ∗ Artist Darryl Tonkin held an exhibition of homoerotic art at the Kensington Art Association Gallery, 4 Kensington Avenue.

[Ken Elliott, "The Unfinished Darryl Tonkin," *Body Politic*, no. 16 (1974), p. 19; Nails, "Interesting Human Beings: An Interview with Darryl Tonkin, Artist, Film Maker," *Metro Community News* 2 (June 1975): 19; "Our Image: Upcoming Events," *Body Politic*, no. 15 (1974), p. 19.]

November 16 ∗ Vancouver ∗ Lord Wolfenden spoke on "Crime and Sin" in an address to the Vancouver Institute, held at the University of British Columbia. Wolfenden had been chairperson of the committee that produced the Wolfenden Report (1957) on laws relating to homosexual offences and which led in 1967 to the passage of the Sexual Offences Bill, which partially decriminalized some same-sex sexual activities in Britain.

["Wolfenden Visits," *Gay Tide* 2 (Autumn 1974): 10.]

November 17 ∗ Toronto ∗ About twenty-five people met at the CHAT centre to discuss the possibility of establishing the first Canadian chapter of Dignity, the group for lesbian and gay Roman Catholics. Jim Leitner of Dignity (Boston) addressed the group, reading Dignity's "statement of position and purpose." About fifteen people signed up to help organize the chapter, and Father Tim Ryan became the group's chaplain. Dignity Toronto began to meet at St. Cecilia's Church but by July 1975 had moved to Our Lady of Lourdes Church, 510 Sherbourne Street.

[Barry B. (Blackburn), "10 years with Dignity: A Retrospective," *Dignity/Dignité Toronto Newsletter*, November 1984, pp. 4–5; Dignity collection, 90–057, Canadian Lesbian and Gay Archives, Toronto; Margaret Fulford, ed., *The Canadian Women's Movement, 1960–1990: A Guide to Archival Resources/Le mouvement canadien des femmes, 1960–1990: Guide de ressources archivistiques* (Toronto: Canadian Women's Movement Archives/ECW Press, 1992), entry 384; Dave G. (Gunton) (interviewing Barry Blackburn), "Dignity/Toronto," *Metro Community News* 2 (7 February 1975): 2, 15; "Welcome to Dignity," *Back/Chat* 4 (22 November 1974): 5.]

November 17 ∗ Vancouver ∗ At a civic all-candidates meeting sponsored by GATE (Vancouver), Alderman Michael Harcourt acknowledged that police had harassed gay establishments at the end of October. Harcourt said that the raids by policemen and city inspectors during checks for liquor rules violations were "dumb and unneccesary and vicious." This was the first acknowledgement by a public official that police harassment of gays had occurred in Vancouver. MLA Gary Lauk (NDP-Vancouver Centre) said that he would investigate. (See also November 20, 23, and December 17, 1974.)

[Maurice Flood, "Double Standard, Double Dealing," *Gay Tide* 2 (March 1975): 3–4; " 'Gay' Clubs Promised Probe," *Vancouver Sun*, four star ed., 2 January 1975, p. 16; Lesley Krueger, "Liquor Raids on Gay Nightclubs 'Dumb,' Says Harcourt," *Vancouver Sun*, four star ed., 18 November 1974, p. 11; "Vancouver Official Reveals Harassment," *Body Politic*, no. 16 (1974), p. 5.]

November 20 * Vancouver * Maurice Flood, chairperson of GATE (Vancouver), was interviewed on "Good Morning Radio" concerning the *Vancouver Sun*'s refusal to print an ad for *Gay Tide*.

["Paper Refuses Ad, Rights Code Invoked," *Body Politic*, no. 16 (1974), p. 7.]

November 20 * Vancouver * The Society for Education Action Research and Counselling on Homosexuality (SEARCH) was formed in reaction to harassment and raids of gay bars and clubs during October. Malcolm Crane and Warren Hague were two of the organizers of SEARCH. The twenty-one people who met at the founding meeting of SEARCH represented a variety of clubs and organizations in Vancouver, although members of GATE (Vancouver) were excluded. The group's aim was to form a coalition to present a united front against official harassment of the gay community. (See also November 23 and December 17, 1974.)

["A Brief History of SEARCH," *SEARCHLight* 1 (April 1978): 4; Maurice Flood, "Double Standard, Double Dealing," *Gay Tide* 2 (March 1975): 3–4; Don Hann and Rob Joyce, "City Police Record: Smash Hit!" *Gay Tide*, no. 16 (1977), p. 4; "Society for Education Action Research and Counselling on Homosexuality (SEARCH)" vertical file, Canadian Lesbian and Gay Archives, Toronto; Jack Wasserman, Column, *Vancouver Sun*, four star ed., 5 November 1974, p. 35.]

November 23 * Vancouver * Thirty-five people demonstrated in front of police headquarters, 312 Main Street, to protest recent police harassment of gay clubs and bars. (See also December 17, 1974.)

[Maurice Flood, "Double Standard, Double Dealing," *Gay Tide* 2 (March 1975): 3–4; "Police Harassing Clubs — Gays," *Vancouver Province*, 25 November 1974, p. 9; "Vancouver Raids Provoke Protest," *Body Politic*, no. 16 (1974), p. 6.]

November 25 * China * During a tour of China, British Columbia Premier David Barrett congratulated Chinese officials for having towns without "any homosexualism, any violence, any idle drifting." GATE (Vancouver) responded in a press release on November 27.

["Vancouver Gays Hit Barrett Slanders," *Body Politic*, no. 17 (1975), p. 6; John Walker, "Chinese Oilfield Villages Blow Barrett's Mind," *Vancouver Province*, 26 November 1974, p. 25.]

November 29–30 * New York, N.Y. * The second annual conference of the Gay Academic Union was held at the Loeb Student Center, New York

University, and was attended by about ten Canadian scholars. The Canadians met to discuss gay studies in Canada and ways to help gay scholars come out, and decided to form a Canadian academic union that would be loosely affiliated with the American group. Dorothy Broderick (Dalhousie Univ.) and John Alan Lee (Univ. of Toronto) were to act as contact people. (See also September 1975.)

["Academics Ponder Community," *Body Politic*, no. 17 (1975), p. 8; John A. Lee, "Gay Academic Union: Toronto Group Forms," *Metro Community News* 2 (30 May 1975): 1.]

December * Ottawa * The Club Baths opened at 1069 Wellington Street.

[Advertisement, *Metro Community News* 1 (18 October 1974): 19; "The Police and the Press," *Body Politic*, no. 25 (1976), p. 17.]

December * Toronto * The Task Force on Gay Liberation was formed by Ron Dayman, Ed Jackson, and Michael Lynch. It was a letterhead organization formed to monitor the press for homophobic content and to write letters protesting discriminatory articles, letters, or advertisements. The group was not very active, and lasted until Summer 1975.

["Task Force on Gay Liberation (Toronto)" vertical file, Canadian Lesbian and Gay Archives, Toronto.]

December * Waterloo, Ont. * When five lesbians (including Candis Graham, Marie Robertson, and Margaret Telegdi) tried to rent a house, the landlord agreed to rent to them only if they paid extra money because of the problems he believed were intrinsic to renting to homosexuals. When the landlord refused to change his position, the women attempted to lodge a complaint with the Ontario Human Rights Commission (OHRC), but were told that the OHRC had no jurisdiction over this form of discrimination. The women then reported the incident to the press; it was reported by the *Kitchener-Waterloo Record* and by a CTV affiliate. Although an informal lesbian drop-in had existed in Waterloo for several months, it was this event that led to the formation of the Waterloo Lesbian Collective, which held a weekly drop-in at the Women's Place, 25 Dupont Street E. The Collective was active in CGRO and was represented by Candis Graham and Marie Robertson at CGRO's founding conference in January 1975.

[P.d.V. (Peter de Vries), "K-W Lesbians Fight Rental Bias," *Gay Rising* 1 (April 1975): 3; Margaret Fulford, ed., *The Canadian Women's Movement, 1960–1990: A Guide to Archival Resources/Le mouvement canadien des femmes, 1960–1990: guide de ressources archivistiques* (Toronto: Canadian Women's Movement Archives/ ECW Press, 1992), entry 419; "Lesbian Collective (Waterloo)" vertical file, Canadian Lesbian and Gay Archives, Toronto; "Lesbian Feminist Group Established," *Body Politic*, no. 17 (1975), p. 7; "Marie Robertson" vertical file, Canadian Lesbian and Gay Archives, Toronto;

Marie Robertson and Ken Popert, "Lesbians Expose Landlord," *Body Politic*, no. 18 (1975), p. 9.]

December 17 ✷ Québec, Qué. ✷ Québec Justice Minister Jérôme Choquette deferred the Human Rights Code at a meeting of the Parliamentary Commission. (See also January 23, 1975.)

["Rapport du Comité des Libertés/Human Rights/Civil Liberties," *Gay-Zette* Christmas Edition (December 1975–January 1976): 3, 23.]

December 17 ✷ Vancouver ✷ Recommendations concerning the treatment of gay clubs and bars by police, licensing and inspection officers, and other city officials were presented to City Council by the Standing Committee on Social Services. The recommendations had been formulated by members of SEARCH during November, in the wake of controversy over the harassment of gay bars and clubs in Vancouver at the end of October. Some members of GATE (Vancouver) were unhappy with the proposals, claiming that they had not been consulted adequately and that the real problem was the homophobic attitude of police and government officials. (See also May 1975.)

[Maurice Flood, "Double Standard, Double Dealing," *Gay Tide* 2 (March 1975): 3–4.]

December 17 ✷ Winnipeg ✷ Chief County Court Judge Allan R. Philp ruled that a homosexual couple cannot be considered married because they are of the same sex. The ruling ended the appeal by Richard North and Chris Vogel, married in a Winnipeg Unitarian Church on February 11, 1974, to legalize their union by having it recorded as a vital statistic. The appeal had been launched after D.W. Matheson, Manitoba's recorder of vital statistics, refused to recognize the marriage.

["Homosexual Marriage Can't Be Recognized, Manitoba Judge Rules," *Globe and Mail*, metro ed., 18 December 1974, p. 1.]

December 18–22 ✷ Edinburgh, Scotland ✷ George Hislop of CHAT attended the first International Congress on Gay Rights, held at the University of Edinburgh, where he chaired a panel discussion on "Problems of the Aging Homosexual."

[Ian Dunn, "International Congress on Gay Rights, Edinburgh," *SMG News* (Scottish Minorities Group, Glasgow), no. 8 (1974), p. 5; Jim Foster, "International Congress Report," *Advocate* (Los Angeles), no. 156 (1975), pp. 5–7.]

1975

——— * Edmonton * The Imperial Court of the White Rose was formed and was incorporated under the Provincial Societies Act of Alberta. The Court provided a social and entertainment outlet through its sponsorship of parties, drag balls, dances, and other activities.

["The Imperial Court of the White Rose," *The Greater Edmonton Pride Pages 1994–95* (Edmonton: n.p., 1994), p. 12.]

——— * Garden City, N.Y.; Toronto * Jane Rule's *Lesbian Images* was published by Doubleday. This was a groundbreaking study of the lives and works of twelve well-known women writers who had significant same-sex experience — from Radclyffe Hall and Gertrude Stein to May Sarton.

["A Bibliography," *Canadian Fiction Magazine*, no. 23 (1976), pp. 133, 137–38; Jane Rule (interview), "Jane Rule: The Woman behind *Lesbian Images*," *Body Politic*, no. 21 (1975), pp. 14–15, 17; Cyn Wright, "*Lesbian Images*," *Other Woman* 3 (October–November 1975): 23.]

——— * Metuchen, N.J. * Ian Young's *The Male Homosexual in Literature: A Bibliography* was published by Scarecrow Press. A second edition was released by the same press in 1982.

[(Ian Young), *Ian Young: A Bibliography 1962–1980*, Canadian Gay Archives Publication no. 3 (Toronto: Pink Triangle Press, 1981), entries A12, E63, E65, E67, E76, E85, E88, E93, E95–E98, E106, E108, E121, and E123.]

——— * Montréal * Four works by Claude Beausoleil were published this year: *Ahuntsic Dream* and *Le sang froid du reptile*, both by Herbes rouges, *Promenade modern style*, by Éditions Cul Q, and *Motilité*, by Éditions l'Aurore.

[Bernard Gilbert, "*Intrusion ralentie* et autre recueils de poésies et de textes en prose de Claude Beausoleil," in *Dictionnaire des oeuvres littéraires du Québec*, ed. Maurice Lemire et al., vol. 5 (1970–75) (Montréal: Fides, 1987), pp. 436–39.]

——— * Montréal * Jovette Marchessault's novel *Comme une enfant de la terre: 1. Le crachat solaire* was published by Leméac. It won the Prix littéraire France-Québec in 1976.

[Marie-Andrée Beaudet, "*Comme une enfant de la terre: 1. Le crachat solaire,*" in *Dictionnaire des oeuvres littéraires du Québec*, ed. Maurice Lemire et al., vol. 5 (1970–75) (Montréal: Fides, 1987), pp. 169–70.]

—— ✴ Montréal ✴ Paul Toupin's *La nouvelle inquisition* was published by Pierre Tisseyre.

[Madeleine Ducrocq-Poirier, "*La nouvelle inquisition,*" in *Dictionnaire des oeuvres littéraires du Québec*, ed. Maurice Lemire et al., vol. 5 (1970–75) (Montréal: Fides, 1987), pp. 600–601.]

—— ✴ Ottawa ✴ David Watmough's *Love and the Waiting Game: Eleven Stories* was published by Oberon.

[Russell M. Brown, "For Every Taste," *Canadian Literature*, no. 73 (1977), pp. 105–07; Paul Denham, "Stories from Oberon," *Journal of Canadian Fiction*, no. 19 (1977), p. 145; Peter Millard, "Books: *Love and the Waiting Game,*" *Body Politic*, no. 26 (1976), p. 16; Patricia Morley, "*Love and the Waiting Game: Eleven Stories,*" *Queen's Quarterly* 83 (Autumn 1976): 519–20.]

—— ✴ Scarborough, Ont. ✴ Gavin Dillard's collection *Twenty-Nine Poems* was published by Catalyst Press.

[Ian Young, *The Male Homosexual in Literature: A Bibliography*, second ed. (Metuchen, N.J.: Scarecrow Press, 1982), entry 1011.]

—— ✴ Toronto ✴ Helene Rosenthal's *Listen to the Old Mother: Poems New and Selected* was published by McClelland and Stewart.

[Tom Wayman, "Mothers, Writers, Instruments and Fathers," *University of Windsor Review* 11 (Spring–Summer 1976): 110–13.]

—— ✴ Vancouver ✴ Jane Rule's collection of short stories *Theme for Diverse Instruments* was published by Talonbooks. Some of the stories had been published previously in *The Ladder*, the American lesbian periodical.

["A Bibliography," *Canadian Fiction Magazine*, no. 23 (1976), pp. 133, 137; Jane Rule (interview), "Jane Rule: The Woman behind *Lesbian Images,*" *Body Politic*, no. 21 (1975), pp. 14–15, 17.]

—— ✴ Vancouver ✴ Two books of poetry by George Stanley were published this year: *Sticks*, by Talonbooks, and *You*, by New Star Books.

[Gerald Hannon, "*You,*" *Body Politic*, no. 18 (1975), p. 24; Ian Young, "The Ivory Tunnel" (column), *Body Politic*, no. 21 (1975), p. 23.]

January ✴ Montréal ✴ "The Myth of Madness," a special forty-two-page issue of *Long Time Coming* about lesbians and the mental health system in Canada, was published. The regular issue of *Long Time Coming* for January 1975 was entirely devoted (thirty-five pages) to a reprinting of the Collective Lesbian International Terrors (CLIT) Statement, a series of short articles on dyke political theory first published in the July 1974 issue of *Off Our Backs* (Washington, D.C.).

[Articles in the "Myth of Madness" issue (January 1975) included "Alternatives" (pp. 17–19), "Annemieke's Story" (pp. 13–16), "Danielle and the Shrink" (pp. 7–11), "An Interview with Dr. Irene Simons" (pp. 23–28), "Interview with Felicity" (pp. 2–6), Jackie, "Gay: Mad, Bad, or Glad?" (pp. 29–31), "Linda's Story" (pp. 21–22), and Erin Shoemaker, "The Homosexual in the New Therapies" (pp. 33–42); "CLIT Statement No. 2," *Long Time Coming* 2 (January 1975): 2–36.]

January * Québec, Qué. * The Service d'entraide homophile de Québec (SEHQ) became an independent counselling and referral service. Although created by CHAL, SEHQ received so many requests for service that it became independent, although it still operated from CHAL's office at 264, rue des Franciscains. SEHQ was devoted to providing consultation and referrals to gay men and lesbians for moral, social, familial, and legal problems. Denise Goyette was the director of SEHQ.

["Denise Goyette: ouvrière de la libération gay," *Gay Montréal* 1 (2 November 1976): 4; "Québec: Service d'entraide homophile de Québec," *Le gai Québec* 1 (15 August 1975): 6; SEHQ, "Le Service d'entraide homophile de Québec (SEHQ)," *Gay Montréal* 1 (30 November 1976): 34; "La vraie nature de Denise Goyette" (interview), *Gay Montréal* 1 (25 January 1977): 18, 26.]

January * St. Lambert, Qué. * The gay studies course "The Homosexual Perspective in Literature" was offered by Prof. Bryan Doubt at Champlain College.

["Gay Studies Survive Obstacles, Others Appear," *Body Politic*, no. 16 (1974), p. 7.]

January * Toronto * Steven Hannah and Guy Roy attempted to start a project aimed at helping to reduce the alienation of elderly gay men.

["Project for Elderly Gays," *Alternative to Alienation*, no. 5 (1975), p. 22.]

January 1 * Saskatoon * The Zodiac Friendship Society and Saskatoon Gay Action became known officially as the Gay Community Centre of Saskatoon.

["Gay Community Centre of Saskatoon" vertical file, Canadian Lesbian and Gay Archives, Toronto.]

January 6 * Ottawa * Member of Parliament Lloyd Francis (Lib.-Ottawa West) claimed that an "irresponsible act" by an office assistant had left the erroneous impression that he considered the Immigration Act discriminatory because it barred gay people. This controversy erupted after a questionnaire sent by the NGEC during the 1974 federal election campaign was returned from Francis's office with a written response supporting several NGEC demands, including one relating to changes to the Immigration Act. GO followed up on this response and received a letter reiterating Francis's support for changes to the Act, which GO then quoted in a press release. When the *Ottawa Citizen* quoted the press release, Francis denied personal knowledge of the letter to GO.

["Francis Denies Letter to Gays: 'Irresponsible Act,' " *Ottawa Citizen*, 6 January 1975, p. 3; "Immigration: Attempted Smear," *Gay Tide* 2 (March 1975): 5; "Politicians Fighting for Homosexuals: Bid to End Discrimination," *Ottawa Citizen*, 3 January 1975, p. 2; "Rights Support Made Public, M.P. Threatens Withdrawal," *Body Politic*, no. 17 (1975), p. 7.]

January 18–19 ∗ Toronto ∗ About sixty people attended the founding conference of the Coalition for Gay Rights in Ontario (CGRO), held at the DonVale Community Centre. Nine groups from five Ontario cities were represented officially; four other political and social service organizations sent delegations. CGRO was formed at the initiative of Tom Warner of GATE (Toronto) to work for law reform in Ontario at the provincial level, and particularly towards the amendment of the Ontario Human Rights Code to protect people from discrimination based on sexual orientation. The formation of CGRO marked the first time that gay and lesbian groups in Ontario had really united to work towards a common purpose. In 1987 the group changed its name to the Coalition for Lesbian and Gay Rights in Ontario/ Coalition pour les droits des lesbiennes et des hommes gais en Ontario (CLGRO/CDLGO). (See also February 22, 1975.)

[Coalition for Gay Rights in Ontario (CGRO) papers, 82–016 and 83–012, Canadian Lesbian and Gay Archives, Toronto; "Coalition Unites Ontario Movement," *Gay Rising* 1 (March 1975): 4; Margaret Fulford, ed., *The Canadian Women's Movement, 1960–1990: A Guide to Archival Resources/Le mouvement canadien des femmes, 1960–1990: guide de ressources archivistiques* (Toronto: Canadian Women's Movement Archives/ ECW Press, 1992), entries 371, 1011; "Gay Coalitions Form," GO *Info* 2 (March 1975): 4; Wendy Johnston, "Ontario Gay Rights Coalition Formed," *Labor Challenge*, 10 February 1975, p. 10; "Ontario Coalition," *Gay Tide* 2 (March 1975): 11; "Ontario Gay Rights Coalition Formed," *Body Politic*, no. 17 (1975), p. 6; Ken Popert, "All Together Now," *Body Politic*, no. 17 (1975), p. 10; "Rights Coalition to Form," *Metro Community News* 1 (17 May 1974): 1.]

January 23 ∗ Québec, Qué. ∗ Parti Québécois House Leader Robert Burns announced his support for the inclusion of a sexual orientation clause in the proposed provincial Human Rights Charter after representatives of three gay organizations (Roger Bellemare, Luc Doré, and Denise Goyette, representing CHUM, AHM/GMA, and SEHQ) presented briefs to the Québec Assembly's Justice Committee. Jérôme Choquette, Québec's Minister of Justice, conceded that gay people had faced discrimination and did not dismiss the possibility that sexual orientation would be included in the proposed Charter. This was the first time that representatives of the gay movement had appeared before a Canadian legislative body. (See also June 25, 1975.)

[Roger B. (Bellemare), "Les droits de l'homme/The Rights of Man," *Gay-Zette* 1 (September 1974): 1–2; "La Chartre des droits de l'homme/An Act Respecting Human Rights . . . ," *Gay-Zette* (Coming Out Edition), November–December 1974, pp. 14, 16; "Civil Liberties," *Gay-Zette* (Christmas Edition), December 1974–January 1975, pp. 2–3; "Coalition Lobbies Support for Gay Civil Rights," *Gay Times* 1 (April 1975): 1–2; Ron Dayman, "Quebec: Five Years of the Movement," *Body Politic*, no. 29 (1976–77), p. 22; "Droits civils pour les homosexuels québécois," *GO Info* 2 (March 1975): 6; "Editorial," *Gay-Zette* 2 (April 1975): 2; Jacques Guay, "Quand Jérôme Choquette reçoit les 'homophiles,' " *Le jour*, 24 January 1975, p. 4; "P.Q. Houseleader Supports Gay Rights," *Body Politic*, no. 17 (1975), pp. 5, 6; "Rapport du Comité des libertés civiles/Human Rights/Civil Liberties," *Gay-Zette*, December 1974–January 1975, pp. 3, 23.]

January 24–26 ✳ Montréal ✳ Between 200 and 300 delegates from Canada and the United States attended the second annual national lesbian conference, organized by Montreal Gay Women (Labyris). Seminars were held on such topics as coming out, lesbian separatism, multiple relationships, self-defence, and directions for gay women in society. One of the highlights of the event was a dance, featuring the New Haven Women's Liberation Rock Band, which was attended by 500 women.

[Pat Blandford and Leslie Orchard, "The Call-in Radio Show Classic," *Long Time Coming* 2 (April 1975): 4–9 (Part 2, *Long Time Coming* 2 [May 1975]: 6–10; Part 3, *Long Time Coming* 3 [July 1975]: 18–22; Part 4, *Long Time Coming* 3 [September 1975]: 8–12; Part 5, *Long Time Coming* 3 [October 1975]: 14–17); Beth Foster, "National Lesbian Conference," *Gay Community of Saskatoon Newsletter*, January 1975, p. 3; Margaret Fulford, ed., *The Canadian Women's Movement, 1960–1990: A Guide to Archival Resources/Le mouvement canadien des femmes, 1960–1990: guide de ressources archivistiques* (Toronto: Canadian Women's Movement Archives/ECW Press, 1992), entries 616, 622; "Gay Women Meet," *Chevron* (Univ. of Waterloo), 7 February 1975, p. 7; Linda Graham, "A Gathering of 350 Gay Women," *Advocate* (Los Angeles), no. 159 (1975), p. 10; "Lesbian Conf.," *Other Woman* 3 (Winter 1975): 19; "Lesbians Meet in Montreal," *Body Politic*, no. 17 (1975), p. 5; "Les lesbiennes s'organisent . . . ," *Le gai Québec* 1 (28 June 1975): 3; Reva, "Lesbian Mothers," *Long Time Coming* 2 (March 1975): 5–6; Sharon Rogers, "Gays at Guelph: Report on the 2nd Annual National Lesbian Conference in Montreal," *Ontarion* (Univ. of Guelph), 11 March 1975, p. 9; "Thoughts on the Lesbian Conference," *Long Time Coming* 2 (March 1975): 2–4; Yvonne, "Dyke Separatism," *Long Time Coming* 2 (March 1975): 8; Yvonne, "Myth of Madness," *Long Time Coming* 2 (March 1975): 7.]

January 25 ✳ Vancouver ✳ Members of GATE (Vancouver) took part in a demonstration against racism organized by the International Committee against Racism. The Committee said that it was pleased with gay participation in the rally, but did not allow a gay speaker.

["Anti-racist Group Closets Gays," *Body Politic*, no. 17 (1975), p. 8; Maurice Flood, "Gays Fight Racism," *Gay Tide* 2 (June 1975): 1, 7.]

February * Guelph, Ont. * Students from the associate diploma course in agriculture at the University of Guelph presented a 100–signature petition to the *Ontarion*, protesting "the favourable publicity that homosexuality in general and the UGHA in particular receives through the *Ontarion*." The paper had published regular "Gays at Guelph" pieces since autumn 1973. The petition referred to homosexuality as "a perversion."

["Homosexuality a 'Perversion,' Says Petition," *Ontarion* (Univ. of Guelph), 25 February 1975, p. 2; "A Petition against Publicity for Gays and Homosexuality," *Body Politic*, no. 18 (1975), p. 9.]

February * Hamilton * The Club Hamilton steambath opened at 542 Barton Street. It operated until August 1977.

[Advertisement, *Metro Community News* 2 (10 October 1975): 14; S.S. Que Hee, "The Chronology of Events during the Existence of the Hamilton McMaster and McMaster Homophile Associations 1972–1977," unpublished typescript, September 1977, 82–013, Canadian Lesbian and Gay Archives, Toronto, pp. 6, 11.]

February * Saskatoon * A rap group for bisexuals began meeting regularly at the Gay Community Centre of Saskatoon.

[Notice, *Gay Community Centre of Saskatoon Newsletter*, January 1975, p. 4.]

February 3 * Ottawa * A Green Paper on Immigration and Population was tabled in the House of Commons by Manpower and Immigration Minister Robert Andras. It was ambiguous with respect to gay people and did not eliminate homosexuals from a list of prohibited classes of persons (including also alcoholics, drug addicts, and pimps) automatically denied entry to Canada. (See also February 15 and March 1975.)

["Clean Up the Act!" (editorial), *Body Politic*, no. 17 (1975), p. 2; Ron Dayman, "Green Paper Ignores Gays," GO *Info* 2 (March 1975): 2, 4; "Gays Say 'End Immigration Bias,' " *Gay Rising* 1 (March 1975): 3–4; Philip Girard, "From Subversion to Liberation: Homosexuals and the Immigration Act 1952–1977," *Canadian Journal of Law and Society* 2 (1987): 1–27; "Immigration: Green Paper," *Gay Tide* 2 (March 1975): 5; "Immigration: Report Avoids Gay Issue," *Gay Times* 1 (May 1975): 8; "What Green Paper Says (or Doesn't Say) about Gays," *Body Politic*, no. 17 (1975), p. 5.]

February 4 * Montréal * Police raided the Sauna Aquarius baths, 1183, rue Crescent, and arrested thirty-five people as being found-ins in a bawdy house. The manager and two employees were charged with being operators of a common bawdy house; no charges were laid against the owners. Of the thirty-five customers charged, one pleaded guilty and was fined $25. The police raid on the Aquarius was part of a campaign to "clean up" Montréal

John Damien.
Photo by Gerald Hannon.

in preparation for the 1976 summer Olympics. In response to the raid, the AHM/GMA publication *Gay-Zette* published a special twelve-page issue that included an interview with one of the people arrested and notes on recent police harassment in Montréal. On February 25, 1976, Harold Walsh, the manager of the Aquarius, was convicted of operating a common bawdy house and faced up to two years in prison; his appeal to the Québec Court of Appeal failed in 1977. (See also April 12, 1975.)

["Aquarius Continues," *Gay-Zette* 2 (April 1975): 1; "Aquarius Raid Start of Police Anti-gay Clean-up Campaign," *Gay Times* 1 (April 1975): 1; "Aquarius Trial Postponed (Again)," *Gay-Zette* 2 (June 1975): 8; "Aquarius Trials: News in Brief," *Montreal Gay Times* 1 (December 1975): 7; John Blacklock and Paul Trollope, "How a Steambath Becomes a Bawdyhouse: 'Scanty' Evidence and 'Undercover' Agents," *Body Politic*, no. 38 (1977), p. 7; *Gay-Zette* Special Issue, March 1975, 12 pp.; "Olympic Crackdown," *Body Politic*, no. 25 (1976), pp. 1, 17; "Police Raid Clubs; Seeking Clues to Montreal's Rising Murder Rate?," *Montreal Gay Times* 1 (December 1975): 5–6 (reprinted in *Body Politic*, no. 22 [1976], p. 4).]

February 7 ✳ Montréal ✳ Slightly Older Lesbians (SOL) was formed for lesbians over thirty years old. By late February 1975 SOL was sponsoring socials every second Friday evening at the Women's Information and Referral Centre/Centre d'information et de références pour femmes, 3595, rue St. Urbain, as well as games evenings, dinners, and dances.

["New Lesbian Group Formed," *Gay Times* 1 (May 1975): 4; "News: Slightly Older Lesbians," *Long Time Coming* 2 (April 1975): 34; "Organization Forms for Older Lesbians," *Body Politic*, no. 19 (1975), p. 9.]

February 7 ✳ Toronto ✳ John Damien was officially fired by the Ontario Racing Commission because he was gay. The Commission was an independent agency of the Ontario government. Damien had worked in racing for twenty years and had been employed by the Commission for five years. At the time of his dismissal Damien held the position of Commission Racing Steward, one of three top racing judges in Ontario. On February 14 GATE (Toronto) began to campaign for Damien's reinstatement, as well as for the formation of a commission of enquiry into his firing and into the status of gay people working in positions under Ontario government jurisdiction. The Committee to Defend John Damien was established February 22, with Christine Bearchell as chairperson. The Damien case was to become one of the most prominent gay civil rights cases in Canadian history. After much legal wrangling the case remained partially unresolved when Damien died in Windsor of pancreatic cancer on December 24, 1986. His suit for wrongful dismissal against the Ontario Racing Commission was settled in 1986; Damien received a year's wages plus interest, about $50,000. A second suit, for loss of income, had been placed against the estate of Thoreau Willard

O'Mulvenny, a Fort Erie racetrack doctor who had informed the Ontario
Jockey Club in 1974 that Damien was a homosexual. The case had not yet
been heard when Damien died. (See also February 22, March 14, 21, May 6,
10, 11, 13, 24–25, June 24, June 28–July 1, August 31, September, September
13, October, October 23, 24, 30, and December 5, 1975.)

[Christine Bearchell, "Damien Case: Minister Interferes, Government Agencies Col-
laborate," *Body Politic*, no. 24 (1976), pp. 6–7; Christine Bearchell (interviewing John
Damien), " 'Fired Because I'm a Homosexual': John Damien Interviewed," *Labor
Challenge*, 17 November 1975, p. 4; Christine Bearchell papers, 83–016, Canadian
Lesbian and Gay Archives, Toronto; " 'Because He's a Homosexual' " (editorial), *Body
Politic*, no. 17 (1975), p. 1; Christie Blatchford, untitled column, *Globe and Mail*, metro
ed., 16 December 1975, p. 36; John Bodis, "Kopyto: A Person Is Defined by His Total
Humanity, Not His Sexuality," *Metro Community News* 3 (2 January 1976): 4–5, 11;
Committee to Defend John Damien papers, 82–026, Canadian Lesbian and Gay
Archives, Toronto; John Damien, "I'm Determined to Win" (interview), *Body Politic*,
no. 18 (1975), pp. 12–13; "John Damien" vertical file, Canadian Lesbian and Gay
Archives, Toronto; "Defend John Damien," *Gay Times* 1 (April 1975): 2; "Defend John
Damien," GO *Info* 2 (March 1975): 1, 5; "Discrimination: The Human Cost. Case 1,"
Body Politic, no. 70 (1981), p. 13; Trent Frayne, "Damien vs. Commission," *Toronto
Sun*, final ed., 18 February 1975, p. 27; "Gay Fights Firing," *Gay Tide* 2 (March 1975):
1, 5; Mary Gooderham, "Legal Fight Will Survive Ex-jockey Dismissed for Being
Homosexual," *Globe and Mail*, metro ed., 1 January 1987, p. A10; Peter Hadekel,
" 'Discrimination' ": Fired for Being a Homosexual, Man Fights Back With $ Million
Suit," *Ottawa Journal*, 30 June 1975, p. 24; "He'll Claim Sex Bias," *Toronto Sun*, 16
February 1975, p. 4; John Hofsess, "Damien's Exile: What John Damien Represents
and Defends Is Not Homosexuality but Human Dignity," *Weekend Magazine*, 21
February 1976, pp. 14–17, 19; "Injustice at the Track" (editorial), *Globe and Mail*, metro
ed., 17 February 1975, p. 6; "John Damien a besoin d'argent pour se défendre devant
la justice," *Gay Montréal* 1 (16 November 1976): 6–7; Ron Lowman, "Homosexual
Loses Track Job, Claims Discrimination," *Toronto Star*, Saturday ed., 15 February 1975,
p. A2; Michael Lynch, "Doctor Leaked Medical Info, Damien Charges," *Body Politic*,
no. 49 (1978–79), p. 9; Lawrence Martin, "Racing Chairman Confirms Steward Fired
as Homosexual," *Globe and Mail*, metro ed., 15 February 1975, pp. 1–2; Tim McCaskell,
"Ontario: John Damien: One Year Later," *Body Politic*, no. 23 (1976), p. 5; Terry Phillips
papers, 82–010, Canadian Lesbian and Gay Archives, Toronto; Ken Popert, "Obituary:
John Damien: Spunky Racing Steward Who Defied Discrimination Succumbs to
Cancer," *Body Politic*, no. 135 (1987), p. 15; "Province-Wide Campaign Demands
Government Uphold Gay Rights, Rehire John Damien," *Gay Rising* 1 (March 1975):
1–2; "Re-instate John Damien" (editorial), *Gay Tide* 2 (June 1975): 2; "This Man, John
Damien," *Metro Community News* 2 (24 October 1975): 1, 3–5; "The Will to Win: John
Damien," *Esprit* 1 (October 1975): 25–26, 29; John Wilson papers, 91–048, Canadian
Lesbian and Gay Archives, Toronto.]

February 14–16 ∗ Winnipeg ∗ Stuart Russell and Chris Vogel of GFE were
elected delegates to the annual provincial NDP conference. GFE was allowed
to operate a literature and information table at the convention after first

being refused and threatening to picket. Russell and Vogel were able to gather some support for a brief recommending changes to the Manitoba Human Rights Act regarding sexual orientation.

["Delegates Support Winnipeg Gays," *Labor Challenge*, 24 February 1975, p. 4; "Gays' Info Booth OK'd for Convention," *Winnipeg Free Press*, final ed., 12 February 1975, p. 3; Bill Lewis, "Gays 'Embarrass' NDP," *Body Politic*, no. 18 (1975), p. 6; Stuart Russell, "NDP Gay Caucus Launched," *Body Politic*, no. 20 (1975), p. 9.]

February 15 ∗ Toronto ∗ About fifty people protested in front of the Manpower and Immigration offices against the Green Paper on Immigration and Population tabled in the House of Commons on February 3. The demonstration was organized by GATE (Toronto).

["Gays Say 'End Immigration Bias,' " *Gay Rising* 1 (March 1975): 3–4; "Toronto Gays Join Immigration Fight," *Body Politic*, no. 17 (1975), pp. 5–6.]

February 19–22 ∗ Ottawa ∗ Mart Crowley's play *The Boys in the Band* was performed at the Camelot Little Theatre. About fifteen members of GO distributed leaflets outside, complaining that the play, first produced in 1968, had become a theatrical cliché in that it did not take into account changing attitudes towards gays.

[Ron Dayman, *"Boys in the Band,"* *Body Politic*, no. 18 (1975), p. 21; "GO Leaflets 'Boys in the Band,' " *GO Info* 2 (March 1975): 4, 6.]

February 22 ∗ Waterloo, Ont. ∗ The Steering Committee of CGRO met to discuss a common program for Ontario's gay groups. Eleven organizations were represented. The Committee adopted a founding statement that urged a public campaign to "obtain full civil and human rights for homosexual men and women." CGRO's immediate goal was to press for protection from discrimination based on sexual orientation to be included in the Ontario Human Rights Code. CGRO also launched its first public action by establishing the Committee to Defend John Damien.

["Coalition Unites Ontario Movement," *Gay Rising* 1 (March 1975): 4; Randy Notte, "Gay Coalition Sets Program," *Body Politic*, no. 18 (1975), p. 7.]

February 24 ∗ Saskatoon ∗ The University of Saskatchewan's student debating team sponsored a debate on gay marriage. Norman Naylor, the Unitarian minister from Winnipeg who had married Richard North and Chris Vogel in February 1974, spoke for the affirmative. Brian Thorpe, a United Church minister based at the University campus, spoke against the motion. The affirmative side won, 44–10.

["Gay Marriages?" *Gay West*, no. 2 (1975), p. 11.]

February 27 ∗ Ottawa ∗ Members of GO demanded the right to speak at a workshop for social workers and doctors entitled "Behaviour Therapy and Sexual Dysfunction," featuring psychiatrists Alan Goldstein and Deborah Phillips from Temple University, Philadelphia, and sponsored by the Centre for Behaviour Therapy and Assessment. GO was determined to speak at the session because the doctors displayed anti-gay prejudices and were interested in "reversing" sexual orientation through the use of treatments such as aversion therapy. Charles Hill, president of GO, was allowed to speak for fifteen minutes.

["GO Protests Psychiatric Conference: ATTENTION Social Workers and Doctors!" GO *Info* 2 (April–May 1975): 2; "Gays of Ottawa Demanded the Right to Speak," *Body Politic*, no. 18 (1975), p. 6.]

February 28 * Vancouver * The first public hearing in Canada of a gay civil rights case under provincial human rights legislation was held at the Hotel Vancouver. The case involved GATE (Vancouver)'s complaint against the *Vancouver Sun* that the paper's refusal to print a two-line classified ad for *Gay Tide* contravened the British Columbia Human Rights Act. During the hearing, testimony was given concerning *Sun* publisher Stuart Keate's notion that homosexuality was a "threat to society" and that it was linked to "problems regarding V.D. and crime." On January 12, 1976, the Board of Inquiry, chaired by Vancouver lawyer Joe Wood, ruled that the *Vancouver Sun* had violated the provincial Human Rights Code; it ordered the *Sun* to pay GATE $500 in costs and "to refrain from committing the same or similar contraventions of the Code in future." GATE organized a victory picket of about fifty people outside of the *Sun*'s Pacific Press building. On July 16, 1976, the *Sun* appealed the ruling to the B.C. Supreme Court, but in August the court rejected the appeal and upheld the Board's ruling. On June 10, 1977, the ruling was overturned by the B.C. Court of Appeal. GATE (Vancouver) took the case to the Supreme Court of Canada, making it the first lesbian and gay rights case ever to make it to the highest court in Canada. On May 22, 1979, in a six to three decision, the Supreme Court of Canada dismissed the appeal of GATE (Vancouver), ruling that freedom of the press allowed the *Sun* "reasonable cause" to refuse the ad. The *Sun* eventually changed its ad policy, however, and printed a classified ad for *Gay Tide* on November 17, 1979.

[The following is a selection of articles; for a comprehensive sampling of articles on the case, see the GATE (Vancouver) papers, 82–005, Canadian Lesbian and Gay Archives, Toronto; "B.C. Paper Ordered to Take Gay-Lib Ads," *Globe and Mail*, metro ed., 13 January 1976, p. 8; Bob Cook, "Gays 2, *The Sun* 0," *Body Politic*, no. 27 (1976), p. 6; Robert Cook, "Gays Win Protection under B.C. Rights Code," *Body Politic*, no. 23 (1976), p. 1; "An Exciting Precedent" (editorial), *Body Politic*, no. 24 (1976), p. 2; "Five Year Battle Comes to an End as the *Sun* Accepts *Gay Tide* Ad," *Body Politic*, no.

59 (1979–80), p. 9; "GATE vs. *Sun*: A Chronology of the Case," *Gay Tide*, no. 17 (1977), p. 3; "GATE vs. *Sun*: The Ruling That Was," *Gay Tide*, no. 17 (1977), p. 7; "GATE Wins First Hearing in Canada under B.C. Human Rights Legislation," *Body Politic*, no. 18 (1975), p. 5; "GATE Wins Leave to Appeal to Supreme Court," *Gay Tide*, no. 18 (1978), p. 2; "*Gay Tide* Washed Out by Supreme Court," *Kinesis*, June 1979, p. 1; "*Gay Tide* Wins Round Two," *Gay Tide*, no. 14 (1976), p. 3; "Gays Triumph over *Sun*," *Gay Tide* 3 (April 1976): 1; "Justice Delayed in B.C.," *Body Politic*, no. 21 (1975), p. 6; "On to the Supreme Court" (editorial), *Gay Tide*, no. 17 (1977), p. 1; Stan Persky, "Gays Blast Publisher's Claim Homosexuality Leads to 'V.D., Crime,' " *Western Voice*, 12–25 March 1975, p. 10; Ken Popert, "Newspaper Appeals Ruling Favouring Gays," *Body Politic*, no. 26 (1976), p. 7; Jeff Richstone and J. Stuart Russell, "Comment: Shutting the Gate: Gay Civil Rights in the Supreme Court of Canada," *McGill Law Journal* 27 (1981): 92–117; "Rights Law Tested," *Advocate* (Los Angeles), no. 166 (1975), p. 6; "Ruff: *Sun* Violates Code; *Sun*: Gays a Threat," *Gay Tide* 2 (March 1975): 1, 10; "*Sun* Censors GATE Ad," *Peak* (Simon Fraser Univ., Burnaby, B.C.) (*Gay Supplement*), 9 July 1975, p. 4; "*Sun* Lawyer Says: Gay Love — 'Unlawful'; Gay Lib — 'Illegal,' " *Gay Tide* 3 (August 1976): 1; "*Sun's* Ad Policy Opposes Homosexuality, Inquiry Told," *Vancouver Sun*, four star ed., 1 March 1975, p. 16; "Supreme Court Considers Gay Rights: Laskin Reserves Judgement," *Gay Tide*, no. 21 (1978), p. 3; "Supreme Court Rejects Gay Rights," *Gay Tide*, no. 22 (1979), p. 1; Paul Trollope, "Supreme Court Dumps *Gay Tide*," *Body Politic*, no. 54 (1979), pp. 9–10; "The Verdict: Heads We Win, Tails They Lose" (editorial), *Gay Tide*, no. 21 (1978), p. 2; "Where *Gay Tide* Draws the Line" (editorial), *Gay Tide* 2 (March 1975): 2; J.W. (John Wilson), "Victory for Vancouver," *Gay Rising* 2 (January–February 1976): 1–2, 4.]

March ✳ Montréal ✳ The Groupe homosexuel d'action politique (GHAP), a lesbian and gay organization with an anti-capitalist perspective, was formed. Members of GHAP participated in several women's and workers' marches, including the International Women's Day march on March 8 and the May Day march on May 1, and in the National Gay Rights Conference in Ottawa, June 28–July 1, 1975. During 1975–76, GHAP attempted to develop a gay Marxist ideology, linking workers, women, and gays, but the group disbanded by the end of 1976.

[Ron Dayman, "Quebec: Five Years of the Movement," *Body Politic*, no. 29 (1976–77), p. 22; "Essai critique sur l'histoire du mouvement gai québécois 1970–1977," in *Contribution sur l'histoire du mouvement gai* (Montréal: Ligue Ouvriere Revolutionnaire Quatrieme Internationale, n.d.), pp. (29–30); "GHAP: The Role of Gays in Social Change," *Montreal Gay Times* 1 (August 1975): 7; "Groupe homosexuel d'action politique (GHAP)" vertical file, Canadian Lesbian and Gay Archives, Toronto; Roger Noël, "Pratiques politiques et formation de l'identité gaie au Québec: l'expérience du Groupe homosexuel d'action politique (1975–1976)," M.A. thesis, Science politique, Université du Québec à Montréal (UQAM), 1993, 208 pp.]

March ✳ Ottawa ✳ The Special Joint Committee on Immigration Policy was appointed by the Trudeau government one month after the introduction of the Green Paper on Immigration and Population, which had been prepared by the Department of Manpower and Immigration as a guide to the revision of the Immigration Act. Various community and political groups had denounced the document as racist, anti-immigrant, and reactionary. Gay groups were angered that the document did not propose removing anti-homosexual references from the Act. (See also November 6, 1975.)

[Robert Cook, "Gays Fight Immigration Policy," *Gay Tide* 2 (August 1975): 4, 11; Philip Girard, "From Subversion to Liberation: Homosexuals and the Immigration Act 1952–1977," *Canadian Journal of Law and Society* 2 (1987): 1–27; "Immigration Continued," GO *Info* 2 (April–May 1975): 7; Ken Popert, "Parliamentary Committee Recommends End to Gay Exclusion," *Body Politic*, no. 22 (1975), pp. 3–4.]

March * Toronto * GATE (Toronto) began publishing the newsletter *Gay Rising*. It was published irregularly until November 1978.

["A Newsletter Is Now Being Published," *Body Politic*, no. 18 (1975), p. 7.]

March * Toronto * A review committee of the Ontario Human Rights Commission was established to recommend changes to the Ontario Human Rights Code.

[Brian Mossop, "Gays Address Rights Review Hearing," *Body Politic*, no. 25 (1976), p. 7.]

March 3 * Ottawa * Michel Gravel, twenty-one, was arrested for running two male nude modelling agencies that were used as a front for a prostitution service involving teenage boys. Seventeen other men, all but one customers of the agencies, were arrested over the next three weeks and charged with contributing to juvenile delinquency, gross indecency, or buggery. None of the prostitutes was charged. The media sensationalized the "Ottawa Sex Scandal," calling the agencies a "white slavery ring" and a "homosexual vice ring." The names, ages, addresses, and occupations of those arrested were published or reported not only locally, but in newspapers across the country and on national radio. On March 18, one of the arrested men, Warren Zufelt, a thirty-four-year-old civil servant, committed suicide by jumping from an apartment building. On March 20, GO organized marches against police headquarters and the offices of the *Ottawa Journal* to protest police persecution of gays and biased reporting in the media, and to urge passing of a uniform age of consent law for all sexual acts. Soon afterwards, Ontario MPP Michael Cassidy (NDP-Ottawa Centre) wrote to Ontario's Minister of Justice John Clement. Troubled by Zufelt's death, Cassidy asked for an explanation of the double standard in charging gay clients of prostitutes with more serious offenses (such as gross indecency and buggery) than heterosexual clients (usually charged as being found-ins) in similar circumstances. Michel Gravel eventually pleaded guilty to charges of operating a common bawdy house and gross indecency; in September 1975 he was sentenced to two years less a day at the Guelph Correctional Centre, where he would be protected from prisoner abuse and receive psychiatric treatment. GO established the Warren Zufelt Memorial Defence Fund to help pay the court costs of the men who were charged. Of the sixteen other men charged, nine were fired, suspended, or changed jobs, and eight required psychiatric care because of the deluge of hate mail and calls they received. When their trials were completed, not one of the sixteen received either a jail term or fine; the charges were dismissed or the men were given absolute discharges or suspended sentences. In March and April 1976 there were calls in the Ontario Legislature from both opposition parties, led by MPPs Michael Cassidy (NDP-Ottawa-Centre) and Albert Roy (Lib.-Ottawa East), for a judicial inquiry into the handling of the case by Ottawa's morality squad. These demands were rejected by Ontario's Solicitor-General John MacBeth, Attorney-General Roy McMurtry, and, finally, Premier William Davis, who declared that "a public inquiry would serve no purpose." (See also March 18, April 9, May 13, June 12, and August 15, 1975.)

[The following is a selection of articles on this affair. For excellent collections of copies of these and other articles, see *The Body Politic* papers, 89–065/01, and the Charles Hill papers, 82–015/03, Canadian Lesbian and Gay Archives, Toronto; "Alleged Sex-Ring Clients' Lawyers Demand Probe of Morality Squad," *Globe and Mail*, metro ed., 9 March 1976, p. 8; Bob Avery, "City Police Blamed for Man's Death after Sex Charge," *Ottawa Journal*, 19 March 1975, p. 2; Bob Avery, "Deputy-Chief Defends Police: Accusations 'Irresponsible,' " *Ottawa Journal*, 21 March 1975, p. 3; Bob Avery, "OPP Investigator Studying Sex Case," *Ottawa Journal*, 9 March 1976, p. 1; Bob Avery, "Police Aware Boy in Need of Help," *Ottawa Journal*, 11 March 1976, p. 1; Bob Avery, "Police Prompted Me, Witness Tells Judge," *Ottawa Journal*, 5 May 1976, pp. 1–2; Bob Avery, "Witness May Face Charges," *Ottawa Journal*, 11 March 1976, p. 8; Peter Bakogeorge, "Gays Claim 'Whitewash': Police Beating Charges Dropped," *Ottawa Citizen*, 25 August 1976, p. 47; Peter Bakogeorge, "Police Lawyer Pushes for Vice Ring Inquiry: 'Manhandled,' " *Ottawa Citizen*, 19 March 1976, p. 33; Peter Bakogeorge, "Probe Demand Renewed," *Ottawa Citizen*, 25 August 1976, p. 1; John Beaufoy, "No Other Choice?" (column), *Globe and Mail*, metro ed., 2 April 1975, p. 29; Mark Bonokoski, "Sex Scandal Man Jumps to His Death," *Toronto Sun*, final ed., 19 March 1975, p. 2; Mark Bonokoski, "Young Boys in Ottawa's 'Most Sordid Crime,' " *Toronto Sun*, final ed., 5 March 1975, p. 3; "Boys Used in City Vice Ring," *Ottawa Citizen*, 4 March 1975, p. 1; Murray Campbell, "Breakup of Ring Spurs Calls for Study: Homosexuals Discriminated Against?" *Ottawa Citizen*, 19 March 1975, p. 5; "Cassidy Out for Gay Rights," GO *Info* 2 (April– May 1975): 6; "Charges by Lawyers about Morality Squad Spark Ottawa Inquiry," *Globe and Mail*, metro ed., 10 March 1976, p. 4; "Charges Dismissed

against Last of 17 Accused in Vice Ring," *Ottawa Citizen*, 11 August 1976, p. 3;
"Davis Rejects Probe into Police Conduct," *Ottawa Citizen*, 3 August 1976, p. 3;
Ron Dayman, "Ottawa: Police and Press Lies End in Death," *Body Politic*, no.
18 (1975), pp. 1, 6; Ron Dayman, "Show Trials Continue," *Body Politic*, no. 21
(1975), pp. 3–4; Ron Dayman, "Witch Hunt Extends to Court," *Body Politic*,
no. 19 (1975), p. 9; p. de V. (Peter de Vries), "Suicide Sparks Ottawa Protest,"
Gay Rising 1 (May 1975): 1, 4; Eric Dowd, "Sex Ring Case Prosecutions Were
'Proper': McMurtry Defends Criticisms," *Ottawa Journal*, 19 March 1976,
pp. 1–2; Eric Dowd, "Vice Ring Public Inquiry Rejected," *Ottawa Journal*, 11
May 1976, p. 17; "18th Arrest in Sex Ring at Ottawa," *Globe and Mail*, metro
ed., 27 March 1975, p. 9; "11th Man Charged in City Vice Ring," *Ottawa Citizen*,
13 March 1975, p. 1; Maurice Flood, "Ottawa Outrage Unravels," *Gay Tide* 3
(April 1976): 11; Steve Forster, " 'Depth of Depravation': Operator of Male
Prostitution Ring in Ottawa Sentenced," *Ottawa Citizen*, 20 September 1975,
p. 3; "Four More Charged in City Vice Ring," *Ottawa Citizen*, 17 March 1975,
p. 1; "Four More Ottawa Men Charged in Teen-aged Homosexual Ring," *Globe
and Mail*, metro ed., 18 March 1975, p. 8; "GO Demonstrates," *Gay-Zette* 2 (April 1975):
5; David Garmaise, "Police Acquittal Causes Public Uproar," *Body Politic*, no. 27
(1976), p. 5; Brian Gory, "Gay Society Protests Vice Case 'Persecutions,' " *Ottawa
Journal*, 21 March 1975, p. 3; Brian Gory, " 'Sex Ring' Sparks Furore," *Ottawa Journal*,
23 May 1975, pp. 1, 4; "Guilty Pleas Entered by Ottawa Man, 22, in Teen-age Sex Case,"
Globe and Mail, metro ed., 1 July 1975, p. 8; Gerald Hannon, "Anatomy of a Sex
Scandal: What Happened in Ottawa," *Body Politic*, no. 24 (1976), pp. 10–11; Bert Hill,
"MLAs Attack Crown: Vice Handling," *Ottawa Citizen*, 19 March 1976, p. 1; "Homo-
sexual Witchhunt," GO *Info* 2 (April–May 1975): 1, 4; "Justice Canadian-style"
(editorial), *Body Politic*, no. 18 (1975), p. 2; "Male Sex Ring Sensation Upstages
Dredging Scandal in Ottawa," *Toronto Star*, four star ed., 14 March 1975, p. C3; "Man
Charged in Vice Case Plunges 13 Floors to Death," *Toronto Star*, four star ed., 18 March
1975, p. A1; Dave McKay, "Boys in 'Slavery' Ring," *Ottawa Journal*, 4 March 1975, p. 1;
Russell Mills, "Police Report on Vice Arrests Should Be Public," *Ottawa Citizen*, 20
March 1976, p. 6; "Mountie Arrested in City Vice Case," *Ottawa Journal*, 10 March
1975, p. 1; "Mountie, Newsman, Four Others Facing Homosexual Ring Charges,"
Globe and Mail, metro ed., 11 March 1975, p. 9; "News: Judge Finds Publicity to be
Punishment Enough," *Esprit* 1 (October 1975): 2–3; "Nine Charged in Sex Ring,"
Ottawa Journal, 11 March 1975, p. 5; "Operator of Sex Ring Is Sentenced to Prison for
2 Years Less Day," *Globe and Mail*, metro ed., 20 September 1975, p. 4; "An Ottawa
MLA Has Endorsed Civil Rights for Gay People," *Body Politic*, no. 18 (1975), p. 6;
"Ottawa Outrage," *Gay Tide* 2 (June 1975): 1; "Ottawa Trials Begin, 2 Dismissed," *Gay
Times* 1 (June 1975): 3; "Ottawa 'Witch Hunt,' " *Gay-Zette* 2 (April 1975): 5; "Ottawa
'Witch Hunt' Gravel Pleads Guilty," *Gay-Zette* 2 (July 1975): 6; "Publicity over
Homosexual Ring Prompts Protest by Ottawa Gays," *Globe and Mail*, metro ed., 21
March 1975, p. 9; C.R., "Ottawa Witch-Hunt" (letter), *Gay-Zette* 2 (June 1975): 7;
M.R. (Michael Riordon), "Prostitution Trials: The Plot Sickens," *Gay Rising* 1 (June
1975): 4; "Second Man Charged in Sex Case," *Ottawa Citizen*, 7 March 1975, p. 2; "Sex
Charge against Councillor Is Dismissed: Witnesses Can't Identify," *Globe and Mail*,
metro ed., 23 May 1975, p. 9; "Stop the Ottawa Queer-Hunt!" (editorial), *Gay Rising*

1 (April 1975): 2; "Substitution of Sex Ring Charges Prompts Complaints from Lawyers," *Globe and Mail*, metro ed., 5 June 1975, p. 8; Paul-François Sylvestre, *Propos pour une libération (homo)sexuelle* (Montréal: Éditions de l'Aurore, 1976); "Tous les dessous du scandale de la prostitution mâle à Ottawa," *Gay Montréal* 1 (2 November 1976): 8; "Two More Charged in Sex Case," *Ottawa Journal*, 25 March 1975, p. 2; "Two More 'Sex Scandal' Victims Absolved," *Body Politic*, no. 25 (1976), p. 6; " 'Vice Ring' Cases May Be Checked: Police Commission," *Ottawa Citizen*, 10 April 1976, p. 1; "War Graves Commission Chief Charged in Ottawa Vice Ring," *Ottawa Citizen*, late ed., 12 March 1975, p. 1; "Warren Zufelt Memorial Defence Fund," GO *Info* 2 (July–August 1975): 3.]

March 8 * Montréal * A group of male members of GHAP participated in the International Women's Day celebration.

["GHAP: The Role of Gays in Social Change," *Montreal Gay Times* 1 (August 1975): 7.]

March 8 * Toronto * Delegates at the International Women's Day conference at Toronto City Hall voted to demand the inclusion of a sexual orientation clause in the Ontario Human Rights Code. They also showed support for the Committee to Defend John Damien.

["Support for Gay Civil Rights," *Body Politic*, no. 18 (1975), p. 7.]

March 11 * Ottawa * B.C. MLA Rosemary Brown (Vancouver-Burrard) appeared as a candidate for the leadership of the federal NDP at a public meeting sponsored by the NDP Ottawa-South Riding Association. She spoke briefly on gay issues and the link between the socialist struggle and gay rights. GO members in attendance reported that the audience reacted with "polite silence and embarrassment." (See also May 6, 1975.)

["GO Members Question M.P.s," GO *Info* 2 (April–May 1975): 6.]

March 14 * Toronto * During question period, MPP P.D. Lawlor (NDP-Lakeshore) asked Ontario's Minister of Consumer and Commercial Relations Sidney Handleman to make a statement on the case of John Damien, who was fired from his job with the Ontario Racing Commission for being gay. Mr. Handleman replied that he had "hoped this matter would not arise in the House," and reiterated the Ontario government's position that Damien "had been compromised by certain contacts."

[T.P. (Terry Phillips), "Defending John Damien: Case Hits Ontario Legislature," *Gay Rising* 1 (April 1975): 4.]

March 15 * Thunder Bay, Ont. * The Mona Lisa Tavern's plate glass door was kicked in and owner Michael Agostinelli was faced by a hostile crowd of youths. Agostinelli discharged a gun and one person in the crowd was hit in the leg. Located at 505 Simpson Street, the Mona Lisa had operated as a gay bar since 1972. It was subjected to continual harassment by people who did not want a gay bar in the area, and had been broken up on numerous occasions while the Thunder Bay police refused to act. In 1978, Agostinelli pleaded guilty to a charge of unlawfully causing bodily harm and was fined $500. The bar was forced to close because of the incident and charges.

["Harassed Gay Bar Owner Fined," *Body Politic*, no. 47 (1978), p. 14.]

March 18 * Ottawa * The Ottawa-Carleton Social Planning Council voted 10–5 to approve a motion by board member Irving Greenberg to study how sexual offence charges were laid in Ottawa. This motion was raised in concern over the suicide of Warren Zufelt, one of the men charged in the "Ottawa Sex Scandal."

[Murray Campbell, "Breakup of Ring Spurs Calls for Study: Homosexuals Discriminated Against?" *Ottawa Citizen*, 19 March 1975, p. 5; "Sex Offence Charge Procedures Queried," *Ottawa Journal*, 19 March 1975, p. 4; "Vice Harassment Investigated," *Advocate* (Los Angeles), no. 163 (1975), p. 14.]

March 20 * Hamilton * Gayline Distress Service, Hamilton's first telephone counselling service for homosexuals, began operation under the direction of the Hamilton-McMaster GLM.

["Gayline Distress Service Announces Commencement of Operation," *Dialogue*, no. 10 (1975), p. 5.]

March 21 * Toronto * John Damien, fired from his job with the Ontario Racing Commission for being gay, filed a wrongful dismissal suit for $350,000 in damages against the Commission in the Supreme Court of Ontario. Damien filed another suit for $1 million in punitive damages against officials of the Ontario Jockey Club, the Commission, and the Ontario Ministry of Consumer and Commercial Relations, claiming that they had injured him at his trade. Damien also sought payment of his legal fees and a court order demanding his reinstatement. His lawyer, Harry Kopyto, also began preparing a brief to the Ontario Human Rights Commission, asking the Commission to expand its definition of "sex" in the Ontario Human Rights Code to include sexual orientation. (See also September 1975.)

["Damien Fights Back with $1,350,000 Suit," *Gay Times* 1 (May 1975): 2; "Homosexual Sues over Firing," *Toronto Star*, Saturday ed., 22 March 1975, p. A2; Ken Popert, "Damien Sues for Rights," *Body Politic*, no. 18 (1975), p. 7; "Race Steward Sues for Job," *Advocate* (Los Angeles), no. 165 (1975), p. 13; M.R. (Michael Riordon), "Damien Suit Asks $1,350,000," *Gay Rising* 1 (April 1975): 1.]

March 21 * Winnipeg * GFE sponsored a forum at the University of Manitoba entitled "Homosexual Oppression and Liberation — Views from the Left." Political parties of the left were invited to present their analysis of the nature of gay oppression and their relationship to the gay movement. Members of the Revolutionary Marxist Group and the League for Socialist Action were present, but NDP and Communist Party members refused to participate.

[Richard North, "Socialists Give Views on Gay Liberation," *Body Politic*, no. 18 (1975), p. 8.]

March 26 ∗ Alberta ∗ A provincial election was held in which the Progressive Conservatives won sixty-nine of seventy-five seats. In the period leading up to the election, members of GATE (Edmonton) questioned candidates about gay civil rights and the inclusion of sexual orientation in provincial human rights legislation. GATE (Edmonton) also sent the brief "Homosexuals: A Minority without Rights" to all candidates. Fifty-five percent of the candidates who returned the questionnaire (mostly NDP candidates) supported including sexual orientation in the legislation. During the campaign, gays were vilified by the president of the Alberta Liberal party, Jack Pickett.

["Gay Alliance toward Equality (GATE) (Edmonton)" vertical file, Canadian Lesbian and Gay Archives, Toronto.]

Spring ∗ Montréal **∗** Raids and arrests made in baths, bars, and public washrooms signalled the beginning of a police crackdown against the gay community in an attempt to "clean up" Montréal in preparation for the thousands of tourists who would visit the city during the 1976 summer Olympics.

["Aquarius Raid Start of Police Anti-gay Clean-up Campaign," *Gay Times* 1 (April 1975): 1; John Blacklock, "Montreal: Olympics Circus Brings More Repression," *Body Politic*, no. 23 (1976), p. 6; "City Cracks Down," *Body Politic*, no. 19 (1975), p. 8; Ron Dayman, "Quebec: Five Years of the Movement," *Body Politic*, no. 29 (1976–77), p. 23; "Police 'Can't Deny' Entrapment," *Gay Times* 1 (May 1975): 1; "Police Deny Harassment, Decline Talks," *Montreal Gay Times* 1 (August 1975): 5; "Police Harassment Declines," *Gay Times* 1 (June 1975): 2.]

Spring ∗ Montréal **∗** Bishop Robert Clement of the Church of the Beloved Disciple, New York, N.Y., visited MCC and delivered a sermon tracing the growth of his gay church.

["Gay Bishop Visits Montreal," *Gay-Zette* 2 (April 1975): 3.]

Spring ∗ New Brunswick **∗** Five English-language daily newspapers refused to print a classified ad for Gay Friends of Fredericton. All of the papers (the *Daily Gleaner*, Fredericton; the *Telegraph-Journal* and the *Times-Globe*, Saint John; the *Moncton Times*; and the *Moncton Transcript*) were owned by the Irving family.

["Gay Friends" vertical file, Canadian Lesbian and Gay Archives, Toronto; "New Brunswick Paper Cartel Closes Ads to Gays," *Body Politic*, no. 19 (1975), p. 6.]

Spring ∗ Ottawa ∗ A chapter of Alcoholics Anonymous geared specifically to gay men began to meet regularly at the MCC church hall.

["Gay A.A. Group Starts," *New Beginnings* 1 (30 May 1975): 4.]

Spring ∗ St. John's ∗ CHAN sponsored a lesbian/feminist workshop at the St. John's Women's Centre.

["History of CHAN . . . ," *Aboutface* 2 (May 1976): 2.]

Spring ∗ Saskatoon ∗ The Committee of Gays for the Re-election of John Richards was formed in preparation for the June 11 provincial election. Richards (Ind. Soc.-Saskatoon-Centre), elected in 1971, had been supportive of the gay community and had raised the issue of gay rights in the legislature. Richards went down to defeat in the election.

["Gays Enter Political Arena," *Gay West*, no. 2 (1975), pp. 7, 15.]

Spring ∗ Toronto ∗ The musical revue *In Gay Company* played at the Teller's Cage theatre.

[Gerald Hannon, "*In Gay Company*," *Body Politic*, no. 18 (1975), p. 20; "*In Gay Company*," *Metro Community News* 2 (30 May 1975): 12; John A. Lee, "*In Gay Company*," *Metro Community News* 2 (16 May 1975): 14.]

Spring ∗ Toronto ∗ Rev. Bob Wolfe announced that MCC would not seek membership in CGRO because the congregation's "diversity on the subject of activism precludes the direct and official participation of our corporate entity at this time." MCC changed its position on October 5, 1975, when the newly elected board of directors of MCC voted to become affiliated with both CGRO and NGRC/CNDH.

["MCC to Join NGRC," *Metro Community News* 2 (10 October 1975): 3; "Toronto MCC Has Decided against Membership in CGRO," *Body Politic*, no. 18 (1975), p. 7.]

April ∗ Montréal ∗ An independent collective (including John Blacklock, Frank Brayton, Robert Burns, Tony Farebrother, and Kelly Rivard) began publishing the English-language monthly newsjournal *Gay Times* in response to increased police harassment of the gay community. The police crackdown was intended to clean up the city's gay life in preparation for the 1976 summer Olympics. *Gay Times* was formed to monitor police actions and to press for organized reaction from the community. The paper ceased publication in spring 1976, after only eight issues.

[Ron Dayman, "Quebec: Five Years of the Movement," *Body Politic*, no. 29 (1976–77), p. 23; "A Monthly Gay Paper Has Appeared in Montreal," *Body Politic*, no. 18 (1975), p. 7; "Time to Organize" (editorial), *Gay Times* 1 (April 1975): 2.]

April ∗ Ottawa ∗ MPP Michael Cassidy (NDP-Ottawa-Centre) endorsed the

Committee to Defend John Damien and also declared his support for the inclusion of a sexual orientation clause in the Ontario Human Rights Code. Cassidy had come to support this position after the death of Warren Zufelt in the "Ottawa Sex Scandal" affair.

["NDP Legislator Joins Damien Defence Cause," *Body Politic*, no. 19 (1975), p. 7.]

April * Ottawa * GO members Denis LeBlanc and Paul Wise prepared the brief "Civil Rights of Homosexuals in City Employment," which was presented to members of Ottawa's Board of Control and to all councillors. (See also June 12 and August 19, 1975.)

["GO Presses for Civic Rights," *Body Politic*, no. 19 (1975), p. 9; "Ottawa: Victory at Ottawa City Hall," *Body Politic*, no. 24 (1976), p. 3.]

April * Québec, Qué. * The Civil Liberties Committee, composed of representatives from AHM/GMA, CHAL, and CHUM, forwarded a 2,600–name petition supporting the inclusion of sexual orientation in the proposed Human Rights Charter to Québec's Justice Minister Jérôme Choquette.

["Petition Sent to Quebec," *Gay Times* 1 (May 1975): 4.]

April * Toronto * The Royal Commission into Metropolitan Toronto Police Practices began hearings under Ontario Supreme Court Justice Donald Morand. Pat Murphy testified concerning mistreatment during her arrest as one of the Brunswick Four. The Commission's report was released on June 30, 1976, and concluded that in the case of the Brunswick Four the police officers had not used excessive force and that the women had been abusive to the police.

[Vianney Carriere, "Heard Fellow Constables Jeering at 4 Women, Policeman Testifies," *Globe and Mail*, metro ed., 10 April 1975, p. 57; Vianney Carriere, "Lawyer, Pub Manager Disagree over Reaction to Song: 'Sophisticated, Witty' or Cause for Riot?" *Globe and Mail*, metro ed., 9 April 1975, p. 4; Vianney Carriere, "Three Women Assaulted, Taunted as Lesbians, Child-Care Worker Testifies at Police Probe," *Globe and Mail*, metro ed., 8 April 1975, p. 5; "Inquiry Told Women Derided as Lesbians," *Toronto Star*, four star ed., 8 April 1975, p. C27; Michael Riordon, "Gay Woman Recounts Police Violence," *Body Politic*, no. 18 (1975), p. 8; Becki L. Ross, *The House That Jill Built: A Lesbian Nation in Formation* (Toronto: University of Toronto Press, 1995), p. 256 n.28.]

April * Winnipeg * The Manitoba Telephone System refused to list either of GFE's numbers in Winnipeg's new telephone directory. Only after several weeks of pressure from lawyers representing GFE and from the Provincial Ombudsman's office did the telephone company agree to list them.

["Gays for Equality (GFE)" vertical file, Canadian Lesbian and Gay Archives, Toronto.]

April 5 * Toronto * Two lesbians, Nancy and Linda, were married at the MCC by Rev. Bob Wolfe. The ceremony was covered by the *Toronto Sun*.

[Helen Bullock, " '... I Now Pronounce You ... Er,' " *Toronto Sun*, 6 April 1975, p. 4.]

April 9 ∗ Ottawa ∗ Ron Dayman of GO filed a complaint with the Ontario Press Council against the *Ottawa Citizen*, complaining of the sensational and biased reporting displayed by the *Citizen* during the "Ottawa Sex Scandal" affair. (See also August 15, 1975.)

[Charles Hill papers, 82–015/01 and /03, Canadian Lesbian and Gay Archives, Toronto.]

April 12 ∗ Montréal ∗ A fire destroyed the Sauna Aquarius baths, 1183, rue Crescent. Three men were killed in the blaze. Arson was suspected, but never proved.

["Aquaris (sic) Fire Inquest Over," *Montreal Gay Times* 2 (Spring 1976): 6; "Aquarius: Tragic End," *Gay-Zette* 2 (June 1975): 6; "Fire Guts Aquarius; Three Fatalities," *Gay Times* 1 (May 1975): 2; "A Fire Killed Three People," *Body Politic*, no. 18 (1975), p. 7; Robert Goyette, "Death Blaze Sauna Had No Fire Alarms," *Montreal Star*, final ed., 24 September 1975, p. A14; "3 brûlés à l'Aquarius," *Gay-Zette* (Special Edition), 12 April 1975, p. 1; Mark Wilson, "Aquarius Made $100,000 a Year Profit: Cause of Fatal Fire Unknown," *Montreal Gay Times* 1 (November 1975): 3, 18.]

April 12 ∗ Québec, Qué. ∗ About fifty lesbians met at CHAL, 264, rue des Franciscains, to discuss problems faced by lesbians in society. The event was organized by Denise Goyette of CHAL. This was the first meeting of its kind held in Québec City.

["CHAL: au féminin," CHALUM 1 (? June 1975): 4.]

May ∗ Montréal ∗ Representatives of *Gay Times* met with Neil Caplan, a member of the executive of the Montreal Citizen's Movement (MCM), to discuss gay civil rights and municipal government in Montréal. At that time, the MCM held almost one-third of the seats on city council.

["MCM: Gays Must Protest Police Abuse," *Montreal Gay Times* 1 (August 1975): 15; "MCM: Possibility of Raising Gay Issues at City Hall," *Gay Times* 1 (June 1975): 8.]

May ∗ Toronto ∗ Issue eighteen of *The Body Politic* was ordered off the newsstands by the Toronto Morality Squad. A full-page cartoon on page eleven entitled "The Continuing Adventures of Harold Hedd," written and drawn by Rand Holmes, showed two men engaged in oral sex. The same cartoon had been published in a censored form in the *Georgia Straight* in October 1971. At that time the sex scenes were removed because the printer refused to print them.

[Gerald Hannon, "Obscenity Laws and the Uses of Sexual Guilt," *Body Politic*, no. 20 (1975), pp. 1, 19; Rand Holmes, "The Continuing Adventures of ... Harold Hedd," *Georgia Straight*, 19–22 October 1971, pp. 1, 11; "Police Censor *Body Politic*," *Gay Tide* 2 (August 1975): 10; "Thought Police" (editorial), *Body Politic*, no. 19 (1975), p. 2; " 'We're Gonna Close You Down,' " *Body Politic*, no. 19 (1975), pp. 1, 12.]

May ∗ Vancouver ∗ After a 5–5 tie vote, Vancouver City Council rejected a grant proposal for $9,000 to sponsor a gay education and counselling service, submitted by SEARCH. The proposal had been recommended to Council by the Director of Social Planning and had already passed Council's Standing Committee on Social Services. It was resubmitted but was rejected again on July 22, 1975, by a 6–5 margin.

> ["Liberal Councillors Manipulate Gays: Analysis," *Gay Tide* 2 (August 1975): 3; "SEARCH Grant Refused," *Gay Tide* 2 (June 1975): 6.]

May 1 ∗ Montréal ∗ A lesbian and gay contingent of about sixty people took part in the annual May Day march for workers' solidarity. The group carried its own banner and placards and was generally well-received by the other marchers. This was by far the largest openly gay contingent in a Montréal demonstration to that time.

> [Ron Dayman, "Quebec: Five Years of the Movement," *Body Politic*, no. 29 (1976–77), p. 22; "Gay May Day Demonstration," *Gay-Zette* 2 (June 1975): 4; "Gays Join May Day Marchers," *Gay Times* 1 (May 1975): 3; S. Gupta, "Gay Mai Day" (photos), *Gay-Zette* 2 (June 1975): 5; " 'May Day' March Draws Gay Solidarity," *Body Politic*, no. 19 (1975), p. 9.]

May 2 ∗ Toronto ∗ The Wages Due Lesbians collective, part of the International Wages for Housework movement, held a demonstration at Toronto City Hall. Eight women from different backgrounds spoke to a noontime crowd of about 250.

> ["Wages for Housework," *Other Woman* 3 (Winter 1975): 6–7, 24; "Wages for Housework Mayday in Toronto: Progress Report," *Other Woman* 3 (Spring Solstice 1975): 22.]

May 6 ∗ Ontario ∗ The Ontario Educational Communications Authority (OECA) (Channel 19) broadcast the documentary *To Be or Not to Be* in its series "The Quiet Furies." Filmed several years earlier in the United States, *To Be or Not to Be* was seen by some to be homophobic in its depiction of gays as superficial, immature, and living hopeless lives. GATE (Toronto) protested to OECA chairperson Ronald Ide, and demanded that the program be withdrawn and never shown again. Later, members of *The Body Politic*, GATE (Toronto), and GAY met with the head of adult programming for OECA in an attempt to influence programming on gay subjects.

> [Michael Riordon, " 'Education' vs. Being Gay," *Body Politic*, no. 19 (1975), p. 7; M.R. (Michael Riordon), "T.V. Bomb," *Gay Rising* 1 (June 1975): 2.]

May 6 ∗ Vancouver ∗ GATE (Vancouver) received a letter from MLA Rosemary Brown (NDP-Vancouver-Burrard), at that time a candidate for the leadership of the federal NDP, expressing her support for the campaign to reinstate John

Damien, who was fired from his job with the Ontario Racing Commission for being gay.

["B.C. NDP Leadership Candidate Is for Damien Reinstatement," *Gay Rising* 1 (May 1975): 3.]

May 8 * Toronto * Members of GATE (Toronto) distributed leaflets to many of the 250 people attending a public meeting of the candidates for leadership of the federal NDP. Michael Riordon of GATE (Toronto) was able to ask the candidates their position on gays and the Canada Immigration Act. All candidates (including Ed Broadbent and Lorne Nystrom), although uncomfortable with the question, admitted that the prohibition of "these people" was unjust and should be eliminated from the Act.

["NDP Leaders Vacillate," *Body Politic*, no. 19 (1975), pp. 5, 12; K.P. (Ken Popert), ". . . and Immigration Change," *Gay Rising* 1 (May 1975): 3.]

May 10 * Montréal; Toronto * Lesbians and gay men took part in the "Women Unite: May 10th March," which was held to publicize International Women's Year and what they saw as the real needs of women — equal pay for equal work, abortion on demand, free daycare facilities, educational opportunities, and the repeal of discriminatory legislation. Marchers also called for equal custody rights for lesbian mothers and justice for John Damien and Dr. Henry Morgentaler.

["Gays Support Rally," *Body Politic*, no. 19 (1975), p. 8; "Le 10 mai: marche militant en défense des droits des femmes," *Le gai Québec* 1 (28 June 1975): 3; "May 10th, Toronto," *Other Woman* 3 (Spring Solstice 1975): 4; "News: The May 10 Women Unite March," *Long Time Coming* 2 (May 1975): 28; Photograph, *Gay Rising* 1 (May 1975): 1; Kathleen Rex, "From Pro-abortionists to Gay Liberation, Many Viewpoints Represented in Women's March," *Globe and Mail*, metro ed., 12 May 1975, p. 13.]

May 11 * Chatham, Ont. * The Southwestern Ontario Regional Conference of NDP Riding Organizations passed resolutions to support the inclusion of a sexual orientation clause in the Ontario Human Rights Code and to support John Damien in his case against the Ontario Racing Commission. The resolutions had been introduced by Windsor-Sandwich delegate Harold B. Desmarais, chairperson of WGU. (See also May 24–25, 1975.)

["And Now the Good News," *Windsor Gay Unity Newsletter* 1 (May 1975): 5–6; "NDP Group Votes Gay Rights," *Gay Rising* 1 (June 1975): 4; "NDP Resolutions O.K.'s Rights," *Body Politic*, no. 19 (1975), p. 6.]

May 13 * Montréal * Representatives of AHM/GMA, CHUM, and CHAL presented a brief protesting the government's stand on homosexuals and immigration to a meeting of the Special Joint Committee on Immigration Policy, held at the Berkeley Hotel. Charlie Thorpe of MCC also made a presentation.

["Gays Present Brief," *Gay-Zette* 2 (June 1975): 8; "L'homosexualité et l'immigration," CHALUM 1 (? June 1975): 3; "Immigration: Brief Presented to Government," *Gay Times* 1 (June 1975): 4.]

May 13 ✶ Toronto ✶ GO had complained to the office of the Attorney General of Ontario regarding police practices in the arrests of the men charged in the "Ottawa Sex Scandal," particularly with regard to the way in which the Ottawa Morality Squad handled the laying of charges and the releasing of the names of the accused. On May 13, W.H. Langton replied in a letter on behalf of the ministry, stating that "the vigilant efforts of the police deserve commendation rather than censure," and that the publication of the names of the accused was the media's "decision and responsibility." GO's request for a probe into the matter was denied.

[Bob Avery, "Police Probe Denied: Province Refuses Gays' Request," *Ottawa Journal*, 23 May 1975, p. 3.]

May 13 ✶ Toronto ✶ The lawyer for John Mooney, president of the Ontario Jockey Club, asked Justice S.M. McBride of the Supreme Court of Ontario to dismiss several parts of John Damien's statement of claim against him, including the allegation that Mooney was motivated by prejudice against Damien's sexual orientation. On June 11, Justice McBride ruled that portions of the claim that alleged anti-gay prejudice be struck out. Damien's lawyers immediately appealed the decision. (See also June 24, 1975.)

[W.B. (Walter Bruno), "Damien Court Motions Begin: Lawyers Charge Government Stall," *Gay Rising* 1 (June 1975): 1, 2.]

May 17 ✶ Montréal ✶ Labyris (formerly Montreal Gay Women) held its first dance at the Powerhouse Gallery. About 110 women attended.

["Labyris Holds Dance, Prepares Centre," *Gay Times* 1 (June 1975): 2.]

May 18–19 ✶ Edmonton ✶ Thirty-five delegates from across the Prairie provinces attended the Second Prairie Gay Liberation Conference, sponsored by GATE (Edmonton). Workshops were held, as well as discussions on campaigns for the inclusion of sexual orientation in provincial human rights codes, gay election activity, and work in the NDP. Delegates passed several resolutions, including a call for coordinated public actions across the Prairies on June 28 to protest the failure of the federal government's Green Paper on Immigration and Population to recommend deletion of anti-gay clauses in the Immigration Act.

["Prairie Gays Blast Green Paper," *Labor Challenge*, 2 June 1975, p. 2; "Prairie Gays Gather," *Gay West*, no. 2 (1975), pp. 9, 11; "Prairie Organizations Gather for Second Annual Conference," *Body Politic*, no. 19 (1975), p. 7.]

May 24–25 ∗ Windsor, Ont. ∗ The Windsor-Sandwich NDP Riding Association passed resolutions supporting the inclusion of a sexual orientation clause in the Ontario Human Rights Code, supporting John Damien's fight against the Ontario Racing Commission, and condemning the failure of the Green Paper on Immigration and Population to recommend the deletion of anti-gay clauses in the federal Immigration Act. These resolutions had been introduced by delegate Harold B. Desmarais, chairperson of WGU. (See also July 4–7, 1975.)

["NDP Resolutions O.K.'s Rights," *Body Politic*, no. 19 (1975), p. 6.]

May 25 ∗ Toronto ∗ GATE (Toronto) participated in the People's Assembly on the Green Paper on Immigration, a gathering of forty community, church, and labour groups that discussed the federal government's proposals for a new Immigration Act.

[B.M. (Brian Mossop), "Let Our People In!" *Gay Rising* 1 (June 1975): 1, 3.]

May 27 ∗ Vancouver ∗ David Jacobs of Gay People of SFU presented a brief to the Special Joint Committee on Immigration Policy. GATE (Vancouver) sent a written submission.

[Robert Cook, "Gays Fight Immigration Policy," *Gay Tide* 2 (August 1975): 4, 11; David Jacobs, "A Gay and the Green Paper on Immigration," *Peak* (Simon Fraser Univ., Burnaby, B.C.) (*Gay Supplement*), 9 July 1975, p. 1.]

June ∗ Calgary ∗ Gay Information and Resources Calgary (GIRC) was formed. Its office, originally located at 2–112A 8th Avenue S.E., offered weekly meetings, a speaker's bureau, political action, and a library. The group's first chairperson was John Windi (a.k.a. Windi Earthworm).

["Community Page: Calgary," *Gay West*, no. 2 (1975), p. 16; "Doug Young" (interview), *Body Politic*, no. 66 (1980), p. 25; "New Group Formed in Calgary," *Body Politic*, no. 20 (1975), p. 9; Ken Popert, "Gay Group Sues for Right to Advertise," *Body Politic*, no. 20 (1975), p. 6.]

June ∗ Calgary ∗ An anti-gay skit performed by a band called The Dandies at the Four Seasons Hotel's Scotch Room cabaret was allowed to continue despite letters of protest from GIRC to hotel management as well as a physical confrontation with the band, members of the audience, and the cabaret's management.

["Calgary Gays Try to Stop Show," *Body Politic*, no. 20 (1975), p. 11; "Gay Information Resources Calgary (GIRC)" vertical file, Canadian Lesbian and Gay Archives, Toronto.]

June ∗ Edmonton ∗ Eight people attended two meetings to discuss the possibility of forming a branch of MCC. The group decided to continue to meet informally.

["Wolfe and Crap," *GAYtuk* 1 (28 January 1976): 2–3.]

June * Edmonton * The Gay Associations of Edmonton (GAE) was formed as a coalition of gay businesses and organizations. Its aim was to encourage closer ties between different segments of the community and to coordinate community-oriented projects.

["Gay Alliance toward Equality (GATE) (Edmonton)" vertical file, Canadian Lesbian and Gay Archives, Toronto.]

June * Mississauga, Ont. * Members of GATE (Toronto)'s educational committee were denied access to Cawthra Park Secondary School, where they had been scheduled to speak. The talk was cancelled at the last minute by principal Allan Pleasance, who declared that because homosexuality is a controversial "moral issue" the invitation would require parental approval.

[Ed Jackson, " 'Education' vs. Being Gay: Toronto," *Body Politic*, no. 19 (1975), p. 7.]

June * New York, N.Y. * Robert Wallace's play *No Deposit — No Return*, about five men who interact when they are trapped in a subway washroom, was performed at the West Side Discussion Group Gay Theatre, 37 Ninth Avenue. The principal character, Sara Lee, was played by Saul Rubinek.

["*No Deposit — No Return*" vertical file, Canadian Lesbian and Gay Archives, Toronto; James Wilson, "*No Deposit — No Return*," *Body Politic*, no. 20 (1975), pp. 21–22.]

June * Toronto * *In the Light*, an extended-play recording of four songs by Sara Ellen Dunlop, was released as the first recording of Sara Ellen's Home-made Records, a label created by Dunlop (and her partner and business manager Shirley Anne Stonehouse) to distribute her own original music. Dunlop, who was born and raised in Alabama, became a legend in Toronto through her co-ownership (with Richard Kerr) of the Music Room and the Melody Room and as the driving force behind the band Mama Quilla. Her company, Sara Ellen's Music Ltd., was one of the earliest recording companies wholly owned and operated by women. Dunlop died of cancer in February 1978.

[John Forbes, "Sara Ellen Dunlop: A Memory," *Body Politic*, no. 41 (1978), p. 16; "Music," *Esprit* 1 (October 1975): 6, 66; Grace Scott, "Music Reviews: Sara and Rita. Interview with Sara Ellen Dunlop," *Other Woman* 3 (October–November 1975): 24.]

June * Vancouver * *Pedestal*, a women's liberation newspaper published since 1969, included much material of interest to feminists and occasional articles on lesbianism. The paper collapsed early in 1974 but was revived in June 1975. Renamed *Pedestal: A Lesbian-Feminist Newspaper*, it was now much more lesbian-oriented. The new venture lasted three issues before collapsing again by the end of 1975.

["News: The *Pedestal* Returns," *Long Time Coming* 2 (May 1975): 29.]

June 4 * St. John's * A member of CHAN gave a verbal presentation before a meeting of the Special Joint Committee on Immigration Policy, held at the Hotel Newfoundland, stating that CHAN supported the brief prepared by GO concerning gays and the Immigration Act.

["CHAN Speaks Out at Immigration Hearings," *Aboutface* 1 (Summer 1975): 1.]

June 5 * Fredericton * Keith Sly of Gay Friends presented a brief to a meeting of the Special Joint Committee on Immigration Policy.

["Gay Friends" vertical file, Canadian Lesbian and Gay Archives, Toronto.]

June 9 * Toronto * Representatives of GATE (Toronto) appeared before a meeting of the Special Joint Committee on Immigration Policy, held at the Park Plaza Hotel. Hundreds of demonstrators marched outside of the hotel on Avenue Road, including a large gay contingent carrying signs and distributing leaflets protesting the federal government's exclusion of gay immigrants.

[Norman Hartley, "Chairman Holds Militant Groups Apart at Green Paper Hearings," *Globe and Mail*, metro ed., 10 June 1975, pp. 1–2; Brian Mossop, "Gay Community Effects Concerted Effort to Protest Failures of Immigration Paper," *Body Politic*, no. 19 (1975), p. 5; B.M. (Brian Mossop), "Let Our People In!" *Gay Rising* 1 (June 1975): 1, 3.]

June 10 * Saskatoon * About twenty men and women demonstrated in front of the *Star-Phoenix* building to protest the paper's refusal to print an ad submitted by the Gay Community Centre. The Centre had sent questionnaires on gay matters to all candidates running in the June 11 provincial election. Nine of the twenty-five candidates in Saskatoon replied: eight were supportive of gay rights, one was negative. The ad refused by the *Star-Phoenix* listed the results of the poll. This was the first gay picket held in Saskatoon.

["During the Past Provincial Election a Campaign Was Undertaken by the GCCS to Poll All the Candidates and Get Their Stand on Gay Rights," *Gay Community Centre of Saskatoon Newsletter*, August 1975, pp. 1–2; "GCCS Polls Candidates," *Gay West*, no. 2 (1975), p. 7; Vern Greenshields, "Gay Community Protests Ad Decision: *Star-Phoenix* Picketed," *Saskatoon Star-Phoenix*, 10 June 1975, p. 3; Doug Hellquist, "First Prairie Picket Held," *Body Politic*, no. 19 (1975), p. 6; "Prairie People Picket Paper," *Gay Tide* 2 (August 1975): 10; "Saskatoon Gays Fight Back," *Gay West*, no. 2 (1975), pp. 6, 15.]

June 12 * Ottawa * Ron Dayman and Charles Hill of GO met with Ottawa Mayor Lorry Greenberg to press for an investigation of police activities in the arrests in the "Ottawa Sex Scandal" affair, and to recommend the adoption of a civil rights clause to protect gay municipal employees in Ottawa. Greenberg appeared to be largely unaware of discrimination against gays and asked GO to submit a brief outlining specific complaints to the Ottawa Police Commission. (See also August 19, 1975.)

[Ron Dayman, "Show Trials Continue," *Body Politic*, no. 21 (1975), pp. 3–4; "Gays Referred to Commission about Inquiry," *Ottawa Citizen*, 13 June 1975, p. 2; "Gays Tell Mayor of Police Brutality: Will Submit Brief," *Ottawa Journal*, 13 June 1975, p. 3; "GO Continues Municipal Efforts," *Body Politic*, no. 21 (1975), p. 6; "GO Goes to City Hall," GO *Info* 2 (July–August 1975): 3.]

June 12 ✳ Windsor, Ont. ✳ Harold B. Desmarais, chairperson of WGU, appeared before a meeting of the Special Joint Committee on Immigration Policy, held at the Holiday Inn. Desmarais presented a brief on behalf of Windsor gays, calling for the implementation of the recommendations made in 1966 by a government commission in Section 61 of a White Paper on immigration. Desmarais was later interviewed by CKLW news.

["Immigration Hearings Provide Television Coverage for WGU," *Windsor Gay Unity Newsletter* 1 (June 1975): 4.]

June 16 ✳ Winnipeg ✳ Members of GFE presented a brief to a meeting of the Special Joint Committee on Immigration Policy.

[Gays for Equality (GFE) papers, 83–024, Canadian Lesbian and Gay Archives, Toronto.]

June 18 ✳ Regina ✳ Peter Millard of the Gay Community Centre of Saskatoon presented a brief to the Special Joint Committee on Immigration Policy. The brief called for the removal of all restrictions on gay people visiting or emigrating to Canada.

["Ignored Again," *Gay West*, no. 2 (1975), p. 5; Untitled news item, *Gay Community Centre of Saskatoon Newsletter*, September 1975, p. 2.]

June 24 ✳ Toronto ✳ John Damien was granted an appeal for reinclusion of major claims in his suit against the Ontario Racing Commission. Reversing Justice S.M. McBride's decision of June 11, Justice J. Lerner restored two important parts of Damien's claim — that he had been fired because he was a homosexual, and that he had been competent in his former position as a steward for the Ontario Racing Commission.

[C.B. (Chris Bearchell), "Round One to Damien," *Gay Rising* 1 (September 1975): 1–2; Robert Trow, "Damien Wins Preliminary Decision," *Body Politic*, no. 20 (1975), p. 5.]

June 25 ✳ Québec, Qué. ✳ Justice Minister Jérôme Choquette and Liberal members of the National Assembly's parliamentary Justice Committee, supported by the Créditistes, defeated a PQ amendment to Bill 50, the province's proposed Charter of Rights, that would have outlawed discrimination based on sexual orientation. Opposition members, particularly Robert Burns (PQ-Maisonneuve) and Jacques-Yvan Morin (PQ-Sauvé), protested the move, declaring that an impressive number of religious, social, legal, and

LE GAI QUÉBEC

Vol. 1 no. 1   Le 28 juin 1975, journée internationale Gaie.
NUMERO GRATUIT—FREE NUMBER.

" ET JE LE REPETE AVEC INSISTANCE,
LA SOLIDARITE EST UNE GRANDE CHOSE
QUI DONNE DE LA FORCE."

(EVA FOREST)

An issue of *Le gai Québec*, edited by Pierre Ducharme.

union organizations had supported the demands of the gay coalition fighting for the amendment. Choquette, however, stated that Québec society was not yet ready for such legal sanctions for homosexuals. The Charter was adopted July 7, 1975, without legal protection on the basis of sexual orientation, and came into effect June 28, 1976. The Charter was eventually amended to include sexual orientation on December 15, 1977, under a PQ government, when only two of the 110 members of the Assembly voted against the amendment. At that time Québec became the first Canadian province and the largest political jurisdiction in North America to provide legal protection for homosexuals.

[Frank Brayton, "Choquette Kills Gay Rights Amendment," *Body Politic*, no. 20 (1975), p. 6; Gilbert Brunet, "Droits et libertés de la personne" (editorial), *Le droit*, 11 July 1975, p. 6; Ron Dayman, "Quebec: Five Years of the Movement," *Body Politic*, no. 29 (1976–77), p. 22; "Editorial," *Gay-Zette* 2 (July 1975): 2; Gilles Gariepy, "Choquette refuse de protéger les homosexuels contre la discrimination," *La presse*, 26 June 1975, p. A6; Jacques Guay, "Le P.Q. tente en vain d'y inclure l'âge et les tendances sexuelles: Charte des droits de l'homme," *Le jour*, 26 June 1975, p. 4; "Liberals Reveal Narrow-Mindedness" (editorial), *Montreal Gay Times* 1 (August 1975): 4; "Liberals Veto Gay Rights Bid," *Montreal Gay Times* 1 (August 1975): 3; "Quebec Total of Homosexuals Put at 300,000," *Toronto Star*, four star ed., 7 July 1975, p. A5; Bernard Racine, "Le caucus libéral aurait refusé d'inclure l'orientation sexuelle: Charte des libertés de la personne," *Le droit*, 7 July 1975, p. 20; Stuart Russell and Michael Lynch, "Quebec: Gay Rights: Oui! Quebec Adds 'Sexual Orientation' to Human Rights Charter in Precedent-Setting Move," *Body Politic*, no. 40 (1978), pp. 4–5; Yvon Thivierge, "Gais québécois pas protégés," GO *Info* 2 (July–August 1975): 5.]

June 26 ✶ **Halifax** ✶ Robin Metcalfe of GAE presented a brief to a meeting of the Special Joint Committee on Immigration Policy.

[Gay Alliance for Equality (GAE) papers, 84–018, Canadian Lesbian and Gay Archives, Toronto.]

June 28 ✶ **Pointe-aux-Trembles, Qué.** ✶ The first issue of *Le gai Québec*, a bilingual monthly tabloid, was published. Edited by Pierre Ducharme, it ceased publication in December 1975, after seven issues.

["Quebec Gets Another Gay Paper," *Body Politic*, no. 20 (1975), p. 7.]

June 28–July 1 ✶ **Ottawa** ✶ The National Gay Rights Coalition/Coalition nationale pour les droits des homosexuels (NGRC/CNDH) was officially formed at the third national gay conference, organized by GO and held at the University of Ottawa. The event was the largest and most geographically representative meeting of lesbians and gays in Canada to that time. About 200 people took part in the conference, which included caucuses, workshops, street theatre, dances, and a demonstration on Parliament Hill (June 30). The 150 registered delegates, of whom only about twenty were women, represented almost every city in Canada, and many points of view. Growing divisions in the gay movement were evident, and at least five distinctive subgroupings were present: religious, service-oriented, rights-oriented, anarchist, and leftist. The groups were able to compromise, however, to reach a consensus on a ten-point programme for the NGRC/CNDH, which included the controversial recommendation to abolish all age-of-consent laws. The conference also voted to support other resolutions: to urge all gay organizations to take up the defence of John Damien; to send a message of support to Dr. Henry Morgentaler, commending his contributions to the struggle for women's rights, and calling for his release from prison; to support the struggle of gays in Québec; and to stage simultaneous demonstrations across Canada in the autumn of 1975 to protest anti-homosexual provisions in the federal Immigration Act. The issue of lesbian participation arose in a resolution, later adopted, which gave the Women's Caucus delegate status and established a person to act as a liaison to encourage lesbian participation in the NGRC/CNDH. As well, this was the first Canadian national conference in which delegates from Québec played a significant role; six groups from Montréal sent delegates, as did one group from Québec City. The NGRC/CNDH originally consisted of twenty-seven member groups and was to be coordinated by GO. Ron Dayman was named the first secretary of the group's national coordinating office. The NGRC/CNDH was renamed the Canadian Lesbian and Gay Rights Coalition/Coalition canadienne pour les droits des lesbiennes et gais (CLGRC/CCDLG) in 1978 and was active until June 1980.

[Chris Bearchall (sic), "Gay Views: National Gay Rights Conference," *Other Woman* 3 (October–November 1975): 12; "Canada's Gays Meet," *Windsor Gay Unity Newsletter* 1 (July 1975): 2; "La conférence des homosexuels mènera à une coalition nationale," *Le droit*, 30 June 1975, p. 3; "Conference: National Gay Conference, 3rd Annual, Ottawa, June 28–July 1, 1975" vertical file, Canadian Lesbian and Gay Archives, Toronto; George Crews, "Canada Coalition Forms," *Advocate* (Los Angeles), no. 169 (1975), pp. 8–9; "Crucial Issue Resolved," *Gay Tide* 2 (August 1975): 6; "Delegates Bury National Coalition as Movement Ponders New Tactics," *Body Politic*, no. 65 (1980), pp. 8–9; "Demands Taken to Public," *Gay Tide* 2 (August 1975): 7; Thérèse Faubert, "National Gay Rights Conference/Nationale pour les droits des homosexuels," *Le gai Québec* 1 (21 July 1975): 2–3; Maurice Flood, "Gay Liberation: Where It's At," *Gay Tide* 2 (August 1975): 8–9; Margaret Fulford, ed., *The Canadian Women's Movement, 1960–1990: A Guide to Archival Resources/Le mouvement canadien des femmes, 1960–1990: guide de ressources archivistiques* (Toronto: Canadian Women's Movement Archives/ECW Press, 1992), entries 24, 41; "Gay Unity: Waiting for Godot," *New Beginnings* 1 (27 July 1975): 1; "Gays Form Rights Group," *Ottawa Journal*, 2 July 1975, p. 17; Gays of Ottawa (GO) papers and inventory, 82–017, Canadian Lesbian and Gay Archives, Toronto; "Gays Seek Coalition: Third Annual Conference in Ottawa," *Ottawa Citizen*, 30 June 1975, p. 3; "Gays Want Uniformity in the Age of Consent," *Globe and Mail*, metro ed., 30 June 1975, p. 12; HALO Gay Rights Committee

(HGRC)," *Homophile Association of London, Ontario Newsletter* 2 (January 1975): 2–4; Peter Hadekel, "Gays Lash Out at News Media," *Ottawa Journal*, 30 June 1975, p. 1; "Homosexual Seeks Help to Sue Ex-bosses," *Toronto Star*, four star ed., 30 June 1975, p. A12; "Homosexuals Demand Rights," *Ottawa Citizen*, 2 July 1975, p. 2; "Homosexuals Demand Rights," *Ottawa Journal*, 2 July 1975, p. 9; "NGRC Demands," *Gay Tide* 2 (August 1975): 8–9; "National Coalition Formed," *Montreal Gay Times* 1 (August 1975): 4; "National Conference: Gays March on Hill," *Gay West*, no. 2 (1975), p. 3; "National Gay Rights Coalition Born," *Gay West*, no. 2 (1975), p. 8; "National Gay Rights Conference," *GO Info* 2 (April–May 1975): 6; "National Gay Rights Conference," special issue of *GO Info*, June 1975, 8 pp.; "National Gay Rights Conference," *Gay-Zette* 2 (July 1975): 3; "National Gay Rights Conference in Ottawa June 28–July 1," *Gay Times* 1 (June 1975): 3; "National Talks to Launch First Cross-Country Coalition," *Gay Rising* 1 (June 1975): 3; "Ottawa Conference 'Unqualified Success,' " *Montreal Gay Times* 1 (August 1975): 2; "Ottawa Sees Largest Gay Rights Congress," *Gay Tide* 2 (August 1975): 6–7; "Out of the Closets, into the Streets, Gay Rights Now!" *Homophile Association of London, Ontario Newsletter* 2 (July 1975): 4; Ken Popert, "Gay Rights Now!/Exigeons nos droits!" supplement to *Body Politic*, June 1975, 4 pp.; Ken Popert, "Third National Conference Launches Gay Rights Coalition," *Body Politic*, no. 20 (1975), pp. 3–5; Patrice Simister, "Gay Views: Gay Rights with Reservations," *Other Woman* 3 (October–November 1975): 13; Merv Walker, " 'Many Faces, One Focus': 4th Annual Conference Planned for Toronto," *Body Politic*, no. 26 (1976), p. 6; "The Weekend of June 28 to July 1 Marked the Happening of the Third National Gay Conference in Ottawa," *Gay Community Centre of Saskatoon Newsletter*, August 1975, p. 1.]

June 28–July 1 ∗ Ottawa ∗ The Canadian Gay Press Service was formed during the third national gay conference. Members of the Service were *The Body Politic* (Toronto), *Gay Times* (Montréal), *Gay West* (Saskatoon), and *Gay-Zette* (Montréal).

["Gay Press Service," *Gay Tide* 2 (August 1975): 11.]

Summer ∗ Calgary ∗ *The Calgary Herald* refused to print an advertisement for GIRC, reasoning that "the *Herald* is a family medium, and it's going to stay that way." *The Albertan*, the *Herald*'s major competitor, printed the ad without comment. GIRC sought the help of the Alberta Human Rights Commission and the Alberta Press Council, but to no avail.

["Gay Information Resources Calgary (GIRC)" vertical file, Canadian Lesbian and Gay Archives, Toronto; Ken Popert, "Gay Group Sues for Right to Advertise," *Body Politic*, no. 20 (1975), p. 6.]

Summer ∗ Ontario ∗ For the second summer in a row, Cora, a women's bookstore and resource centre on wheels, travelled around rural and small-town Ontario with the aim of helping women in smaller centres overcome isolation from the women's movement. In Orillia, the bookmobile was searched by police after a man complained it was distributing "pornography" such as *The Other Woman* and birth control and V.D. handbooks; no charges were laid.

["A Feminist Bookmobile Will Travel around Ontario," *Body Politic*, no. 18 (1975), pp. 8 (photo), 9; "Lies the CBC Told You," *Body Politic*, no. 21 (1975), p. 18; "News: Feminist Bookmobile Runs into Problems," *Long Time Coming* 3 (September 1975): 29.]

Summer * Ottawa * The management and employees of the Lord Elgin Hotel's bars attempted to discourage gay customers by barring obviously gay people and by imposing arbitrary dress codes. This led to a brief gay boycott of the hotel. The Lord Elgin's lounge (main floor) and tavern (downstairs) had been gay meeting places for years.

[Ian Maclennan, "Lord Elgin = Homophobia," GO *Info* 2 (July–August 1975): 4.]

Summer * Saskatoon * An Opportunities for Youth grant for $7,200 was awarded to the project "Community Understanding." Doug Hellquist, Ann Lawrence, Lesley Noton, and Doug Wilson were hired to produce educational material (mostly pamphlets) about gay lifestyles.

["The Gay Community Centre Has Received an Opportunities for Youth Grant from the Federal Government for the Sum of $7,200," *Gay Community Centre of Saskatoon Newsletter*, August 1975, p. 1; "OFY Grant for Saskatoon," *Gay West*, no. 2 (1975), p. 9; "Two Media Projects Win Government Funding," *Body Politic*, no. 19 (1975), p. 9.]

Summer * Toronto * At least sixty-two bathers were arrested for being nude in a public place at the gay beach at Hanlan's Point on the Toronto Islands. This was part of an apparent increase in arrests and incidents of harassment directed against the gay community by the Toronto police and morality squad.

[Gerald Hannon, "War on Sin Produces Gay Casualties,"*Body Politic*, no. 20 (1975), p. 8; "In Brief," GAY*tuk* 1 (Christmas 1975): 4; "Sunbathed Nude on Island, 5 Fined," *Toronto Star*, Saturday ed., 13 September 1975, p. A8.]

Summer * Toronto * An Opportunities for Youth grant for $6,610 was awarded to the project "About Gay People." Sue Ann Chousky, Peter Lancastle, Stephen Moyse, and Steve Quagliariello produced two thirty-minute video presentations about gay oppression, coming out, and lesbian and gay liberation in the Toronto area. The videos included interviews with delegates to the third national gay conference (June 28–July 1, 1975).

["Homosexual Film, Refurbished Rail Car, Two OFY Projects," *Globe and Mail*, metro ed., 21 June 1975, p. 5; "News: Gay Grants," *Esprit* 1 (October 1975): 2; "Two Media Projects Win Government Funding," *Body Politic*, no. 19 (1975), p. 9.]

Summer * Toronto * "Marxism from a Gay Perspective" was offered by the Marxist Institute, 200 Bedford Road, as part of its summer course series. The instructors included Walter Bruno and Tim McCaskell. The course was offered again (by McCaskell) during the autumn session.

["Marxist Institute of Toronto" vertical file, Canadian Lesbian and Gay Archives, Toronto; "Marxist Institute Offers Gay Course," *Body Politic*, no. 20 (1975), p. 7.]

Summer ∗ Toronto ∗ The Ontario Arts Council awarded grants totalling $3,500 to seven writers recommended by the writers' cooperative Catalyst. The writers were Gavin Dillard, Michael Higgins, Graham Jackson, E.A. Lacey, Wayne McNeill, Richard Phelan, and Ian Young.

["Grants for Gay Writers," *Body Politic*, no. 21 (1975), p. 5; "Money for Gay Writers," *Gay Tide* 3 (November 1975): 3.]

Summer ∗ Vancouver ∗ City police escalated a campaign of entrapment, surveillance, and intimidation of gay men, laying numerous charges against people caught cruising beaches, parks, and public washrooms.

["Police Entrapment on Upswing" (editorial), *Gay Tide* 2 (August 1975): 1.]

Summer ∗ Windsor, Ont. ∗ The Ritz Hotel Tavern, a mixed bar located at 88 Pitt Street E., became mostly gay after a series of successful gay dances were held there by WGU. This was the first gay bar in Windsor.

[Jim Monk, "Windsor: Bar Sparks Tensions in Gay Community," *Body Politic*, no. 23 (1976), p. 4; Zipp Zero, "Talk of the Town," *Windsor Gay Unity Newsletter* 1 (September 1975): 2.]

Summer ∗ Windsor, Ont. ∗ WGU opened a drop-in centre at 137 Park W., complete with a gayline and a library.

["Gay Drop-in Centre," *Windsor Gay Unity Newsletter* 1 (July 1975): 6; "Windsor Opens Drop-in Centre," *Body Politic*, no. 20 (1975), p. 11.]

July ∗ Montréal ∗ After a three-month search, the AHM/GMA found a home for its drop-in centre and library in an apartment at 6–3425, rue Peel. The group had been evicted from its rented premises in the wave of harassment leading up to the 1976 summer Olympics. AHM/GMA was forced to vacate the rue Peel premises in December 1975; by February 1976, the group had disbanded.

[John Blacklock, "Montreal: Olympic Circus Brings More Repression," *Body Politic*, no. 23 (1976), p. 6; "Gay Montreal Drop-in Centre Opens," *Body Politic*, no. 21 (1975), p. 7; Eric Hill, Letter, *Montreal Gay Times* 1 (December 1975): 18.]

July ∗ Montréal ∗ A proposal was drafted for a Gay Social Services Project to be operated under the Family Service Association at the Ville Marie Social Service Centre, 5 Weredale Park, Westmount. The Project would formalize the services to lesbians and gay men that the Family Service Association had been providing since 1973. It became operational by September 1975 and by mid-1976 had expanded through additional funding. The Project provided a variety of services to the anglophone gay community, including a gayline, individual and group counselling, community relations groups, a foster children's project, a gay youth group, and educational seminars. It was coordinated by Miriam Boghen and employed two gay social workers (Bruce Garside and Joanne Stitt) as well as about forty male and female volunteers recruited from the gay community. Although it was meant to serve all members of the community, there were some complaints early on that the Project was male-oriented and did not serve lesbians well.

["Association Offers Free Counselling," *Gay Times* 1 (April 1975): 4; John Blacklock, "Government Finances Gay Counselling Service," *Body Politic*, no. 24 (1976), p. 4; Ron Dayman, "Quebec: Five Years of the Movement," *Body Politic*, no. 29 (1976–77), p. 21; "Gay Lines from The Gay Social Services Project . . . ," brochure, (1976), 6 pp., Canadian Lesbian and Gay Archives, Toronto; Terry Last, "Ville Marie Social Service Centre Works for Gay Counselling," *Montreal Gay Times* 1 (December 1975): 9; Jackie Manthorne, "FSA Says No to Lesbians," *Long Time Coming* 3 (April–May 1976): 12–14; Stuart Russell, "Montreal: Gay Social Services Project," *Body Politic*, no. 31 (1977), p. 6.]

July * Montréal * André Roy's book of poetry *Vers mauve* was published by Herbes rouges.

[Roger Chamberland, "*N'importe quelle page* et autres recueils de poésies d'André Roy," in *Dictionnaire des oeuvres littéraires du Québec*, ed. Maurice Lemire et al., vol. 5 (1970–75) (Montréal: Fides, 1987), pp. 594–96.]

July * Toronto * MCC opened the Gay Community Services Centre at 20 Trinity Square with the establishment of a drop-in centre and the continuation of its personal counselling service phone line.

["Gay Center: Its (sic) Coming," *Metro Community News* 2 (June 1975): 1; "Gay Services Center — We're Here!" *Metro Community News* 2 (18 July 1975): 5; "MCC Starts Counselling Service," *Body Politic*, no. 20 (1975), p. 11.]

July * Vancouver * SEARCH opened a community services centre at 301–1367 Richards Street in space donated by the Play Pen Club. From there the group sponsored an information service on counselling and legal assistance, a drop-in, community education seminars and discussions, a gay Alcoholics Anonymous meeting, the Have a Gay Stay housing service, and a newsletter.

["SEARCH Opens Office," *Gay Tide* 2 (August 1975): 11; "Society for Education Action Research and Counselling on Homosexuality (SEARCH)" vertical file, Canadian Lesbian and Gay Archives, Toronto.]

July 2 * Burnaby, B.C. * A lesbian drop-in group began meeting at the Women's Centre at Simon Fraser University.

["Lesbian Drop-in," *Peak* (Simon Fraser Univ.), *Gay Supplement*, 9 July 1975, p. 1.]

July 3 ✳ Montréal ✳ Labyris Montreal (formerly Montreal Gay Women) officially opened its new drop-in centre at 4391, rue Laval with a potluck supper. About thirty women attended. By August 1975, Labyris had eighty-two members, but on August 19 the group's centre was destroyed by fire. Arson was suspected. The group met temporarily at the Women's Information and Referral Centre, 3595, rue St. Urbain. Labyris Montreal did not easily recover, as members drifted away. By the spring of 1976 the group was almost dormant and in July 1976 changed its name to Gay Women of Montreal — Labyris.

["Labyris," *Le gai Québec* 1 (21 July 1975): 4; "Labyris Holds Dance, Prepares Centre," *Gay Times* 1 (June 1975): 2; "Labyris Is Almost Dead: News in Brief," *Montreal Gay Times* 2 (Spring 1976): 6; "Labyris Montreal" vertical file, Canadian Lesbian and Gay Archives, Toronto; "Labyris Women's Centre Burned Out," *Montreal Gay Times* 1 (September 1975): 7; Janet MacDonald, "New Labyris Center Opens," *Montreal Gay Times* 1 (August 1975): 5; "News: Labyris Burnt Out," *Long Time Coming* 3 (September 1975): 27; "News: Labyris Montreal Reopens," *Long Time Coming* 3 (July 1975): 34; "News: Montreal Gay Women Open New Center," *Esprit* 1 (October 1975): 2.]

July 4–7 ✳ Winnipeg ✳ A Gay Caucus was formed at the national NDP convention, held at the Winnipeg Convention Centre and attended by more than 1,600 delegates. The Gay Caucus campaigned for the election of Harold B. Desmarais of WGU, who was running for the NDP Federal Council on a gay rights platform (he was unsuccessful), and launched a campaign to mobilize support for gay rights resolutions in the NDP.

["Gay Rights and the NDP," *Windsor Gay Unity Newsletter* 1 (July 1975): 3; Stuart Russell, "NDP Gay Caucus Launched," *Body Politic*, no. 20 (1975), p. 9.]

July 9 ✳ Burnaby, B.C. ✳ *The Peak*, a student newspaper at Simon Fraser University, published a special gay supplement. The four-page insert, prepared by Gay People of SFU, included articles by gay students, faculty, and Vancouver gays covering many aspects of the gay experience.

["Student Paper Publishes Gay Supplement," *Body Politic*, no. 20 (1975), p. 9.]

July 21 ✳ Ottawa ✳ Justice Minister Otto Lang introduced Bill C-72, The Canadian Human Rights Act, in the House of Commons. The Bill would establish an Ottawa-based Canadian Human Rights Commission to fight discrimination in areas under federal jurisdiction. Discrimination based on sexual orientation would not be covered by the Commission. (See also July 31, 1975.)

[Ron Dayman, "Gays Ignored Again!" GO *Info* 2 (July–August 1975): 2; "Federal Code Ignores Gays," *Montreal Gay Times* 1 (August 1975): 3; "Human Rights Commission Bill Would Bar Bias, Make Records Public," *Globe and Mail*, first ed., 22 July 1975, pp. 1–2; Don Sellar, "Human Rights Legislation Target: Discrimination in Federal Sphere," *Ottawa Citizen*, 22 July 1975, pp. 1, 4.]

July 21–September 26 * Ottawa * GO was awarded a grant for $4,485 from the Secretary of State under the Student Community Services Program to fund Project Community Outreach. The project was designed to help educate people in the Ottawa area about homosexuality and to conduct seminars about GO and the gay community for local social service agencies. Ron Dayman, Ian Maclennan, Marie Robertson, and Greg Spurgeon participated in the project, which included the production of the bilingual booklet *Understanding Homophobia/Pour bien comprendre l'homophobie*. On September 4, Project Community Outreach held a public forum on homosexuality at the Ottawa Public Library Auditorium.

["Activists Win Grant," *Gay Tide* 2 (August 1975): 5; Ron Dayman, "Government Grant for Gay Education," *Body Politic*, no. 21 (1975), p. 5; "$4,485 Given to Tell Public about Gay Life," *Globe and Mail*, metro ed., 1 August 1975, p. 4; "The Public Fears Gays, Forum Told," *Ottawa Journal*, 5 September 1975, p. 26; Greg Spurgeon, "GO Receives Govt. Grant," GO *Info* 2 (July–August 1975): 2.]

July 23 * New Westminster, B.C. * Members of GATE (Vancouver) participated in a picket organized by the Prisoners' Union Committee in support of striking inmates at the penitentiary in New Westminster. The inmates were on strike to demand recognition of a prisoners' union and the right to collective bargaining. GATE (Vancouver) supported sexual rights for prisoners, particularly the right of conjugal visits from wives or lovers.

["For a Prisoners' Union," *Gay Tide* 2 (August 1975): 5.]

July 31 * Ottawa * GO announced the launching of a public campaign to press for the protection of lesbians and gay men under the Canadian Human Rights Commission proposed in Bill C-72, given first reading in the House of Commons on July 21, 1975.

[GO press release, 31 July 1975, Gays of Ottawa/Gays d'Ottawa (GO) vertical file, Canadian Lesbian and Gay Archives, Toronto.]

August * Calgary * At a Western Canada Policy Conference of Progressive Conservative Youth, delegate Wayne Madden introduced a resolution calling for an end to the exclusion of gay people from Canada under the Immigration Act. The resolution was passed at the committee stage but met with a tie vote in the full conference, and was thus defeated.

["Gay Resolution Ties Young P.C.s," *Body Politic*, no. 21 (1975), p. 5.]

August * Montréal * The female manager of Baby Face Disco was accused of physically assaulting patrons of the bar on several occasions. At this time,

Baby Face was the sole women-only bar in Montréal.

["News: Violence at Babyface," *Long Time Coming* 3 (September 1975): 27.]

August ∗ Pointe-aux-Trembles, Qué. ∗ A group for gay Mormons called Groupe Mormon gai/Gay Mormon Group was in operation.

["Montréal: Églises-Churches," *Le gai Québec* 1 (12 August 1975): 5.]

August ∗ Saint John, N.B. ∗ The gay helpline Speak Easy was in operation, with D.R. Reardon acting as one of the coordinators.

["Speak Easy" vertical file, Canadian Lesbian and Gay Archives, Toronto.]

August 11 ∗ Vancouver ∗ Members of GATE (Vancouver) marched under their own banner in a demonstration of 150 people demanding the release of Dr. Henry Morgentaler. The march was organized by the Vancouver office of the Canadian Association for the Repeal of Abortion Laws (CARAL).

["Gays Back Morgentaler," *Gay Tide* 3 (November 1975): 4.]

August 15 ∗ Toronto ∗ Ron Dayman and Charles Hill of GO appeared before the Ontario Press Council to present a complaint against the *Ottawa Citizen* regarding its coverage of the "Ottawa Sex Scandal" in March 1975. GO complained that the paper had engaged in an anti-homosexual witch-hunt, using sensational and irresponsible reporting and terms like "vice ring" to create a rumour mill of national proportions. On December 12, 1975, the Council ruled that the *Citizen* had not given undue prominence to the reporting of charges laid in the "Ottawa Sex Scandal."

[Ron Dayman, "Show Trials Continue," *Body Politic*, no. 21 (1975), pp. 3–4; Ron Dayman, "Witch Hunt Extends to Court," *Body Politic*, no. 19 (1975), p. 9; Charles Hill papers, 82–015/01 and /03, Canadian Lesbian and Gay Archives, Toronto; "Male Prostitute Stories Cleared by Press Council," *Toronto Star*, four star ed., 12 December 1975, p. A13; Russell Mills, "Closed Courts, Secret Justice: Naming Names (Revisited)," *Ottawa Citizen*, 13 December 1975, p. 6; "Press Council Decision," GO *Info* 2 (November–December 1975): 10; "Press Council Supports Witchhunt," *Body Politic*, no. 22 (1976), p. 7.]

August 15 ∗ Toronto ∗ Michael Riordon lodged a complaint with the Ontario Press Council against the *Toronto Star*, accusing the paper of publishing a letter to the editor written by him but with substantial alterations of content. The original letter had criticized the *Star* for its continuing prejudice against gay people; when it appeared in the paper's "Voice of the People" section on February 28, 1975, the criticisms of and references to the *Star* were deleted without acknowledgement. The complaint was later dismissed by the Council.

["Criticism of *Star* Rejected: Press Council," *Toronto Star*, four star ed., 16 September 1975, pp. A1–A2; "Gay Letter-Writer Tackles Newspaper Distortions," *Body Politic*, no.

20 (1975), p. 7; "Press Council Rejects Complaint," *Body Politic*, no. 21 (1975), p. 5.]

August 19 ✶ Ottawa ✶ Marie Robertson and Ron Dayman of GO met with the Ottawa Board of Control to present the brief "Civil Rights of Homosexuals in City Employment" and to make an oral presentation calling for a ruling barring discrimination based on sexual orientation in the employment of municipal workers. Mayor Lorry Greenberg said that the city solicitor and personnel department would examine the brief. After much delay the matter was sent before the full city council for consideration and on April 5, 1976, Ottawa became the second Canadian city to officially ban discrimination based on sexual orientation in municipal employment.

["City of Ottawa Bans Gay Discrimination," *Gay Rising* 2 (April 1976): 1; "GO Continues Municipal Efforts," *Body Politic*, no. 21 (1975), p. 6; "GO Presses for Civic Rights," *Body Politic*, no. 19 (1975), p. 9; "Jobs Open to Gays," *Ottawa Citizen*, 30 April 1975, p. 3; "Ottawa Considers Non-discrimination Motion," *Gay Times* 1 (May 1975): 4; "Rights Move Ahead in Ottawa," *Advocate* (Los Angeles), no. 169 (1975), p. 5.]

August 22–23 ✶ Montréal ✶ A large community dance entitled Gay Dance Party was held at 57, rue Prince Arthur. It was privately sponsored by Outrageous Sound.

["Gay Dances Again in Montreal," *Montreal Gay Times* 1 (September 1975): 7.]

August 31 ✶ London, Ont. ✶ HALO sponsored a fundraising dinner for John Damien, which was attended by about ninety people. Damien, who was fired from his job with the Ontario Racing Commission for being gay, addressed the gathering and was given a standing ovation.

["Damien Benefit," HALO *Grapevine* 2 (August 1975): 7.]

August 31 ✶ Windsor, Ont. ✶ WGU hosted a convention of the Steering Committee of CGRO to discuss strategies in approaching candidates during the campaign for the September 18 Ontario provincial election. (See also September 1975.)

["Coalition for Gay Rights in Ontario," *Windsor Gay Unity Newsletter* 1 (August 1975): 2–3.]

September ✶ Ontario ✶ During the campaign leading up to the September 18 provincial election six NDP MPPS (Ted Bounsall, Michael Cassidy, Pat Lawlor, Stephen Lewis, Ross McClellan, and David Warner) declared their support for amending the Ontario Human Rights Code to include protection based on sexual orientation. Margaret Campbell (Lib.-St. George) also made public statements supporting gay rights. CGRO had produced an updated ten-page brief, "The Homosexual Minority in Ontario," which it sent to all sitting members of the Legislature, and to newly elected members after the election. As well, "Toward Equality," a pamphlet containing CGRO's list of demands, was sent with a covering letter to all candidates in the election. (See also September 13, 1975.)

[W.B. (Walter Bruno), "Who Will Speak for Gays?" *Gay Rising* 1 (September 1975): 4; "Dress Rehearsal" (editorial), *Body Politic*, no. 21 (1975), p. 2; Edward Jackson, "Ontario Coalition Plans Rights March," *Body Politic*, no. 20 (1975), pp. 8–9; Ken Popert, "Election Campaign Yields Gains," *Body Politic*, no. 21 (1975), p. 3; M.R. (Michael Riordon), "Decision for Gays Sept. 18," *Gay Rising* 1 (September 1975): 1–2; I.T. (Ian Turner), "Seven Pro-gay MPPs Elected to Queen's Park," *Gay Rising* 1 (November 1975): 3; Tom Warner, "Dress Rehearsal" (letter), *Body Politic*, no. 22 (1976), p. 2; J.W. (John Wilson), "No Gay Votes for Tories!" *Gay Rising* 1 (September 1975): 3.]

September ✳ Ottawa ✳ Members of GO received a letter from Justice Minister Otto Lang in reply to their query concerning sexual orientation and the proposed Canadian Human Rights Act. Lang indicated that the legislation would exclude gays from protection.

[Ron Dayman, "Lang Replies," GO *Info* 2 (September–October 1975): 2; Connie Harris, "Lang Rejects Gay Protections," *Body Politic*, no. 21 (1975), p. 6.]

September ✳ Toronto ✳ A chapter of the Gay Academic Union (GAU) was officially formed at the University of Toronto. The first executive included Albert Gedraitis, John Alan Lee, Vicky Pullam, and R.T. Wallace. Dorothy Broderick and John Alan Lee had acted as Canadian contacts with the GAU in New York since 1974. An organizing committee (including Barry Adam, Clarence Barnes, John Alan Lee, Michael Lynch, and Jim Quixley) met in May 1975 to formulate goals, which included the "creation of a visible gay presence on campus, an end to discrimination on the basis of sexual orientation or gender, the promotion of gay studies and the improvement of library holdings on gay subjects." The Toronto GAU was seen as an independent group with fraternal ties to the GAU in the United States.

["Academics Organize," *Gay Tide* 2 (August 1975): 11; "Canadian Gay Academics Planning National Body," *Body Politic*, no. 19 (1975), p. 9; Mike Edwards, "U. of T. Academic Union Starts to Fight Discrimination," *Varsity* (Univ. of Toronto), 15 October 1975, p. 3; Margaret Fulford, ed., *The Canadian Women's Movement, 1960–1990: A Guide to Archival Resources/Le mouvement canadien des femmes, 1960–1990: guide de ressources archivistiques* (Toronto: Canadian Women's Movement Archives/ECW Press, 1992), entry 519; "Gay Academic Union," GAY*tuk* 1 (October 1975): 14; "Gay Academic Union (Toronto)" vertical file, Canadian Lesbian and Gay Archives, Toronto; "Gay Academic Union to End Sexism in School," *Metro Community News* 2 (October 1975): 1; John A. Lee, "Gay Academic Union: Toronto Group Forms," *Metro Community News* 2 (30 May 1975): 1; "News: Gay Academic Union Formed," *Long Time Coming* 3 (October 1975): 23; "Towards Gay Education," *Body Politic*, no. 21 (1975), p. 4.]

September ✳ Toronto ✳ The Ontario Human Rights Commission (OHRC) refused to investigate John Damien's complaint against the Ontario Racing

Commission on the grounds that it did not deal with cases related to sexual orientation. The OHRC maintained that the word "sex" in the Code referred to gender only. This was in contradiction to the OHRC's agreement in March 1974 that it would investigate and mediate individual, well-documented complaints of discrimination based on sexual orientation. The Commission, however, was willing to hear a submission from Harry Kopyto, Damien's lawyer. (See also October 24 and December 5, 1975.)

["Legal Jockeying Begins in Damien Discrimination Case," *Body Politic*, no. 19 (1975), p. 7; "News," *Montreal Gay Times* 1 (November 1975): 3–4; "OHRC Reneges," *Body Politic*, no. 20 (1975), p. 11; "OHRC Yawns at Discrimination," *Body Politic*, no. 14 (1974), p. 6; "Once and for All" (editorial), *Body Politic*, no. 22 (1976), p. 2; Ken Popert, "Damien: Central Issue Posed," *Body Politic*, no. 21 (1975), p. 6.]

September ∗ Toronto ∗ The University of Toronto Graduate Teaching Assistants Association included a clause banning discrimination in employment based on sexual orientation in its contract demands.

["University Employees Ask for Ban on Gay Discrimination," *Body Politic*, no. 22 (1976), p. 6.]

September 13 ∗ Toronto ∗ A gay rights march was organized by CGRO to demand the reinstatement of John Damien and the inclusion of a sexual orientation clause in the Ontario Human Rights Code. The 250–300 people who marched from Queen's Park to City Hall were addressed by more than a dozen speakers, including John Damien. Although almost one-third of the marchers were women, Chris Bearchell of GATE (Toronto) and the Committee to Defend John Damien was the only female speaker. The march was not reported in Toronto's mainstream media. This event was part of CGRO's preparations for the September 18 Ontario provincial election.

["CGRO March," *Gay Tide* 3 (November 1975): 3; "The Gay Blade Is Tempered" (editorial), *Gay Rising* 1 (November 1975): 2; "Gay Rights," *Metro Community News* 2 (September 1975): 3; "Gay Rights Demonstration," *Other Woman* 3 (October–November 1975): 12; "Gay Rights Demonstration in Toronto," *Labor Challenge*, 22 September 1975, p. 2; " 'Gayhound' for Gay Rights," GO *Info* 2 (September–October 1975): 1, 6; M.L.H., "News Flash. Date Line Toronto, Sat. 13 Sept. 75," *New Beginnings* 1 (19 September 1975): 9; Edward Jackson, "Ontario Coalition Plans Rights March," *Body Politic*, no. 20 (1975), pp. 8–9; Caitlin Kelly, "Gays Rally for Rights," *Varsity* (Univ. of Toronto), 15 September 1975, p. 1; Gary Kinsman, "Gays, Women and All Workers Unite!" *Old Mole* (RMG, Toronto), October 1975, p. 7; "News: Gay Rights March," *Long Time Coming* 3 (October 1975): 22; Ken Popert, "Election Campaign Yields Gains," *Body Politic*, no. 21 (1975), p. 3; "Successful Gay Rights March in Toronto," *Montreal Gay Times* 1 (November 1975): 20.]

September 19 ∗ Vancouver ∗ Twenty women and men picketed the offices of the *Vancouver Sun* to protest the *Sun*'s reprinting on September 15 of a

Doug Wilson, 1975.
Photo by Gerald Hannon.

pro-family, anti-gay article by conservative Columbia University psychiatrist Herbert Hendin. The article had originally appeared in the *New York Times*. The protest was organized by GATE (Vancouver).

[Herbert Hendion (sic), "Homosexuality and the Family," *Vancouver Sun*, four star ed., 15 September 1975, p. 5; "*Sun* at It Again," *Gay Tide* 3 (November 1975): 4.]

September 22 ⋆ Saskatoon ⋆ Doug Wilson, a graduate student in the Department of Educational Foundations at the University of Saskatchewan, was told by James Kirkpatrick, dean of the university's College of Education, that he would not be allowed to go into the school system to supervise practice teachers because of his public involvement with the gay liberation movement. At that time, Wilson was the first vice-president of the Gay Community Centre of Saskatoon and had been trying to start a gay academic union at the university. Although he was qualified to do the job, Wilson was disqualified solely on the basis of his sexual orientation. Wilson protested, but the decision was upheld by University of Saskatchewan president R.W. Begg. Members of the Department of Educational Foundations immediately protested the decision and a Committee to Defend Doug Wilson was established. The Wilson case generated much support from groups and organizations in Saskatchewan (and elsewhere) and considerable coverage in the media. (See also October, October 2, 3–5, 7, 9, 11–13, 18, 19, 22, 23, 25, 30, and November 9, 1975.)

["The Committee to Defend Doug Wilson," GCCS *Newsletter*, October 1975, p. 1; "Committee to Defend Doug Wilson" vertical file, Canadian Lesbian and Gay Archives, Toronto; "Convocation Protested," *Sheaf* (Univ. of Saskatchewan), 28 October 1975, p. 1; Jim Duggleby, "Begg Supports Decision to Limit Homosexual Teacher," *Saskatoon Star-Phoenix*, 1 October 1975, p. 3; Jim Duggleby, "Organizations Deny Support Given to Wilson Group," *Saskatoon Star-Phoenix*, 13 November 1975, p. 22; Jim Duggleby, "U. of S. Restricts Lecturer," *Saskatoon Star-Phoenix*, 30 September 1975, p. 3; Jim Duggleby, "Wilson Committee Issues Apology," *Saskatoon Star-Phoenix*, 21 November 1975, p. 25; Doug Hellquist, "Discrimination: A Teacher Fights Back," *Body Politic*, no. 21 (1975), p. 1; "Join Us" (editorial), *Body Politic*, no. 21 (1975), p. 2; Peter Millard, "Assault on the Ivory Tower: Doug Wilson vs. the University of Saskatchewan," *Body Politic*, no. 24 (1976), pp. 12–13; Chris Mushka, "Wilson Declared Unfit to Supervise," *Sheaf* (Univ. of Saskatchewan), 26 September 1975, p. 1; "Saskatchewan U. Head Backs Barring Deviate from Education Post," *Toronto Star*, four star ed., 2 October 1975, p. A6; Don Thomson, "College Dean Discriminates," *Sheaf* (Univ. of Saskatchewan), 30 September 1975, p. 1; "University Bans Gay Teacher as Supervisor," *Globe and Mail*, metro ed., 2 October 1975, p. 16; Judy Varga, "Wilson Petition Gains Support," *Sheaf* (Univ. of Saskatchewan), 17 October 1975, p. 1; Doug Wilson papers, 93–053, Canadian Lesbian and Gay Archives, Toronto; Bob Wolfe, "Going Public: Doug Wilson's Human Issue Becomes a Public Issue in Saskatoon," *Esprit* 2 (January 1976): 22–23.]

September 24 * Toronto * The first issue of *Esprit* (October), a national monthly magazine for gay men and lesbians, was published in an edition of 10,000 copies. Published by George Hislop and Peter Maloney and edited by Mary Axten, *Esprit* was an ambitious seventy-two-page, general-interest magazine. Its intention was "to present to the gay community, and to the community at large, a positive perspective of people who are going places and doing things, who are sometimes gay and sometimes not." *Esprit* folded in January 1976, after three issues. (See also October 9, 1975.)

["*Esprit*," *Metro Community News* 2 (October 1975): 3; "*Esprit*: A Negative Perspective," GAY*tuk* 1 (28 January 1976): 2; K.B.G., "Mary Axten: *Esprit*," *Metro Community News* 2 (10 October 1975): 1, 3; Gary Kinsman, *The Regulation of Desire: Sexuality in Canada* (Montréal: Black Rose Books, 1987), p. 184; Robert Martin, "Canada's First Gay Magazine, *Esprit*, Aimed at Both Sexes," *Globe and Mail*, metro ed., 25 September 1975, p. 15; "New Publication Appears," *Body Politic*, no. 21 (1975), p. 7.]

Autumn * Halifax * The Alternate Book Shop opened at 1585 Barrington Street, Suite 301. Operated by Tom Burns, secretary of GAE, it was the first gay bookstore in Atlantic Canada.

[Robin Metcalfe, "Liberation through Education," *Body Politic*, no. 21 (1975), p. 4.]

Autumn * Montréal * The Club Montreal baths opened at 173, rue Ste. Catherine E.

[Advertisement, *Montreal Gay Times* 1 (September 1975): inside back cover.]

Autumn * Saskatchewan * Three NDP constituency associations passed motions requesting that the government include a sexual orientation clause in the provincial Human Rights Code. The motions were passed on for discussion at the NDP convention to be held in Saskatoon in November. The Saskatchewan Young New Democrats also indicated their support for the inclusion of sexual orientation in human rights legislation.

["Support from New Democrats in Saskatchewan," *Body Politic*, no. 21 (1975), p. 7.]

Autumn * Saskatoon * Neil Richards, a member of the Gay Community Centre of Saskatoon, became the first openly gay person to be appointed to the constituency executive and the sixteen-member Metro Council of the NDP in Saskatoon.

["NDP in Saskatoon Promotes Open Gay," *Body Politic*, no. 21 (1975), p. 7.]

Autumn * Toronto * Toronto Area Gays (TAG) was organized, with the intent of sponsoring counselling of lesbians and gays through a phone line as well as informal drop-ins. The first phone call on TAG's gayline was taken on January 29, 1976.

[Margaret Fulford, ed., *The Canadian Women's Movement, 1960–1990: A Guide to*

LESBIAN AND GAY LIBERATION IN CANADA 1975

Archival Resources/Le mouvement canadien des femmes, 1960–1990: guide de ressources archivistiques (Toronto: Canadian Women's Movement Archives/ECW Press, 1992), entry 497; David Gibson, "Toronto: Homosexual? Feeling Isolated? We're Here to Listen," *Body Politic*, no. 23 (1976), p. 6; Harvey and Stan, "Care to Share?" *Body Politic*, no. 25 (1976), p. 2; "New Gay Phoneline," *Body Politic*, no. 21 (1975), p. 7; Peter Zorzi, *What We Did, and Why We Did It: From the Cheap Seats at the Revolution. A Monologue on TAG in the 1970s, with Entertaining Supplementary Harangues* (Toronto: The Author, 1990), 168 pp.]

Autumn ⋆ Vernon, B.C. ⋆ A gay drop-in and sexuality workshop for men and women was held; it was organized through the Women's Centre and North Okanagan Aid (NOA).

[Advertisement, *Pedestal: A Lesbian-Feminist Newspaper* 7 (October–November 1975): 24.]

Autumn-Winter ⋆ Mississauga, Ont. ⋆ Gays of Mississauga was organized by Elgin Blair. The group was later renamed Gay Equality Mississauga (GEM).

[Elgin Blair papers, 85–003, Canadian Lesbian and Gay Archives, Toronto; "New Group Formed," *Body Politic*, no. 22 (1976), p. 7.]

October ⋆ Halifax ⋆ GAE was reorganized and revitalized after almost a year of inactivity. Regular meetings were held at MOVE, a coalition of citizen's groups, at 1712 Argyle Street. By November, a volunteer telephone gayline was established.

[Robin Metcalfe, "Halifax: Movement Aids Gay Community Development," *Body Politic*, no. 23 (1976), p. 4.]

October ⋆ Peterborough, Ont. ⋆ A discreet lesbian group known as the "Women" was formed at Trent University. It was a social group and sponsored informal meetings, discussions, and parties. In September 1976 it reorganized to form the Trent Homophile Association (THA).

[Margaret Fulford, ed., *The Canadian Women's Movement, 1960–1990: A Guide to Archival Resources/Le mouvement canadien des femmes, 1960–1990: guide de ressources archivistiques* (Toronto: Canadian Women's Movement Archives/ECW Press, 1992), entries 511, 547, 1087; "Gay Organization Re-groups," *Peterborough Common Press* 2 (14 September 1976): 10; "Homosexuals Form Social Association," *Peterborough Examiner*, 8 December 1976, p. 3; "Lesbian Group (Peterborough) 1975–76" vertical file, Canadian Lesbian and Gay Archives, Toronto.]

October ⋆ Saskatoon ⋆ Peter Millard and others attempted to form a gay academic union at the University of Saskatchewan in the wake of the Doug Wilson affair. On January 27, 1976, a meeting of the University of Saskatchewan Gay Academic Union was held at which Millard, a professor of English at the university, was elected president. Jim Avandt, Neil Richards, and Doug Wilson were elected to the executive.

[Doug Hellquist, "Academic Group Elects First Officers," *Body Politic*, no. 23 (1976), p. 3; "Ignorance Promotes Formation of Union," *Sheaf* (Univ. of Saskatchewan), 23 January 1976, p. 3; "Union for Gays or Bi-sexuals Suggested," *Sheaf* (Univ. of Saskatchewan), 17 October 1975, p. 3.]

October ＊ Toronto ＊ *The Body Politic* was refused a grant from the Ontario Arts Council, reportedly due to its low standards of writing, editing, and graphic design.

["Arts Council Refuses Grant," *Body Politic*, no. 21 (1975), p. 7.]

October ＊ Toronto ＊ A Symposium on Sexual Preference and Sexual Identity was sponsored by the Department of Psychiatric Education at the University of Toronto. During a discussion of homosexuality as an alternate lifestyle, Dr. Vivian Rakoff, the Symposium's organizer, revealed that he had originally planned to have an additional discussion of homosexuality as a psychopathology but could not find anyone interested in making such a presentation.

["Shrinks Regain Sanity," *Body Politic*, no. 21 (1975), p. 7.]

October ＊ Waterloo, Ont. ＊ The issue of gay rights was raised at the annual convention of the Ontario Federation of Labour. Guelph Gay Equality (formerly the UGHA) distributed 800 leaflets; resolutions to support the inclusion of a sexual orientation clause in the Ontario Human Rights Code and to support John Damien never reached the floor.

["OFL Convention," *Body Politic*, no. 22 (1976), p. 5.]

October 2 ＊ Saskatoon ＊ At a rally of 300–400 people in support of Doug Wilson, MLA Paul Mostoway (NDP-Saskatoon-Centre) pledged his support for gay rights and said that he would work towards the inclusion of sexual orientation in provincial human rights legislation. This was the largest gay rights rally held in Canada to that time.

[Jim Duggleby, "Student, U. of S. Say Publicity Cause for Restriction," *Saskatoon Star-Phoenix*, 2 October 1975, p. 3; Doug Hellquist, "Discrimination: A Teacher Fights Back," *Body Politic*, no. 21 (1975), p. 1; "Rally Supports Homosexual in Job Dispute," *Toronto Star*, four star ed., 3 October 1975, p. A12; "Saskatoon: 400 Rally in Defence of Teacher," *Gay Tide* 3 (November 1975): 1.]

October 3–5 ＊ Waterloo, Ont. ＊ The first Canadian men's liberation conference was held at the University of Waterloo. More than 150 participants attended a workshop on men and homosexuality, during which a resolution was passed to support the inclusion of a sexual orientation clause in the Ontario Human Rights Code. The conference also expressed solidarity with Doug Wilson.

[Harvey Hamburg, "Men's Liberation Support Gays," *Body Politic*, no. 21 (1975), p. 5; Bill Robinson, "Men and Liberation," *Other Woman* 4 (December 1975–January 1976): 8, 22; Elliott Sokoloff, "First Men's Liberation Conference Promising," *Montreal Gay Times* 1 (December 1975): 7.]

October 7 * Saskatoon * The Saskatchewan Association on Human Rights called for changes in provincial human rights legislation to prohibit discrimination based on sexual orientation. The Association cited the case of Doug Wilson as an example of discrimination faced by gay people.

["Prohibition of Discrimination on Sex Orientation Basis Urged," *Saskatoon Star-Phoenix*, 7 October 1975, p. 3.]

October 7 * Saskatoon * In response to the Doug Wilson case, *The Sheaf*, a student newspaper at the University of Saskatchewan, published "*Sheaf* Gay Special," a four-page supplement dealing exclusively with gay liberation. Members of the Gay Community Centre of Saskatoon were involved in its production.

[Doug Hellquist, "Discrimination: A Teacher Fights Back," *Body Politic*, no. 21 (1975), p. 1; "*Sheaf* Gay Special," *Sheaf* (Univ. of Saskatchewan), 7 October 1975, 4 pp.]

October 9 * Toronto * Mary Axten, editor of *Esprit*, was interviewed by Helen Worthington in the *Toronto Star* as part of the "Women of Our Times" series on the changing roles of women in society.

[Helen Worthington, "Lesbian Feels Way of Life Right for Her," *Toronto Star*, four star ed., 9 October 1975, p. E3.]

October 9 * Vancouver * Doug Wilson spoke about his case before a public meeting of fifty people at Fisherman's Hall, sponsored by GATE (Vancouver).

[" 'Gay' Graduate Demands Reinstatement," *Vancouver Sun*, four star ed., 10 October 1975, p. 31.]

October 9–December 11 * Toronto * Professor of sociology John Alan Lee offered a gay studies course, "The Gay Experience: A Sociological Perspective," through the University of Toronto's School of Continuing Studies.

["Gay Studies at University of Toronto," *Body Politic*, no. 20 (1975), p. 9; "Gay Studies Course," *Metro Community News* 2 (October 1975): 13; "Sexual Identity Course," *Metro Community News* 2 (September 1975): 3.]

October 11–13 * Saskatoon * The first National Gay Community Services Conference was held, sponsored by the Gay Community Centre of Saskatoon. Delegates representing gay organizations from Montréal to the west coast met to discuss how community services and education should relate to gay men and lesbians. The conference passed a resolution supporting the reinstatement of Doug Wilson.

[John Argue, "Community Services Conference Held," *Body Politic*, no. 21 (1975), p. 7; "Conference: National Gay Community Services Conf., Saskatoon, October 11–13, 1975" vertical file, Canadian Lesbian and Gay Archives, Toronto; "Gay Community Seeks Assistance of Agencies," *Saskatoon Star-Phoenix*, 14 October 1975, p. 33; "National Gay Community Backs Wilson's Protest on Restriction," *Saskatoon Star-Phoenix*, 14 October 1975, p. 37; "National Gay Services Conference," *Montreal Gay Times* 1 (November 1975): 19; "News: National Gay Community Services Conference," *Long Time Coming* 3 (October 1975): 22.]

October 17 ✳ Montréal ✳ Five gay bars (The Lime Light, Le Mystique, P.J.'s, Le Rocambole, and Au Taureau d'Or) were raided by police. This was part of a series of police raids designed to drive gay people from downtown bars and public places in an attempt to "clean up" Montréal for the 1976 summer Olympics.

["Olympic Crackdown," *Body Politic*, no. 25 (1976), pp. 1, 17; "Police Raid Clubs; Seeking Clues to Montreal's Rising Murder Rate?" *Montreal Gay Times* 1 (December 1975): 5–6 (reprinted, *Body Politic*, no. 22 (1976), p. 4).]

October 18 ✳ Saskatoon ✳ The Saskatchewan Federation of Labour passed a resolution to amend its constitution to prohibit discrimination based on marital status or sexual orientation. This action was influenced by the Doug Wilson case.

[Doug Hellquist, "Discrimination: A Teacher Fights Back," *Body Politic*, no. 21 (1975), p. 1.]

October 19 ✳ Fredericton ✳ The National Union of Students passed a resolution calling upon all of its constituent members to send a letter to R.W. Begg, president of the University of Saskatchewan, to condemn his actions in the Doug Wilson affair.

[Doug Hellquist, "Discrimination: A Teacher Fights Back," *Body Politic*, no. 21 (1975), p. 1.]

October 22 ✳ Toronto ✳ In response to the John Damien and Doug Wilson cases, *The Varsity*, a student newspaper at the University of Toronto, devoted two full pages to articles concerning gay liberation under the general title "Homosexuals — Healthy, Sane Victims of Prejudice."

[John B. Argue, "Saskatoon: Support for Gay," *Varsity* (Univ. of Toronto), 22 October 1975, p. 7; Christine Bearchell, "Lesbians and Gay Liberation: A Feminist Perspective," *Varsity* (Univ. of Toronto), 22 October 1975, pp. 6–7; Christine Bearchell, "Only Eunuchs Can Be Trusted," *Varsity* (Univ. of Toronto), 22 October 1975, p. 6; Doug Hellquist, "Discrimination: A Teacher Fights Back," *Body Politic*, no. 21 (1975), p. 1.]

October 23 ✳ Toronto ✳ The Committee to Defend John Damien, along with several other organizations and prominent individuals, sponsored a public meeting on the Damien case. About 200 people attended the meeting, held at the University of Toronto, which was addressed by fourteen speakers, including Damien, Harry Kopyto, Doug Wilson, and representatives of local lesbian and gay groups and institutions. Both Damien and Wilson received standing ovations.

["Damien Rally," *Metro Community News* 2 (24 October 1975): 17; "The Gay Blade Is Tempered" (editorial), *Gay Rising* 1 (November 1975): 2; "Homosexuals Unprotected, Lawyer Says," *Toronto Star*, four star ed., 24 October 1975, p. C12; "MCC Comes Out," GAYtuk 1 (12 November 1975): 2; "News: Toronto Rally Supports Damien," *Esprit* 2 (January 1976): 2; T.P. (Terry Phillips),"Rally Cheers John Damien," *Gay Rising* 1 (November 1975): 1–2; Ken Popert, "Damien: Central Issue Posed," *Body Politic*, no. 21 (1975), p. 6.]

October 24 * Toronto * Lawyer Harry Kopyto submitted a brief to the Ontario Human Rights Commission on behalf of John Damien, arguing that the Commission should interpret the word "sex" in the Ontario Human Rights Code broadly enough to include sexual orientation. (See also December 5, 1975.)

["Harry Kopyto," GAYtuk 1 (12 November 1975): 3, 8; "In Brief: Gay Rights Brief Presented," *Labor Challenge*, 3 November 1975, p. 2; "News," *Montreal Gay Times* 1 (November 1975): 3–4.]

October 25 * Ottawa * A march of 150 people on Parliament Hill protested government inaction during International Women's Year. About thirty lesbians and gay men participated, and were particularly vocal concerning the issues of gay liberation and custody rights for lesbian mothers. Marie Robertson of GO was one of the speakers, and Doug Wilson was introduced to the crowd.

["Call for Abortion Law Repeal" (photo), *Globe and Mail*, metro ed., 27 October 1975, p. 16; Ron Dayman, "It Hasn't Been Done . . . Why Not?" GO *Info* 2 (November–December 1975): 4; Ron Dayman, "Lesbian Rights — Why Not!" *Body Politic*, no. 22 (1976), p. 6; "Gay Front Activist Fired as Lecturer Pushes Case in Ottawa," *Ottawa Citizen*, 27 October 1975, p. 2; "Lesbians Demonstrate," *Gay Rising* 1 (November 1975): 3; "News: October 25 Demonstration," *Other Woman* 4 (December 1975–January 1976): 6; "Toronto Women Join March to Protest Ottawa's 'Inaction,' " *Globe and Mail*, metro ed., 25 October 1975, p. 15.]

October 26 * Toronto * Leonard Matlovich, the United States Air Force sergeant dismissed for being gay, spoke at MCC.

[" 'Matt,' " GAYtuk 1 (12 November 1975): 3.]

October 29 * Toronto * The *Globe and Mail* printed its first birth announcement involving a same-sex couple. The notice announced the birth on October 27 of Justine Sarah Jane Greenland "to Erika and Diann."

[Greenland birth notice, *Globe and Mail*, metro ed., 29 October 1975, p. 47.]

October 30 ✴ Montréal ✴ Gilles Carle's film *La tête de Normande St-Onge* premiered at Le Parisien theatre. One of the characters, portrayed by Reynald Bouchard, was a gay conjurer-musician.

[Charles Ryweck, "*Normande/La tête de Normande St-Onge*," *Hollywood Reporter*, November 1979, p. 2; Jean-Pierre Tadros, "Le jeu de la séduction: 'La tête de Normande St-Onge,' " *Cinéma Québec* 4 (1976): 6–8; D.J. Turner and Micheline Morisset, eds., *Canadian Feature Film Index, 1913–1985/Index des films canadiens de long métrage* (Ottawa: Public Archives, National Film, Television, and Sound Archives, 1987), entry 583; Thomas Waugh, "Nègres blancs, tapettes et 'butch': les lesbiennes et les gais dans le cinéma québécois," *Copie zéro*, no. 11 (1981), p. 21.]

October 30 ✴ Toronto ✴ About 140 people attended a benefit dinner in support of John Damien, Leonard Matlovich, and Doug Wilson, held at the Four Seasons Sheraton Hotel. The three men appeared on various local television and radio programmes in the few days surrounding the event. The *Toronto Star*'s report of the dinner used the noun "deviates" in its title, which led to protests from members of the gay community. On November 4, Mary Axten, George Hislop, Rev. Bob Wolfe, and Peter Maloney met with Borden Spears, senior editor and ombudsman at the *Star*, to discuss the paper's inadequate coverage of news events in the gay community. (See also November 8, 1975.)

["Do More to Protect Deviates U.S. Official Tells Ontario," *Toronto Star*, four star ed., 31 October 1975, p. B6; Gerald Hannon, "Gourmets Hear Damien, Wilson, Matlovich," *Body Politic*, no. 22 (1976), pp. 5–6; " 'My Only Claim to Fame . . . Is That I'm Gay,' " *Toronto Sun*, final ed., 31 October 1975, p. 66; "News: Benefit Dinner Held for Matlovich, Damien and Wilson," *Esprit* 2 (January 1976): 5–8; "News: Toronto: Gays Make Good Use of Radio, T.V. Forums," *Esprit* 2 (January 1976): 9; "News: Toronto: Gays Pressure Press," *Esprit* 2 (January 1976): 2–3; Poncho, "M.D.W. Benefit," *Metro Community News* 2 (7 November 1975): 12–13.]

October 31 ✴ Montréal ✴ Police raided P.J.'s bar and Baby Face, a popular women's bar, as part of a crackdown on the gay community, leading up to the 1976 summer Olympics.

["Olympic Crackdown," *Body Politic*, no. 25 (1976), pp. 1, 17; "Police Raid Clubs: Seeking Clues to Montreal's Rising Murder Rate?" *Montreal Gay Times* 1 (December 1975): 5–6 (reprinted, *Body Politic*, no. 22 (1976), p. 4).]

October 31–November 1 ✴ Vancouver ✴ Eight lesbian rights policy proposals (ranging from child custody to housing and the age of consent), developed by the Rights of Lesbians Subcommittee of the British Columbia Federation of Women (BCFW), were presented for adoption at the second annual convention of the BCFW, held at Capilano College. One proposal rejecting the abolition of age-of-consent laws, arguing that such a move would worsen the sexual exploitation of young women, was particularly controversial in that it opposed the stand taken by the NGRC/CNDH.

["Lesbian Rights Policy Proposals to the B.C. Federation of Women," *Pedestal: A Lesbian-Feminist Newspaper* 7 (October–November 1975): 6–7; "News: Lesbian Rights Recognized," *Long Time Coming* 3 (April–May 1976): 37; Ken Popert, "Lesbian Group Supports Age-of-Consent Laws," *Body Politic*, no. 23 (1976), p. 1.]

October–November ∗ Vancouver ∗ The Rights of Lesbians Subcommittee of the BCFW, in conjunction with the Women's Office at the University of British Columbia, sponsored a series of six seminars held at UBC entitled "Perspective on Lesbianism," which explored various aspects of lesbian life from a feminist viewpoint.

["Perspective on Lesbianism" (advertisement), *Pedestal: A Lesbian-Feminist Newspaper* 7 (October–November 1975): 17.]

November ∗ London, Ont. ∗ HALO approved funds for a distress and counselling phone line, to be operated from its community centre at 649 Colborne Street beginning in 1976.

["London Group Starts Counselling Line," *Body Politic*, no. 22 (1976), p. 7.]

November ∗ Montréal ∗ Police arrested about eighty men in raids on public washrooms in the downtown core as part of the ongoing crackdown on the gay community leading up to the 1976 summer Olympics.

["Olympic Crackdown," *Body Politic*, no. 25 (1976), pp. 1, 17; "Police Raid Clubs: Seeking Clues to Montreal's Rising Murder Rate?" *Montreal Gay Times* 1 (December 1975): 5–6 (reprinted, *Body Politic*, no. 22 (1976), p. 4).]

November ∗ Ottawa ∗ The Ottawa Knights, a gay leather and denim fraternity, was formed.

["Ottawa Knights" vertical file, Canadian Lesbian and Gay Archives, Toronto.]

November 2 ∗ Toronto ∗ Dave Gunton became the first Canadian-born citizen to be ordained a minister in the Universal Fellowship of Metropolitan Community Churches (MCC).

[Dave Gunton, "On Being First," *Metro Community News* 2 (7 November 1975): 3; "More News & Events: Nov. 2," *GAYtuk* 1 (12 November 1975): 8.]

November 3 ∗ Scarborough, Ont. ∗ Adrienne Potts (one of the Brunswick Four) and one other woman, members of Radical Lesbian Feminists, disrupted the televised 1975 Miss Canada Pageant at the CFTO studio by storming onto the stage and protesting the sexism of the event. They were part of a group of ten lesbians who arrived to protest the pageant. Television viewers did not see the protest.

["Beauty Contests" (editorial), *Other Woman* 4 (December 1975–January 1976): 2; Dennis Braithwaite, "CFTO Ignored a Great Moment," *Toronto Star*, four star ed., 5 November 1975, p. E20; "Lesbians Storm Beauty Pageant," *Toronto Sun*, final ed., 4 November 1975, pp. 1 (photo), 20; "*The Other Woman* Speaks to the Miss Canada Pageant Protesters" (interview), *Other Woman* 4 (December 1975–January 1976): 3, 22; Untitled photograph, *Body Politic*, no. 22 (1975), p. 7.]

November 4 ∗ Toronto ∗ Wages Due Lesbians held a public meeting at St. Paul's Centre about lesbianism and why there should be wages for housework.

["Public Meeting," *Body Politic*, no. 21 (1975), p. 7.]

November 6 ∗ Ottawa ∗ The Special Joint Committee on Immigration Policy presented its final report to Parliament, which advised the federal government to delete from the Immigration Act the provision (under section 5e) that prohibited foreign gays from entering Canada either as visitors or as immigrants. This decision was influenced by the presentations of fifteen gay organizations and numerous individuals made before the Committee in public hearings held across Canada during May–June 1975. The *Immigration Act, 1976*, which removed the prohibition against homosexuals, was passed into law on July 25, 1977.

[Philip Girard, "From Subversion to Liberation: Homosexuals and the Immigration Act 1952–1977," *Canadian Journal of Law and Society* 2 (1987): 1–27; William Johnson, "Immigration Scheme Proposes Quotas, Altered Categories," *Globe and Mail*, metro ed., 21 October 1975, pp. 1, 2; Gary Kinsman, *The Regulation of Desire: Sexuality in Canada* (Montréal: Black Rose Books, 1987), pp. 123–24; Ken Popert, "Parliamentary Committee Recommends End to Gay Exclusion," *Body Politic*, no. 22 (1976), pp. 3–4.]

November 6–9 ∗ Toronto ∗ Rev. Troy Perry, the founder of MCC, visited Toronto and participated in several events, including radio and television interviews. On November 8, 130 people attended a dinner held in Perry's honour, which was followed by a large dance.

["A Busy Schedule," *Metro Community News* 3 (28 November 1975): 5; "Gay Church Leaders Meet," *Metro Community News* 3 (28 November 1975): 4; "News: Religion: Troy Perry Visits Toronto," *Esprit* 2 (January 1976): 3; "Rev. Perry to Visit Here," *Metro Community News* 2 (October 1975): 5; "Troy Perry," GAYtuk 1 (12 November 1975): 9–10; "Troy Perry Dinner," *Metro Community News* 3 (28 November 1975): 1, 3, 14 (photographs).]

November 7 ∗ Montréal ∗ Police raided the Lime Light bar as part of a crackdown on the gay community leading up to the 1976 summer Olympics.

["Olympic Crackdown," *Body Politic*, no. 25 (1976), pp. 1, 17; "Police Raid Clubs; Seeking Clues to Montreal's Rising Murder Rate?" *Montreal Gay Times* 1 (December 1975): 5–6 (reprinted, *Body Politic*, no. 22 (1976), p. 4).]

November 7 ∗ Ottawa ∗ Twenty-five members of GO picketed the national convention of the Liberal Party, meeting at the Chateau Laurier, to demand inclusion of a sexual orientation clause in the federal government's proposed Canadian Human Rights Act. The demonstration was held to coincide with Prime Minister Pierre Trudeau's arrival at the convention. When confronted by the picketers, Trudeau just waved and smiled. The protesters also distributed the NGRC/CNDH's pamphlet "The Homosexual Minority and the Canadian Human Rights Act" to convention delegates.

[Ron Dayman, "GO Pickets . . . Liberal Convention . . . and Federal-Provincial Conference," GO Info 2 (November–December 1975): 3; Ron Dayman, "P.M. Smiles and Waves at Same Time," Body Politic, no. 22 (1976), p. 6.]

November 8 * Toronto * The *Toronto Star*, for years an opponent of gay activists, seemingly reversed its stand on gay liberation when it published an editorial calling for the inclusion of sexual orientation in the revised Ontario Human Rights Code. The *Star* confirmed the same position in an editorial published on January 5, 1976, in which it used the John Damien case as an example of the dangers imposed by not having sexual orientation in the Code. However, at that time the *Star* still refused to use the word "gay" as an alternative to "homosexual."

["For a Broader Definition of Human Rights" (editorial), *Toronto Star*, Saturday ed., 8 November 1975, p. B2; "More Human Rights Need Law's Protection" (editorial), *Toronto Star*, four star ed., 5 January 1976, p. C4; "News: Toronto: Gays Pressure Press," *Esprit* 2 (January 1976): 2–3; T.P. (Terry Phillips), "Protect Gays, Says *Star*," *Gay Rising* 1 (November 1975): 1, 4; Borden Spears, "Homosexuals Find Publicity Is Not an Unmixed Blessing," *Toronto Star*, Saturday ed., 8 November 1975, p. B2.]

November 9 * Montréal * Leonard Matlovich, the United States Air Force sergeant who had been dismissed because of his homosexuality, spoke at the Saidye Bronfman Centre. Between 300 and 400 people attended the event, which included a panel discussion featuring local activists Miriam Boghen, Bruce Garside, and Joan Richardson.

[Ron Daymon (sic), "Matlovich Tells of 'Coming Out,'" *McGill Daily* (McGill Univ.), 10 November 1975, p. 1; "Sgt. Matlovich Speaks in Montreal," *Montreal Gay Times* 1 (December 1975): 5.]

November 9 * Saskatoon * After conducting a preliminary investigation into the Doug Wilson case, the Saskatchewan Human Rights Commission ruled that the rights of gay people were protected under the Saskatchewan Human Rights Act, in that the term "sex" contained in the Act included sexual orientation. As a result of this ruling, lawyers for the University of Saskatchewan sought a court injunction in December 1975 to prevent the Commission from holding a formal inquiry into the Wilson case. On January 30, 1976, the injunction was granted after Justice F.W. Johnson ruled that the word "sex" in the Human Rights Act referred to gender only and that the

Saskatchewan Human Rights Commission did not have the jurisdiction to proceed with a hearing. Wilson vowed to appeal the decision, while the Committee to Defend Doug Wilson continued to raise funds for legal costs. By March 1976, however, Wilson and the Committee decided to cease pursuing his case because of high legal costs and a low chance of success.

[Marsha Erb, "Wilson May Appeal Queen's Bench Ruling," *Saskatoon Star-Phoenix*, 6 February 1976, p. 3; Doug Hellquist, "Breakthrough in Prairie Gay Rights Case," *Body Politic*, no. 22 (1976), p. 4; Doug Hellquist, "Court Halts Rights Inquiry, Wilson Will Appeal Decision," *Body Politic*, no. 23 (1976), p. 3; "U. of S. Seeks Injunction to Halt Wilson Hearing," *Saskatoon Star-Phoenix*, 18 December 1975, p. 20; "Wilson Case Abandoned," *Body Politic*, no. 24 (1976), p. 4; "Wilson Case Ruled Outside Limits of Rights Group," *Saskatoon Star-Phoenix*, 5 February 1976, p. 4; "Wilson Rejects Decision Appeal," *Saskatoon Star-Phoenix*, 6 March 1976, p. 4.]

November 11 * Ottawa * Denis LeBlanc and Marie Robertson of GO laid a wreath at the National War Memorial. The wreath was inscribed with a pink triangle to commemorate the thousands of homosexuals who had been interned in Nazi concentration camps, as well as the thousands of gay men and lesbians who had served in the Canadian Armed Forces during both world wars. This was the first time that a gay group was allowed to participate formally in the official Canadian Remembrance Day ceremonies.

[Denis LeBlanc, "Lest They Forget," *Body Politic*, no. 22 (1976), p. 6; Denis LeBlanc, "Remembrance Day," GO *Info* 2 (November–December 1975): 6.]

November 11 * Toronto * The first public meeting of Integrity, a group for lesbian and gay Anglicans, was held at St. Stephen's Parish Hall. More than seventy-five people attended and heard a panel discussion on "Homosexuality in/and the Church."

["Integrity," *Metro Community News* 2 (24 October 1975): 6; "More News & Events: Nov. 11," GAY*tuk* 1 (12 November 1975): 8; A. W.-H., "Integrity Panel Discussion," *Metro Community News* 3 (28 November 1975): 13.]

November 14 * Toronto * Ontario's newly appointed Minister of Labour Bette Stephenson (PC-Don Mills) declined an invitation to meet with representatives of CGRO. On September 10, during an all-candidates meeting for the provincial election, Stevenson had said that, if elected, she would look into the matter of discrimination against gay people. Stephenson was elected, and by becoming minister of Labour she became the Cabinet minister responsible for the administration of the Ontario Human Rights Code. (See also December 4, 1975.)

[Ken Popert, "Gays Keep Pushing for Equal Rights," *Body Politic*, no. 22 (1976), p. 5; D.S. (Dan Stainton), "Labour Minister Has No Time for Gays: More Promises; Still No Rights," *Gay Rising* 1 (December 1975): 3.]

November 20 ∗ Toronto ∗ CUPE Local 1230, representing non-professional library workers at the main campus of the University of Toronto, went on strike to back contract demands that included a clause to prevent discrimination in employment based on sexual orientation. They were unsuccessful in securing this protection when the strike was settled on December 9, 1975.

[W.B. (Walter Bruno), "Library Workers Seek Gay Rights," *Gay Rising* 1 (May 1975): 3; "Library Workers Abandon Strike," *Body Politic*, no. 22 (1976), p. 6; Tim McCaskell, "Library Union Seeks Protection for Gays," *Body Politic*, no. 21 (1975), p. 5; D.S. (Dan Stainton), "CUPE Local Demands Gay Rights," *Gay Rising* 2 (January–February 1976): 1, 3; Karl Vaughan, "In Brief," GAY*tuk* 1 (26 November 1975): 2.]

November 21 ∗ Grande Prairie, Alta. ∗ For the first time in Canada, an openly lesbian mother was awarded custody of her child. In the case of K. vs. K., Justice D.W. Rowe of the Alberta Provincial Court granted custody to the lesbian mother, reasoning that the child's chances of becoming a homosexual would not increase solely by being raised by a homosexual parent.

[Christine Boyle, "Custody, Adoption and the Homosexual Parent," *Reports of Family Law* 23 (1976): 129–45; "K. v. K.," *Reports of Family Law* 23 (1976): 58–65; Chris MacNaughton, "Who Gets the Kids?: Usually Not Lesbian Mothers, at Least Not in the Courts as They Are Being Conducted Today," *Body Politic*, no. 34 (1977), pp. 12–13; "News: Alberta Lesbian Mother Wins Custody," *Long Time Coming* 3 (April–May 1976): 35.]

November 22 ∗ Toronto ∗ At its founding convention, the Movement for Municipal Reform agreed to add sexual orientation to its non-discrimination clause in the area of education. The amendment had been moved by delegate Herb Spiers, a member of *The Body Politic* collective.

["New Political Force Upholds Gay Rights," *Body Politic*, no. 22 (1976), p. 6.]

November 23 ∗ Ottawa ∗ A Parti Québécois Outaouais regional convention rejected a resolution to establish a committee to study gay oppression and the inclusion of a sexual orientation clause in the Québec Human Rights Code.

["P.Q. Convention Withholds Support," *Body Politic*, no. 22 (1976), p. 7; Yvon Thivierge, "Congrès du P.Q.," GO *Info* 2 (November–December 1975): 5.]

November–December 11 ∗ Vancouver ∗ Members of GATE (Vancouver) and SEARCH were active in questioning candidates about sexual orientation and the provincial Human Rights Act during various all-candidates meetings leading up to the British Columbia provincial election, held December 11.

[Bob Cook, "B.C. Election: Gays Put Forward Independent Politics," *Gay Tide* 3 (April 1976): 5; Bob Cook, "NDP Record on Rights Attacked by Gays," *Body Politic*, no. 22 (1976), pp. 7, 17.]

December ∗ Ottawa ∗ The GO Centre moved to the second floor of 378 Elgin Street. The new location was larger and provided space for a wider range of activities. It officially opened January 2, 1976.

["GO Centre Moves," GO *Info* 2 (November–December 1975): 1.]

December ∗ Toronto ∗ Plans were made for the formation of the independent social and support group Gay Women Unlimited. The group's first official meeting was January 5, 1976, at the CHAT Centre, 201 Church Street.

["Flash!! Gay Women Unlimited," *Other Woman* 4 (December 1975–January 1976): 20; Margaret Fulford, ed., *The Canadian Women's Movement, 1960–1990: A Guide to Archival Resources/Le mouvement canadien des femmes, 1960–1990: guide de ressources archivistiques* (Toronto: Canadian Women's Movement Archives/ECW Press, 1992), entry 395; "Local News: Gay Women Unlimited," *Other Woman* 4 (March–April 1976): 8; Becki L. Ross, *The House That Jill Built: A Lesbian Nation in Formation* (Toronto: University of Toronto Press, 1995), pp. 52–53.]

December ∗ Toronto ∗ Pink Triangle Press was established as a non-profit corporation to oversee the operation of *The Body Politic* and the Canadian Gay Archives.

[Pink Triangle Press papers, 82–002, Canadian Lesbian and Gay Archives, Toronto.]

December 3 ∗ Toronto ∗ Representatives of GATE (Toronto) and *The Body Politic* met with MPP Margaret Campbell (Lib.-St. George). Campbell told Tom Warner that she intended to introduce a resolution in the Legislature that would call for the inclusion of the terms "sexual orientation" and "affectional preference" in the Ontario Human Rights Code.

[Ken Popert, "Gays Keep Pushing for Equal Rights," *Body Politic*, no. 22 (1976), p. 5; D.S. (Dan Stainton), "Labour Minister Has No Time for Gays: More Promises; Still No Rights," *Gay Rising* 1 (December 1975): 3; T.W. (Tom Warner), "GATE Meets Margaret Campbell," *Gay Rising* 1 (December 1975): 1–2; J.W. (John Wilson), "Gays Picket Queen's Park," *Gay Rising* 1 (December 1975): 1.]

December 4 ∗ Toronto ∗ CGRO organized a demonstration of about fifty people at Queen's Park to protest Ontario Labour Minister Bette Stephenson's refusal by letter on November 14 to meet with CGRO representatives. Members of CGRO were pressing for protection for gays in the Ontario Human Rights Code. (See also December 5, 1975.)

[Ken Popert, "Gays Keep Pushing for Equal Rights,"*Body Politic*, no. 22 (1976), p. 5; J.W. (John Wilson), "Gays Picket Queen's Park," *Gay Rising* 1 (December 1975): 1.]

December 5 ∗ Toronto ∗ The Ontario Human Rights Commission (OHRC) announced that it had rejected lawyer Harry Kopyto's submission on behalf of John Damien to appoint a Board of Inquiry to investigate the Damien case. It ruled that the word "sex" in the Ontario Human Rights Code referred to gender only. Kopyto then filed a suit in Divisional Court on behalf of Damien, asking the court to overrule the OHRC and to reverse the decision. During a preliminary hearing before the Ontario Supreme Court held on March 11, 1976, lawyers for the OHRC defended its position by revealing that Ontario Minister of Labour Bette Stephenson, whose department administered the Ontario Human Rights Code, had recommended that the OHRC refuse to appoint a Board of Inquiry in the Damien case. This suit was eventually abandoned, in July 1976.

[Christine Bearchell, "Damien Case: Minister Interferes, Government Agencies Collaborate," *Body Politic*, no. 24 (1976), pp. 6–7; T.P. (Terry Phillips), "No Hearing for Damien," *Gay Rising* 1 (December 1975): 1–2; Ken Popert, "As Damien Gets to Court, Money Runs Out," *Body Politic*, no. 26 (1976), p. 6; Ken Popert, "Gays Keep Pushing for Equal Rights," *Body Politic*, no. 22 (1976), p. 5.]

December 11 * Ottawa * Twenty-five members of the NGRC/CNDH picketed a federal-provincial conference on human rights, demanding the inclusion of a sexual orientation clause in the proposed Canadian Human Rights Act. This was the first public action by the NGRC/CNDH.

[Ron Dayman, "GO Pickets . . . Liberal Convention . . . and Federal-Provincial Conference," *GO Info* 2 (November–December 1975): 3; Ron Dayman, "NGRC Protests Rights Conference," *Body Politic*, no. 22 (1976), pp. 6–7.]

December 13 * London, Ont. * A meeting of the Steering Committee of CGRO was held, during which a letter from Ontario Minister of Education Thomas Wells was read. Wells stated that health and physical education classes at Ontario's high schools could include a full unit on homosexuality, but that the inclusion of the unit and its contents would be the responsibility of local school boards.

[John Bodis, "CGRO Meeting," *Metro Community News* 3 (19 December 1975): 1, 7.]

December 19 * Toronto * The Richmond Street Health Emporium officially opened at 260 Richmond Street E. as one of the largest gay steambaths in North America.

["Richmond Street Health Emporium" vertical file, Canadian Lesbian and Gay Archives, Toronto.]

December 26 * Toronto * The Three of Cups, a women's coffeehouse popular with lesbians, opened at 20 Scadding Square.

[Margaret Fulford, ed., *The Canadian Women's Movement, 1960–1990: A Guide to Archival Resources/Le mouvement canadien des femmes, 1960–1990: guide de ressources archivistiques* (Toronto: Canadian Women's Movement Archives/ECW Press, 1992), entry 495; "News: Coffee House," *Other Woman* 4 (December 1975–January 1976): 6; Becki L. Ross, *The House That Jill Built: A Lesbian Nation in Formation* (Toronto: University of Toronto Press, 1995), pp. 51–52.]

A Checklist of Lesbian and Gay Organizations in Canada, 1964–1975

NOTE: This list concentrates on lesbian and gay homophile and liberation groups. It has been compiled with the following limitations:

- Listings are by city from west to east and chronological; national groups are at the end.
- Commercial establishments, bars, and clubs have been excluded. For a listing of Canadian lesbian and gay periodicals, see Appendix Two; for bars and clubs, see Appendix Three.
- I have listed groups active sometime during the period 1964 through 1975 only. Their years of activity during this period have been calculated using articles and advertisements in Canadian lesbian and gay periodicals and, in some cases, the papers of the organizations themselves. The notations - and + denote that the group was also active before (-) or after (+) the date(s) listed.

Victoria, B.C.
Royal Thunderbird Court (1972–75 +)
Gay People's Alliance (GPA) (April 1974–Autumn 1974)

Burnaby, B.C.
Gay People of SFU (Simon Fraser University) (Autumn 1974–75 +)

Vancouver, B.C.
Association for Social Knowledge (ASK) (April 1964–Summer 1965; 1966–early 1969)
The Circle (- 1968–71 +)
Gay Action Committee (August 1970–late 1970)
Gay Liberation Front (GLF) (November 1970–Autumn 1971)
Gay Sisters (1971 +)
Border Riders M.C. (January 1971–73 +)
Canadian Gay Activists Alliance (CGAA) (February 1971–73)
Dogwood Monarchist Society and Imperial Dogwood Court (Spring 1971–75 +)
Gay Alliance toward Equality (GATE) (May 1971–75 +)
Gay People's Alliance (became Gay People of UBC [University of British Columbia] in September 1972) (October 1971–September 1972)
Gay People of UBC (University of British Columbia) (September 1972–75 +)
Gay People Together (November 1972–75 +)
Zodiac M.C. (January 1973–75 +)

Gay Transient Referral and Information Centre (Gay TRIC)
(May 1973–March 1974)
Greater Vancouver Business Guild (- June 1973–75 +)
Have a Gay Stay Transient Housing and Gay Information Service
(March 1974–75 +)
Vancouver Gay Information Service (Van-Gay) (March 1974–75 +)
Rights of Lesbians Subcommittee, B.C. Federation of Women
(October 1974–75 +)
Society for Education Action Research and Counselling on Homosexuality
(SEARCH) (November 1974–75 +)

Calgary, Alta.
Scarth Street Society (1970–75 +)
People's Liberation Coalition (January 1973–75)
Gay Information and Resources Calgary (GIRC) (June 1975 +)

Edmonton, Alta.
Gay Alliance toward Equality (GATE) (Summer 1971–75 +)
Edmonton Lesbian Feminists (ELF) (1972–74 +)
Office of Gay Affairs, Unitarian Church (December 1973–75 +)
Imperial Court of the White Rose (1975 +)
Gay Associations of Edmonton (GAE) (June 1975 +)

Saskatoon, Sask.
Gay Alliance toward Equality (GATE) (1971 — merged into Saskatoon Gay
Action in October 1972)
Gay Students Alliance (GSA), University of Saskatchewan (Autumn 1971 —
merged into Saskatoon Gay Action in October 1972)
Zodiac Friendship Society (January 1972 — renamed Gay Community Centre
of Saskatoon in January 1975)
Saskatoon Gay Action (October 1972 — renamed Gay Community Centre of
Saskatoon in January 1975)
Gay Women's Group (December 1972–March 1973)
Lesbian Feminists (Autumn 1973 +)
Gay Community Centre of Saskatoon (January 1975 +)
Committee of Gays for the Re-election of John Richards (Spring 1975 — June
1975)
Committee to Defend Doug Wilson (September 1975 +)
Gay Academic Union, University of Saskatchewan (October 1975 +)

Regina, Sask.
Atropos Friendship Society (February 1972–75 +)
University of Saskatchewan Homophile Association (USHA; renamed
the University of Regina Homophile Association in 1974)
(February 1973–75 +)

Winnipeg, Man.
Mutual Friendship Society (Summer 1971–75 +)
Campus Gay Club, University of Manitoba (renamed Gays for Equality [GFE]
in 1973) (February 1972–75 +)

Thunder Bay, Ont.
Lakehead Gay Liberation, Lakehead University (January 1974–June 1974)

Windsor, Ont.
Windsor Homophile Association (renamed Windsor Gay Unity [WGU] in 1973) (November 1972–early 1974; November 1974–75 +)

London, Ont.
University of Western Ontario Homophile Association (Gay Lib Union) (UWOHA) (February 1971 — merged into HALO in Autumn 1974)
Homophile Association of London, Ontario (HALO) (March 1974–75 +)

Kitchener–Waterloo, Ont.
Waterloo Universities' Gay Liberation Movement (Waterloo GLM) (University of Waterloo and Wilfrid Laurier University) (February 1971–75 +)
Waterloo Lesbian Collective (December 1974–75 +)

Guelph, Ont.
University of Guelph Homophile Association (UGHA; renamed Guelph Gay Equality in 1975) (February 1971–late 1971; September 1973–75 +)

Hamilton, Ont.
Hamilton-McMaster Gay Liberation Movement (GLM; renamed the McMaster Homophile Association [MHA] in January 1976) (January 1973–75 +)

Mississauga, Ont.
Gays of Mississauga (Autumn–Winter 1975/76 +)

Downsview, Ont.
York University Homophile Association (YUHA; renamed the Gay Alliance at York [GAY] in 1975) (October 1970–75 +)
NOTE: A separate chapter of YUHA was formed at Glendon College in Autumn 1971

Toronto, Ont.
Homophile Reform Society (planned in July 1964 to begin in October 1964 but may not have been active)
University of Toronto Homophile Association (UTHA) (October 1969–73)
Spearhead Toronto (May 1970–75 +)
Community Homophile Association of Toronto (CHAT) (December 1970–75 +)
Toronto Gay Action (TGA) (June 1971–73)
Gay Fellowship Discussion Group, First Unitarian Congregation (September 1971–72 +)
Homophile Information Media (HIM; later renamed the Homophile Information Media of Canada/Centre d'information homophile du Canada) (Autumn 1971–January 1974)
Ontario Campaign for Sexual Equality (Autumn 1971)
Ontario Homophile Federation (October 1971–1972)
Gay Youth Toronto (Spring 1972–75 +)
Gays against the War (- April 1972 +)
ANIK (February 1973–75 +)
Gay Alliance toward Equality (GATE) (February 1973–75 +)
Metropolitan Community Church (MCC) (July 1973–75 +)
Radical Lesbians (- 1974–75 +)
HASP (Heather, Adrienne, Sue, Pat) (January 1974–75)

Gay Media (February 1974–75 +)
Lanyards (May 1974–75 +)
Amazon Workshop (June 1974–75 +)
Brown Breast Brigade (BBB) (Summer 1974)
Labyris Collective (Autumn 1974)
Committee for Media Fairness to Gays (October 1974–75 +)
Wages Due Lesbians (October 1974–75 +)
Dignity (November 1974–75 +)
Task Force on Gay Liberation (December 1974–Summer 1975)
Coalition for Gay Rights in Ontario (CGRO) (January 1975 +)
Committee to Defend John Damien (February 1975 +)
Gay Academic Union (September 1975 +)
Toronto Area Gays (TAG) (Autumn 1975 +)
Integrity (November 1975 +)
Gay Women Unlimited (December 1975 +)
Pink Triangle Press (December 1975 +)

Peterborough, Ont.
"Women," Trent University (became the Trent Homophile Association [THA] in 1976) (October 1975 +)

Kingston, Ont.
Queen's University Homophile Association (QUHA) (October 1973–March 1975; September 1975 +)

Stittsville, Ont.
Committee on Social Hygiene (- 1964–May 1965)

Ottawa, Ont.
Canadian Council on Religion and the Homosexual (May 1965–Autumn 1966)
Gays of Ottawa/Gays d'Ottawa (GO; Gays of Ottawa/Gais de l'Outaouais from 1975) (September 1971–75 +)
Gay Club, Carleton University (a branch of GO) (September 1972–75 +)
Gay Caucus, Unitarian Church (Autumn 1973–75 +)
Metropolitan Community Church (MCC) (September 1974–75 +)
Warren Zufelt Memorial Defence Fund (April 1975 +)
Ottawa Knights (November 1975 +)

Saint-Laurent, Qué.
Gay Vanier (Autumn 1972–73)

Pointe-aux-Trembles, Qué.
Groupe Mormon gai/Gay Mormon Group (- August 1975 +)

Montréal, Qué.
International Sex Equality Anonymous (ISEA) (- August 1967–71)
Kemo M.C. (1970–75 +)
Front de libération homosexuelle (FLH) (March 1971–Autumn 1972)
Iron Cross M.C. (April 1972–75 +)
GAY, McGill University (later Gay McGill) (September 1972–75 +)
Trident M.C. (February 1973–75 +)
Montreal Gay Women (renamed Labyris Montreal by December 1974) (Spring 1973–75 +)

Northern Lights M.C. (April 1973–75 +)
Association homophile de Montréal/Gay Montreal Association (AHM/GMA)
(June 1973–75 +)
Centre d'accueil homophile/Gay Community Centre (June 1973–75 +)
Egaylity, Loyola College (Autumn 1973–75 +)
L'Église communautaire de Montréal/Montreal Community Church
(ECM/ MCC) (December 1973–75 +)
Centre homophile urbain de Montréal (CHUM) (January 1974–75 +)
Gay Dawson, Dawson College (- February 1974–75 +)
Front homosexuel québécois de libération (FHQL) (March 1974–late 1974)
Jewish Gay Discussion Group (later known as Naches) (November 1974–75 +)
Slightly Older Lesbians (SOL) (February 1975 +)
Montreal Lesbian Mothers (- March 1975 +)
Groupe homosexuel d'action politique (GHAP) (March 1975 +)
Gay Social Services Project, Family Service Association, Ville Marie Social
Service Centre (July 1975 +)

Québec, Qué.
Centre humanitaire d'aide et de libération (CHAL) (May 1972–75 +)
Service d'accueil d'information et de référence du CHAL Inc. (renamed Service
d'entraide homophile de Québec [SEHQ] in January 1975) (January
1974–75 +)

Fredericton, N.B.
Gay Friends (February 1974–August 1975)

Saint John, N.B.
Speak Easy Gayline (- August 1975 +)

Halifax, N.S.
Gay Alliance for Equality (GAE) (June 1972–December 1974; October 1975 +)

St. John's, Nfld.
Community Homophile Association of Newfoundland (CHAN)
(May 1974–75 +)

National Groups
National Gay Election Coalition (NGEC) (September 1972–74)
Canadian Gay Liberation Movement Archives (later renamed the Canadian
Gay Archives) (September 1973–75 +)
Canadian Gay Press Service (July 1975 +)
Gay Caucus, New Democratic Party (NDP) (July 1975 +)
National Gay Rights Coalition/Coalition nationale pour les droits des
homosexuels (NGRC/CNDH) (July 1975 +)

A Checklist of Canadian Lesbian and Gay Periodicals, 1964–1975

I have attempted to examine every issue of all known lesbian or gay periodicals published in Canada between 1964 and 1975. To ensure that news material relating to the latter part of 1975 was not missed, I also examined issues of selected periodicals for early 1976.

For the purposes of this project I defined a lesbian or gay periodical as a publication issued serially by self-declared lesbians or gay men and intended for an audience of like-minded people. This definition includes a wide variety of works: from *The Body Politic*, a newsmagazine of national scope, to the most obscure newsletters published by individuals or private clubs. Numerous publications with incidental gay or lesbian material have been excluded on the grounds that they were not produced for a lesbian or gay audience. Thus, crime and scandal tabloid publications such as *Allo Police*, *Hush*, *Justice Weekly*, and *Tab* and feminist or women's publications such as *The New Feminist*, *On Our Way*, and *The Other Woman*, although containing some material of interest to lesbians or gay men, have been excluded. The only exception I have permitted is for Canadian physique magazines. Although not self-declared gay publications, they were read primarily by gay men and so have been included.

The following list details the known Canadian lesbian and gay periodicals for the period. Each entry includes:

- the title of the publication
- the sponsoring group (if any, or if known)
- the address of the publication listed on the latest issue examined
- the number and date of the earliest issue examined
- the number and date of the latest issue examined
- the total number of issues examined, and whether this represents a complete run of the publication for the time period under consideration
- miscellaneous notes, including changes in title and notes on locations of copies

The periodical collection at the Canadian Lesbian and Gay Archives (CLGA) in Toronto was the core collection examined, and Alan Miller's *Our Own Voices: A Directory of Lesbian and Gay Periodicals, 1890–1990, Including the Complete Holdings of the Canadian Gay Archives* (1991) was useful in compiling the basic list. All of the titles listed here are located at the CLGA unless otherwise noted. The CLGA collection is incomplete, and numerous other collections were consulted also. I was unable to locate any copies of several periodicals, and have given the source of my information about them.

Aboutface
   Community Homophile Association of Newfoundland (CHAN)
   Box 613, Station C, St. John's, Nfld.
   Earliest: vol. 1, no. 4 (Summer 1975)
   Latest: vol. 2, no. 4 (May 1976)
   • two issues examined (incomplete run)

Alhumanact
   c/o John C. Sullivan
   24 Baldwin Street, Toronto, Ont.
   Earliest: no. 1 [1972]
   • one issue examined (complete run ?)
   • literary

Archangel
   Association homophile de Montréal/Gay Montreal Association (AHM/GMA)
   Montréal, Qué.
   ca. 1974
   • no issues located; see *"Archangel," Long Time Coming* 1 (March 1974): 23

ASK Newsletter
   Association for Social Knowledge (ASK)
   Box 4277, Vancouver, B.C.
   Earliest: vol. 1, no. 1 (April 1964)
   Latest: vol. 5, no. 2 (February 1968)
   • thirty issues examined (complete run ?)
   • see also *Blue Sheet*

Association homophile de Montréal/Gay Montreal Association Bulletin Newsletter
   Association homophile de Montréal/Gay Montreal Association (AHM/GMA)
   C.P. 694, Succ. N, Montréal, Qué.
   Earliest: May 1974
   Latest: June 1974
   • two issues examined (complete run)
   • the first issue (May 1974) was entitled *Nous nous préparons/Getting Ready*
   • continued by *Gay-Zette*

Back Chat Newsletter
   Community Homophile Association of Toronto (CHAT)
   223 Church Street, Toronto, Ont.
   Earliest: vol. 1, no. 1 (February 1971)
   Latest: [May 1976 ?]
   • twenty-seven issues examined (complete run)
   • also called *Back Chat, Back/Chat,* and *Back/Chat Newsletter*

Bed
   1247 W. 7th Avenue, Vancouver, B.C.
   Earliest: August 1975
   Latest: October 1975

- two issues examined (complete run)
- literary; edited by Stan Persky, George Stanley, and Scott Watson

Bisexus
Les Éditions Berima Inc.
C.P. 160, Longueuil, Qué.
Earliest: vol. 2, no. 22 [1972 ?]
Latest: vol. 3, no. 10 (July 1973)
- six issues examined (incomplete run)
- four issues are located at the Archives gaies du Québec: vol. 3, no. 3 (April 1973); vol. 3, no. 4 (May 1973); vol. 3, no. 9 (July 1973); and vol. 3, no. 10 (July 1973)
- continued by *Le nouveau bisexus*

Blue Sheet
Association for Social Knowledge (ASK)
Box 4277, Vancouver, B.C.
Earliest: [April 1964]
Latest: [June 1965]
- ten issues examined (incomplete run ?)
- ASK published *Blue Sheet* as a single-leaf information sheet on upcoming events, usually printed on blue paper
- none of the issues examined were dated; internal evidence suggests seven monthly issues in 1964 (April–October) and three in 1965 (February, May, and June); there may have been more but no other issues have been located
- see also ASK *Newsletter*

The Body Politic
Pink Triangle Press
Box 7289, Station A, Toronto, Ont.
Earliest: no. 1 (November–December 1971)
Latest: no. 24 (June 1976)
- twenty-four issues examined (complete run)

Brite Lite: GLF Newsletter
Gay Liberation Front (GLF)
Box 15, Station A, Vancouver, B.C.
Earliest: [February–March ?] 1971
- one issue examined (complete run ?)

Carousel Capers
Scarth Street Society
1632 Centre Street N., Calgary, Alta.
Earliest: vol. 3, no. 6 (June 1972)
Latest: unnumbered, undated issue [March 1975 ?]
- thirteen issues examined (incomplete run)

Le Chaînon
Centre humanitaire d'aide et de libération (CHAL)
C.P. 596, Haute-Ville, Québec, Qué.

Earliest: vol. 1, no. 2 (December 1973)
Latest: vol. 2, no. 4 (April 1974)
• five issues examined (incomplete run)
• continued by CHALUM

CHALUM
Centre humanitaire d'aide et de libération (CHAL)/Centre homophile urbain de
    Montréal (CHUM)
[Montréal, Qué. ?]
Earliest: vol. 1, no. 2 [June 1975 ?]
• one issue examined (incomplete run)
• continued Le Chaînon

Closet Burner
6–1419 Fort Street, Victoria, B.C.
Earliest: vol. 1, no. 8 (4 April 1975)
• one issue examined (incomplete run)
• newsletter of the Royal Victorian Court

Club '70 News
Club '70
Box 1716, Main Post Office, Edmonton, Alta.
Earliest: vol. 2, no. 5 [misnumbered 6] (August 1971)
Latest: February 1976
• twenty-five issues examined (incomplete run)
• some issues entitled *'70 News, Headline Seventy*, and *Club '70 Newsletter*

Coming Out
Vancouver, B.C.
ca. 1972
• no issues located; see "Why Have We Re-opened *Open Doors?*" *Open Doors* 2
    (December 1972): 12

Coup-de-poing
Front homosexuel québécois de libération (FHQL)
2126, rue Amherst, Montréal, Qué.
ca. 1974
• no issues located; this may never have been published; see "Information:
    Front homosexuel québécois," *Long Time Coming* 1 (May–June 1974): 34

Crossroads
Iron Cross M.C.
Box 1721, Station A, Montréal, Qué.
Earliest: vol. 5, no. 3 (1976)
• one issue examined (incomplete run)

Dialogue
Hamilton-McMaster Gay Liberation Movement (GLM) [from 1976: McMaster
    Homophile Association (MHA)]
Box 44, Station B, Hamilton, Ont.

Earliest: no. 1 (October 1973)
Latest: February 1976
• fourteen issues examined (complete run)

Duo
Les Agences F.L.
4835, rue Jean Talon E., St. Leonard, Qué.
Earliest: vol. 1, no. 1 (Summer 1974)
• one issue examined (complete run ?)
• issue located at the Archives gaies du Québec, Montréal

Dynamic Duals
Frank Borck Enterprises
P.O. Box 637, Station F, Toronto, Ont.
Earliest: [1966 ?]
• one issue examined (complete run ?)
• physique magazine

Esprit
Esprit Publishing Company
105 Carlton Street, 4th floor, Toronto, Ont.
Earliest: vol. 1, no. 1 (October 1975)
Latest: vol. 2, no. 1 (January 1976)
• three issues examined (complete run)

Evolution
International Sex Equality Anonymous (ISEA)
Montréal, Qué.
ca. 1969
• no copies located; this may never have been published; see Levy Beaulieu, "Une explosion de joie chez les 70,000 homosexuels du Québec," *La semaine*, 17–23 June 1969, p. 6

Exclusive Male
Exclusive Male Publications
Box 154, Toronto, Ont.
Earliest: [vol. 1, no. 1] (January 1972)
Latest: vol. 1, no. 10 (October 1972)
• ten issues examined (complete run)

Face and Physique
Mark-One
Box 32, Lachine, Qué.
Earliest: no. 9 (Winter 1964)
• one issue examined (complete run ?); only no. 9 was published during the period for this study
• physique magazine

Flash: The International Guide to Gay Living
Big Brother Communications Corporation

219–5871 Victoria Avenue, Montréal, Qué.
Earliest: vol. 40, no. 4 (23 March 1976)
Latest: vol. 40, no. 15 (24 August 1976)
• seven issues examined (incomplete run)
• no issues located for the period before 1976, although they probably existed
• Big Brother Communications also had an office at 313 W. 53 Street, New York, N.Y.
• printed in Canada, but content was mostly American

GAE *Monitor*
Gay Alliance for Equality (GAE)
207–1585 Barrington Street, Halifax, N.S.
Earliest: November 1972
Latest: January 1974
• eight issues examined (incomplete run)
• some issues entitled *Newsletter*, GAE/Y *Information Service,* GAE/Y *Information Services,* or GAE/Y *Monitor*

Gai-kébec
Les Éditions Hochelaga Enr.
C.P. 42, Lasalle, Qué.
Earliest: vol. 1, no. 1 (Spring 1974)
Latest: vol. 1, no. 4 [August 1974 ?]
• four issues examined (complete run ?)
• all four issues located at the Archives gaies du Québec, Montréal

Le gai Québec
C.P. 161, Pointe-aux-Trembles, Qué.
Earliest: vol. 1, no. 1 (June 28, 1975)
Latest: vol. 1, no. 7 (December 1975)
• seven issues examined (complete run ?)
• issues vol. 1, no. 6 (November 1975) and vol. 1, no. 7 (December 1975) located at the Archives gaies du Québec, Montréal

The Gaily Planet
University of Guelph Homophile Association (UGHA)
University of Guelph, Guelph, Ont.
Earliest: vol. 1, no. 1 (October 1974)
Latest: vol. 1, no. 2 (November 1974)
• two issues examined (complete run ?)
• continued *University of Guelph Homophile Association Newsletter*

Gay
Gay Publishing Company
122 Wellington Street W., Toronto, Ont.
Earliest: vol. 1, no. 1 (30 March 1964)
Latest: vol. 1, no. 11 (15 October 1964)
• eleven issues examined (complete run)
• continued by *Gay International*

Gay: A Newsletter
GAY
McGill University, 3480 McTavish Street, Montréal, Qué.
Earliest: vol. 1, no. 1 (1 January 1973)
Latest: vol. 1, no. 5 (24 February 1973)
• five issues examined (complete run ?)
• continued by *Gay News*

Gay Book News
Catalyst Press
315 Blantyre Avenue, Scarborough, Ont.
Earliest: no. 1 (August 1973)
• one issue examined (complete run)

The Gay Canadian
Anjou Publications
Box 426, Burnaby, B.C.
Earliest: vol. 1, no. 1 (7 September 1972)
Latest: vol. 1, no. 2 (November 1972)
• two issues examined (complete run ?)
• distributed by the CGAA

Gay Community Centre of Saskatoon Newsletter/News
Gay Community Centre of Saskatoon (GCCS)
Box 1662, Saskatoon, Sask.
Earliest: [January] 1975
Latest: December 1975
• five issues examined (complete run)
• some issues entitled GCCS *Newsletter*
• continued *Gay West* and *Zodiac Friendship Society Information*

Gay Directions
Community Homophile Association of Toronto (CHAT)
223 Church Street, Toronto, Ont.
Earliest: August 1973
Latest: August 1974
• two issues examined (complete run)
• a directory to the gay scene in Toronto published for Gay Pride Week

Gay Giggle
Kamp Publishing Company
Box 842, Adelaide Station, Toronto, Ont.
ca. 1964
• no issues located; see Alan V. Miller, *Our Own Voices: A Directory of Lesbian and Gay Periodicals, 1890–1990, Including the Complete Holdings of the Canadian Gay Archives*, Canadian Gay Archives Publication no. 12 (Toronto, CGA, 1991), p. 228

Gay International
Gay Publishing Company
980 Queen Street E., Toronto, Ont.

Earliest: vol. 1, no. 12 (1964)
Latest: no. 15 (1965)
• four issues examined (complete run)
• each issue was printed with two different covers, but with identical content
• continued *Gay*

Gay News
Gay McGill
McGill University, 3480 McTavish Street, Montréal, Qué.
Earliest: vol. 2, no. 1 (21 November 1973)
Latest: vol. 2, no. 4 (January 1974)
• four issues examined (complete run)
• continued *Gay: A Newsletter*

Gay Rising
Gay Alliance toward Equality (GATE)
193 Carlton Street, Toronto, Ont.
Earliest: vol. 1, no. 1 (March 1975)
Latest: vol. 2, no. 1 (January–February 1976)
• eight issues examined (complete run)

Gay Tide
Gay Alliance toward Equality (GATE)
Box 1463, Station A, Vancouver, B.C.
Earliest: vol. 1, no. 1 (August 1973)
Latest: vol. 3, no. 2 (April 1976)
• twelve issues examined (complete run)

Gay West
Saskatoon Gay Action/Gay Community Centre of Saskatoon
Box 1662, Saskatoon, Sask.
Earliest: no. 1 (June 1974)
Latest: no. 2 (1975)
• two issues examined (complete run)
• continued by *Gay Community Centre of Saskatoon Newsletter/News*

Gayokay
University of Toronto Homophile Association (UTHA)
SAC Office, University of Toronto, 12 Hart House Circle, Toronto, Ont.
Earliest: January 1971
Latest: no. 5 (November 1972)
• five issues examined (complete run)
• continued UTHA *Newsletter*

GAYtuk
South of Tuk International
Box 1267, Station A, Toronto, Ont.
Earliest: vol. 1, no. 1 (12 November 1975)
Latest: vol. 1, no. 5 (January 1976)
• five issues examined (complete run)

Gay-Zette
Association homophile de Montréal/Gay Montreal Association (AHM/GMA)
C.P. 694, Succ. N, Montréal, Qué.
Earliest: vol. 1, no. 3 (September 1974)
Latest: vol. 2, no. 6 (July 1975)
• nine issues examined (complete run)
• continued *Association homophile de Montréal/Gay Montreal Association Bulletin Newsletter*

Gemini
Waterloo Universities' Gay Liberation Movement (GLM)
c/o Federation of Students, University of Waterloo, Waterloo, Ont.
Earliest: vol. 1, no. 1 (June 1971)
Latest: vol. 1, no. 3 (October 1971)
• three issues examined (complete run ?)
• continued by *Gemini II*
• see also GLM *Newsletter*

Gemini News
Gemini Club
Box 1662, Saskatoon, Sask.
Earliest: vol. 1, no. 1 (13 November 1971)
Latest: vol. 1, no. 5 (May 1972)
• five issues examined (complete run)
• issues vol. 1, no. 1 and 2 had the cover title *Gemini Club News*
• continued by *Zodiac Friendship Society Information*

Gemini II
Waterloo Universities' Gay Liberation Movement (GLM)
c/o Federation of Students, Room 217C, Campus Centre,
University of Waterloo, Waterloo, Ont.
Earliest: vol. 1, no. 2 (March 1973)
Latest: vol. 2, no. 2 (February 1974)
• seven issues examined (incomplete run)
• continued *Gemini*

Geo. Marshall's Queen City Gazette
George Marshall Associates
Suite 1, 1495 Queen Street W., Toronto, Ont.
Earliest: no. 1 (June 1965)
Latest: July 1965
• two issues examined (complete run ?)
• issue one was published as a four-page insert to *Gay International*, no. 14 (June 1965)

Glad Day Books
Glad Day Books
4 Collier Street, Toronto, Ont. [shop address]

Earliest: [December 1974]
Latest: [1975]
• three issues examined (complete run ?)
• annotated sales catalogues for Glad Day Bookshop, all undated

GLM *Newsletter*

Waterloo Universities' Gay Liberation Movement (GLM)
c/o Federation of Students, University of Waterloo, Waterloo, Ont.
Earliest: vol. 1, no. 1 (22 March 1971)
Latest: vol. 2, no. 1 (12 January 1972)
• nine issues examined (incomplete run)
• see also *Gemini*

GO *Info*

Gays of Ottawa/Gais de l'Outaouais (GO)
P.O. Box 2919, Station D, Ottawa, Ont.
Earliest: vol. 1, no. 1 (July 1972)
Latest: vol. 3, no. 1 (February–March 1976)
• fifteen issues examined (complete run)

The Graphic Sapphic

5021, av. du Parc, Montréal, Qué.
ca. 1974
• no issues located; see *"The Graphic Sapphic," Long Time Coming* 2
(December 1974): 11

The Great Monarch Butterfly

Elgin F. Blair
P.O. Box 6248, Station A, Toronto, Ont.
Earliest: vol. 1, no. 1 [1973]
• one issue examined (complete run)
• a mimeographed letter mailed to members of the U.U. Gay Caucus
• see also *Magenta Moth*

HALO *Grapevine*

Homophile Association of London, Ontario (HALO)
649 Colborne Street, London, Ont.
Earliest: vol. 2, no. 8 (July 1975)
Latest: February–March 1976
• four issues examined (incomplete run)
• some issues entitled *The Grapevine*
• continued *Homophile Association of London Ontario Newsletter*

Homomundo

Les Distributions Patricia Inc.
C.P. 294, Montréal-Nord, Qué.
Earliest: vol. 1, no. 1 [1975]
• one issue examined (complete run ?)
• issue located at the Archives gaies du Québec, Montréal

Homophile Association of London Ontario Newsletter
Homophile Association of London, Ontario (HALO)
649 Colborne Street, London, Ont.
Earliest: vol. 1, no. 1 (September 1974)
Latest: vol. 2, no. 7 (July 1975)
• eleven issues examined (complete run)
• May 1975 issue misnumbered vol. 2, no. 4
• continued UWOHA Newsletter
• continued by HALO Grapevine

Jeux d'hommes
ca. 1972–74
• no issues located; see the finding aid "Périodiques: Liste,"
  Archives gaies du Québec, Montréal, 27 February 1992, p. 2

Lambda
Front homosexuel québécois de libération (FHQL)
2126, rue Amherst, Montréal, Qué.
ca. March 1974
• no issues located; see "Front homosexuel québécois de libération (FHQL)"
  vertical file, Canadian Lesbian and Gay Archives, Toronto

The Lanyard Newsletter
Lanyards
P.O. Box 272, Station M, Toronto, Ont.
Earliest: issue [vol.] 2, no. 3 (15 June 1975)
• one issue examined (incomplete run)

Lesbomonde
Les Publications Patricia
C.P. 305, Succ. C, Montréal, Qué.
ca. 1973–74
• no issues located; see Alan V. Miller, *Our Own Voices: A Directory of Lesbian and Gay Periodicals, 1890–1990, Including the Complete Holdings of the Canadian Gay Archives*, Canadian Gay Archives Publication no. 12 (Toronto, CGA, 1991), p. 363

Lezbeen News
Third National Gay Conference, Ottawa, Ont.
Earliest: 30 June 1975
• one issue examined (complete run)
• humorous publication issued at the Conference

Long Time Coming
Montreal Gay Women
Box 218, Station E, Montréal, Qué.
Earliest: vol. 1, no. 1 (July 1973)
Latest: vol. 3, no. 4 (April–May 1976)
• twenty issues examined (complete run)

Magenta Moth
Elgin F. Blair
Box 6248, Station A, Toronto, Ont.
Earliest: 19 August 1974
- one issue examined (complete run)
- a mimeographed letter mailed to a number of Blair's friends
- see also *The Great Monarch Butterfly*

The Male Nude
Kamp Publishing Company
P.O. Box 842, Adelaide Station, Toronto, Ont.
Earliest: no. 1 [ca. 1964]
Latest: no. 8 [ca. 1968]
- seven issues examined (incomplete run)
- issues were numbered but not dated
- physique magazine

Masculin: pour feminin
Les Publications Patricia Inc.
B.P. 337, Succ. C, Montréal, Qué.
Earliest: vol. 2, no. 1 (May 1972)
- one issue examined (incomplete run)

Metro Community News
Metropolitan Community Church — Toronto (MCC)
20 Trinity Square, Toronto, Ont.
Earliest: vol. 1, no. 1 (15 November 1973)
Latest: vol. 3, no. 3 (2 January 1976)
- fifty-five issues examined (incomplete run)
- some issues entitled *Metropolitan Community News*

Montreal Gay Times
P.O. Box 36, Station C, Montréal, Qué.
Earliest: vol. 1, no. 1 (April 1975)
Latest: vol. 2, no. 1 (Spring 1976)
- eight issues examined (complete run)
- cover title vol. 1, no. 1–3 (April–June 1975): *Gay Times*

Montreal Gay Women Newsletter
Montreal Gay Women
3664, rue Ste. Famille, Montréal, Qué.
ca. 1974
- no copies located; see "Montreal Gay Women News,"
  Long Time Coming 2 (December 1974): 30
- title uncertain; the group appears to have published a newsletter
  other than *Long Time Coming*

Montréalités
Montreal Community Church/Église communautaire de Montréal
C.P. 610, Succ. N.D.G., Montréal, Qué.

Earliest: vol. 1, no. 1 (February 1975)
Latest: vol. 2, no. 2 (February 1976)
• six issues examined (incomplete run)

Music Room Newsletter
The Music Room
575 Yonge Street, Toronto, Ont.
ca. 1964
• no copies located; see "Late Bulletin," ASK *Newsletter* 1 (August 1964): 9
• title uncertain; described as "their own newsletter" and that it was not *Two* magazine

New Beginnings
Metropolitan Community Church of Ottawa (MCC)
Box 868, Station B, Ottawa, Ont.
Earliest: vol. 1, no. 1 (30 May 1975)
Latest: vol. 1, no. 13 (28 November 1975)
• five issues examined (incomplete run)

Newsletter of the Royal Dogwood Court
Royal Dogwood Court
Vancouver, B.C.
ca. 1973–74
• no issues located; title uncertain; see *Thrust* 1 (January 1974): 9

NGEC Newsletter
National Gay Election Coalition (NGEC)
Toronto, Ont.
Earliest: no. 1 (May 1974)
Latest: no. 4 (18 July 1974)
• four issues examined (complete run)

Le nouveau bisexus
Les Éditions Berima Inc.
C.P. 160, Longueuil, Qué.
Earliest: vol. 3, no. 12 (August 1973)
Latest: vol. 5, no. 3 (1975)
• four issues examined (incomplete run)
• continued *Bisexus*

Nympho: journal pour les disciples de Lesbos
Les Publications Patricia
C.P. 66, Montréal-Nord, Qué.
Earliest: vol. 1, no. 3 (March 1972)
• one issue examined (incomplete run)

The Odyssey News
Atropos Fellowship Society
Box 3563, Regina, Sask.
Earliest: vol. 1, no. 4 (14 May 1975)
• one issue examined (incomplete run)

Omnibus

Les Publications Patricia

C.P. 66, Montréal-Nord, Qué.

[1973: C.P. 305, Succ. C, Montréal, Qué.]

Earliest: vol. 1, no. 20 (1972)

Latest: vol. 6, no. 33 (September 1975)

• twenty-four issues examined (incomplete run)

• issue for vol. 6, no. 33 is at the Archives gaies du Québec, Montréal

Omnimag

Les Éditions Hero Inc.

C.P. 294, Montréal-Nord, Qué.

Earliest: vol. 5, no. 12 [1976 ?]

• one issue examined (incomplete)

• issue located at the Archives gaies du Québec, Montréal

• issue examined is too late for this study, but earlier issues probably existed

Open Doors

Canadian Gay Activists Alliance (CGAA)

Box 284, Station A, Vancouver, B.C.

Earliest: vol. 1, no. 1 [1971]

Latest: vol. 3, no. 1 (January 1973)

• seven issues examined (complete run)

• continued by *Your Thing*

Ozomo

Gourmet Publishing Company Ltd.

C.P. 615, Succ. N, Montréal, Qué.

Earliest: vol. 1, no. 1 [1972 ?]

Latest: vol. 1, no. 12 [1973 ?]

• eight issues examined (incomplete run)

• issues were numbered but not dated; internal evidence suggests *Ozomo* was published during 1972–73

• Archives gaies du Québec, Montréal, has vol. 1, nos. 1, 2, 3, 7, 8, 10, 11, 12

Pedestal: A Lesbian-Feminist Newspaper

6854 Inverness Street, Vancouver, B.C.

Earliest: vol. 7, no. 1 (June–July 1975)

Latest: vol. 7, no. 3 (October–November 1975)

• three issues examined (complete run)

• *Pedestal* was a feminist newspaper published by the Vancouver Women's Caucus starting in 1969. It contained some articles on lesbianism, but only incidentally, and could not be considered a lesbian newspaper. *Pedestal* collapsed in 1975 but was revived by June–July 1975 as *Pedestal: A Lesbian-Feminist Newspaper* (vol. 7, no. 1), with content much more focussed on lesbianism. It survived only three issues, until October–November 1975 (vol. 7, no. 3)

Phalia

Spearhead Toronto

Box 293, Station A, Toronto, Ont.

Earliest: no. 1 (June 1970)
Latest: no. 18 (May 1973)
- nine issues examined (incomplete run)

The Phoenix
Vancouver, B.C.
Earliest: vol. 1, no. 1 (30 September 1971)
- no issues located; see Alan V. Miller, *Our Own Voices: A Directory of Lesbian and Gay Periodicals, 1890–1990, Including the Complete Holdings of the Canadian Gay Archives*, Canadian Gay Archives Publication no. 12 (Toronto, CGA, 1991), p. 483

Publication of the Gay People of UBC
Gay People of UBC
Box 9, Student Union Building,
University of British Columbia,
Vancouver, B.C.
Earliest: vol. 1, no. 1 (1 December 1972)
- one issue examined (incomplete run ?)

Queen's University Homophile Association Newsletter
Queen's University Homophile Association (QUHA)
c/o Terry Watson, Victoria Hall,
Queen's University, Kingston, Ont.
Earliest: January 1974
- one issue examined (incomplete run ?)
- continued by QHA *News* (February 1976)

La revue om
Les Éditions Berima Inc.
C.P. 160, Longueuil, Qué.
Earliest: vol. 1, no. 15 (1971)
- one issue examined (incomplete run)
- issue located at the Archives gaies du Québec, Montréal

SEARCH: The Society for Education Action Research and Counselling on Homosexuality
Society for Education Action Research and Counselling on Homosexuality (SEARCH)
Box 48903, Bentall Centre, Vancouver, B.C.
Earliest: vol. 1, no. 1 (September 1975)
- one issue examined (incomplete run ?)
- continued (?) SEARCH *Community Events Calendar*

SEARCH Community Events Calendar
Society for Education Action Research and Counselling on Homosexuality (SEARCH)
Box 48903, Bentall Centre, Vancouver, B.C.
Earliest: June–August 1975
- one issue examined (incomplete run ?)

• continued (?) by SEARCH: *The Society for Education Action Research and Counselling on Homosexuality*

Sapho

Montréal, Qué.

ca. 1973

• no issues located; see Alan V. Miller, *Our Own Voices: A Directory of Lesbian and Gay Periodicals, 1890–1990, Including the Complete Holdings of the Canadian Gay Archives*, Canadian Gay Archives Publication no. 12 (Toronto, CGA, 1991), p. 526

Sexus

4383, rue Christophe Colomb, Montréal, Qué.

Earliest: no. 1 (August–September 1967)

Latest: no. 3 (January–February 1968)

• three issues examined (complete run ?)

• issues examined are located at the Archives gaies du Québec, Montréal

Teen' Nude

Kamp Publishing Limited

Box 842, Adelaide Station, Toronto, Ont.

Earliest: no. 1 [ca. 1964]

Latest: [no. 3, ca. 1964]

• four issues examined (complete run ?)

• physique magazine

• there are two variant issues of no. 1, published in different formats and with different content

• three of the issues examined are in a private collection

Thrust

Box 5213, Vancouver, B.C.

Earliest: vol. 1, no. 7 (December 1973)

Latest: vol. 1, no. 10 (March 1974)

• three issues examined (incomplete run)

• issue for vol. 1, no. 7 (December 1973) is located in the IGIC Collection, Manuscripts Division, New York Public Library, New York, N.Y.

Le tiers: le magazine homophile du Québec

Publications Andant Inc.

C.P. 148, Vanier, Châteauguay, Qué.

Earliest: vol. 1, no. 1 (September 1971)

Latest: vol. 1, no. 2 (December 1971–January 1972)

• two issues examined (complete run)

Town Crier

c/o Greater Vancouver Business Guild

Box 5104, Vancouver, B.C.

ca. 1973–74

• no issues located; see *Thrust* 1 (January 1974): 9

Two

Kamp Publishing Company
292 Yonge Street, Toronto, Ont.
Earliest: no. 1 [1964]
Latest: no. 11 (July–August 1966)
• ten issues examined (incomplete run)

University of Guelph Homophile Association Newsletter

University of Guelph Homophile Association (UGHA)
Bursar Hall, University of Guelph, Guelph, Ont.
Earliest: no. 1 (March 1971)
• one issue examined (complete run ?)
• continued by *The Gaily Planet*

UTHA *Newsletter*

University of Toronto Homophile Association (UTHA)
c/o SAC Office, University of Toronto, 12 Hart House Circle, Toronto, Ont.
Earliest: no. 1 (April 1970)
• one issue examined (complete run)
• continued by *Gayokay*

U.U. Gay Caucus Newsletter

Unitarian Universalist (U.U.) Gays
c/o Elgin Blair, Box 6248, Station A, Toronto, Ont.
Earliest: vol. 1, no. 1 (September 1971)
Latest: vol. 3, no. 2 (June 1973)
• eight issues examined (complete run)
• a *Gay Caucus Newsletter — Supplement* was also occasionally published, for
  caucus members only, starting in July 1972. I have examined issues for July,
  September, and December 1972, and March and September 1973;
  the editor was Rev. Richard Nash of Los Angeles, Ca.
• continued by *Unitarian Universalist Gay Caucus Newsletter* (starting with vol.
  3, no. 3 [October–November 1973], published in Los Angeles, Ca.), which
  was continued by *U-U Gay World* (starting with vol. 4, no. 5 [Spring 1975],
  published in Washington, D.C.)

UWOHA *Newsletter*

University of Western Ontario Homophile Association (UWOHA),
University of Western Ontario, London, Ont.
Earliest: no. 1 (10 February 1971)
Latest: vol. 3, no. 7 (July 1974)
• thirty-six issues examined (complete run)
• note change in numbering of issues; there was a first series of issues with
  numbers only: no. 1 (10 February 1971) to no. 15 (9 March 1972); a second
  series, with volume and number, ran from vol. 1, no. 1 (October 1972)
  through vol. 3, no. 7 (July 1974)
• some issues were entitled *University of Western Ontario Homophile Association
  Newsletter*
• continued by *Homophile Association of London Ontario Newsletter*

Waterloo University Gay Liberation Movement
Waterloo University Gay Liberation
University of Waterloo, Waterloo, Ont.
Earliest: January 1972
- no issues located; see Alan V. Miller, *Our Own Voices: A Directory of Lesbian and Gay Periodicals, 1890–1990, Including the Complete Holdings of the Canadian Gay Archives*, Canadian Gay Archives Publication no. 12 (Toronto, CGA, 1991), p. 610.

What's Happening!: Happenings Club Newsletter
Happenings Social Club; Mutual Friendship Society
Box 1262, Winnipeg, Man.
Earliest: vol. 2, no. 8 (April 1973)
Latest: August 1975
- eleven issues examined (incomplete run)

Windsor Gay Unity Newsletter
Windsor Gay Unity (WGU)
Box 2, Sandwich Station, Windsor, Ont.
Earliest: vol. 1, no. 1 (December 1974)
Latest: vol. 2, no. 1 (January 1976)
- twelve issues examined (complete run)

York University Homophile Association Newsletter
York University Homophile Association (YUHA)
CYSF Office, Ross Building,
York University, Downsview, Ont.
Earliest: November 1970
Latest: [November 1971]
- four issues examined (incomplete run ?)

Young Flesh
Jock of South Africa [Peter Bromfield]
Toronto, Ont.
Earliest: vol. 1, no. 1 [ca. 1964]
- one issue examined (incomplete run ?)
- physique magazine

Your Thing
Open Doors
Box 284, Station A, Vancouver, B.C.
Earliest: vol. 1, no. 12 (5 July 1973)
Latest: vol. 2, no. 32 (4 April 1974)
- four issues examined (incomplete run)
- continued *Open Doors*

Zodiac Friendship Society Information
Zodiac Friendship Society
Box 1662, Saskatoon, Sask.

Earliest: vol. 1, no. 6 (June 1972)

Latest: vol. 2, no. 9 (December 1973)

- eighteen issues examined (complete run)
- two issues were misnumbered: there were two issues numbered vol. 2, no. 5 (May 1973) and two numbered vol. 2, no. 8 (August and September 1973)
- cover title varied: *Zodiac Friendship Society Gemini Club Newsletter*, *Zodiac Friendship Society News*; *Zodiac Friendship Society*
- entitled *Zodiac Friendship Society Information* (vol. 2, no. 2–8 [1973])
- continued *Gemini News*
- continued by *Gay Community Centre of Saskatoon Newsletter*
- see also *Gay West*

A Preliminary Checklist of Lesbian
and Gay Bars and Clubs in Canada,
1964–1975

NOTE: Three questions arise in any attempt to compile a checklist of lesbian and gay bars and clubs in Canada. First, what qualifies as a lesbian and/or gay bar? Undoubtedly almost every bar and club in the land has been visited by at least one lesbian or gay man. Second, is it possible to be entirely accurate in recording the addresses of these establishments, in light of sometimes unreliable or conflicting sources? The third problem is a related one: Is it possible to establish the years when these places were frequented by lesbians and/or gays? With these questions in mind, I have attempted to compile as complete a checklist as possible, but must qualify it as a "preliminary" listing. There may be errors and omissions. In addition, it has been compiled with the following limitations:

- Only establishments in Canadian metropolitan areas with the most active lesbian and gay communities during the period have been listed (twenty-seven cities in total).
- Many of the bars, beverage rooms, and clubs listed here had a mixed lesbian, gay, and straight clientele. These were the places where lesbians and gays would typically meet in the days before communities developed exclusively lesbian- and gay-oriented bars and clubs. Although lesbians and gays would meet there, many of these places could not be described as "gay bars"; in some cases the gay presence was very discreet. Establishments that were most popular with lesbians or gays have been marked L and G; all others were mixed.
- I have attempted to list complete street addresses. These have been checked when possible against the appropriate city directories or telephone books.
- The dates listed refer only to the period between 1964 and 1975 when the establishments were most active as lesbian/gay meeting places. Some of the dates are approximate, and have been calculated using ads and articles from Canadian lesbian and gay periodicals (see Appendix Two) as well as the sources listed below. The symbols - and + denote that the establishment was active before (-) or after (+) the date(s) listed.

Sources:
Barfly. Eastern edition. Los Angeles: Advocate Publications, 1973.
Damron, Bob. *Bob Damron's Address Book*. San Francisco: Bob Damron Enterprises, 1965–76.
Gaia's Guide. San Francisco: Gaia's Guide, 1975–76.
Green, Roedy. *A Guide for the Naive Homosexual*. 13th edition. Vancouver: The Author, 1971.
International Guild Guide. Washington, D.C.: Guild Press, 1964–72.

Victoria, B.C.

Churchill Hotel, Bastion Inn Pub. 1140 Government St. (downstairs) (- 1964–75 +)

Empress Hotel, Bengal Room. 721 Government St. (- 1971–75 +)

Sappho's. 734 Fort St. (- 1973–75 +)

Strathcona Hotel, Old Forge Tavern. 919 Douglas St. (- 1966–73 +)

Vancouver, B.C.

Abbotsford Hotel, Bar. 921 W. Pender St. (- 1960s +)

Alcazar Hotel, Bar. 337 Dunsmuir St. (- 1972–73 +)

Ambassador Hotel, Pub. 773 Seymour St. (- 1972–75 +)

August Club. 818 Richards St. (L, G) (1968–72)

B & B [Betwixt and Between] Club. 1369 Richards St. (G) (- 1970–72)

B.J.'s Show Club. 339 W. Pender St. (downstairs) (L, G) (1970–75 +)

Boogie Man's Rock Palace. 1066 Seymour St. (1975 +)

Bullring. 887 Seymour St. (G) (1970–73)

Castle Hotel, Puss 'n Boots Room. 750 Granville St. (G) (- 1964–75 +)

Champagne Charlie's. 612 Davie St. (L, G) (- 1970–75)

Cheiros [also known as B&B 11 or Charles 111]. 728 Robson St. (L) (- 1970–73 +)

Club 752. 752 Thurlow St. (G) (1964–69)

Corral Club. 887 Seymour St. (G) (1973–75)

Dance Machine. 887 Seymour St. (1975 +)

Devonshire Hotel, Tavern. 849 W. Georgia St. (downstairs) (- 1964–73 +)

Faces. 795 Seymour St. (G) (1970–75 +)

Gastown Inn, Bar. 314 Cambie St. (- 1971–73 +)

George 11. 1156 Denman St. (- 1973 +)

Georgia Hotel, Tavern. 801 W. Georgia St. (downstairs) (- 1964–73 +)

Hampton Court Club. 1066 Seymour St. (G) (1973)

Kingston Hotel, Tavern. 757 Richards St. (- 1970 +)

Montreal Club. 163 E. Hastings St. (- 1964–73 +)

Mrs. Goguen's Pool Parlour. 1066 Seymour St. (L) (1973–75)

Ms. Club. 2089 W. 4th Ave. (L) (1974 +)

Music Room. 1066 Seymour St. (G) (1973–74)

Nelson Place Hotel, Bar [formerly the Belmont Hotel]. 1006 Granville St. (1970–73 +)

New Fountain Club. 45 W. Cordova St. (- 1967–69)

Phase 111 [also known as Cabaret 71]. 823 Granville St. (1971 +)

Play Pen. 856 Seymour St. (upstairs) (1975 +)

Play Pen North. 571 Seymour St. (G) (- 1975 +)

Play Pen South. 1369 Richards St. (G) (1973–75 +)

P.S. Club. 571 Seymour St. (1974 +)

Queenie's Truck Stop. 1135 Howe St. (upstairs) (L) (- 1975 +)

616 Club. 616 Robson St. (L, G) (- 1973–75)

Talk of the Town. 1275 Seymour St. (- 1975 +)

Thunderbird Club. 856 Seymour St. (G) (- 1972–75)

Twiggy's 795 Club. 795 Seymour St. (- 1970)

Up-Stares. 804 W. Pender St. (G) (- 1972–73 +)

Vancouver Hotel, Tavern. 900 W. Georgia St. (1960s)

Vanport Hotel, Pub. 645 Main St. (L) (- 1967–75 +)

Calgary, Alta.
Carlton Hotel, Bar. 126 9th Ave. S.W. (- 1964–75 +)
Cecil Hotel, Bar. 401 4th Ave. S.E. (L) (- 1968–75 +)
Club Carousel. 1207 1st St. S.W. (downstairs) [from October 1972:
  1632 Centre St. N. (upstairs)] (L, G) (1970–75 +)
Club Marquis. 815 8th Ave. S.W. (- 1973–75 +)
Holiday Inn, Red Fox Pub. 708 8th Ave. S.W. (- 1971–75 +)
October '69 Club [also called the 1207 Club]. 1207 1st St. S.W. (1969–70)
Palliser Hotel, King's Arms Pub ("The Pit"). 133 9th Ave. S.W. (downstairs)
  (- 1964–75 +)
Parkside Continental. 1302 4th St. S.W. (L, G) (1973–75 +)
Royal Hotel, Bar. 8th Ave. and 2nd. St. S.W. (- 1971–72 +)
Sheraton-Summit Hotel, Summit Lounge. 202 4th Ave. S.W. (- 1971–75 +)
620 Club. 620 8th Ave. S.W. (L, G) (- 1970–73 +)

Edmonton, Alta.
Ambassador Motor Inn, Bar. 10041 106th St. N.W. (- 1972–73 +)
Club '70. 10242 106th St. N.W. (L, G) (1970–75 +)
Corona Hotel, Bar. 10625 Jasper Ave. N.W. (- 1964–75 +)
Flashback Social Club. Jasper Ave. and 116th St. N.W. (downstairs) (G)
  (- 1975 +)
Grand Hotel, Bar. 10266 103rd St. N.W. (- 1971 +)
King Edward Hotel, Tavern. 10180 101st St. N.W. (- 1971–75 +)
Macdonald Hotel, Bar. 10065 100th St. N.W. (- 1968–75 +)
Mayfair Hotel, Tavern. 10815 Jasper Ave. N.W. (- 1971–75 +)
Pig 'n Whistle Restaurant and Bar. 10548 Jasper Ave. N.W. (- 1973 +)
Royal George Hotel, Tavern Lounge. 10229 101st St. N.W. (- 1964–72 +)

Regina, Sask.
Georgia Hotel, Bar. 1927 Hamilton St. (1960s)
Gold Night Club. Albert St. (1972–75 +)
Odyssey Club. 2242 Smith St. (L, G) (1972–75 +)
Plains Motor Hotel, Bar. 1965 Albert St. (1960s)
Regina Inn, Night Club. 1975 Broad St. (1970s +)
Saskatchewan Hotel, Coachroom Beverage Room. 2125 Victoria Ave.
  (downstairs) (- 1964–75 +)

Saskatoon, Sask.
Bessborough Hotel, Harlequin Room and the Library Lounge. Spadina Cres.
  and 21st St. E. (- 1970–75 +)
Gemini Club, Zodiac Friendship Society. 502 Main St. E. [from March 1973:
  124A 2nd Ave. N. (upstairs)] (L, G) (1972–75 +)
King George Motor Hotel, Cove Lounge. 157 2nd Ave. N. (- 1970–75 +)
Ritz Hotel, Apollo Room. 118 21st St. E. (- 1971–75 +)
Sheraton Cavalier Motor Inn, Bar. 612 Spadina Cres. (- 1970–75 +)

Winnipeg, Man.
Club Morocco, Bar. 573 1/2 Portage Ave. (- 1964–73 +)
Club 654. 654 Erin St. (G) (1971–73 +)
Detour. 90 Albert St. (1975 +)
Empire Hotel, Cocktail Lounge. 171 Main St. (- 1967–72 +)

Happenings Club. Various locations until October 1973: 242 Manitoba Ave.
(L, G) (1971–75 +)
Mall Hotel, Pickwick Room. 469 Portage Ave. (- 1967–71 +)
Mardi Gras Restaurant, Bar. 287 Portage Ave. (upstairs) (L, G) (- 1964–75 +)
Midnight Hours. 185 Bannatyne Ave. (- 1975 +)
Moore's Restaurant, Bar. 297 Portage Ave. (- 1964–69 +)
Mount Royal Hotel, Bar. 186 Higgins Ave. (L, G) (- 1967–75 +)
St. Regis Hotel, Outside Inn Pub. 285 Smith St. (L, G) (- 1975 +)
Second Story Club. 90 Albert St. (G) (- 1972–73 +)
Town 'n Country Cabaret and Night Club. 317 Kennedy St. (- 1966–73 +)
Zoratti's Restaurant, Bar. 423 Portage Ave. (- 1967–71 +)

Thunder Bay, Ont.
Back Street Athletic Club. 539 Simpson St. (upstairs) (L, G) (1975 +)
Mona Lisa Tavern. 505 Simpson St. (G) (1972–75)
Prince Arthur Hotel, Fountain Room. 17 Cumberland St. N. (- 1970s +)
Royal Edward Hotel, Dominican Room. 114 May St. S. (- 1975 +)

Sudbury, Ont.
Nickel Range Hotel, Matador Room. 8–12 Elm St. W. (- 1971–75 +)

Windsor, Ont.
Imperial House Hotel, Tavern. 191–93 Riverside Dr. (- 1973 +)
Ritz Hotel, Tavern. 88 Pitt St. E. (G) (1975 +)
West Side House Hotel, Tavern. 623–29 Riverside Dr. W. (L, G) (- 1973–75 +)

London, Ont.
400 Club. 398 Clarence St. (- 1968–72 +)
Grapevine Club. 674 Wellington Rd. S. (- 1971 +)
HALO Club. 649 Colborne St. (L, G) (1974 +)
Holiday Inn, Flanagan's Bar. 299 King St. (downstairs) (- 1970–75 +)
Iroquois Hotel, Bar. 369–77 Clarence St. (- 1968–70 +)
London Hotel, Camelot Lounge and Pump Room. Dundas St. and
Wellington Rd. (- 1968–72 +)

Kitchener, Ont.
Walper Hotel, Men's Pub and Hofbrau Room. 1 King St. W. (- 1975 +)

Guelph, Ont.
Royal Hotel, Rebel Room and August Club. 106 Carden St. (L, G)
(- 1974–75 +)

St. Catharines, Ont.
Harding Hotel, Fontana Room. 70 James St. (- 1970–73 +)
Mansion House Tavern. 5 William St. (- 1970–75 +)
Montebello Inn, Bar. 286–88 St. Paul St. (- 1975 +)
New Murray Hotel, Cameo Royale Lounge. 58–60 James St. (G) (- 1968–73 +)
Twilight Villa Social Club. 117 Chetwood St. (L, G) (- 1973–75 +)
Welland House Hotel, Alibi Room. 30 Ontario St. (- 1968–75 +)

Hamilton, Ont.
Club Nite Lite. 126 James St. N. (G) (- 1964 +)
Golden Rail Restaurant, Bar. 93 King St. E. (- 1964–65 +)
Windsor Hotel, Bar. 31 John St. N. (- 1975 +)

Toronto, Ont.

Algonquin Tavern. 5795 Yonge St. (- 1971–73 +)
Alternate. 19 St. Joseph St. (1972)
Astronaut Club. 511 Yonge St. (- 1964 +)
August Club. 530 Yonge St. (upstairs) (G) (1970–72)
August 11. 1 Isabella St. (G) (1973–74)
Bay House. 572 Bay St. (- 1968–73)
Bimbo's. 530 Yonge St. (upstairs) (G) (1975 +)
Blackbeard's. 2087 Yonge St. (1975 +)
Bluejay Club. 336 Pape Ave. (L) (1972–75 +)
Brown Derby Tavern. 311-13 Yonge St. (- 1971–73 +)
Cameo Club. 1130 Queen St. E. [later at 95 Trinity St. (downstairs)] (L) (1975 +)
Carriage House Motor Hotel, Bar. 306 Jarvis St. (L, G) (1971–75 +)
Les Cavaliers. 418 Church St. (G) (ca. 1975 +)
Charley O's Keg. 572 Bay St. (1973–74)
Club 511. 511A Yonge St. (downstairs) (G) (1964–74)
Club Manatee. 11A St. Joseph St. (G) (1970–75 +)
Colonial Tavern. 203 Yonge St. (downstairs) (- 1974–75 +)
Continental House, Bar. 150 Dundas St. W. (L) (- 1964–73 +)
David's. 16 Phipps St. (G) (1975 +)
Famous Door Tavern. 665 Yonge St. (G) (1964–72)
Ford Hotel, Tropical Room and Men's Beverage Room. 595 Bay St. (G)
    (- 1964–73)
Gasworks. 585 Yonge St. (- 1971–73 +)
Gateways. 1 Howard Park Ave. (L) (- 1973–74 +)
Isabella Hotel, Bar. 556 Sherbourne St. (- 1975 +)
Jo-Jo's. 83 Granby St. (upstairs) (G) (1975 +)
King Edward Hotel, Times Square Lounge and Pickwick Room.
    37 King St. E. (- 1964–75 +)
Kit Kat Klub. 1 Howard Park Ave. (L) (1974–75 +)
Letros Lounge, Nile Room. 50 King St. E. (downstairs) (G) (- 1964–72)
Make Believe. 530 Yonge St. (rear) (- 1970–71 +)
Malloney's Studio Tavern. 66 [later, 85] Grenville St. (G) (- 1964–75 +)
Maygay Dance Club. 488 Yonge St. (upstairs) (G) (1970–75 +)
Melody Room. 457 Church St. (L, G) (1964–66)
Metropole Hotel, Bar. 141 King St. W. (- 1964 +)
Milkbar. 530 Yonge St. (upstairs) (G) (1973–74)
Momma Cooper's. 530 Yonge St. (upstairs) (G) (1972–73)
Municipal Hotel, Essex Bar. 67 Queen St. W. (- 1964–66)
Music Room [previously the Maison de Lys]. 575 Yonge St. (upstairs) (L, G)
    (- 1964–66)
Park Plaza Hotel, King Cole Room. 4 Avenue Rd. (- 1960s)
Parkside Tavern. 530 Yonge St. (G) (- 1965–75 +)
Parkway Club. 1 Howard Park Ave. (L) (- 1975)
Penthouse Club. 575 Yonge St. (upstairs) (L, G) (1967–71)
Pink Pussycat Club. 450 Spadina Ave. (L) (1975)
Quazimoto's. 530 Yonge St. (upstairs) (G) (1974–75 +)

Quest. 665 Yonge St. (L, G) (1971–75 +)
Regency Club. 31 Prince Arthur Ave. (L, G) (- 1964–66?)
St. Charles Tavern. 488 Yonge St. (G) (- 1964–75 +)
Selby Hotel, Bar. 592 Sherborne St. (G) (- 1971–75 +)
Snuggles. 17 St. Joseph St. (1971)
Spoken Cycle Club. 19 St. Joseph St. (1972)
Strange Door. 174 Avenue Rd. (G) (- 1968–69 +)
Sugar's Disco. 593 Yonge St. (upstairs) (1974–75 +)
Sutton Place Hotel, Royal Hunt Room and Stop 33 (thirty-third floor).
    955 Bay St. (- 1971–75 +)
Le Trique. 14 Breadalbane St. (G) (ca. 1969–70 +)
Union House Hotel, Tavern. 71–73 Queen St. W. (- 1964–65 +)
Westbury Hotel, Red Lion Room. 475 Yonge St. (- 1964–68)

Kingston, Ont.
Grand Public House, King's Landing. 76 Princess St. (1970s)
La Salle Hotel, Cat's Meow. Princess and Bagot Sts. (1960s-71)

Ottawa, Ont.
Bytown Inn, Tavern. 73–75 O'Connor St. (G) (- 1966–70 +)
Capital House Hotel, Ray's Discotheque. 202 Rochester St. (- 1972–73 +)
Cellar Club. 30 Nicholas St. (downstairs) (G) (- 1971–75 +)
Club Private. 227 Laurier Ave. W. (penthouse) (L, G) (1971–75)
Coral Reef. 30 Nicholas St. (G) (- 1971–75 +)
Lord Elgin Hotel, Lounge (main floor) and Tavern (downstairs).
    100 Elgin Boul. (- 1964–75 +)
Windsor House. 134 Queen St. (- 1975 +)

Hull, Qué.
Chez Henri Hotel, Taverne (downstairs) and Salon d'Or. 179, rue Principale.
    (G) (- 1966–75 +)
Ottawa House, Taverne. 35, rue Principale. (- 1972–73 +)
Spotlight Discotheque. (1975 +)
Terrace du Potage Club. 66, rue Notre-Dame. (- 1975 +)
Texas Taverne ("The Pub"). 29, rue Eddy. (upstairs) (L) (- 1975 +)

Montréal, Qué.
Arlequin aux Deux Masques, 75, rue Ste. Catherine E. (- 1967–1972 +)
L'Axe Disco Club. 1755, rue St. Denis. (- 1975 +)
Baby Face Disco. 1235, boul. Dorchester. O. (L) (1968–75 +)
Bar Labyris. 3896, rue St. Denis. (L) (1970s +)
La Bâton Rouge. 1254, rue St. Denis. (L) (- 1973–75 +)
Beau Brummel. 1465, rue Metcalfe. (G) (- 1970–71)
Béret Bleu. 173, rue Ste. Catherine E. (- 1970)
Berkeley Hotel, Bar. 1188, rue Sherbrooke O. (- 1964–75 +)
Le Bistro. 2071, rue Ste. Catherine O. (- 1973 +)
Black Bottom. 22, rue St. Paul E. (L) (- 1970–75 +)
Bud's Lounge. 1250, rue Stanley. (L, G) (- 1968–75 +)
Le Cachot. 1204, rue Drummond. (G) (- 1970–72 +)
Café Canasta. 1232 boul. St. Laurent. (L) (1960s)
Café Casa Loma. 96, rue Ste. Catherine E. (L) (1960s)

Café Casbah. 286, rue Ste. Catherine E. (L) (- 1967–69 +)
Café Lincoln. 4479, rue St. Denis. (three floors) (- 1967–75 +)
Café Monarch. 162, rue Ste. Catherine E. (- 1966–75 +)
Café Only. 57, rue Ste. Catherine O. (L) (1965–72 +)
Café Rodéo [later, the Lodéo]. 1050, boul St. Laurent. (L) (1960s)
Casino de Paris Club. 136, rue Ste. Catherine O. (- 1964–69 +)
La Cave. (L) (ca. 1967)
Chez Fernand. 1484, boul. Dorchester O. (downstairs) (1971–75 +)
Chez Madame Arthur. 2170, rue Bishop. (L) (- 1971–75)
Chez Paree. 1258, rue Stanley. (- 1970)
Le Choc. 1473, boul. Dorchester O. (- 1970–73 +)
Club Cabaret. 281, rue Ste. Catherine E. (- 1970 +)
Club Cherrier. 847, rue Cherrier. (1967–68)
Club 1160. 1160, rue Sherbrooke E. (- 1974–75 +)
Club Esperanza. 1418, rue Guy. (third floor) (L, G) (- 1970–71 +)
Club Zanzibar. 1311, rue St. Christophe. (L) (early 1960s)
Crazy Cat Disco. 5868, av. du Parc. (- 1973 +)
Le Cruiser 750. 1419, rue Drummond. (third floor) (- 1975 +)
Downbeat Cabaret. 1422-24, rue Peel. (- 1964–65)
Edifice. 1218, rue Stanley. (upstairs) (- 1970 +)
L'Etoile de l'Est Disco. 4490, rue Ontario E. (- 1975 +)
Le Gant de Velours. 2077, rue Victoria. (upstairs) (1973–75 +)
La Garçonnière. 1600, boul. St. Laurent. (1975 +)
Gemini 1 Club. 1285, boul. de Maisonneuve O. [later Alexandre de Seve] (later
    moved) (L, G) (- 1969–72 +)
La Grande Discotheque. 77A, rue Ste. Catherine E. (- 1974–75 +)
La Guillotine. 1174, rue de la Montagne. (L) (- 1971–72 +)
Hawaiian Lounge. 1254, rue Stanley. (upstairs) (L, G) (- 1967–72 +)
Holiday Inn, Lounge. 420, rue Sherbrooke O. (- 1970–72 +)
Le Jardin. 1258, rue Stanley. (G) (1975 +)
Jilly's. 1426, rue Bishop. (L) (- 1975 +)
Latin Quarter. 1177, rue de la Montagne. (- 1964–70 +)
Lime Light. 1254, rue Stanley. (upstairs) (1973–75 +)
Lorelei. 1226, rue Stanley. (- 1974–75 +)
Monterey Lounge. 1108, rue Ste. Catherine O. (- 1964–70 +)
Le Mystique. 1424, rue Stanley. (- 1975 +)
Le Palais d'Or. 1226, rue Stanley. (1975 +)
Peel Pub. 1107, rue Ste. Catherine O. (downstairs) (G) (- 1966–75 +)
Penthouse. 1194, rue Peel. (upstairs) (- 1967–69 +)
P.J.'s. Cabaret. 1422, rue Peel. (upstairs) (- 1971–75 +)
Les Ponts de Paris. 1276, rue St. André. (L) (- 1964–75 +)
Puccini Restaurant and Bar. 1250, rue Stanley. (early 1960s)
Les Quatre Coins du Monde. 1218, rue Stanley. (G) (- 1966–70 +)
Regent Apollo Club. 5116, av. du Parc. (- 1971–75 +)
Le Rocambole. 1426, rue Stanley. (G) (- 1971–75 +)
Le Rose Rouge. 2042, rue MacKay [from 1975: 2112, rue Ste. Catherine O.].
    (- 1973–75 +)

Le Sabre. 405, rue Craig O. (L) (- 1974–75 +)
Le Saguenay. 984, boul. St. Laurent. (- 1974–75)
St. John Bar. 984, boul. St. Laurent. (- 1964–69 +)
Scandinavian Club. 1183, rue Crescent. (- 1969 +)
Sheraton Mt. Royal Hotel, Kon Tiki Bar. 1455, rue Peel. (- 1973–75 +)
La Source. 2150, rue Guy. (L) (1960s).
Le Stork Club. 1433, rue Guy. (- 1975 +)
Studio 1. 968, rue Ste. Catherine O. (upstairs) (G) (- 1975 +)
Tapis Rouge Bar. 1484, boul. Dorchester O. (early 1960s)
Le Tarot. 1459, rue St. Alexandre. (- 1971–75 +)
Au Taureau d'Or. 1419, rue Drummond. (second floor) (G) (- 1968–75 +)
Taverne Altesse. 100, rue Ste. Catherine O. (G) (- 1966–73 +)
Taverne Bellevue. 151, rue Ste. Catherine E. (- 1973–75 +)
Taverne les Carabiniers. Plaza Alexis Nihon. (- 1973–75 +)
Taverne Dominion Square. 1243, rue Metcalfe. (G) (- 1967–75 +)
Taverne Gambrinus. 1151, rue Ontario E. (- 1975 +)
Taverne le Gobelet. 8405, boul. St. Laurent. (- 1967–71 +)
Taverne des Immeubles. 804, rue Ste. Catherine E. (- 1967 +)
Taverne de Montréal. 1415, boul. St. Laurent. (- 1971–75 +)
Taverne Neptune. 121, rue de la Commune O. (- 1969–75 +)
Taverne de la Paix. 330, rue Ste. Catherine E. (- 1967–75 +)
Taverne la Patrie. 214, rue Ste. Catherine E. (- 1967–69 +)
Taverne le Plateau. 71, rue Ste. Catherine E. (- 1969–75 +)
Taverne St. Regis. 484, rue Ste. Catherine O. (- 1964–69 +)
Taverne Ste. Catherine. 1703, rue Ste. Catherine E. (- 1975 +)
Taverne Victoria Square. 726, rue St. James O. (- 1969–73 +)
Tropical Lounge. 1422, rue Peel. (upstairs) (- 1964–70 +)
Le Tunisie. 1204, rue Drummond. (third floor) (G) (- 1970–72 +)
Valentin Disco. 291, rue Mont-Royal O. (- 1975 +)
Vendome Cocktail Lounge ("Bachelor's Den"). 1202, rue Ste. Catherine O.
    (upstairs) (G) (- 1970–72 +)
Le Vieux Budapest. 3481, boul. St. Laurent. (1975 +)
Yakis. 2150, rue Guy. (L, G) (- 1970–71 +)
Zodiac Disco-Club. 1418, rue Guy. (- 1971 +)
Sherbrooke, Qué.
Sherbrooke Hotel, Bar. 9, rue Dépôt. (- 1973 +)
Wellington Hotel, Flamingo Bar. 68, rue Wellington S. (- 1967–75 +)
Trois-Rivières, Qué.
St. Louis Hotel, Pub Taverne. 119, rue des Forges. (upstairs) (- 1967–75 +)
Québec, Qué.
L'Alouette. 1169, rue St. Jean. (L, G) (- 1970–75 +)
Le Ballon Rouge. 811, rue St. Jean. (G) (1971–75 +)
Le Barillet Restaurant and Pub. 333, boul. Charest E. (- 1966 +)
Brasserie Houblonnière. 1110, rue St. Jean. (- 1973 +)
Brasserie O'Koin. 896, rue du Roi. (- 1975 +)
Cabaret Elle et Lui. 49, rue. St. Nicolas. (- 1975 +)
Le Cabaret Vénus. 157, chemin Ste-Foy. (- 1975 +)

Cercle des Amazones. (L) (1975 +)
Château Frontenac, Bar. 1, rue des Carrières. (- 1964–70s +)
Château View Hotel, Bar. 8, rue Laporte. (- 1973–75 +)
Chez Paul Cocktail Lounge. 28-30, rue St. Nicolas. (G) (- 1967–72 +)
Cirque Electrique. 27, Côte du Palais. (- 1973–75 +)
Clarendon Hotel, Bar (downstairs) and Lounge. 57, rue Ste. Anne. (- 1966–75 +)
Dante Restaurant, Cave au Vin Piano Bar. 17, rue St. Stanislas. (downstairs)
   (- 1969–75 +)
La Gorgendière. 13, place Royale. (G) (- 1975 +)
Le Gueuleton. 106, av. St. Sacrement. (L, G) (- 1966 +)
L'Intendant. 13, place Royale. (G) (- 1971–75 +)
Kajama. 895, Côte d'Abraham. (G) (- 1968–69 +)
Le Périgord. rue St. Stanislas. (- 1975 +)
Restaurant l'Esplanade, Lounge. 1084, rue St. Jean. (upstairs) (G) (- 1967 +)
Restaurant Pompernik Saloon Bar. 680–84, Côte d'Abraham. (L) (- 1970–73 +)
St. Roch Hotel, Taverne. 360, rue St. Joseph E. (- 1967–71 +)
Taverne Capitol. 980, rue St. Jean. (- 1966 +)
Taverne Chez Baptiste. 815, rue St. Augustine. (- 1967–75 +)
Taverne Chien d'Or. 8, rue Fort. (- 1966–73 +)
Taverne Coloniale. 1087, rue St. Jean. (- 1966–73 +)
Taverne Couronne d'Or. 305, rue de la Couronne. (- 1966 +)
Taverne Foyer. 1044, rue St. Jean. (- 1970–73 +)
Taverne Léo Bourgeault. 1190, rue St. Jean. (- 1966–70)
Taverne Limoilou. 472, 3ème Av. (downstairs) (- 1966 +)
Taverne du Quartier Latin. 1190, rue. St. Jean. (1970–75 +)
Taverne Sélect. 925, Côte d'Abraham. (- 1967–75 +)
Taverne Unek. 896, rue du Roi. (G) (1973 +)
Taverne du Vieux Québec. place du Marché Finley. (G) (- 1968–73)
Le Temple Discotheque. 25, rue St. Stanislas. (upstairs) (- 1970–73 +)
Le Vagabond. 69, boul. Charest E. (- 1975 +)
Fredericton, N.B.
   Cosmopolitan Club. 546 King St. (- 1973 +)
   Lord Beaverbrook Hotel, River Room Bar. 659 Queen St. (- 1970–75 +)
Saint John, N.B.
   Admiral Beatty Motor Hotel, Marco Polo Lounge. 14–22 King Sq. (L)
      (- 1968–75 +)
   Royal Hotel, Tavern. 61 Germain St. (downstairs) (- 1967–73 +)
Halifax, N.S.
   Candlelight Lounge. 5507 Spring Garden Rd. (- 1969–73 +)
   Captain's Cabin Lounge. 5680 Spring Garden Rd. (- 1967–73 +)
   Carleton Hotel, Jury Room Lounge. 1685 Argyle St. (- 1969–73 +)
   Carousel Showboat. 1873–75 Barrington St. (- 1972–73 +)
   Comeau's Tavern. 2776 Gottingen St. (- 1972–73 +)
   Dresden Arms Moter Hotel, Fore and After Lounge. 5530 Artillery Pl. (- 1973–75 +)
   Heidelberg Restaurant and Lounge. 1479 Dresden Row. (L, G) (- 1975 +)
   Klub 777 [also known as Thee Klub]. 1585 Barrington St., Suite 207. (L, G)
      (1973)

Lord Nelson Hotel, Victory Lounge and Tavern. 1515 S. Park St. (- 1964–75 +)
Piccadilly Tavern. 1599 Grafton St. (G) (- 1964–73 +)
Sea Horse Tavern. 1663 Argyle St. (- 1968–70 +)

St. John's, Nfld.
Newfoundland Hotel, Admiral's Keg. Cavendish Sq. (- 1969–73 +)
Porthole. Water St. W. (- 1966–73 +)

INDEX

NOTE: The Appendices have not been indexed. Also, some of the entries in this index appear more than once on the pages listed.

287